MW01040918

The Leasing Process: Landlord and Tenant Perspectives

Professional Review
Shannon Alter, CPM©
Mez R. Birdie, CPM©, CCIM, SCSM
Chris Mellen, CPM©, ARM©
Susan Sgrignoli, CPM©

Tulie O'Connor
Editorial Director, Education Publishing

Amanda Hellenthal
Editor, Education Publishing

The Leasing Process: Landlord and Tenant Perspectives

Richard F. Muhlebach, CPM©, SCSM, CRE, RPA
Alan A. Alexander

IREM Institute of Real Estate Management

Library of Congress Cataloging-in-Publication Data

Muhlebach, Richard F., 1943–
   The leasing process : landlord and tenant perspectives / Richard F. Muhlebach, Alan A. Alexander.
      p. cm.
   Includes index.
   ISBN-13: 978-1-57203-139-5 (hbk.)
   ISBN-10: 1-57203-139-5 (hbk.)
   1. Real estate management—United States. 2. Commercial leases—United States.
3. Landlord and tenant—United States. I. Alexander, Alan A. II. Title.
   HD1394.M844 2008
   333.33'8750973—dc22

                                                                              2008035747

To our second generation of leasing professionals, two outstanding retail brokers: my daughter Katherine Burns in Seattle and my son Eric Muhlebach in San Francisco. To our third generation: Joseph, Daniella, Jimmy, Allison, and Luccas. And to my loving wife and partner in life for over 39 years, Maria.

R.F.M.

To my loving wife, Jeanne, who provides me with support, backup, love, and encouragement in all that I do: thank you. I could not do it without you.

A.A.A.

Special Thanks
To my good friend Richard Muhlebach, who has been an inspiration, a friend, and a partner for over 30 years. There is no one in this field whom I respect more. I am a better person for having known you.

A.A.A.

Preface

The Leasing Process: Landlord and Tenant Perspectives has been written to provide landlords, tenants, and real estate professionals with a practical guide to successfully bring the leasing process to its intended conclusion: a fully executed lease. This book is a hands-on resource that takes the reader through the entire leasing process with problem-solving practices and tips. Suggestions come from the combined experiences of the authors, who have over 75 years in the leasing, marketing, and managing of all types of commercial properties.

The book begins with an overview of the role of the players in the leasing process in Chapter 1. The lease transaction, or "deal," has a pulse, and each player has a responsibility to maintain the rhythm of that pulse in order to keep the lease transaction moving to completion.

The second chapter discusses the responsibilities of each player in the leasing process. It reviews the pro and cons of assigning the leasing of a building to a leasing agent, an in-house leasing person, or the building's property manager. The chapter ends with a discussion of ethics in real estate and leasing.

Chapter 3 introduces the basics of marketing and prospecting, including evaluating the market, finding prospective tenants, developing marketing materials, and how best to advertise a commercial property. It delves into publicity and a wide range of networking opportunities that can lead to mutually beneficial deals in the future.

The fourth chapter reviews the leasing agreement and discusses issues to negotiate from the landlord's perspective. This chapter also discusses several important documents including the tenant registration letter and agreement, the recognition of the leasing agent's status in a "deal" and the tenant's request for proposal to lease space in a building. The chapter concludes with a discussion of the commission in a deal.

Chapter 5 reviews the process for landlords and tenants to prepare for negotiating a lease. This chapter discusses methods for landlords to qualify tenants and for tenants to qualify landlords. Negotiating tips are also discussed.

Chapter 6 discusses the importance of the landlord and the tenant understanding the commercial real estate market, as well as methods for becoming knowledgeable of market conditions and recently completed deals.

The seventh chapter provides successful practices along with tips for tenants on increasing their profitability in different types of commercial properties.

The next chapter reviews how landlords operate their buildings. This is important to tenants in order to know what to expect when their business operates in a multi-tenant commercial property.

The ninth chapter reviews industry methods for measuring space in office buildings, medical office buildings, industrial properties, and shopping centers. This is important because the amount of space a tenant occupies is one of the factors used to determine monthly rent and pass-through charges.

The tenth chapter discusses monetary issues that will affect the tenant's business as well as the net operating income and value of the landlord's building.

Chapter 11 discusses a frequently overlooked lease transaction: the lease renewal. This chapter provides insight into the challenges of preparing for the lease renewal process for both the landlord and the tenant.

The next chapter thoroughly reviews each lease provision, discusses how they impact the tenant's business and the landlord's building, and provides negotiating strategies for both the landlord and the tenant.

And the last chapter, Chapter 13, discusses the importance of lease administration and provides methods and practices for establishing efficient lease administration.

This book approaches the leasing process with the philosophy that the best outcome is a "win-win" situation for the landlord and the tenant, and a rewarding transaction for all the players involved in the "deal."

Acknowledgements

Professionals in the real estate industry have always been willing to share their knowledge and experiences. This has enabled the real estate industry to grow and prosper and its professionals to better serve their clients and their communities.

We would like to acknowledge and express our appreciation for the insights with which the following commercial real estate professionals have provided us: Eric Muhlebach, Fandel Retail Group, San Francisco; Katherine Burns, Burns and Associates, Seattle; Gail Duke, New York Life, New York; Shannon Alter, Orange County, California; Dave Paperd, Green Ridge Fund, Spokane; Mez Birdie, NAI Realvest, Maitland, Florida; Rick Page and Don MacLean, Office-lease, Seattle; and Jason Smith, GVA Kidder Mathews, Seattle.

We also would like to express our appreciation to the Institute of Real Estate Management (IREM©), the Building Owners and Managers Association (BOMA) International, and the International Council of Shopping Centers (ICSC) for the knowledge we gained attending their courses, reading their publications, and networking at their local and national meetings.

We are grateful for the advice and expertise of our fellow leasing professionals who reviewed our manuscript and served as editorial consultants: Susan Sgrignoli, CPM©, Chris Mellen, CPM©, ARM©, Shannon Alter, CPM©, and Mez R. Birdie, CPM©, CCIM, SCSM.

We are especially grateful for the excellent editing of this publication by Amanda Hellenthal, Editor, and Tulie O'Connor, Editorial Director, Education Publishing, at IREM.

Alan A. Alexander
Richard F. Muhlebach, CPM©, SCSM, CRE, RPA

About the Authors

Richard F. Muhlebach, CPM©, SCSM, CRE, RPA, has over 37 years of experience leasing and managing commercial properties. He was the Senior Managing Director of Kennedy Wilson Properties, Bellevue, Washington, a division of Kennedy Wilson International, Beverly Hills, which is a public real estate company responsible for leasing, management, and development activities in the northwest. Previously, for 19 years, he served as the founder and president of TRF Management Corporation, a commercial leasing and management firm, which he sold to Kennedy Wilson. His prior experiences include serving as the vice president for Tishman West Management Corp and The Lusk Company, developers in California.

Mr. Muhlebach started his career leasing and managing a diverse portfolio that included a regional mall, grocery-anchored shopping centers, office buildings, and medical office buildings. He also served as the general manager of a two-million-square-foot mixed-use development on 175 acres. He developed a leasing and management firm specializing in shopping centers, enclosed malls, high-rise office buildings, and mid-rise medical office buildings. He has supervised leasing and management professionals for over 35 years.

Mr. Muhlebach has served on the faculty of the Institute of Real Estate Management (IREM©), the Building Owners and Managers Association (BOMA) International, and the International Council of Shopping Centers (ICSC), teaching leasing, management, and ethics courses. He has taught leasing and property management at the University of Washington for over 20 years. Mr. Muhlebach has lectured or taught seminars in Singapore, China, Taiwan, Spain, Hungary, and Poland. He is a frequent speaker at real estate conferences across the United States.

The author of more than 100 articles on leasing and property management that have been published in the United States, Asia, and Europe, Mr. Muhlebach also has co-authored 17 books on commercial real estate. These books include *Shopping Center Management and Leasing, Managing and Leasing Commercial Properties,* and *Business Strategies for Real Estate Man-*

agement Companies, published by IREM, as well as *Operating Small Shopping Centers* and *Shopping Center Tenant Relations,* published by ICSC. He is a member of IREM's Academy of Authors.

Mr. Muhlebach has served on the editorial review board for several real estate books and for the *Commercial Lease Law Insider, Journal of Property Management (JPM©), Shopping Center Management Insider,* and *Office Building Manager.*

He was IREM's national president in 1998. He also served as the president of the Washington State Commercial REALTORS© Association, the Western Washington Chapter of IREM, the Seattle King County Building Owners and Managers Association, and the Northwest Chapter of the Real Estate Educators Association.

Mr. Muhlebach has served on the board of the Washington State Real Estate Research Foundation, and for several years chaired the Real Estate Advisory Board of North Seattle Community College. He is a graduate of San Francisco State University, and he is a CERTIFIED PROPERTY MANAGER©, Senior Certified Shopping Center Manager, Counselor of Real Estate, and Real Property Administrator.

Alan A. Alexander is the President of Alexander Consultants, Scottsdale, Arizona, which specializes in the managing, leasing, and consulting for income-producing properties. He has provided problem-solving consultation on properties throughout the United States. He is the former senior vice president of Fox & Carskadon Management Corporation, where he had responsibilities for a portfolio of properties worth in excess of $100 million in four western states. As director of leasing for Fox & Carskadon Financial, Mr. Alexander was responsible for the leasing of all shopping centers owned by the company throughout the United States.

Mr. Alexander was a member of the national faculty of the Institute of Real Estate Management (IREM) from 1982 through 1997, and was a frequent speaker and instructor at the International Council of Shopping Centers (ICSC) programs, including the school for professional development, the University of Shopping Centers, the annual convention, and international classes in Hong Kong, Taiwan, the Philippines, Malaysia, China, Singapore, India, Dubai, Holland, South America, Jamaica, Canada, and Mexico. He has been the moderator and speaker for more than 200 seminars on developing, managing, and leasing shopping centers and small office buildings for the Northwest Center for Professional Education.

He is the author of several articles published in the *Journal of Property Management (JPM)* and is a co-author of the books *Shopping Center Management and Leasing* and *Managing and Leasing Commercial Properties,* published by IREM. Mr. Alexander was inducted into IREM's Academy of Authors in February 1984, and is a past president of IREM's San Francisco Bay Area Chapter. In 1992, he received the Distinguished Service Award for educational service to ICSC.

Contents

1

An Introduction to the Leasing Process

A commercial lease transaction is a complicated and important transaction between the landlord and the tenant. Lease negotiations require both parties to engage in extensive analyses, discussions, negotiations, and compromises. The best outcome is a win-win situation in which both parties are confident that their objectives have been met.

A completed lease transaction is the rewarding result of several real estate professionals using their expertise, knowledge, and experience. They all work together to achieve their client's leasing goals and objectives. The leasing process these professionals go through takes several months and either culminates in a completed lease or ends with the landlord and/or the tenant being disappointed that they were unable to complete the transaction.

The lease transaction is also important to many individuals who provide information to help the landlord and tenant make their best decisions during lease negotiations. Though these professionals do not control the decisions made by the landlord and the tenant, they must fulfill their responsibilities in a timely manner. Their goal is to bring the leasing process to fruition through a fully executed lease.

There are many beneficiaries of a completed lease. The community benefits every time a new business enters the area. Jobs are created, services are provided, the tenant mix of shopping centers is enhanced, and other businesses in the area benefit when a new business brings employees and attracts customers to the area. The new business and its employees often become customers of other businesses in the area. And each business contributes to the tax base of the community.

Yet lease negotiations do not just effortlessly transition through the many steps needed to arrive at an executed lease. The landlord and tenant must be prepared for the important process of negotiations, and all the players involved must use their skills diligently to achieve the successful completion of a lease transaction.

THE PULSE OF THE DEAL

Every lease transaction, also known as a "deal," takes on an often precarious and fragile life of its own. Any number of events can slow a deal, create barriers to completing negotiations, and make it difficult, if not impossible, for landlords and tenants to complete a lease transaction. Every deal has a pulse that must be maintained by all the players. Any player in the deal can slow its pulse and unintentionally place the deal at risk of failing. If the pulse of the deal is allowed to stop for even a short time, it may not be revived. If the pulse stops for an extended time, it is almost never revived.

When the transaction dies, it is often the result of either the landlord or the tenant not being able to afford the terms of the deal. The proposed lease restrictions may be too onerous to one of the parties. At other times, a better alternative arises during the early stages of the leasing process. The tenant may find a better location or the landlord may find a tenant who either is a better fit for the building or will lease additional space. In this case, the saying "Sometimes the best deal is the one that did not happen," often applies.

Players in the Pulse of the Deal

A lease transaction can have just a couple players or it can have several players. The landlord and the tenant are the main players in the deal, and occasionally the only players. But they typically call upon the expertise of several professionals in addition to their *leasing agents* to complete the leasing process.

Each player in the leasing process has a responsibility to keep the lease transaction moving towards a completed lease at the pace established by that player's client. Most landlords hand over to leasing professionals the responsibility to develop and implement a leasing plan for their buildings. These professionals may be employees of the landlord, but typically they are professionals working for commercial real estate firms.

Tenants also may look for space and negotiate a lease independently. Large corporations often have a real estate division that handles all their real estate transactions. Most tenants, however, use the services of a leasing agent. The respective leasing agents, representing the landlord's search for tenants and the tenant's search for a location, usually introduce the main players to each other.

Leasing agents play a critical role in the success of their clients' businesses. The landlord's leasing agent is assigned the responsibility of developing and implementing the building's marketing and leasing plan. This plan, similar to the marketing and sales plan of most businesses, will ultimately determine the success of the landlord's business: the building. The leasing agent has a wealth of knowledge concerning market conditions, including rental rates, concessions, and buildings' *pass-through charges,* along with recent deals in the area, buildings' vacancies, and the strengths and weaknesses of each competing building.

The leasing agent's advice and recommendations are important during the initial lease-up of a building and its ongoing leasing. The landlord depends on the leasing agent to keep the building operating at a high occupancy. When a building has a vacancy problem, the landlord is likely to supplement the building's income stream with a cash infusion or risk losing the building to its lender.

The landlord may hire a space planner to efficiently design and lay out the tenant's premises while considering the building's budgeted *tenant improvement (TI) allowance* and the required tenant contribution to the TIs. In the absence of space planning, tenants are likely to have space designs that will not optimize the use of their premises, possibly negatively impacting operations and increasing *occupancy costs.* The tenant or landlord may hire a designer to select the interior finishes, furniture, and accessories.

A *general contractor* is hired by the landlord of office, medical office, and industrial properties to estimate the cost to build out the premises. The general contractor or TI contractor is needed to take the plans for the premises through the city's permitting process and secure the necessary building permits. These professionals also build out the premises to the space planner's specifications, and they are often called upon to "value engineer" the build-out within the landlord's and the tenant's budgets. Retail tenants usually have contractors who build out all their stores and provide cost estimates to complete their TIs.

Attorneys are hired by the landlord and the tenant to protect their respective interests when negotiating the lease document. Since the lease is a legal document with rights and obligations for the landlord and the tenant, attorneys protect clients' interests by negotiating the lease in their clients' best interests.

Other consultants or players to the transaction may be hired for their specific knowledge or technical skills. Each of these players must be aware of the pulse of the deal and work to ensure that the deal flow continues at a pace that will bring the leasing process to a successful transaction.

The Leaders

Each of the players in the transaction fulfills a critical role in bringing the deal to completion. Yet every transaction needs a leader to ensure that all the players are performing their tasks in a timely manner and no one is slowing the leasing process. One of the players in the deal needs to take charge of the deal flow and maintain the pulse of the deal. This person is often one of the leasing agents. Both leasing agents may assume a leadership role in keeping all the players focused on completing their part of the deal. Each player in the deal is working on several transactions or deals concurrently, and it is easy for one or more of them to lose track of the pulse of a specific deal by focusing their attention on other lease transactions.

The leasing agent (or agents) in charge of the deal creates a timeline with targeted goals for each player to ensure that all are aware of their deadlines and that the pulse of the deal maintains it rhythm. Though leasing agents should lead the deal process, the ultimate responsibility for the deal flow rests with the landlord and the tenant.

The Timeframe

Decade after decade, leasing agents say it takes longer to do a deal than in the past. It may not seem possible that it requires more and more time to complete the leasing process, but leases become more complicated every few years as new provisions are added. The hazardous substance provision did not exist in the early 1980s, yet now it makes up two pages of the lease and is often one of the most contested provisions.

In the first decade of the 21st century, green building provisions were new to leases. Today, more governmental initiatives have produced regulations or laws to protect the environment and prevent unscrupulous individuals from taking advantage of others and of society. When new building regulations and codes are enacted, the permitting process takes longer than ever before.

A lease transaction, starting with the tenant's initial search for space and ending with the tenant occupying the premises, typically takes months to complete. The leasing agent may spend weeks searching for several locations that meet the tenant's needs. Then the tenant needs at least a few weeks to visit and analyze alternative locations. A space planner requires about a week to interview the tenant and understand the tenant's business, as well as a couple of weeks to prepare the space layout.

A tenant improvement contractor needs two weeks to price the cost of the build-out. The premises must be built out based on the timeline for the tenant's move-in date. If tenants are relocating from another space, they will be in a difficult position if their new space is not completed on time. The landlord needs the space built out and occupied as soon as possible to generate rent from the premises. If the space is not delivered on time, the tenant may require the landlord to pay a penalty for the delay. Many retailers open stores only during specific periods of the year, and if their space is not ready during one of those windows they will delay their move-in and store opening to avoid opening during the "wrong" time of the year.

While it takes just a few hours to draft a lease, it can take months for the attorneys, the leasing agents, the tenant, and the landlord to negotiate the document. Once the lease has been executed, it takes a month or longer to have the plans reviewed and approved by the city and a building permit issued. Depending on the extent of the build-out, which can range from just cleaning or replacing the carpet and painting the walls to removing all existing improvements and building out the premises to the specifications of the new tenant, the tenant improvement contactor may need a few weeks or months to build out the premises.

When the leasing process has finally been successfully completed, all the players can move on to other assignments with a tremendous feeling of a job well done.

THE IMPORTANCE OF THE LEASE

A lease is an important transaction for the landlord and tenant. Landlords have substantial investments in their buildings. The investment in a ten-thousand-square-foot office building by an individual is just as important as the multi-million-dollar investment a *real estate investment trust (REIT)* makes in a major shopping center. Small investors acquiring buildings on their own are likely to have more personally at risk than do investors in larger investment groups.

The Landlord's Investment

A landlord acquires a building by either developing it or purchasing it. Development is a high-risk and high-reward business. The final and most critical factor in determining whether a development is successful is the time it takes to lease the building and the rental rates that are achieved. Most of the other components of developing a project can be estimated with a fair degree of accuracy, but the leasing projection requires forecasting what the market conditions will be several years in the future, when the building will be ready for occupancy.

Most landlords acquire their buildings by purchasing them. Their risks are not as great as those of developers; but their buildings, which will have a physical life of several decades to well over 100 years, will go through multiple real estate cycles that can threaten their financial stability. During these cycles the buildings are subject to many influences, some of which the landlords have control over and others that are out of their control.

Based on how they operate and maintain their buildings, landlords determine what they will charge within the market range of rental rates. They also determine which concessions, if any, they will offer to prospective tenants, and they establish the building's management and operations standards. Landlords select the members of their leasing teams and monitor their performance.

There are many issues landlords cannot change that affect their building's performance. Landlords have no control over the commercial real estate market, new competing buildings that are developed in the area, the area's economy, interest rates, or governmental regulations that impact building operations. A poor economy affects job growth, new business formation, and the ability of businesses to develop and expand. These issues have a direct effect on the demand for space in a building or an area.

High interest rates also slow business expansions—especially for retailers. When this occurs, the demand for space declines and vacancies increase, causing rental rates to drop and concessions to increase. High interest rates increase the risk involved in developing buildings and reduce the *return on investment (ROI)*. Governmental regulations can affect the cost to build and operate buildings. Tax laws influence the return on real estate investments.

Regardless of the market conditions, the strength or weakness of the economy, and all the other factors that can positively or negatively affect buildings, *tenants* are a building's most valuable asset and ultimately determine the success of an income-producing real estate investment. The rent tenants pay generates the building's income, pays its operating expenses and debt service, and produces the cash flow and the return on the landlord's investment. The quality and the quantity of the building's income stream, which is provided by all the tenants, are two key components in determining the building's value.

Landlords have always been aware of the importance of their tenants to the success of their investments. However, this was never more evident than in the late 1980s and early 1990s when the commercial real estate market was in a depression in many areas of the country. Office buildings' rents throughout the country plummeted, and vacancy rates soared. Other commercial real estate property types—medical office buildings, industrial properties, and shopping centers—did not experience the same devastation that the office building markets experienced, but they also suffered from high vacancies and falling rental rates. Many properties were lost to their lenders, either through foreclosures or deeds in lieu of foreclosures. During this period real estate loans were difficult to obtain, so fewer properties were sold and purchased.

Every landlord became keenly aware, through firsthand experience, of the cost of losing a tenant. The number one responsibility of property managers became tenant retention. Regular visits with tenants from property managers, tenant satisfaction surveys, and tenant appreciation events were just a few of the components that became part of a building's tenant retention program. Today those programs are still in place, and property managers continue to focus their attention on meeting the needs of the building's most valuable asset: its tenants.

The Tenant's Business

Landlords and tenants have much in common. They are both operating a business, and each one's business is dependent upon the other for its success. A landlord's building is a business with the same management, marketing, and operational issues faced by tenants operating their own business. A building is operated with the same management principles used to operate any other business successfully; and without a steady and sufficient income stream, the landlord's business will fail.

A lease is important to the tenant's business plan. A lease "puts the tenant in business." It provides a tenant with the right to occupy and use space in a building for a defined period of time. Tenants negotiate for their business's first location and then either renew their lease or find another location about every three to five years.

The rent and other elements that add to the occupancy cost of a lease, such as pass-through building operating expenses, utilities, etc., are significant expenses for a tenant. Rent or occupancy cost in excess of the tenant's budget can place a financial strain on the operating expenses of a start-up business. This can create financial hardship and threaten the survivability of a new venture.

For many businesses, location is a critical component of their operations. A long-term lease in a good location can have value beyond the rent the tenant is paying. Most retailers need to be located where there is high pedestrian traffic. Industrial tenants who require multiple transportation channels require a location that can facilitate the efficient and cost-effective transportation of their products. If their business is not located near a freeway or port, they usually incur additional—and needless—operational costs.

The tenant's location also may be part of the business's brand image. For instance, a merchant may want a prominent location in Union Square in San Francisco or on Michigan Avenue in Chicago. These locations are seen by millions of people each year and serve as a form of advertising. A retailer can create brand awareness by operating in a prominent location. A law firm or a consulting firm may locate in a prestigious high-rise office building, or in an upscale office park with the best address in the city.

Leasing and operating buildings is a landlord's business, while tenants often have limited knowledge of the commercial real estate market conditions, the operations of buildings, and the lease document. No two leases are alike, and some are drafted to be fair to each party while others are drafted solely for the benefit of the party preparing the document. A lease should be an asset to a tenant's business but, depending on how it is negotiated, it can be a liability to the operations of the business. The tenant should consult with an attorney or a person who is familiar with commercial leases when negotiating this complex document. Three to ten years is a long time to live up to a lease that is onerous and negatively affects business operations.

Lease negotiations can place significant strain on the tenant. The process may require time commitments from the tenant's key employees beyond their regular responsibilities. The uncertainty of where and when a new location will be found can create stress for top management. In addition, the next location may not be as advantageous to the tenant's business operations.

The lease has many provisions that affect tenants' occupancy costs. These provisions also place restrictions on tenant business operations. Financial strain will arise if rental rates and occupancy costs are beyond a tenant's budget.

Tenants do have significant motivation to complete the lease transaction and "do the deal." A start-up business typically needs to find space that is economical yet meets the business's space and location requirements. A retailer growing his business from its first location needs to be certain that the second store is located in the best area for his business, that it is in the right type of retail property (e.g., a grocery-anchored shopping center, a lifestyle shopping center, or an enclosed mall), and that his customer profile is represented in the shopping center's *trade area.*

A national retailer entering a market for the first time has the same concerns as a local retailer looking for additional locations. These retailers understand their merchandise niche, their customers, and the correct pricing of their products; but they do not know the many retail property submarkets of the area, each submarket's customer base, the performance of other retailers in each submarket, and the occupancy costs for several alternative locations. Retail brokers who understand their clients' products and customer bases are able to provide an invaluable service in analyzing market data, shopper profiles, and the performance of other retailers in each local submarket.

When industrial or office tenants' businesses grow and need to expand, the tenants must either lease additional space in their current building or relocate to another building. Occasionally tenants have the opposite need: to downsize their operations and reduce the size of their space. These tenants have similar options: remaining in their present building and negotiating for less space by renegotiating their current lease, relocating to another building when that lease expires, or buying out of their lease. In these situations, the tenant must acquire the necessary amount of space at the right rental rate to operate an efficient and cost-effective business.

Tenants are not commercial real estate professionals. They are often the only players in the leasing process who are not real estate professionals or affiliated industry professionals. All the other players in the transaction earn their livelihood working the leasing process. In this respect, tenants are at a disadvantage when looking for space for their business, going through the leasing process, and negotiating the business terms of a lease on their own.

Because tenants do not always know the leasing market or which buildings have space to lease, they frequently need to rely on leasing agents to find them the best location with the most advantageous lease terms. Tenants should select a leasing agent (or agents) to represent them and protect their business interests in their initial search for a location, during their analysis of spaces, through the conclusion of lease negotiations, and up to the moment of their move to the new premises.

EXECUTING THE LEASE DOCUMENT

A lease provides each party with rights and obligations, and if the lease is poorly negotiated, either the landlord or the tenant is likely to suffer financially. Some lease obligations may negatively affect either the operations of the building or the tenant's business. The landlord and the tenant must carefully select the right players to represent them in the transaction to achieve their goals and the objective of bringing the leasing process to a fully executed lease.

The landlord and the tenant need to prepare for lease negotiations. The first phase of preparation is for each party to determine its needs and establish its leasing goals and objectives. Next, the parties need to understand the market conditions and the strengths and weaknesses of the other party's position. This will allow both parties to develop their leasing strategies and tactics.

The lease needs to be carefully negotiated by landlords and tenants. It is a legal document that provides rights and obligations to both parties. Since a lease is for the use of the landlord's property, it will almost always benefit the landlord. A building's income stream and *net operating income (NOI)* are dependent on how each of its leases has been negotiated.

Depending on how the lease is negotiated, tenants may be able to assign their *leasehold* rights to another tenant for a substantial profit. For instance, anchor tenants, such as supermarkets in shopping centers, enter into 20- to 30-year leases with multiple five-year options. It is not uncommon for supermarkets to evolve and change their format and store size over time, and build state-of-the-art stores in the immediate area of their older stores. They will relocate to their state-of-the-art store in a new location and sublease their original store for a rent which could be well above what they are paying, allowing them to retain the difference. They know the value of their space to the landlord, and they may offer to cancel their lease for a substantial lease *buyout* payment from the landlord. Though this situation is not common in the commercial real estate industry, it emphasizes the value of a lease for a good location with favorable terms.

Almost all leases are prepared by the landlord. Landlords have their own lease form or document prepared by an attorney and modified or updated every few years. Landlords want one lease for all their tenants so they do not have to administer dozens of different leases in their buildings. An exception to using the landlord's lease is national retail anchor tenants and governmental agencies who insist on using their own lease document. The party whose lease is used usually begins with the advantage of a lease that has been drafted to protect their interests. If the landlord's lease form is used and the tenant is not a real estate expert, that tenant often starts at a disadvantage in the negotiating process.

The landlord and the landlord's leasing agent will enter into a *leasing agreement* that establishes their respective responsibilities and obligations. Leasing agreements (or *brokerage agreements*) are almost always provided by the leasing agent's *brokerage firm*. These agreements favor the brokerage firm, so the landlord should carefully review the agreement and offer changes and modifications where needed. The leasing agreement is negotiable just as the lease document is negotiable.

Leasing agents will provide their clients with their cost of doing the deal and, when appropriate, their cost of *not* doing the deal. Deals have the obvious costs of base rent and the expenses of TIs. Other costs that are frequently overlooked are the building pass-through charges, possible percentage rent for retailers, and other lease obligations that affect the operations of the building and the tenant's business.

Once the lease is executed by the landlord and the tenant, it needs to be administered by each party. Two new players enter the leasing process, one representing the landlord and the other representing the tenant, to ensure that both parties honor their lease obligations and enjoy the benefits of the lease. Lease administrators and property managers have an important responsibility through the life of the lease.

Business Terms of the Lease

Often tenants believe that finding the right space for their business is the end of the leasing process. In fact, when the right location in the best building is found, the leasing process merely enters into another phase. The business terms of the lease, many of which are dependent on the cost to prepare the premises for the tenant's occupancy, must be negotiated. Tenant improvements for office and medical office buildings—and sometimes industrial properties and shopping centers—are often the most costly part of the deal for the landlord.

Usually retail properties are either leased in "as is" condition or a small TI allowance is provided to the tenant. In office buildings, medical office buildings, and industrial properties, the landlord usually provides the tenant with an allowance to build out the premises. This allowance, which is a substantial cost for the landlord, may cover all the costs to build the premises to the tenant's specification; or the tenant may pay for a portion of the build-out. The cost of TIs needs to be known or estimated before the business terms of the lease are fully negotiated. After the entire lease document has been negotiated, the tenant's premises are built out as designed, agreed to, and negotiated.

The landlord and the tenant usually focus solely on the business terms of the deal. Yet these issues are just a few of the many lease provisions in a commercial real estate lease. All of the other provisions are rights and obligations of the landlord and the tenant, and these impact the operations and *cash flow* of the building as well as the operations and profitability of the tenant's business.

Lease Renewals

The lease renewal is a lease transaction that is often overlooked or prepared for improperly. Renewals are often taken for granted; but imagine the potential negative impact to a business if the landlord chooses not to offer a lease renewal.

The cost to move to another location is usually greater than tenants realize. A new location may negatively impact the morale of employees and (depending on the location) affect employee recruitment. Tenants who have lost their lease are in a difficult position; they can be out of business if a new location is not found, a lease negotiated and fully executed, and the space built out to their specifications before the previous lease expires.

Landlords also need to establish a plan to renew or replace tenants whose leases are expiring. The least expensive deal for a landlord is a lease renewal. In contrast to a new lease, a renewal has no downtime or lost rent, fewer TI expenses, and a lower commission cost.

A lease renewal should be approached by the tenant and the landlord with the same diligence and analysis as a new lease. Both parties almost always want to renew the lease, and each party should negotiate for the best terms possible.

RESOURCES

There are several resources available that provide guidance, knowledge, and market information to allow landlords, tenants, and leasing agents to successfully work through the many challenges they confront in a deal.

Leasing agents provide the best source of market data to landlords and tenants. Leasing agents are "in the field" everyday, working on lease transactions and networking with other leasing agents. Networking provides them with up-to-date information on deals that have occurred in the area. The real estate industry has a wealth of resources available for leasing agents to improve their leasing skills. There are several real estate professional associations that provide great networking opportunities. They allow leasing agents to meet and discuss market conditions and recently completed deals.

Major commercial brokerage firm research departments conduct and publish their *market surveys* quarterly, allowing landlords and tenants to stay abreast of market conditions. Local newspapers use the data from these surveys to write articles on the commercial real estate market. Brokerage firms also place their surveys on their websites for everyone to access. Many brokerage firms develop and publish one- to four-page color reports on the market conditions and lease transaction data for each property type or the property type of their specialty. Some brokerage firms publish their own booklets, with charts and graphs as well as narratives describing the market conditions, for each property type in every major and secondary city in the United States.

The Institute of Real Estate Management (IREM; www.irem.org) has chapters in every metropolitan area across the United States and Canada, and many of these chapters conduct an annual market forecast meeting towards the end of the year. These meetings are open to the public, and the speakers discuss the current market conditions and predictions for the coming years for each property type.

IREM offers seminars—regionally, nationally, and internationally—on leasing office buildings, medical office buildings, shopping centers, and retail properties. IREM has also published *Shopping Center Management and Leasing, Office Building Management,* and *Managing and Leasing Commercial Properties,* which are "how-to" books on developing marketing and leasing plans. Several issues of IREM's *Journal of Property Management (JPM)* have articles on leasing. And IREM publishes annual Income/Expense Analysis Reports for office buildings and shopping centers that provide the operating expenses for these property types. These data are important to tenants for knowing what the pass-through charges are likely to be in their area.

The International Council of Shopping Centers (ICSC; www.icsc.org) annually conducts the University of Shopping Centers. This program has a track on leasing shopping centers. ICSC also publishes books on leasing shopping centers. Every year, ICSC conducts a spring convention in which the main attraction is a "leasing mall" where retailers, developers, and brokerage firms have booths and meet with each other to discuss—and often start the leasing process for—specific sites and shopping centers. Additionally, ICSC offers the only commercial real estate leasing designation, the Certified Leasing Specialist (CLS).

The Building Owners and Managers Association (BOMA) International (www.boma.org) and the BOMI Institute (www.bomi-edu.org) offer office building leasing seminars and publish books on the subject. ICSC and BOMA International also publish analyses of operating expenses in buildings. The Certified Commercial Investment Member (CCIM) Institute (www.ccim.com) offers courses on real estate financial analysis and market analysis.

Some major publishing houses have a real estate division that publishes commercial real estate leasing books. There are monthly newsletters on leasing and lease negotiations. "Commercial Lease Law Insider" is a monthly newsletter for landlords and their attorneys, leasing agents, and property managers. "Commercial Tenant's Lease Insider" is a newsletter for tenants and their attorneys. Each of these newsletters provides lease provisions that favor their audience and recent court rulings on leasing issues. These newsletters are published by Vendome Group, LLC in New York City.

Just about every area has at least one community college with a real estate program. Most of these colleges offer a course on managing and leasing commercial properties. Many universities have a real estate program, and some of their courses are open to real estate professionals and tenants.

In brief, there is no shortage of information on the commercial real estate market and lease documents. A little time invested in understanding the leasing process, market conditions, and the commercial real estate lease will pay great dividends when landlords and tenants are negotiating for space.

2

The Players in a Lease Transaction

BUILDING A TEAM

Leasing space requires the expertise of several professionals from different disciplines in the real estate industry working together to achieve their client's leasing goals and objectives. Landlords assemble leasing teams to find tenants for their buildings, while tenants assemble leasing teams to find space to operate their businesses.

The landlord's team will include *leasing agents,* administrative support, attorneys, space planners, tenant improvement contractors, the building's property manager, and possibly the building's lender. When the landlord is a developer, the team developing and building the project will expand to include the developer's employees, designers, construction contractors, finance professionals, leasing agents, and property managers.

The number of players on the tenant's team will vary depending on whether the tenant is a local business or a national company. A local business will hire a leasing agent and may require the services of a space planner and designer. Regional and national companies have real estate representatives, site selection committees, construction coordinators, and lease administrative personnel, and they often contract with a local leasing agent to find alternative locations to consider.

THE PLAYERS

Many of the key players in a lease transaction are discussed in the sections below.

The Landlord

An income-producing building is a business. Operating a building is no different than operating any other type of business. And of all the issues a landlord must address while operating a building, none is more important than leasing. Landlords need to lease space in their buildings in order to generate income for paying the building's operating expenses and debt service.

Being aware of the many reasons landlords need to operate their buildings at a high occupancy will assist tenants and their leasing agents in finding the right space and negotiating the best lease. It is assumed that all landlords want to lease their space as quickly as possible and at the highest rent. While this is true for most landlords, many have additional objectives. These may include exceeding occupancy requirements to prevent existing retail tenants from exercising a *co-tenancy provision;* achieving a lender's required occupancy or *net operating income (NOI);* and sustaining a desirable tenant mix.

Most landlords do not want to lease to tenants who are likely to create management issues such as excessive use of building services, violating the building's rules and regulations, paying rent late, and unkempt stores. This is a major issue with landlords of shopping centers and retail properties, who are concerned with securing the right tenant mix for their targeted customer base. They will often avoid leasing to certain tenants, leaving spaces vacant until the right tenant is found. Additionally, landlords of shopping centers and malls will offer favorable lease terms to the most desirable retailers.

Just as tenants should find out the leasing objectives of the landlord to make their best deal, the landlord should also discover the leasing objectives and the needs of prospective tenants. For instance, landlords of retail properties can facilitate the leasing of their properties and the lease transaction by understanding what motivates a retailer or service tenant. Retailers analyze whether a location will be profitable for them based on their anticipated sales volume, the rent and *occupancy cost,* labor cost, and the cost to build out their space. This information is necessary to arrive at their projected net profit.

The landlord is well advised to provide prospects with all the information they need to determine whether the building is the best place for them to locate their business. A retailer needs building-specific information, such as:

- The building's physical condition and utility capacity
- *Americans with Disabilities Act (ADA)* compliance

- An accurate set of as-built drawings
- Data about the trade area

Some questions for the retailer to ask include:

- Does traffic arrive at the shopping center or retail property primarily by auto, by public transportation, or by foot?
- How have other retailers in the shopping center and/or immediate area performed?
- What are the *demographics* and *psychographics* of the primary, secondary, and tertiary trade areas of the property?

Leasing agents will gather this necessary information on their clients' properties and the surrounding areas, and will make it available for prospective tenants.

To facilitate the leasing of their building and to be fair to prospective tenants, landlords should establish standards to qualify prospects. No one wants to spend time on deals that have little or no chance of happening. It is almost always in the landlord's best interest to let the tenant's leasing agent know up front where the client stands with the desired use and/or financial criteria. If there are multiple offers on a single space, the landlord should let each leasing agent know the tenant's standings. The landlords who are always "moving the goal posts" will discourage leasing agents from bringing them prospectives.

It is in the best interest of all parties to have everyone dealing fairly and openly. Landlords should develop a reputation in the brokerage community as being deal makers rather than deal killers. This can be achieved by assembling a team prepared to promptly provide all the information the tenant needs to decide whether or not to lease space in the building. Likewise, the tenant can facilitate the transaction by providing the necessary business information to facilitate the landlord's decision.

The Developer

Developers are visionaries and risk takers. Where others see a vacant lot or dilapidated eyesore of a building, they envision a new or rehabbed building generating revenue. Developers typically hire six different teams to bring their vision to reality. These teams are (1) the developer and developer's associates; (2) the design team; (3) the finance team; (4) the construction team; (5) the leasing team; and (6) the property management team.

Architects and engineers are hired to transform the developer's vision into a building design. A *general contractor* is hired to assemble the construction team and to build the building. A mortgage broker is selected to find the best financing available based on the developer's financing goals and objectives. One or more leasing agents are chosen to provide market information, project rental rates, and find tenants. An attorney is needed to protect the developer's interests and negotiate the land sale, the financing documents, and the leases. A property manager is hired to develop the building's operating budget and manage the building through different real estate cycles, based on the developer's goals and objectives. Other consultants may be brought on to address specific issues and to validate the economics of the developer's vision.

The development business is a high-risk and high-reward business. The developer often personally guarantees the loan to build the project. If the development is initially successful or is successful over time, the developer is handsomely rewarded. If the development is significantly over budget, has significant construction delays, or leases well below the lease-up projections, the project will not come close to achieving its projected *pro forma* and the developer will most likely need to make cash contributions to keep the project's loan current. If the cash drain continues for a long time or is beyond the developer's financial capabilities, that developer is likely to lose the property to foreclosure or deed in lieu of foreclosure. In addition to losing the property, the lender may go after the developer's other assets. Few people are willing to take such risks for the rewards of developing a property. Yet successful developers are continually taking these risks.

The overall cost of developing a building can often be quantified with a relatively high level of confidence before construction commences. The cost of the land is negotiated well in advance. Financing is arranged and the loan payments can be fixed. The construction costs can be negotiated with a guaranteed price contract. Of course, there may be expensive cost overruns for changes in the scope of the project. The cost to operate the building upon opening can be determined by using the operating costs of similar buildings in the area and applying an inflation factor. The only element that cannot be projected with confidence during the planning stage is leasing.

Leasing has two components: rate and time. A small building can take a couple of years to progress from the developer's initial vision to the time the first tenant takes occupancy. A large building can take four to seven years from that initial vision to final build-out and occupancy. During this time the leasing market can change from a landlord's market to a tenant's market, and it may be impossible for the leasing pro forma to be achieved.

What will rental rates be several years from the time the project starts? How long will it take to lease up the building? The answers to these questions are the key to a profitable development. The successful leasing of the project validates the developer's vision. Developers are highly motivated to lease their buildings, and they ideally will reduce their risk by preleasing. Tenants can negotiate their best deals by knowing what motivates developers and where the project is in its lease-up.

The Tenant

Tenants, like developers, are entrepreneurs and risk takers who create and operate businesses. They need the best space, in the right location, at acceptable rental terms to optimize their operations, income, and profits. The best space and location vary depending on the type of business and the preferences of that business's owner(s). Most tenants are not knowledgeable of the commercial real estate market and are wise to add to their team a leasing agent.

The leasing agent has a wealth of knowledge about market conditions, knows the reputation of different buildings and their landlords, and is aware of the terms of current lease deals in the market. Many national corporations—especially national retailers—contract with tenant-rep brokers (also called *tenant-rep leasing agents*) to represent them in specific geographic areas of the United States.

Real estate is a local product, and markets are different throughout the country. National retailers need specific market data for each area in which they are considering opening a store. And leasing agents are the best people to gather this data and supply market knowledge. Once the data has been obtained, the retailer's site selection committee will review and either approve or reject all sites and leases presented to their company. Some retailers have regional site selection committees (e.g., a West Coast committee to approve sites and leases that are then sent to a national selection committee for final approval).

It is in their best interest for tenants to "sell" themselves to the landlord as an asset to the property. Landlords want to have confidence that tenants will pay rent on time, live up to their lease obligations, and not create any problems. Landlords know that tenants generate the building's income stream, but they want to lease to the best tenants possible. Some landlords will reject lease proposals until they find what they define as a "good" tenant. Others are only concerned with filling a rent roll and will accept any tenant and any use.

Because landlords are concerned about the creditworthiness of tenants, prospects should explain why they are good for the building, making sure to present their business in the best possible light. They should organize their financial data, which the landlord will review to determine their financial condition and payment history, and would be wise to have financials professionally prepared. The retail tenant also needs to be realistic concerning projected sales.

If the tenant is a startup business, a business plan should be provided for the landlord, who can benchmark a retail prospect's expected sales by either reviewing that company's sales at other locations or comparing the projections to local tenants with similar uses. This business plan is especially important for a startup *retail* business. The landlord can compare the retailer's sales projections to the national averages for that category of business. This data can be found in *Dollars & Cents of Shopping Centers,* which is copublished biannually by the Urban Land Institute (ULI) and the International Council of Shopping Centers (ICSC).

All prospective tenants should quantify their current and future space needs. A space planner can estimate the amount of space needed and then provide sample space layouts depending on the configuration of the leased space. The tenant should have available business and financial references, and be responsive to questions from the landlord when negotiating deal points and signing the lease.

It will also benefit the tenant to do homework on the landlord. The leasing agent can gather this information. First, check into the landlord's ability to manage and operate the property. The building operations—especially for a shopping center—can have an impact on a tenant's business and profitability. If the landlord is using a third-party property management company, find out what experience and reputation that company has with the property type. Each commercial property type requires specific knowledge and experience to be managed efficiently and effectively.

The goal of tenants is to find the best place and terms available for operating their business. By studying the market, comparing alternative buildings, gathering information on the landlords and the manner in which their properties are operated, and ultimately "selling" their business and tenancy to the landlord, tenants' location goals and objectives can be achieved.

THE LEASING AGENT

Many leasing agents specialize as either a landlord or a tenant agent. Some leasing agents will have both landlords and tenants as clients, but they usually spend the majority of their time representing one or the other.

The Landlord Leasing Agent

Most landlords do not have a leasing team or the time to lease properties themselves, so they contract with a brokerage firm to lease their buildings. An exception would be large developers and real estate investment trusts (REITs) with in-house leasing departments.

One of the advantages of contracting with a brokerage firm is that its leasing agents are "in play" at all times, looking for prospects, networking with other leasing agents (from their own firm as well as from competing firms), and discovering deals that have taken place. They are constantly monitoring changes to the market conditions.

Leasing space is more than a sign on a property and an ad in the local newspaper. Most leasing agents who represent landlords devote all their time to finding tenants. They usually have a number of buildings listed, each with varying amounts of space available for lease. Sometimes leasing agents assume the leasing of very large, new buildings that require all of their time for an extended period. A few leasing agents will also list properties for sale while they are working their leasing listings.

Leasing agents are compensated only after a deal is completed, necessitating aggressive tenant searches for their currently listed buildings while planning ahead to find new listings that will generate commission for the following year. Sometimes other players in the lease transaction will envy or resent the commission paid to the leasing agent—especially when it is substantial. It is easy for the other players to overlook the fact that leasing agents are the only players who have to spend their time prospecting for tenants and then negotiating leases. The leasing agent often spends months looking for tenants before a deal is even brought to the leasing team, while all the other players on the landlord's team are paid a fee or salary for their role in every deal—including the ones that don't result in an executed lease.

Leasing agents go through a long apprenticeship and start-up period in which they learn the business and build their "book of business." During this time, which is easily three years or longer, they have no salary, working only for commission and often struggling to survive financially. However, those leasing agents who are eventually able to build a leasing practice typically earn a substantial income. Successful leasing agents consistently earn in the low- to mid-six figures, and top leasing agents will earn even more. Yet even the most successful leasing agents often work on several deals each year that extend for months before falling apart; and they receive no compensation for these efforts.

There are a few disadvantages to contracting with a leasing agent. Leasing agents may be more focused on earning a commission than on maximizing rents and finding optimal tenants for the building. If there are just a few spaces remaining to lease, they may focus their attention on other buildings with greater leasing opportunities. The landlord must be confident that the leasing agent does not have a conflict of interest derived from leasing buildings in direct competition with the landlord's building.

Leasing agents build their business without hiring a staff or renting space. They work for free until a deal is completed, and then they wait a month or longer to be paid. They are entrepreneurs and risk takers.

The Tenant Leasing Agent

The tenant's leasing agent, referred to as a *tenant rep,* provides a valuable service. Tenants are not in the real estate business, and they seldom have more than a cursory knowledge of the commercial real estate market. They often do not have the time or interest to educate themselves on market conditions, nor do they have the resources or the contacts to know the terms of comparable deals. The tenant rep fills this gap by providing a wealth of knowledge about the market along with the ability to select and analyze buildings that meet certain space and location needs. This allows a tenant to focus on business operations, knowing that a real estate professional is looking for space that will meet the specified business requirements on the best possible terms.

Like the landlord leasing agent, the tenant leasing agent spends a majority of time locating space. After interviewing new clients to discover their reasons for relocating or opening new locations, this agent is charged with searching the market to find and compare several suitable options. If the tenant is a retailer, for example, the space must be located in an area where the tenant's customer base is represented. The leasing agent will then compare these spaces using the tenant's criteria. In addition, the leasing agent compares the rent and other charges for each building. Building features are examined along with amenities in the area. The reputation of the landlord is included in the analysis.

During this process, the tenant relies on the leasing agent to provide current market and rental information. Leasing agents have a tremendous influence over which buildings their tenants select. Once a decision has been made, leasing agents negotiate the business terms of the lease. They may also either provide advice on certain lease provisions or negotiate the entire lease. However, many leasing agents prefer to negotiate only the business terms, devoting their time to leasing rather than negotiating the other lease provisions.

The tenant leasing agent will either be paid a commission directly by the landlord or, if the building is listed with another broker, share the commission received by the listing broker. Usually this commission is shared equally or the tenant's agent receives the greater percentage. In a few situations, when the tenant's leasing agent receives no more than a nominal commission from the landlord, the tenant pays a fee to the agent.

The Tenant's In-House Leasing Representative

Some large tenants have their own in-house leasing agents. These real estate professionals are responsible either for managing the leasing process or for working directly with landlords to locate and negotiate leases.

When managing the leasing function, the in-house rep hires brokerage firms to direct the leasing effort; find locations; work with an in-house attorney or law firms to review the lease document; coordinate the build-out of the premises; and negotiate the lease. These brokers must be knowledgeable on multiple markets and have trust in the in-house agent's recommendations and knowledge of the market.

In some situations, in-house reps will work directly with the landlord to negotiate the lease. This may occur, for example, when national retailers negotiate with shopping center and mall developers. These large retailers usually have an established relationship with a developer's leasing team because they have multiple stores in that developer's shopping centers or malls.

The Landlord's In-House Leasing Agent

Though the great majority of landlords use brokerage firms to lease their properties, some benefit from having an in-house leasing team. There are potential advantages and disadvantages to having an in-house leasing agent.

The in-house leasing agent is part of the landlord's team developing or acquiring properties. This allows the benefit of focusing only on leasing the employer's properties, giving the in-house agent a better understanding than an independent agent would have of the landlord's goals and objectives for each property. In-house leasing agents also don't have to continually look for new business to fill a business development pipeline with future deals for future commissions. They are able to focus all efforts on leasing the properties.

The landlord's in-house leasing agents also often get the attention of the brokerage community by continually having space to lease. Tenant leasing agents need to know of buildings that have (or will have) available space to place them, and consequently they need to develop a good working rapport with these in-house leasing agents.

The environment in many brokerage firms is very competitive. Often leasing agents at these firms will not discuss their current deals or clients with other agents for fear those clients or deals will be stolen. In contrast, a team environment exists for in-house leasing agents working with the landlord, other in-house leasing agents, administrative personnel, and the property manager, because they are all focused on the same goals.

In-house leasing agents usually have the advantage of having several properties to present to a prospect. If they are leasing several shopping centers, for example, they can often negotiate multiple deals at several locations with a retailer who seeks increased market penetration. Often prospects give in-house leasing agents more respect because they are part of the landlord's team and therefore perceived as having more authority to do the deal. This is especially the case when the property owner—whether a REIT, private investment group, or a developer—is well-known and respected in the real estate community.

Some in-house leasing agents do have the authority to fully negotiate deals without final approval from anyone else. This allows unique advantages; for example, if such agents are leasing shopping centers and a retailer with multiple locations wants to lease space, the leasing agent may be able to leverage the best shopping centers in the portfolio by requiring that retailer to also lease space in some of the portfolio's more average shopping centers. During these negotiations, the tenant negotiates with the landlord's representative, so both parties have the additional benefit of negotiating "principal to principal."

One of the greatest advantages to being an in-house leasing agent is the elimination of the need to "fight" for commissions earned and wait months for payments from some landlords. In-house agents have 100 percent loyalty to one client: their employer; and their employer has loyalty to them. Their compensation is a good base salary with additional incentive pay tied to their leasing performance. They also have all of their expenses paid for, which can easily amount to more than $30,000 per year.

There are many who benefit from the in-house leasing agent's services. For example, it can be efficient and cost-effective for landlords with large portfolios to hire in-house leasing agents to lease their properties directly. Landlords who have large office building or industrial property portfolios in a metropolitan area may have an in-house leasing team to work with the brokerage community and solicit tenants independently.

There are also advantages for landlords of multiple properties—or properties with leasing problems—who have an in-house leasing agent (or agents). The in-house agent will allow a landlord greater control of the marketing plan and leasing effort. If the landlord is also the developer, that person will likely benefit from the leasing agent's understanding of the market, tenant mix, tenants' space requirements, and building amenities.

In addition, many REITs and large development firms have an in-house leasing team. For instance, developers and landlords of regional malls will almost always have their own leasing team. Landlords of regional and super-regional malls and their leasing team are able to network with all the national retailers and most of the regional retailers. This is because the leasing division for mall developers and REITs has negotiated leases with most of these retailers, and so they do not need to be represented by a third-party leasing agent to find tenants. Their leasing team will work out of their headquarters or a regional office and be responsible for the initial lease-up of their new malls and for re-leasing their existing malls.

Regional malls often have a specialty leasing agent, usually located on-site at the mall or at a nearby mall, who is responsible for leasing to temporary tenants. The specialty leasing agent is responsible for leasing space in kiosks, carts, and vacant stores for a short term during the holidays and the best selling seasons.

Grocery-anchored shopping center REITs that have a large concentration of properties in a metropolitan area will also employ an in-house leasing agent. This person is responsible for re-leasing space and renewing leases on all their properties in that metropolitan area. In this situation, the leasing agent could handle the re-leasing and the renewal leasing on 15 to 20 shopping centers.

Another good (but seldom-used) opportunity to employ an in-house leasing agent is when a landlord has a property with a high vacancy rate or a serious leasing problem. When a landlord has a property that is difficult to lease, and one or more third-party leasing agents have not been successful in leasing it, a viable option is to hire an on-site leasing agent. This person will have a relatively short leasing assignment (e.g., six months to one year) and will focus the entirety of his or her efforts on leasing the challenging property. These leasing agents are paid a salary as well as an attractive incentive for spaces leased.

Even with all the aforementioned benefits, there are some disadvantages to having—or to being—an in-house leasing agent. First and foremost, there is a ceiling on the income that these agents can earn. Though their net compensation is often greater than the average brokerage firm's leasing agent, they will never have the opportunity to earn what the top producers at brokerage firms earn. And because they do have a salary, in-house leasing agents may not be as aggressive seeking tenants. They may rely too much on outside leasing agents.

Some leasing agents believe that being an in-house agent is an easy job, but in-house leasing agents must justify their cost to the company through their production. Another disadvantage to working in-house is that these leasing agents may be assigned property management tasks simply because they are "part of the team" and there is no one else to do the job.

The Property Manager

The property manager is responsible for the daily operations of either one substantial property or a portfolio of several small- to medium-sized properties. Managing a property is managing a business. All of the activities and responsibilities involved in managing a business are required to manage a property. One of the activities in managing a business is selling a product or service; in property management, the parallel activity is leasing space. The property manager may be responsible for any level of responsibility in leasing the property: acting as the leasing agent, supervising the leasing agent, or providing support to the leasing agent. The landlord will assign one of these roles to the property manager.

The Asset Manager

An *asset manager* is responsible for the management and overall performance of an investment. *Asset management* involves enhancing the property's cash flow and value by developing and executing a long-term strategy consistent with the landlord's goals and objectives. In the real estate industry, asset managers are usually employed by financial institutions, REITs, real estate funds, and other companies. They select and hire the property's leasing agent, property manager, and other real estate professionals.

While the property manager is responsible for the daily property operations, the asset manager assumes the role of a landlord, setting strategy and monitoring the performance of a portfolio of properties. Asset managers are the property's team leader, directing the management and leasing activities. They are responsible for supervising the leasing of the properties in their portfolio, and make leasing decisions in their role as the landlord's representative.

Real estate is a profession of specialists, and no one has expertise in every type of property. Because asset managers are often responsible for a portfolio of multiple property types, they must frequently rely on their leasing agent and property manager for recommendations during a lease transaction. Some asset managers are responsible for a portfolio of one classification of property, such as office buildings, while others are assigned a geographic area in which they handle multiple property types.

There is a risk element in every transaction, and the asset manager measures that risk against the value the lease brings to the property. Asset managers act on behalf of another party or entity, and by nature of this responsibility are often cautious and deliberate in decision making. Tenants and their representatives will want to know the asset manager's authority in the lease transaction. Can the asset manager approve the transaction, or must it be sent up the line with recommendations for approval? It will take more time if another person or committee has to review and approve or reject the deal.

Asset managers work in several markets and are rarely located near their properties; hence, the property manager and/or leasing agent should keep the asset manager current on market conditions and deals occurring in the area. Asset managers must be aware of the pulse of a transaction and keep the transaction alive by providing direction to the leasing team. They must give timely decisions to lease offers and negotiate changes to lease terms and provisions.

The Administrative Assistant

The administrative assistant supports the leasing agent's search for buildings or tenants, providing invaluable research and marketing support. Administrative assistants gather the data tenants need to determine their best business site. They are responsible for finding the right person to contact for each site under consideration, which is often a very time-consuming activity. The administrative assistant gathers market data, develops marketing materials, assembles a tour book of alternative sites, and gathers property information for each site. If the property is a shopping center or another type of retail property, the assistant collects demographic and psychographic reports on the trade area around each alternative site, traffic counts on streets adjacent to the property, and a list of similar properties in the area.

When the landlord and tenant agree to a transaction, the administrative assistant is occasionally the one who prepares the lease documents. Inevitably lease provisions are negotiated and changes are made to the lease— often by an attorney or the leasing agent—and the administrative assistant then tracks the relined lease copy, comparing it to the original lease. The administrative assistant's most important responsibility is to keep the deal moving by gathering the necessary data for the leasing team to decide which location is best for the tenant's business (or which prospective tenant is best if the team represents the landlord), and then to provide support to keep the lease document moving from party to party.

The Attorney

Attorneys are hired to protect the interests of their clients—whether those clients are landlords with hundreds of millions of dollars invested in properties or small business owners with their life savings invested in their business. The parties to any transaction should know and understand the responsibilities of the attorney. The attorney's role is often misunderstood by leasing agents, and occasionally by landlords and tenants.

When landlords and tenants use an attorney, they should clearly communicate the attorney's responsibilities for negotiating the lease. If these expectations are not stated, attorneys are left to assume what their responsibilities are. Usually attorneys are hired to review and negotiate only the lease provisions, but they may occasionally be expected to negotiate the business terms (including the length of the lease, the rental charge, tenant improvement [TI] allowances, and concessions) as well.

The lease document is typically provided by the landlord, and the tenant's attorney reviews the lease, discusses issues of concern with the client, and then provides suggested modifications and eliminations for the lease provisions. Most attorneys are not current with market conditions and have not been a party to the negotiations of the business terms. Once these business terms have been established and the lease has been sent to the attorneys, the parties involved do not want to renegotiate the business terms based on the attorney's comments. If attorneys are assigned the role of negotiating the business terms, they should be part of the original negotiations.

Attorneys should not assume what is important to their clients. What may seem important to the attorney may not be as important to the client. However, attorneys *should* inform their clients about the lease provisions' short- and long-term legal and business consequences to the clients' business operations or their building and cash flow. Attorneys should also know their clients' expectations on lease turnaround time so the deal stays on the planned time schedule. Every deal has a life cycle and a timeline to which the attorney must be able to respond. The timely preparation of the lease document and its changes is a critical element in keeping the deal moving forward.

When the landlord selects an attorney, it is best to select one who has experience with the specific type of property the landlord owns. The needs and issues that are important are not the same for office, retail, and industrial tenants. Some issues that are not important to an office tenant are critical to a retail tenant's success. An attorney who has negotiated several leases with major retailers will have an advantage over one who has never negotiated a lease with an anchor retail tenant. Even within some property types, the needs and requirements of tenants are vastly different. In retail properties, for example, the needs of tenants in lifestyle shopping centers are much different than those in grocery-anchored neighborhood shopping centers. The attorney needs to understand the tenant's space and operational needs.

An attorney from a large firm may have a conflict of interest when representing either the landlord or the tenant. It is best to notify the attorney of all the players in the transaction up-front so that the attorney can determine if they have ever been the firm's clients. If a potential conflict arises, attorneys may either withdraw from the assignment or agree with their client that this past representation at the firm does not present a conflict of interest.

Design and Construction Professionals

The Architect. Architects have the assignment of designing buildings that will maximize the efficiency of a site, which translates into designing buildings with the greatest amount of income-producing space. Developers often struggle with making a site "pencil" (or be economically viable), and they need this profitable space to support the project's costs and provide a reasonable return to investors. This must be balanced with care to avoid building more space than the market can absorb.

The architect needs to be an active member of the leasing team. The landlord and leasing agent must work with the building design to lease the space as configured by the architect. From a leasing perspective, the primary role of the architect is to design a building that will be accepted in the market and meet the space requirements of its targeted tenants. When a major tenant commits to a building before it is designed, such as a department store or a supermarket in a mall or shopping center, that tenant will have input in the store's location on the site and the surrounding parking field. The tenant wants to be assured that there is adequate parking in front of the building and that there are acceptable sightlines from the street. It is the architect's job to meet these needs.

It seems obvious that office buildings should be designed by office building architects, and shopping centers should be designed by shopping center architects; and this is usually what happens. These specialized architects understand the latest building technologies, the changing space requirements of tenants, and the relationship between the cost to build and the amount of rent the developer must charge to support the building's operating expenses and debt service while earning a fair return for the investors. Sometimes, however, buildings are designed by architects who do not have the necessary experience.

Architects may not have the knowledge needed to design a certain classification of building or a particular use within a mixed-use development. Many multi-use and mixed-use buildings, which have become popular again in the early 21st century, have a residential component as the primary use along with ground floor retail space. Some mixed-use developments are office buildings with ground floor retail, while others have an equal distribution of two or three property types. Many experienced office building and residential architects have limited experience designing retail space and may not design the ground floor retail space to meet the store size and depth requirements of targeted retailers. As a result, developers who are planning to build a vertical multi- or mixed-use development with more than limited ground retail floor space should hire a retail consultant—usually a retail leasing agent—or a consulting retail architect to be part of the design team.

An architect is also a valuable member of the leasing team when a building is being renovated. The architect can redesign space that is difficult to lease because it no longer meets the space requirements of today's tenants. This eliminates obsolescence in the building and once again maximizes the site's efficiency and revenue-generating potential.

The Space Planner.   *Space planning* is the process of designing an office configuration for maximum functional efficiency based on a prospective tenant's space utilization needs, aesthetic requirements, and budget. It is an important part of a lease transaction's early stages. The process involves determining the amount of space the tenant needs for efficient business operations. It may also include addressing not only the tenant's current space needs, but future expansions as well. Space planning ensures a balanced relationship between space and workflow.

The space planner is an important player in completing the lease transaction. This person can demonstrate how efficiently designed space will optimize the tenant's operations, streamlining workflow and increasing office productivity. An efficient space plan can often reduce a tenant's space requirements and lower occupancy costs. The space planner's layout and design can assist in controlling the cost to build out the premises, thus facilitating the deal-making process. The space planner may also assist with the color, materials, and furniture selection, as well as with the furniture layout.

Space planners are usually needed to assist office and medical office tenants in planning their space requirements. Landlords of office and medical office buildings will select a space planner to work with prospective tenants to show them how the building and specific spaces can meet their space requirements.

Landlords of shopping centers and other retail properties almost never work with a space planner. Most merchants have a store format that has been developed and tested, and they will use their store planner to "fit" their format into the dimensions of the space they are leasing. Retailers may hire an architect to perform a site survey to determine the store dimensions, verify if their client's format will "fit" into the space, and determine if the building meets current codes and Americans with Disabilities Act (ADA) requirements.

Space planning meetings are conducted with the prospective tenant and leasing agent(s). The purpose of these meetings is to show the prospect—on paper—where the office or medical office space will be situated and how the people, furniture, and equipment will fit into the premises. An efficient space plan will streamline the flow of work to increase productivity; optimize leased space for the tenant, thus reducing occupancy costs including rent and pass-through charges; and, in some situations, reduce labor costs.

Some tenants will use their own space planner. When selecting a space planner, the landlord or tenant should preliminarily qualify candidates based on ability, reputation, references, and prior assignments. There are then additional assignment-specific issues to consider. Space planners must be able to keep the design cost within a determined range and meet the time requirements of the lease transaction so that lapsed time does not kill the deal. They should understand the tenant's operational needs as well as the codes, permitting process, and timeline for the jurisdiction in which the building is located. An additional consideration for landlords' space planners is their desire to convince prospective tenants to lease space in the building.

The space planning process, as outlined in Exhibit 2.1, starts with an understanding of the client's needs. The space planner assesses the tenant's needs and then uses them to develop a schematic design. *Computer-aided design (CAD)* allows for easy modifications to the design, which are likely to occur multiple times. From the final design, construction documents are prepared, approved, and sent out for bids. A contract is eventually entered into with a general contractor selected by the landlord. The entire process, from the first space-planning interview to the time the tenant moves in, usually takes from three to six months.

The leasing agents representing the landlord and the tenant should attend the initial meeting between the space planner and the tenant. It is important that the space planner and the tenant keep the landlord's TI allowance and the cost for additional improvements in focus. The space planner must be aware of the deal's timeline and keep the pulse of the deal active. The client should establish the maximum number of space plan drafts that are expected before a final space plan is approved.

Space planning services can be provided by many types of companies, including architectural firms, interior design firms, office furniture com-

---

Exhibit 2.1
Phases in the Space Planning Process

1. Evaluation (assigning definition)
   - Interview the client/tenant
   - Visit the client's existing premises
   - Conduct an employee count and calculate future staffing needs
   - Determine employees' space needs
   - Develop an equipment list
   - Note specialized equipment and maintenance needs
   - Discuss the client's planned growth
2. Schematic design
3. Design development
4. Developing construction documents
5. Client approval and signing off of the construction documents
6. Bidding and negotiations
7. Construction
8. Tenant move-in

---

panies, and smaller firms that specialize in space planning. Even after the space planner's job is complete, the landlord or property manager can keep track of how space is used in a building by compiling a *plan book* that shows each tenant's floor plans as well as all the floor plans by floor.

The Interior Designer.   Office and medical office tenants may use the services of an interior designer. The criteria for selecting an interior designer are similar to those mentioned above for choosing a space planner. It is important that the interior designer understands the prospective tenant's budget and what amount, if any, the landlord is contributing to the design of the space.

The landlord usually has a list of two or three interior designers to refer to prospective tenants. Some landlords will offer to pay for the initial meeting between the prospective tenant and the designer, but seldom will they pay for the tenant's designer. Typically the landlord will have color and material pallets available for the most popular color and material combinations. These usually include a building standard (usually within the tenant allowance) as well the next few upgrades, which come at an additional cost to the tenant.

The General Contractor.   A general contractor—who constructs the tenant build-out—may be referred to as a *tenant finish contractor* or TI contractor. The general contractor provides an estimate to build out the premises and, if a lease is executed, is responsible for completing the improvements within the specified timeframe. These contractors may be large construction firms that also build buildings, or they may be small contractors who specialize in TI work.

Landlords of office or medical office buildings contract for work performed in their buildings to maintain the integrity of electrical and mechanical systems. Retail tenants in shopping centers and other types of retail properties use their contractors to build out their premises and install fixtures. Industrial tenants, on the other hand, may perform their own TIs, or the landlord may provide this service through the contractor.

Occasionally, major tenants insist on using their own contractor. Ground floor retail or service tenants in multistory buildings typically use their own contractors to build out their premises. When a tenant contracts directly for TIs, that tenant must conform to the building's rules and regulations. These guidelines include stipulations for elevator use, work that must be performed after normal business hours, approved contractors, contractors' insurance requirements, and so forth.

As with space planners and contractors, there are several issues to be addressed when selecting a general contractor or tenant finish contractor. The first consideration is the contractor's reputation. This can easily be checked by calling property managers of other buildings who have hired the contractor. Another concern is whether the contractor can build out the premises at the required standard with the allocated budget. The timeframe that the contractor needs to complete the build out must be determined. The contractor's understanding of the inspections and permitting requirements in the building's municipality should be verified. An additional consideration— if the building requires union workers—is whether or not the contractor is unionized. It is also necessary to ensure that the contractor is licensed by the state, is bonded, and has proper insurance. Additionally, there are many issues to consider that are specific to the building and/or the tenant.

The On-Site Tenant Improvement Supervisor. Large office buildings, medical office buildings, and business parks will often have an on-site tenant improvement supervisor. This person works with the prospective tenant, the space planner, the interior designer, and the general contractor.

The tenant improvement supervisor arranges and attends the initial meeting between the tenant and the space planner. The space planner is made aware of the tenant's budget as well as the allowance the landlord has offered the prospective tenant for building out the premises, and it is the tenant improvement supervisor's job to work with the space planner and interior designer to stay within each party's budget.

When a lease is executed, the tenant improvement supervisor will contract for the build-out of the premises and supervise the general contractor, ensuring that the premises are built on time and in keeping with the lease requirements. After the premises have been constructed, the tenant improvement supervisor inspects them along with the tenant and the property manager; together they develop the "punch list" of construction items that need correcting.

Exhibit 2.2
Considerations for Loan Underwriting

- Minimum lease rates
- The percentage of common area maintenance (CAM) and building operating expenses that are reimbursed by the tenants
- The minimum length of the lease
- Required periodical rent step-ups
- Staggered lease expiration dates
- Loan-to-value ratios
- The loan's expiration (Retail anchor tenant leases may be required to expire a year after the loan matures.)
- The quality of the tenant
- The contribution the tenant(s)—especially the retail tenant—makes to the building
- The credit rating of the tenants

The Lender

A lender can influence the leasing of a building by attaching specific lease requirements to the loan. The developer's—and sometimes the landlord's—lender may place restrictions on the terms of a lease. Lenders underwrite loans based on several criteria, a few of which are listed in Exhibit 2.2 below. They may then turn these criteria into lease term restrictions that are placed on the property. Often these restrictions are more arduous for new developments than for existing buildings.

The lender is concerned with the financial condition of prospective tenants because the mortgage is paid from tenants' rents. The lender is also concerned with onerous lease provisions that might interrupt the property's income flow: the lease cancellations right, the co-tenancy provision, operating covenants of anchor stores, and other lease encumbrances. Most lenders require that tenants sign an estoppel on approved forms to enable a more clear understanding of the status of the lease. An estoppel covers the business terms of the lease, whether or not rent has been prepaid, and default of the lease by either the landlord or the tenant.

To minimize risk, lenders considering a loan on a new development want to be certain the developer has experience building that particular type of building and can execute the project on time and within budget. Lenders also want to know that the architect has relevant design experience and that the general contractor has previously built within the specified property classification. It is preferable that the architect and general contractor have worked together in the past. Lenders are concerned about the financial strength of these players. They should also inquire about the leasing team's experience. There may be leasing restrictions that require the team's approval to circumvent, and lenders need to be aware of the importance of responding promptly to related requests and approval of the lease terms.

Other Players

There are others who may have a role in the lease transactions.

The Mall Marketing Director. A mall is two rows of stores that face each other, separated by a walkway. Malls, whether they are community, regional, or super-regional malls, have marketing directors. A strip shopping center, on the other hand—such as a grocery-anchored shopping center—is a row of stores facing a parking lot. Not all shopping centers have marketing directors: lifestyle shopping centers, specialty shopping centers (such as Ghirardelli Square in San Francisco), and outlet shopping centers generally do have a person in this position, while power shopping centers and grocery-anchored shopping centers typically do not.

The role of the marketing director is to develop an effective marketing strategy and successfully execute its advertising and promotional programs. This person has the responsibility of continually evaluating the mall's (or shopping center's) tenant mix and making recommendations to the leasing agent concerning which categories of merchants need upgrading, which new retailers are needed to strengthen the mall's tenant mix, and which existing merchants should be replaced for poor performance.

The marketing director should have a prominent position on the leasing team. No one is more familiar with the mall's (or the shopping center's) trade area, the dynamics of its tenant mix, and the strengths and weaknesses of competing malls and shopping centers. The marketing director has the best understanding of each merchant and which merchants are contributing to the synergism of the mall's tenant mix.

Brokerage Firms. Brokerage firms provide valuable information and services to their clients. They hire and train leasing agents to develop the skills and knowledge to represent landlords and tenants. Brokerage firms provide tenants with market data, alternative building analyses, and the terms of recent deals that are critical for deciding where to locate their business.

These firms gather market and building data that is indispensable for developers and investors in the selection of sites and buildings. They provide information for their clients to develop the project's pro forma and lease-up projections. Most brokerage firms also offer additional services, such as sales, financing, and consulting. Some offer property management and appraisal services.

There are several different types of commercial brokerage firms. National and international full-service brokerage firms have leasing agents who specialize in each property sector—office, industrial, and retail. National firms have offices in cities across the United States and refer clients between cities. Regional brokerage firms offer services that are similar to the national firms, and are sometimes affiliated with a national network and referral system. Local brokerage firms may also operate like national firms in the services they offer, but serve a limited geographic area—usually a metropolitan area or a group of smaller communities.

There are also sole proprietors: one-person brokerage firms with a specialty-market niche. They work with just a few clients at a time. And boutique brokerage firms specialize in a single property type; they may lease shopping centers or provide tenant-rep services to office users. These boutique firms may represent clients locally, regionally, or nationally. A high-end specialty retailer may hire retail leasing agents to find the best space in several major metropolitan areas.

Technology has leveled the playing field among these firms. All brokerage firms, regardless of size, can now provide current market data. Before the evolution of current technology, only the larger firms could afford research departments to develop this information. Today, however, they all have access to the same global market data provided by Internet real estate listing firms and service providers. Technology has also enabled all types of brokerage firms to produce professional-looking marketing materials.

National and regional brokerage firms may have research departments to create their own market data; but through Internet listings, local commercial multi-listing services, opportunities to network within the brokerage community, and market surveys, every leasing agent has access to the market information on rental rates and comps needed to consult with clients. Larger brokerage firms may offer more opportunities for networking among leasing agents; however, within the commercial real estate industry there are several professional associations that offer networking opportunities at meetings, educational offerings, and social events for all leasing agents.

Therefore, the decision concerning which brokerage firm to use often comes down to relationships or referrals. Leasing is a service business and, regardless of the size of the brokerage firm, the level of service a landlord or tenant receives is dependent on the selected leasing agent that the firm provides.

The four key issues to inquire about when selecting a leasing agent are: (1) the person's experience with the subject property type; (2) the agent's knowledge and experience working in a specific area; (3) how long it will take to complete the assignment; and (4) whether this assignment will create a conflict of interest. Often less experienced leasing agents will provide better service because they have lighter workloads and place more importance on the assignment. However, experienced leasing agents have track records of completing deals, and they probably have more tenant and landlord contacts. There are several factors to consider when selecting a leasing agent.

WHAT TO EXPECT FROM A LEASING AGENT

Landlords and tenants should know what to expect from their leasing agents.

Leasing Reports

Leasing reports, or leasing activity updates, provide current information about leasing efforts to both landlords and tenants. Because leasing agents have different assignments when leasing a building for a landlord than when finding space for a tenant, landlords and tenants receive different reports. The information provided in a landlord's leasing report is in some ways opposite from the information provided in a tenant's leasing report. The purpose of each report, however, is the same: to inform the client of market conditions and leasing activities. Both reports inform the leasing agent's client of the status of all activities to date.

Depending on the amount of vacant space in a building, the landlord will want to receive a leasing report anywhere from weekly to monthly, often via email. During the lease-up of a new or renovated building, the report is usually provided weekly. The landlord's leasing report provides a short comprehensive summary of the leasing activities and status of each prospect, as outlined in Exhibit 2.3 below. It is brief to allow leasing agents to spend time more effectively in the field searching for prospects, communicating with the brokerage community, showing space, and negotiating leases rather than filling out elaborate reports.

Tenants will also receive leasing reports anywhere from weekly to monthly. The tenant's leasing report is presented in a brief summary format (as detailed in Exhibit 2.4 below) for the same reason as the landlord's is: to allow the leasing agent to spend more time searching for alternative locations, comparing buildings and their asking lease terms, and negotiating the deal.

Leasing reports are computerized and can easily be updated. The landlord and the tenant may use their leasing reports to evaluate the efforts of their leasing agent. Sometimes a leasing agent's efforts will be redirected to another assignment if leasing activities slow on a building or a search for sites.

Dual Agency

The regulatory agency (often called the state's real estate department, division, or commission) of many states requires licensed leasing agents to state, in writing, which party to the transaction they represent. This is to avoid the situation where both parties believe the leasing agent is representing them solely. When a leasing agent is representing the landlord *and* the tenant in a lease transaction, many states require the agent to acknowledge this

---

Exhibit 2.3
The Landlord's Leasing Report

The landlord's leasing report may include the following information:

- A description of the market conditions for the subject property type
- A list of leasing deals and their terms that have been recently completed in the market
- The amount of space that was available to lease in the building at the beginning of the leasing assignment
- The amount of space that has been leased
- The amount of space that is available
- The average rent achieved on the space leased in the building
- The square footage of tenants' spaces expiring this year and each of the next five years
- The amount of TI dollars budgeted for the building
- The amount of TI dollars paid to date
- The amount of TI dollars remaining and offered to prospects
- Each prospect, listed with the following:

  ○ Name
  ○ Use
  ○ Square footage requirements
  ○ Required occupancy date
  ○ The status of the deal (e.g., "inquiry," "space shown to prospects," "letter of intent," "lease being drafted," "lease out for signature," as well as the square footage of each deal and the cumulative square footage of all the deals in each status category)
  ○ Terms of the deal (e.g., rental rate, concessions, TI allowance, length of the lease)

- Each prospect's rating, on a scale of 1–5 or 1–10, for likelihood of completing a deal
- Exceptions to lease terms or provisions (e.g. exclusives, caps on pass-through charges)
- The name of the tenant's leasing agent

---

dual agency and receive written acknowledgement and consent from both parties. Even if the state does not require such approval, the leasing agent should obtain their written permission.

When leasing agents are acting as dual agents, they must not take any action detrimental to either party's interest in the transaction, nor disclose confidential information about either party. From a practical standpoint, one or both parties may believe their best interests are not served if one leasing agent is representing them both. If there is any doubt that one of the party's interests are not best served, that party should not agree to the terms of dual agency.

In the real estate industry it is customary for the tenant leasing agent to be compensated by the landlord or to share the commission paid to the landlord's exclusive agent. In many cases, the tenant receives free service because the landlord pays the commission. If the leasing agent is also the

Exhibit 2.4
The Tenant's Leasing Report

The tenant's leasing report may include the following information:

- A brief description of the market conditions
- A list of recent deals and their terms
- The momentum of deals in the market—more or fewer deals completed
- A list of each building under consideration
- The name of the building's landlord and the leasing agent
- A description of the building, its tenant mix, amenities, and location
- If the tenant is a retailer, the sales of either the anchor tenants and similar tenants in the shopping center or sales of other retailers the client uses to benchmark projected sales
- If the tenant is a retailer, a summary of the demographics and psychographics in the trade areas of each property under consideration
- A comparison of the asking and, if the negotiations are far enough along, the deal-making terms of each offer, including:

  - The rentable and usable rates for office and medical office buildings
  - All concessions and TI allowances
  - The effective rental rate when concessions are factored into the rental
  - The tenant's pass-through charges
  - The tenant's occupancy cost

- Discussion on which building(s) best meets the occupancy needs of the tenant

---

building's listing agent, however, the landlord may forbid that agent from representing prospective tenants. The tenants will then either represent themselves or hire a leasing agent or attorney. They are wise to hire someone unless they are knowledgeable about market conditions and negotiating leases. Even if they are educated on such matters, it is in their best interests to have a local expert represent them. Tenants will benefit from a real estate professional's perspective on alternative buildings and the business terms of the deal.

The advantages for leasing agents acting as a dual agent are that commission is not shared with another leasing agent and the deal may transpire faster. Some brokerage firms prefer that their agents not act as dual agents because it may be difficult at times to avoid a conflict of interest—or the perception of such a conflict—when an agent is representing both parties to a lease. The leasing agent's best policy is therefore always full disclosure.

SELECTING THE PROPERTY MANAGER AS THE LEASING AGENT

A third option when selecting a leasing agent is to contract with the property manager to provide this service. Property managers are often hired to re-lease space when tenants vacate and to handle lease renewals on build-ings they manage. There are many times when this is the best choice. The property manager probably understands the goals and objectives of the landlord, knows the building and its tenants better than anyone, and com-prehends the best tenant mix for the building. If property managers have been conducting market surveys regularly, they understand the market and how their building competes in its *micromarket* or trade area.

There are also times when the property manager should *not* have the dual role of the building's manager and leasing agent. Six review factors, presented in the following paragraphs, exist to help determine whether the property manager is the right choice to be building's leasing agent.

The first factor is the amount of space available to lease in the building. If the building is new or has excessive space available, it is unlikely that the property manager will have the time necessary to manage and lease the build-ing. If the building has only a few smaller vacancies, however, it is often not cost-effective for a leasing agent—whose income is derived solely from com-missions—to spend the time marketing and leasing. The amount of income required to support these efforts for a particular building varies by agent, but the property manager is often the best choice for such an assignment.

For example, the last 10 to 15 percent of a building is often composed of the least desirable spaces, and hence is the most difficult to lease. Yet the income from this last 10 to 15 percent of building space usually generates the building's cash flow. Many property managers who either are on-site managers or visit the property regularly can most effectively lease this last portion of a building and re-lease the space as it becomes available.

The second review factor is the property manager's experience. Some of the knowledge, skills, and personal traits needed to manage a building are naturally different than those needed to lease a property. Property man-agers may be good managers but lack the sales skills necessary to lease a building. There are many, however, who do have the skills and personal traits to handle the different tasks of managing as well as leasing. If a prop-erty manager appears to have this aptitude, a safe check is to make sure it has been proven through experience.

The third consideration for review is the time the property manager will have available to lease the building. Property management is an all-consuming assignment. Property managers must be available 24/7, and they have demanding clients. The determining factors for whether or not quali-fied property managers have the time to lease additional properties are the number of properties they currently manage, the number of tenants in their managed portfolio, whether any of their properties has issues that may require an extraordinary amount of time to resolve, and the amount of as-sistance they have available for handling these tasks.

For example, the extent of the support staff provided to a property manager will make a huge difference in the amount of responsibility she can handle. There is no industry standard as to the type and level of support that property managers receive from their firms. If property managers have limited administrative support, it is unlikely that they will have time to lease any of the buildings they manage. There are scores of issues that must be handled when managing a large building or a portfolio of small to medium-sized buildings. An administrative assistant can handle many of these issues, freeing the property manager to either manage more properties or take on specific leasing assignments.

The next consideration is how involved the property manager is in the leasing market. Does the property manager have relationships within the brokerage community? These connections are necessary in order to most effectively and efficiently perform a leasing assignment.

The fifth consideration is how the property manager will be compensated for taking on the additional task of leasing, which will add responsibilities and time to his or her day. Since property managers have a base salary and all or most of their expenses are reimbursed, the commission split with the firm will be less for property managers than for full-time leasing agents. If property managers are not adequately compensated for the added responsibilities and time away from their family and personal life, they may not be properly motivated to devote the necessary time to leasing the property.

The final factor to consider when determining if the property manager is the right choice for leasing the building is the type of marketing resources provided by the property management firm. Is the firm a member of the local commercial multiple listing service if one exists in the area? Does it use Internet listing services and sites? Does the firm have the ability to develop marketing materials? If property managers do not have access to these marketing resources, it may be difficult for them successfully to perform a leasing assignment.

When landlords are evaluating who should lease their buildings, and businesses are seeking a leasing agent to represent them in finding building space, they should consider the above six factors to decide if the property manager is truly the best person to handle the assignment. There are many times when the property manager is the best person to lease the building, and there are also times when someone else is the better option.

THE BROKERAGE COMMUNITY

The brokerage community plays an important role in facilitating lease transactions. Many tenants are represented by leasing agents, and landlords almost always use an agent to lease their buildings. It is therefore important for tenants and landlords to establish good relations with the brokerage community.

When a building is listed with a brokerage firm, many of the deals will be co-brokered with leasing agents who work for other firms. Landlords will therefore often develop and foster good working relationships with the brokerage community. It is essential that they are knowledgeable of leasing agents' concerns and priorities, and that they use this awareness to avoid any potential problems.

Landlords would be wise to establish a reputation for honoring all commission agreements and paying all commissions on time if not early. Leasing agents do not receive a salary and are paid only after a lease has been completed. Naturally they want to be protected in the deal. They do not want the landlord bypassing them to get to a client, denying their role in the transaction. Rather, leasing agents want landlords to keep their word regarding commission arrangements and protect their position in the deal. It is important to remember that leasing agents have a tremendous influence on their clients, and tenant reps can encourage their clients to work with or avoid certain landlords.

Leasing agents also prioritize working with landlords who are deal makers instead of deal killers. Time kills deals, and so it is important to leasing agents that everyone involved maintains the pulse of the transaction. A landlord who is motivated and knowledgeable about the market can often overcome the obstacles that may cause a deal to come to a halt, thus reducing the likelihood that one of the parties will lose interest before the deal can be executed.

It is also important for tenants to develop good relationships with their leasing representatives. Tenant leasing agents want to be certain that the tenant is serious about searching for alternative space. They will spend many hours learning about the tenant's business needs, searching for multiple buildings that meet these needs, contacting building leasing agents to gather rental data, analyzing each building, developing a comparison chart and report showing each building's strengths and weaknesses, and recommending the best deal for the tenant. Tenants will usually work with just one leasing agent and have little contact with the brokerage community. However, if they develop a reputation for being difficult to work with, many leasing agents and landlords may be reluctant to deal with them in the future.

WHAT PREVENTS DEALS FROM HAPPENING?

There is an endless list of reasons why transactions never become deals. Some of these reasons are unavoidable, but many others could be prevented. Deals often fail due to needless factors such as poor communication between the parties involved, one party not responding in a timely manner, and people allowing their personalities or egos to get in the way

Exhibit 2.5
Common Reasons Deals Fail

- One party cannot afford the deal. This is a legitimate reason why a transaction dies. Either the landlord cannot or will not reduce the building's rent or provide the concessions the prospective tenant requires. The prospective tenant may not perceive the same value in the space that the landlord does, or the tenant may not be able to afford the rent.

- One party does not have an understanding of the market. The landlord may perceive value in a building that the market doesn't reflect, or the landlord may be stubborn in asking a rental rate that has no relationship to the market. On the other hand, prospective tenants are not real estate professionals and are usually not up-to-date on market conditions. Their frame of reference for rental rates may be the rate they are paying on a lease negotiated years ago. Rental rates quoted in a good market can easily cause sticker shock, so leasing agents need to make sure their clients are aware of the market conditions and the rental rates in similar buildings.

- A landlord or asset manager who does not live in the area and visits infrequently may lack sufficient market expertise to recognize the right deal. Often asset managers are responsible for a portfolio of properties located in several cities, and they do not have the same market expertise for each market. This can easily occur when an asset manager or landlord of an office building is evaluating an offer from a retail tenant for ground floor space. The landlord or asset manager may understand the office market but have limited knowledge of the retail market.

- A retailer may be overly conservative in sales projections, and consequently pass on a good location. Leasing agents should obtain the sales of other tenants in the immediate area so that their clients can use those figures as a benchmark.

- The tenant may not understand the market. The leasing agent needs to provide the client with all available data so the tenant can accurately decide whether the building or space is a good location and the terms are acceptable.

- A lease that is too one-sided may be prohibitively onerous for the tenant. In a strong market the landlord may effectively use an aggressive lease, while in a weak market it may have to be converted to a "tenant-friendly" lease.

- The decision makers may not be party to the negotiations or be too far removed from the transaction, resulting in the deal never getting approved.

- Sometimes attorneys, in the zeal to protect their clients' interests, become a hindrance to completing the transaction. No attorney wants to be called a deal killer.

- One party may have a hidden agenda. If this is the case, the transaction is likely to fall apart somewhere during negotiations.

- Time can kill a deal. A lack of a timely response from any party to the negotiations provides the prospective tenant with an opportunity to find alternative space or the landlord to find another prospective tenant with a more attractive offer.

- Personalities can clash, and people may develop a dislike for one another that causes interest in completing the transaction to fade.

- An ego can kill a transaction.

- Gloating over a deal can prevent the next deal with the same parties from happening.
(*continued*)

of a successful transaction. The list in Exhibit 2.5 outlines a few of the most common explanations—both the inevitable and avoidable—for transactions failing to become deals.

ETHICS AND PROFESSIONAL STANDARDS

For centuries, societies have defined good and bad behavior. *Ethics* is the discipline dealing with what is right or wrong, good or bad, and is often related to duty or obligation. Ethics provides a guide for behavior, the foundation of which is simply honesty. Without honesty in business and in relationships, people cannot interact openly and must protect themselves when dealing with one another. Without standards of behavior, the public would be at the mercy of the unscrupulous.

Our society, the media, and special interest groups monitor the actions of business leaders, governmental officials, and politicians to ensure that their power is not used to harm others and that they meet the expected standards. The standards of good and bad behavior govern the conduct of industries and professions. Ethical practices are a critically important part of the business and social fabric of the United States.

Today our society is more aware of ethical behavior and professional standards than in any time in our country's history. In the 1990s and the beginning of this century's first decade, leaders in high-profile corporations violated the trust of their employees, customers, and stockholders. Political leaders exploited the confidence of the people they governed through greedy and self-serving actions. The many corporate scandals of 2002 reinforced the need for every business and every professional association to establish and follow ethical practices.

For real estate professionals, the presumption of a strong ethical approach is the basis of action for each player in a transaction. Clients place a great deal of trust in their leasing agent, and have every right to expect that their interests will be first and foremost in the mind and activities of the leasing agent. Sometimes real estate professionals are acting in situations that cannot be completely defined by a specific set of policies and procedures, and they must rely on their professional standards and the real estate industry's code of ethics to proceed honestly, legally, and ethically. One of the best principles to guide a person's behavior when confronted with a difficult situation is "full disclosure, and give the bad news first."

The Players in Real Estate Ethics

There are three constituencies that benefit from ethical behavior in the commercial real estate industry. The first is the group of clients, landlords, and commercial tenants who are served by and interact with commercial real estate professionals on a daily basis. A code of ethics protects this group from real estate professionals who may use their position and knowledge to cause financial or personal harm to those they serve. The second constituency that is protected is the commercial real estate industry. People seek the services and advice of others who will place their clients' best interests ahead of their own. The third constituency is the firm that employs the commercial real estate professional. Ethical behavior allows firms to secure the confidence and trust of potential clients while retaining the confidence and trust of existing clients. This allows the firm to grow and prosper.

A real estate lease transaction has three primary players: the real estate professional, the landlord, and the tenant. The real estate professional—the leasing agent—must at all times place the interests of his or her client ahead of his or her own interests. This can be challenging at times for some leasing agents, because their compensation is earned only when the lease transaction is completed. Leasing space only to earn a commission and not necessarily to find a good tenant for the landlord or a good location and deal for the tenant is not acting in the best interest of the client.

There are several ways that leasing agents might place their interests before their clients' interests, and these usually center around getting a deal done that may not be in a client's best interest. They need to make certain the economic terms of the lease are the market terms, and if not, they need to make their client aware of this discrepancy. Leasing agents must have the patience to find the right deal for the client regardless of how long it takes, assuming the timeline meets the client's needs. They should be honest with the information they provide to the client.

The landlord and the tenant are also expected to act ethically and honestly in a lease transaction. There are many opportunities for the landlord to violate ethical standards and deal dishonestly with a tenant. A landlord can overstate the size of the spaces in the building. Most landlords will state that their spaces are approximately so many square feet. They do this because every time a space is measured the total square feet in the space may be a few feet different. However, there are landlords who will deliberately add a couple hundred feet to the size of their spaces. If a space leased for $35 per square foot including base rent and pass-through building expenses and a landlord claimed the space was 150 square feet larger that its actual size, the tenant would annually be charged an additional $5,250 per year: an additional $26,250 over the life of a five-year lease.

Landlords may also cheat their tenants by charging expenses to the building pass-through charges that are not allowed in the pass-through lease provision. Another way a landlord can cheat tenants is by not crediting to the building's pass-through charges reimbursement such as insurance proceeds for damage to the common areas or building, refunds from utilities companies, and real estate tax refunds from appealing the property's tax assessment. Keeping funds that belong to someone else is stealing; overcharging someone for a service or charging for an expense that has not been agreed upon is also stealing.

Tenants also have an ethical responsibility to be honest and fair in their dealings with the landlord. Tenants should be honest with the landlord regarding their intended use of the premises. Most landlords are concerned with the tenant mix of their building and do not want to lease to a tenant whose use may be detrimental to the other tenants and the building. A tenant may overstate the business's net worth or financial situation. A retail tenant with a *percentage rent* provision in the lease may understate sales to avoid paying percentage rent. A tenant who does this is stealing from the landlord just as a landlord steals from tenants by including expenses in the building's pass-through charges that are not authorized or are prohibited by the lease. Once the confidence of trust has been violated, the relationship between the parties becomes a struggle. Not knowing when the other party is telling the truth leads to animosity and distrust. Ethics in business is the practice of goodwill in both intent and actions. Ethical behavior is a long-term business strategy. Honesty in one's dealings is a prerequisite for establishing trust, for without trust there can be no cooperation.

Determining Ethical Behavior

Real estate practitioners have come to realize they will only prosper by building relationships and not taking advantage of their clients. They are professionals who want to render quality service and generate repeat business. Real estate professionals will only be able to accomplish this if they treat each client in the manner in which they expect to be treated.

Obviously one's actions can be legal and still not be ethical. A leasing agent placing the opportunity to earn a quick commission ahead of finding the right tenant for a landlord's building is not performing an illegal act but is not acting in the best interest of the client. The ethical response in this situation would be to explain to the client the risk in leasing to a tenant whose financial situation is marginal or whose use is not the best for the building. The landlord makes the decision of whether to accept or reject the prospect, and should be provided with all the information necessary to make the best choice.

The area of ethics can be complicated and has many gray areas. If there is any doubt about an action in a transaction—if you have to ask yourself, "Should I or shouldn't I?"—it is very likely that the answer is you should not. If you have questions about a transaction involving a client, you cannot go wrong if you make the decision to fully disclose the issues.

There are two well-known self-tests an individual can take to determine whether a behavior is ethical or fair. The first is the front-page test. Would you be ashamed if your proposed behavior was fully reported on the front page of your area's daily newspaper accompanied by your photo? The second is the family test. Would you be embarrassed to explain the proposed behavior or actions to your entire family? If the answer to either of these questions is yes, the behavior in question should not be undertaken.

Professional Standards

Professional standards create the rules of conduct or code of principles recognized in a particular activity. Real estate professional and trade associations have adopted codes of ethics and professional standards. These codes and standards cover matters of fiduciary obligation to clients, disclosure, confidentiality, protection of funds, compliance with laws and regulations, equal opportunities, and competence.

The NATIONAL ASSOCIATION OF REALTORS (NAR), founded in 1908, was one of the first business groups in our country to adopt an ethical code. It adopted its Code of Ethics in 1913, and amended it 31 times through 2006 at its annual conventions. The REALTOR Code of Ethics is based on the "let the public be served" concept. Many states have based their real estate license laws on the standards established by NAR.

Many leasing agents are members of real estate professional associations that are affiliates of NAR, including the Certified Commercial Investment Member (CCIM) Institute, the Society of Industrial and Office REALTORS, the Counselors of Real Estate, and the Institute of Real Estate Management (IREM). Members of these associations are required to abide by the REALTOR Code of Ethics; and the Society of Industrial and Office REALTORS, the Counselors of Real Estate, and IREM also have their own codes of ethics and professional standards that their members must follow. The Institute of Real Estate Management, for example, awards several designations, including the CERTIFIED PROPERTY MANAGER (CPM) designation, and requires all members to abide by its Code of Professional Ethics.

The International Council of Shopping Centers (ICSC) offers several designations, including the industry's only leasing designation, and requires those who receive their designations to agree in writing to abide by their code of ethics. The Building Owners and Managers Association (BOMA), a trade association representing landlords and property managers of office buildings, also has a code of ethics. The REALTORS require that their members take an ethics course every four years; IREM and BOMA require that their members take a full-day ethics course as one of several requirements for earning the professional designations they award.

Enforcing Ethics

The NATIONAL ASSOCIATION OF REALTORS and many other real estate professional and trade associations have a mechanism for enforcing their ethical codes. When a complaint is filed with NAR, their Grievance Committee conducts the initial review. If the committee determines that there may have been a violation of the ethics code, the case is then sent to the Professional Standards Hearing Panel. This panel conducts a hearing and decides whether there was a violation of the Code of Ethics. If the panel determines that a violation has been committed, it then determines the discipline to be imposed on the violator. Once a decision has been rendered, either party to the complaint has 20 days to appeal the decision to the Appeals Committee.

The Institute of Real Estate Management's Code of Professional Ethics includes a statement about the consequences to its members for violations, and provides for disciplinary action to be taken in accordance with IREM regulations and bylaws. The Institute has a mechanism in place to investigate, conduct hearings, and enforce violations of its code of ethics.

When IREM receives a complaint of an alleged violation of its Code of Professional Ethics by a member, the complaint is referred to its Board of Ethical Inquiry. This board will review the complaint and determine if one or more articles of the Code of Professional Ethics have been violated. If the board rules in the affirmative, the case is sent to the Ethics Hearing and Discipline Board. The complainant and the respondent are allowed to present their cases in writing and/or appear in person. Often the respondent will be represented by an attorney at the hearing. If the board rules that the respondent has violated the IREM Code of Professional Ethics, the respondent may request a second hearing by the Ethics Appeal Board. The Ethics Hearing and Discipline Board, by secret vote, can discipline a violator via a letter of censure or suspend or terminate the person's IREM designation.

There are more than 18,000 IREM individual members. During the 25-year period from 1978 to 2002, 315 ethical complaints were reported to the Institute. The Board of Ethical Inquiry dismissed 157 complaints and referred 158 to the Ethics Hearing and Discipline Board. Among the latter, no action was taken on 22 of the complaints, a letter of censure was issued on 31 cases, 23 CPM Members were suspended, and 74 individuals had their CPM designations terminated.

The State Commissioner's Code of Ethics

Any member of a real estate firm who sells, leases, or exchanges real estate or collects rents must also be licensed. In addition, at least one member of the firm must be a licensed real estate broker, and all licensees are subject to the commissioner's code of ethics. The commissioner's regulations cover areas of representation, disclosure, and other client relations with similar intent and requirements to those outlined by NAR, IREM, and other real estate associations in their codes. Anyone may file a complaint with the real estate commissioner.

Real estate brokerage firms are subject to being audited periodically by their state's real estate licensing department. The purpose of the audit is to ensure that the firm is operating within the state's administrative codes and to protect the public from illegal actions by real estate licensees. Violations of the state's codes and laws can result in fines and/or suspensions or revocations of a person's or a firm's real estate license. When individuals lose their real estate license, they are no longer allowed to practice the profession.

3

Prospecting

THE BASICS OF PROSPECTING

Few activities in the operation of commercial properties are more important than leasing, and leasing starts with prospecting. Prospecting is more than just calling on potential tenants. It requires the leasing agent to have a full understanding of the property's position in the marketplace, the clientele it plans to service, what management plan will be followed, and the terms of the lease document.

The leasing agent must be prepared to lease before going out to face potential tenants. Initial marketing strategies often consist of one-page flyers that can be handed out to each person contacted, emails sent to leasing agents and prospects, listings on Internet sites and with commercial multiple listing services, signs on the property, billboards for larger properties, publicity releases, on-site receptions for leasing agents, and meetings with brokers and prospective tenants. In addition to a full understanding of the property and the lease document, the agent must have effective marketing materials to present and leave with potential tenants. Creating these materials is the responsibility of the landlord's leasing agent.

Developing Effective Marketing Materials

Marketing materials include brochures, one-page flyers, property websites, plot plans, demographic information, renderings, business cards, advertising and promotional materials, and, in some cases, even model offices. These materials need not be inordinately expensive, but should be very professional and reflect the quality of the property being offered. They allow tenants and their leasing agents to stay aware of what is available in the marketplace.

Tenant leasing agents often keep marketing materials to serve as a "mini" market survey when looking for locations for prospective tenants. If the information being presented is likely to change often, it is a good idea either to print a limited supply of the materials so they can be changed easily, or to make a basic package with inserts that can be added to reflect changes in the current situation. It does not reflect well on the property to cross out information or make additions in pencil or ink. Desktop publishing software makes it easy to update and modify flyers and other marketing materials.

The Property Brochure

The property brochure should be professionally prepared and should reflect the quality of the project. If the brochure is to be handed out by more than one leasing agent, there should be a place for the business card so many agents can use the same brochure. Even if it is only a one-page brochure or flyer, the materials should be easy to read, be clear, and contain basic information to help prospects decide if this is a property they want to consider further. For shopping centers, it is most helpful to identify the anchor tenants and other tenants whose presence may entice a prospect to consider locating in the shopping center. All leasing materials should contain the name of the leasing agent(s), along with a phone number and email address, to make it easy for the prospect to make contact.

The Property Layout

The building layout is important for tenants in a shopping center. The layout of the building(s) determines traffic flow in the shopping center and parking lot and the visibility of each space from the parking lot and the street. Is parking convenient and adequate? Are ingress and egress convenient? Does the flow of both automobile and pedestrian traffic seem reasonable?

In the case of high-rise office buildings, is internal transportation efficient? The size and configuration of the office building and office medical building's floor plate are a major factor in how the tenants' spaces are designed and the efficiency of these spaces. The size of the floor plate is also a factor for what size of tenants will lease space in the building. Floor plates with shallow depth from the core to the exterior of the building attract smaller tenants, while floor plates with a large depth attract larger tenants.

Exhibit 3.1

The Contents of a Good Leasing Package

A good leasing package includes:

1. A transmittal letter customized for each prospect
2. The property brochure
3. The plot plan (layout) of the property
4. The tenant list
5. Aerial photos
6. The layout of the space being considered
7. A rendering of the property
8. A map of the area
9. Accessibility and transportation information
10. A summary of the building's unique features
11. A disclaimer stating that the landlord may change the layout of the site plan and the design of the parking lot, and the tenants listed might not remain tenants in the building.

The Leasing Package

A leasing package is used once interest in a property has been established. There is no reason to provide a leasing package to every person contacted, as the percentage of contacts that will actually lead to an executed lease is quite small. Instead, a one-page flyer on the building may be left with prospects. However, once a tenant prospect has shown interest in the property, a leasing package is presented with all of the relevant information about the property. The leasing package should also be available as an email attachment, because many companies prefer to communicate via email rather than U.S. mail. The contents of a good leasing package are outlined in Exhibits 3.1 and 3.2.

MARKETING AND PROSPECTING FOR TENANTS

Marketing and prospecting for tenants is the critical element in a leasing plan. Potential tenants are everywhere. The art and the science of marketing and prospecting lie in target marketing, which gives prospecting a higher probability of resulting in a completed deal. For any building, there are only certain tenants who are viable prospects to lease space in that building. The leasing agent must determine which uses and tenants are compatible with the building and its location, tenant mix, and amenities. National office tenants seldom lease space in older Class B buildings, for example, and upscale retailers do not lease space in low- to moderate-income areas.

A very successful leasing agent once said that he usually made one

---

Exhibit 3.2
The Contents of a Shopping Center Leasing Package

In addition to the regular leasing package, the following information is included in a good leasing package for a shopping center:

1. The trade area's demographic and psychographic information
2. Traffic counts
3. General sales information on the performance of the shopping center
4. A calendar of marketing events, if they exist

---

lease for every 100 prospects he met with; so his job was to talk to as many people as possible, weeding out the 99 who wouldn't sign the lease to get to the one who *was* going to make the deal. As an added bonus, some of those 99 who originally declined a lease could well be persons of interest in a future leasing assignment, so the effort was not wasted.

Evaluating the Market

There are many ways to evaluate a market, several of which are listed below.

Commercial Multiple Listing Services.   Many major metropolitan areas now have a commercial multiple listing service that is subscribed to by brokers in the area. These services provide a centralized database listing commercial properties with space for lease, and are a good source for information on what is available in the market.

Employment Ads.   Checking with employment ads in a community can tell the leasing agent who is hiring and therefore possibly expanding. These companies become targets to contact.

Business Directories.   Most business associations and chambers of commerce have directories of their membership. Many of these members are community leaders, and they are excellent contacts. Even if they are not in the market for space, they likely know of someone who is.

Government Space Requirements.   Governmental agencies frequently put out requests for bids on office and industrial space that they will need in the near future. Depending on the type of buildings being leased, one should get on all of the relevant mailing lists and at a minimum be prepared to discuss an agency's needs. Even if there is not an immediate fit for a specific need, that contact may well pay off for future projects.

Signs and Billboards

Signs are a common and often very effective way to attract potential tenants.

Leasing Signs.   It is generally held that the leasing sign is one of the most effective leasing tools for commercial properties. Most tenants who are looking for space have a specific area in mind, and leasing signs tell them what is available. Leasing agents will drive an area looking for vacant space for their clients, and so a sign is especially helpful to tenants who are out looking for new locations without the help of a leasing agent. It quickly tells them what is available in that area.

A leasing sign should be as large as the local authorities allow. It should contain relevant information, including the name of a leasing person and a very visible phone number and/or email address. If the project is new and the developer is a recognized and respected name, that should be prominent on the sign as well. It is generally agreed that it is not a good idea to include the available square footage, as many prospects are not sure of how much space they need. However, in cases where a large amount of space is available, indicating that square footage can be helpful.

The leasing sign should be kept in good repair during the entire leasing process, and its visibility should be checked from time to time. It is not unusual to have a sign for a building under constructed become hidden. Even in newer projects, landscaping can easily obscure a sign.

Project Signs.   A "coming soon" project sign can generate a lot of interest in a specific project. The sign should be very well done and quite visible. The names of the developer, general contractor, architect, and lender are often included in the text. Somewhere on the sign should also be the name, phone number, and email of the leasing agent, because substantial interest in a coming project may be generated with "coming soon" signs.

Billboards.   Very large projects, such as regional malls or high-rise office buildings, can benefit from the use of a billboard in the area or directly on-site. The billboard should have a rendering of the building, names of anchor tenants (if already signed), and the name of the developer and leasing agent. A phone number and email address should also be included.

Direct Mail

Direct mail is an easy way to reach a large number of prospects, but the returns are fairly small. A return of 1 to 2 percent of the total mailing is considered a good response, and not all of those who respond will wind up signing a lease. However, it is also fairly inexpensive to reach a large pool of potential tenants through direct mail, so the effort is usually worthwhile. Many leasing companies will include a postage-paid response card to make it easy for the prospect to get more information. Of course, email is another form of direct mail.

Radio and TV Advertising

Radio and TV are generally not used for leasing. This is because both radio and TV are quite expensive, and it is very difficult to target the ad to any specific tenant or group of tenants.

Canvassing

Canvassing is calling on tenants in person. Cold canvassing is one of the most effective tools in leasing, but one that many leasing agents prefer not to do. It is time consuming—especially getting to the responsible party—but a wealth of information is gathered in the process, and much of this information can be used in future leasing efforts. Leasing agents should start each outing with a goal of a minimum number of calls to be accomplished. They should be armed with calling cards and the property flyer, and these should be handed out to anyone who will accept them, along with the request that they be passed along to the responsible party. If a chat seems like it might lead to a deal, a follow-up phone call should be made a week or so after the initial contact.

Phone Prospecting

Telephone canvassing is a good use of a leasing agent's time, but it yields success in a very low percentage of the contacts made. However, this approach allows the leasing agent to talk with a large number of people in a short period of time and, when interest is shown, the leasing agent can either put information in the mail or deliver it in person. It is not likely that a deal will be made during the initial phone call, but interest can be established and a follow-up arrangement reached. One in-house leasing agent for a grocery-anchored shopping center REIT was known as a "killer cold caller" for the number of phone calls she made in a day and her excellent percentage of deals generated from the calls.

The yellow pages are an excellent source for identifying prospects in specific business categories and telephone prospecting. Returns may be low, but a lot of prospective tenants can be contacted in a relatively short period of time. This holds true for retail, office, and industrial tenants.

Print Ads

Print ads can be used to attract potential tenants to a commercial property.

Trade Journal Ads.   Every profession and trade has a journal, and these can be excellent sources for reaching tenant prospects. These types of advertisements are generally more effective for larger projects. A regional mall may take out an ad in *Women's Wear Daily;* or, when looking for a restaurant, an ad in *Restaurant News* may prove to be effective. When leasing up a high-rise office building, ads in various trade journals for the desired types of tenants can be quite effective. Ads for a new medical office building in the state AMA's directory can be an effective means to reach doctors.

Classified Ads.   Classified ads are not a particularly effective means of finding tenants; however, they are inexpensive and can be targeted to specific tenants. Rather than advertising a 1,200-square-foot shop for lease, one might use the classifieds to promote a delicatessen location or an ice cream store location of 1,200 square feet. If classified ads are used, it is a good idea to change them often, as readers get used to seeing the same ad and can easily ignore it.

Display Ads

Display advertising is a type of advertising that usually contains graphic information beyond text. Display advertising can appear in a variety of formats—in a periodical, as a web banner, as interactive media, etc. They are meant to capture the attention of prospective tenants by announcing the coming of a project, the grand opening, the signing of recognized tenants, the revealing of impressive building amenities, and so forth.

Electronic Marketing

Electronic marketing is becoming ever more popular as a means of prospecting.

Email.   Email has become a very effective tool for informing brokers of a building's available space and special promotions. It can be used to send a newsletter to the brokerage community, or it can provide special alerts for space that is available. Email lists can be targeted to reach brokers specializing in a particular property type.

Websites.   In today's electronic age, it is almost essential to have a company and/or project website. A website can present a whole story, including the history of the developer and the development. It is a great opportunity to tell one's story at the convenience of the potential client. Much like the property sign, simply having a website by itself is not likely to generate a lot of deals; however, it is a productive tool when used as a complement to other approaches.

Internet Listings. Almost every major metropolitan area now has Internet listings of commercial properties that are available for lease or sale. Some of these sites are better than others, but all of them provide a good cross-section of what is available in the marketplace, and most of them provide general terms. Internet listings can serve as a good way to narrow down the buildings in a search before setting out to see them.

Open Houses

There is nothing like an open house to display exactly what a property is all about. This approach is especially effective for leasing office buildings, but can also be effective in retail and industrial properties. An open house can be held in conjunction with a ground breaking, a grand opening, the setting of important artwork, and/or the "topping off" of the building.

There are separate open house events held for prospective tenants and existing tenants, as well as different open houses for the brokerage community. An open house usually includes refreshments and is staffed with sufficient personnel to make sure everyone is welcomed and provided with essential information. It is not unusual for the developer or landlord to offer small incentives to those who attend such open houses, such as coffee shop gift cards or being entered into a drawing to win an iPod or flat-screen TV.

The Model Office

A model space is especially helpful for office building leasing. The model office should be furnished and finished approximately at building standard. This can be an effective sales tool with individual tenant prospects; and the local brokerage community can also be invited to stop by and view the model office.

Marketing for Medical Office Buildings

There are specific aspects to be taken into account when finding prospective tenants for medical office buildings.

Contacts at Local Hospitals. Medical office buildings and office buildings with medical space should be marketed to hospital administrators in the general area. The hospital administration is aware of doctors who either have been approached about affiliating with the hospital or have ap-

proached the hospital themselves. In either case, these doctors may well
need space near the hospital.

Medical Journal Ads.   Local and regional medical journals provide a
good way to contact doctors in a general area. The ads therein can be very
general in order to appeal to a broad audience, or they can feature a specific
space. These ads should be quite prominent and eye-catching, and placement is suggested on either the back page or the inside cover.

Marketing for Retail Tenants

Retail tenants are often procured through the following means.

Merchant Ads.   Watch the local papers for retailer ads to see who is growing and who is promoting business. These ads will provide a good idea of
the market niche in which specific retailers are operating, and should provide the leasing agent with good direction concerning which retailers will
fit best into a given property.

ICSC Conventions and Meetings.   International Council of Shopping
Centers (ICSC) meetings and conventions are great meeting places for landlords and tenants alike. The annual May convention held in Las Vegas, with
upwards of 50,000 attendees, can be a bit overwhelming, but there is no better place to meet many retailers. Retailers, brokerage firms, and developers
have booths while the majority of attendees do not have booths but walk
the convention floor meeting each other. Many deals are started at ICSC's
conventions and meetings.

Retail Tenant Directories.   There are a few retail tenant directories available, both in print form and on electronic disks. These provide a valuable
source for target marketing.

Publicity

Publicity is a very effective leasing and marketing tool. Good publicity coverage does not happen by accident. Property ownership and their property
management staff should cultivate relationships with the staff of local papers and radio stations, and work with them to place positive publicity at
every opportunity. Good occasions for telling the property's story arise with
a variety of events and details, including the announcement of the project,
special amenities, the signing of important tenants, the groundbreaking,
placing of financing, the addition of important artwork, the building topping off, the grand opening, charitable contributions, and the naming of

the building property manager or the property management company. Any chance for good publicity should never be ignored.

Networking

Networking is an absolute essential for the leasing agent. The leasing professional should be active in the community as well as active in the trade associations that serve their market niche. All contacts should be treated with courtesy and respect, and staying in touch can be very beneficial. Leasing agents do not have to attend all of these functions and "sell" their projects, but rather they should simply go to the meetings, let people know who they are and what they do, and conduct themselves in a businesslike manner. Good things are likely to happen from there.

Civic and Business Meetings.   Either the on-site property manager or the marketing director of a mall—or both—should be involved in local civic groups, charitable organizations, and/or social clubs. It is important to be active in these organizations and to be involved for the good of the organizations. When that is accomplished, the property will benefit from the contacts and the positive influences encountered. Professionals should not go to these meetings just to promote their property; but this promotion is likely to happen as a byproduct of being involved and answering questions about the building, especially if the property is a large mall or a lifestyle or specialty shopping center.

Hosting a Luncheon.   Hosting a luncheon for a small number of business managers who represent the desired types of tenants can be a very good networking experience. The connections made can easily build relationships that will have benefits for future projects.

Prospective Tenant Sources

There are many sources for finding prospective tenants, a few of the most effective of which are listed below.

Working with the Brokerage Community.   Some landlords prefer to do their own leasing instead of being involved with the brokerage community. This can be an effective strategy. However, there are some lease deals that are in the hands of specific brokers, and these deals will not be concluded without them. In addition, brokers often come into contact with people looking for space to whom the landlords may not have access. For these reasons, it is a good idea for landlords to work with the brokerage community. Even when doing their own leasing, this connection facilitates the potential capture of those few elusive deals that only a broker can bring to the property.

Working with Other Managers and Leasing Agents.   While real estate professionals are competitors with others at similar buildings in their area, they also share a common interest in seeing that the area is well-leased and that the vacancy factor is as low as possible. If one building cannot accommodate a tenant, it is a good idea for the landlord to steer the tenant to a nearby building. Hopefully that building's property manager or leasing agent will return the favor. Such referrals can either be done on a "favor" basis, or each can act as a broker on the cross-deals. The important thing is to keep the lease deal in the local market.

Suppliers.   Suppliers of goods and services can make attractive prospective tenants. If, for example, a leasing agent has a good restaurant space to lease, she can contact restaurant equipment and supply firms and inquire if they know of any restaurant operators who are looking to open another restaurant. If a lease is signed with an operator, the equipment supplier is likely to sell the equipment to the operator.

This creates an ideal situation for the supplier and, likewise, for the restaurant tenants in the area who are looking to expand. Similar arrangements can be made with suppliers of beauty shop or ice cream store equipment, manufacturers of shoes, clothing, or jewelry, etc., and their clients.

Existing Tenants.   Existing tenants are almost always a good source of prospects. Current tenants should be visited on a regular basis, and management should use this "chat" opportunity to share what the building's future holds, ask the tenants how they are doing, and find out about their future plans. It is always a good idea to ask an existing tenant for thoughts about who might be a good prospect for an existing or upcoming vacancy.

The Goal of Prospecting

Marketing and prospecting for tenants is a never-ending task, but it is absolutely essential to the success of any commercial property. The effective leasing agent does not just make contacts for a current project, but also thinks about future projects and/or alternative options for prospects.

The goal of every leasing contact is to establish credibility as an expert in the tenant's marketplace. The effective leasing agent presents opportunities in an effort to show the prospect why his property will meet the location needs of this business. This paves the way for an established relationship that could well produce mutually beneficial deals in the future.

4

Negotiating the Brokerage Agreement

A *leasing agreement* is necessary when landlords select a brokerage firm to lease their property, or when brokers or their leasing agents present a prospective tenant to the landlord. The leasing agreement between a landlord and a broker will state what the broker or the broker's leasing agent must do to represent a tenant or the landlord, how a commission is earned, the method for determining the amount of the commission, and the rights and obligations of the landlord and the broker.

One of the reasons landlords prefer to enter into a leasing agreement is to protect themselves from leasing agents claiming they are owed a commission when they have not represented a tenant who entered into a lease. Brokers likewise want an agreement to protect their leasing agent's position in the transaction. Both parties to the agreement should understand the specific responsibilities of each party. This chapter will discuss the different types of agreements from the landlord's and the broker's perspectives.

When a broker or leasing agent represents a tenant, both parties will enter into an agreement that almost always gives the brokerage firm and its leasing agent the exclusive right to represent the tenant in the tenant's search for space. Leasing agents may prepare a *request for proposal (RFP)* to outline the location, building, and space requirements of their client. A landlord will either acknowledge the leasing agent's role in representing the tenant or not accept the leasing agent's representation. These agreements will be discussed from the perspective of both parties.

TYPES OF LISTING AGREEMENTS

There are several types of listing agreements, as discussed below.

Exclusive Right to Lease Listing Agreement

The *exclusive right listing agreement* is the most common agreement used by landlords when they contract with a broker to lease their building. It is also the agreement preferred by brokerage firms. This agreement gives the brokerage firm the *exclusive right to lease* the building. If another broker or leasing agent brings a tenant to the building and a lease is signed, the listing broker will still be paid a commission. Usually the listing leasing agent will enter into an agreement with the tenant's broker or leasing agent to share the commission. Even if the landlord, or anyone else, finds a prospect and a lease is entered into with that prospect, the listing broker is nevertheless paid a commission.

Since lease listing agents invest a considerable amount of their time and some expense in marketing a building, they want to be sure that they will be paid a commission—or a portion of the commission—regardless of who brings a prospect to the building and finalizes a lease. They do not want to be competing, but cooperating with the brokerage community to find tenants for the building. The advantage of this type of agreement to the landlord is the assurance that the leasing agent(s) are committed to spending the necessary time marketing and leasing the property.

Exclusive Agency Lease Listing Agreement

The *exclusive agency listing agreement* is similar to the exclusive right listing agreement, except in the case of the landlord finding a tenant. If the landlord finds the tenant, a commission is not paid to the listing brokerage firm. Landlords benefit from this arrangement by not having to pay commission if they find a tenant. The disadvantage, however, is that leasing agents are more likely to believe that landlords are competing with them to find tenants for the building. A dispute over who first contacted a tenant or how the tenant became aware of the building can easily develop.

When an exclusive agency listing agreement is used, it is in the interest of both parties to have an addendum to the agreement that lists which prospective tenants the landlord is working with or intends to contact. The addendum may state that the broker will not be paid a commission if any of these prospects enters into a lease with the landlord. An alternative to not paying the brokerage firm for tenants the landlord finds is for the landlord to pay only a partial commission to the brokerage firm for those tenants.

The landlord must be careful not to compete or give the perception of competing with the brokerage firm, which might discourage the firm's leasing agents from providing a 100 percent effort for marketing and leasing the building. The brokerage firm will want to have its "For Lease" sign on the property and be the only party to list the property with commercial multiple listing services and online Internet listing services. The firm will also want to receive all inquiries from prospects and other leasing agents. It is important for landlords to recognize these preferences and comply with all reasonable requests so that there are no conflicts between landlords and their broker(s).

Open Lease Listing Agreement

Open lease listing agreements do not provide a broker with the exclusive right to lease the landlord's building. The landlord will pay a commission to any broker who brings a prospect who enters into a lease. In theory, this type of agreement will encourage all leasing agents to "work" the landlord's property, searching for tenants for the building.

In reality, though, few if any leasing agents will market a building under an open listing agreement. If leasing agents invest their time in marketing a building, they want the assurance that they will be paid a commission when a lease is executed. If leasing agents represents tenants, however, they may present their clients to landlords with an open listing agreement. Tenant leasing agents prioritize the best building and location for their clients, and they are consequently just as likely to respond to an open listing as to another type of listing if their client's needs are met.

Single Party Lease Listing Agreement

When a leasing agent represents a tenant, or when a landlord gives the leasing agent an assignment to contact a specific prospective, the parties may enter into a *single party lease listing agreement.* This agreement may also be used when leasing agents present a prospective to landlords who have no exclusive leasing agent and prefer to lease their building with an open lease listing agreement. A *registration letter,* which is discussed later in this chapter, may be used in lieu of a single party lease listing agreement.

THE LEASING AGREEMENT

Once the landlord and the brokerage firm have agreed upon the type of listing arrangement, a leasing agreement needs to be executed by both parties. The agreement will formalize in writing each party's rights and obligations, as well as the broker's compensation.

The leasing agreement is usually provided by the brokerage firm. Most brokerage firms have developed their own agreement, and in some markets a commercial multiple listing service will provide an agreement for its members. Few landlords—usually only those who have a large portfolio of properties—have their own leasing agreement.

The leasing agreement should be carefully reviewed by each party. Many of the provisions are standard for all types of agreements, and there is little to negotiate in these provisions. There are others provisions, though, that need careful scrutiny and may require negotiations. A discussion of the issues and provisions in a leasing agreement, from both the landlord's and the broker's perspectives, is provided below.

Leasing Agreement Issues and Provisions

1. **Parties to the Agreement.** The landlord and the broker are named.

2. **Exclusive Agreement.** The brokerage firm is appointed as the exclusive leasing agent for the property. The issue to discuss is whether the broker is granted the exclusive right to lease the property or an exclusive agency. (These two types of listing agreements are discussed above.)

3. **Description of the Property.** This provision describes and provides the property's legal address. If the agreement is for a specific space or spaces in the building, this agreement will describe those areas. A *metes and bounds* description may be necessary for a parcel of land such as a *pad* or an *out parcel*. A *site plan* of the property may be an addendum to the agreement.

4. **Leasing Agreement Term.** The length of the agreement and its commencement and expiration dates are stated. The brokerage firm usually prefers a one-year agreement, which will enable the firm to develop and implement a marketing plan, contact prospective tenants, show space, and negotiate leases. A landlord may prefer a shorter agreement—usually six months. Most agreements will provide both parties with a 30-day written cancellation right, with or without cause.

5. **Registration of Prospects.** This registration provision will usually state that the broker and the landlord agree on a *registration list*. When an agreement is cancelled, or expires and is not renewed, the broker and landlord may establish such a list. It is to the broker's advantage to register a list of prospects with the landlord so that, if a lease is entered into with any of those listed, the broker will receive a commission. Brokers benefit from making sure that every prospect they contact or show space to is included on the registration list.

The landlord, on the other hand, is concerned that the broker will provide a list including prospects who do not yet have a serious interest in the building. The landlord wants to protect against future disputes, and so wants only those prospects actually involved in lease negotiations on the list. If another broker represents a listed prospect in the future and a lease is entered into, the landlord does not want two brokers claiming a commission for the same prospect.

One method to settle any possible disputes over which prospects should be included is to review the last few leasing reports and include only those prospects who are shown with serious interest or are in lease negotiations. A timeframe for executing the lease may also be stated, and those deals not completed within the given limits will be taken off the broker's list. The opportunity for the leasing agent to earn commissions for these prospects will then expire.

6. **Commissions.** This provision states the commission rate and the commission payment schedule. The agreement may exclude from the commission calculations income derived from the following: parking, percentage rent, *consumer price index (CPI)* increases, over-standard or after-hours utility charges, late payments and fees, security deposits, payment for over-standard improvements, etc. The agreement also may state that commissions are paid only on base or minimum rent.

A negotiable issue is whether or not the broker is to be paid a commission if the tenant expands or renews the lease. (Renewals are discussed in more detail in Chapter 11, "Lease Renewals.") The brokers' position is that they brought the tenant to the building and therefore should be paid a commission on all transactions between the tenant and landlord. The landlords' position is that they have already paid the broker for the initial transaction, so any subsequent transactions— such as expansion and lease renewal—should be strictly between the landlord and the tenant. Additionally, any subsequent transactions are likely to occur several years after the initial lease is executed, and the broker is typically long gone by then. The landlord is usually in a strong negotiating position on this issue, and will often prevail.

Some brokerage firms' agreements will state that, if the landlord intends to sell the property during the lease listing agreement, the leasing broker will receive the exclusive right to sell the property. Most landlords will not agree to this request. They may believe another broker is more qualified to sell the property; they may want to sell the property themselves; or they may not want to commit to doing something in the future they have not yet decided is best. This is another issue that brokers are usually willing to delete from their leasing agreements.

7. **Cooperating Brokers.** The landlord authorizes the broker to cooperate with other brokers, and the broker agrees to market the property and cooperate with other brokers.

8. Rent Schedule. Some lease listing agreements state either the anticipated asking rental rate or the anticipated deal-making rental rate. These rates are derived from a conversation between the broker and the landlord about the market rate for the building. The agreement may also state other lease terms, such as the minimum and maximum lease length and the tenant charges.

9. Advertising. The landlord authorizes the broker to advertise the property and list it with commercial multiple listing services and Internet services. The landlord will want full approval of all ads. The issue to negotiate is who pays for this advertising.

10. Signs. The broker is authorized to place "For Lease" signs on the property. The cost of these signs is usually the broker's expense.

11. Leasing Meetings and Reports. The broker will meet with the landlord a specific number of times to discuss the marketing plan and leasing progress. If the building is in initial lease-up, or if there is excessive vacancy, the landlord may want to meet with the broker weekly or biweekly. If a building has limited space to lease, a monthly meeting will usually suffice. If the landlord's office is not near the property or the broker's office, the meeting can be in the form of a conference call. A few days prior to the meeting, the broker should provide the landlord with a leasing status report, which may be formatted as an addendum to the agreement.

12. Property Disclosure. The landlord agrees to fully disclose to the broker and prospects all known information regarding zoning, land restrictions, existing lease restrictions, and environmental and hazardous issues affecting the property.

13. Deposits. The broker is authorized to accept deposits from prospects on behalf of the landlord. If the deposit is nonrefundable, the broker will want to keep a portion—possibly half—of the money in case the tenant does not complete the transaction and forfeits the deposit.

14. Dual Agency. The agreement may state that the landlord chooses to allow the broker to act as a *dual agent,* representing both the landlord and the tenant in a lease transaction. The landlord may not agree to this provision, however, believing that the broker may not serve the best interest of the landlord when acting for both parties. If the parties do decide on a dual agency agreement, the broker will agree not to disclose confidential information of either party. Some states require that the broker provide the landlord with a pamphlet on the law of real estate agency. In these states, the agreement will affirm that the landlord acknowledges receiving and reading the pamphlet.

15. Lease Form. The parties agree either that the landlord will provide the lease agreement or that the brokerage firm will provide its standard agreement, which the landlord must approve. A few areas also have commercial multiple listing services that provide their standard lease agreement for the parties to use. The *lease agreement* is between the landlord and the tenant, while the *leasing agreement* is between the landlord and the brokerage firm. There is no industry standard lease agreement.

16. Referrals. The landlord agrees to immediately refer all inquiries to the broker.

17. Right to Reject Prospects. The landlord reserves the right, in his or her sole and absolute discretion, to reject any prospective tenant or any proposed lease terms presented by any broker. The landlord is not obligated to pay a commission on any rejected prospects.

18. Assignment. Often the landlord enters into a leasing agreement because of his or her relationship with a leasing agent. If the agreement is assigned, the landlord may want the option to cancel the agreement.

19. Sale of Property. The leasing agreement is usually cancelled upon sale of the property. The broker asks that, in the event of a sale, the landlord will attempt to get the purchaser to agree to continue listing the property with the broker.

20. Disputes. The parties agree on how a dispute will be settled. Often the parties will agree to binding arbitration, with the prevailing party being reimbursed for costs. If the issue in dispute can not be arbitrated or the parties have not agreed to arbitration, the prevailing party is reimbursed for its legal fees as well as costs.

21. Nondiscrimination. The landlord and the broker agree to comply with all applicable antidiscrimination regulations and laws.

22. Governing Law. This agreement is governed by the laws of the state in which the property is located.

23. Indemnity. There is usually a mutual indemnity provision. The landlord agrees to *indemnify* the broker for his or her performance, and the broker agrees to indemnify the landlord for any incorrect information provided.

24. Competition. The landlord may want to include a provision stating that the broker will not lease any property in direct competition with the landlord's property. However, such a request may not be in the landlord's best interest because it will likely exclude many of the larger brokerage firms. If the brokerage firm is leasing a property that is in competition with the landlord's property, the two parties should first resolve whether or not the properties are in direct competition, and then decide how the landlord's property can be marketed and leased without a conflict of interest. Seldom do both buildings have identical features, location, and available space size, so they can be marketed by the same broker without conflict. Often marketing two similar buildings in close proximity to each other enables the leasing agent to devote *more* time and marketing expense to each building.

25. Confidentiality. The broker agrees to keep all information provided by the landlord confidential, except for that which the landlord authorizes for use in the property's marketing and leasing efforts. The landlord may also require that the broker keep all data regarding existing and future tenants confidential. The landlord does not want his or her tenants' information used in the brokerage firm's leasing database, or in any other listing that the firm might develop to market and lease other properties or find tenant representation.

26. Independent Contractor. The agreement may state that the broker and the leasing agent are independent contractors, and not employees of the landlord.

27. Lien Law. In specific situations, some states provide the broker with the right to file a *lien* on the property for commission that is owed and not paid. This provision makes reference to that law.

28. Notices. This provision states where notices will be sent for each party, as well as the delivery method.

29. Entire Agreement. This provision states that the listing agreement constitutes the entire agreement, supersedes any prior written or oral agreements, and is the prevailing agreement.

30. Exhibits. The agreement may refer to exhibits such as site plans, commission schedules, etc.

THE LETTER OF ENGAGEMENT

When a leasing agent represents a business seeking space, the brokerage firm for which the leasing agent works will enter into an agreement with the tenant to find that space. This agreement is formalized through the *letter of engagement,* which appoints the brokerage firm as the exclusive agent to represent the tenant.

The scope of the space-finding assignment will vary depending on the needs of the tenant. When office tenants need to relocate, leasing agents meet with them to determine their existing and future needs, go into the market and survey office buildings, and then present their findings and recommendations to the tenants. A retail leasing agent may have a similar assignment when a tenant requests space to open an additional store in a specific trade area's shopping center.

A retail leasing agent may also be given an expanded assignment that includes developing a market penetration strategy for a retailer either entering a market or attempting to grow its market share. This assignment may include developing an understanding of the client's core customers, determining the number of stores to maximize market opportunities, deciding on the sequencing of store openings, surveying the market for rental rates and lease terms, recommending which trade areas to enter, finding locations within those trade areas, and negotiating the leases.

The letter of engagement may be as simple as a one-page agreement on the tenant's letterhead, designating the brokerage firm as the exclusive agent to represent the business in locating space of a designated size in a specific area. The agreement will also state how the leasing agent will be compensated. Usually a commission is paid by the landlord; but if the landlord refuses to pay a commission or agrees to only a small amount, the tenant may pay all or a portion of the commission. If the assignment is broader than just finding a location, the tenant may also pay for the travel expenses of the leasing agent and possibly pay a *retainer.* Commissions the leasing agent receives from landlords could offset the retainer.

THE REGISTRATION LETTER AND AGREEMENT

When a leasing agent represents a tenant and they have selected a building in which to negotiate a lease, the leasing agent will present a registration letter to the landlord. This letter formalizes the *registration and commission agreement,* stating that the brokerage firm and leasing agent exclusively represent the tenant. It also includes the terms of this agreement and the commission schedule. The registration letter is usually one or two pages in length, but for major transactions it can be several pages long and include issues beyond those discussed below.

Registration Letter Issues and Provisions

1. **Registration.** This provision states that the brokerage firm represents the tenant, and the landlord agrees to pay a commission if a lease is executed between the landlord and the tenant.

2. **Term.** This provision states the length of the agreement. These agreements are often for three to six months, and they are extended

if the parties are pursuing or negotiating a lease. The leasing agent wants sufficient time to complete the transaction. The landlord may want a shorter term in order to motivate the leasing agent to facilitate the transactions in as short a time as possible, thus avoiding any unnecessary lost rent on the vacant space under consideration.

3. **Commission.** The commission rate and payment schedule is stated.

4. **Renewals and Expansions.** This provision states whether or not a commission is paid if the tenant renews the lease or expands the premises.

5. **Signature.** All three parties—the tenant, the landlord, and the brokerage firm—sign the agreement. The tenant may prefer not to sign the agreement and instead have an engagement letter with the brokerage firm. In this case, the tenant will provide the landlord with a letter on the tenant's letterhead, stating that the brokerage firm is its exclusive agent in the transaction.

RECOGNITION OF THE BROKER'S STATUS

When leasing agents claim that they represent a tenant interested in leasing space in a landlord's building, that landlord should ascertain the statement's validity. Making sure that the leasing agent is indeed the tenant's exclusive representative can prevent the situation in which two leasing agents both claim to represent the same tenant. To this end, the landlord requests that the leasing agent either bring the tenant to the building and introduce the tenant to the landlord, or provide a letter from the tenant—on the tenant's letterhead—stating that the leasing agent is the tenant's exclusive agent.

In response, the landlord will send the broker a letter either acknowledging the broker as the tenant's representative or denying the agent's representation. If the leasing agent provides a letter of registration and agreement that the landlord accepts and signs, the landlord does not need to sign a separate letter acknowledging that the leasing agent represents the tenant.

THE TENANT'S REQUEST FOR PROPOSAL

A leasing agent may develop a request for proposal (RFP) for a tenant's space needs and provide it to several landlords whose buildings appear to meet the tenant's space and location requirements. The questions on the RFP will vary depending on if the tenant is an office, medical, industrial, or retail user. The following presents sample elements of an RFP that a landlord would complete for an office tenant.

Sample Elements of an RFP

1. **Building Name.** The name of the building.

2. **Building Address.** The building's street address.

3. **Landlord Name and Address.** The entity that owns the building and its address.

4. **Tenant Name.** The name of the prospect.

5. **Building Size.** The building's square footage or, if there are multiple buildings in the complex, the size of each building as well as the total square footage of all the buildings.

6. **Premises Size Measured in Usable and Rentable Square Feet.** The size of the space the landlord is offering the tenant, measured in usable square feet and in rentable square feet.

7. **Building Load Factor.** The building's usable/rentable factor, also know as its *load factor.*

8. **Initial Lease Term.** The length of time included in the initial term of the lease.

9. **Tenant's Use.** The tenant states the intended use for the space, and will want it to be as broad as possible.

10. **Exclusive or Other Restrictions.** This includes the exclusive use restriction or any other restriction for which the tenant asks.

11. **Base Rent.** The monthly and annual base rent and rent step-ups.

12. **Pass-Through Building Expenses.** This section states how the building operating expenses are billed to the tenant and the tenant's prorated share of the expenses.

13. **Security Deposit.** This element discloses whether or not there will be a security deposit and, if so, the amount and due date.

14. **Tenant Improvement Allowance.** The amount of allowance that the landlord will provide to the tenant to build out the premises.

15. **Space Planning Allowance.** The amount of allowance that the landlord will provide to the tenant for space planning and possibly interior design.

16. **Time to Build Out Tenant Improvements.** The landlord will state the time required to build out the tenant's premises.

17. **Time to Set Up the Office.** The tenant will want time to make equipment installations and set up the business without paying rent.

18. **Rent Commencement Date.** The day rent commences, which may not be the same day the tenant takes occupancy of the premises.

19. **Lease Renewal Options.** The tenant will want one or multiple options to renew the lease. The option may be at market rent; it may be a percentage of market rent, such as 95 percent; or the rent for the option period may be predetermined.

20. **Lease Expansion Options.** The tenant will want the option to expand the premises or take additional space elsewhere in the building.

21. **Lease Cancellation Option.** The tenant will want the right to cancel the lease under certain circumstances.

22. **Tenant Parking.** This includes the number of parking stalls or spaces the tenant will receive, whether they are reserved or unreserved, and the parking charges to the tenant, if any.

23. **Assignment and Subleasing Rights.** The tenant will want the right to assign or sublease its lease. (These rights are discussed in more detail in Chapter 12, "Negotiating the Lease.")

24. **Signage.** This lists whether or not the tenant will have signage rights on the building or in any other place on the property. The tenant may request that the building name be changed to include the tenant's name.

25. **Tenant's Insurance Requirements.** Covers the building's insurance requirements for the tenant.

26. **Relocation.** The tenant prefers that the landlord does not have the right to relocate the tenant.

27. **Nondisturbance Agreement.** The landlord will provide a nondisturbance agreement from the lender benefiting the tenant.

28. **Hazardous Substances.** A statement either that the property has no known hazardous substances or providing a list of hazardous substances in the building, such as asbestos in the fireproofing, etc.

29. **Building Services.** This section provides a list of the building's services, such as the frequency of janitorial service, etc.

30. **Building Hours.** A list of the building's standard hours.

31. **After-Hours HVAC Charges.** The hourly rates for heating, ventilating, and air conditioning after hours.

32. **Building Security.** A description of the building's security and emergency procedures.

33. Building Amenities. A list of the building's amenities that are available to the tenant.

34. Area Amenities. A list of amenities within walking distance of the building, such as restaurants, shopping facilities, banks, etc.

35. Public Transportation. A listing of nearby public transportation.

36. Structural Defects. A statement either declaring that there are no known structural defects or, if there are, providing a list of the defects.

37. ADA and Code Compliance. A statement that the building is in compliance with the *ADA* and all other building codes and ordinances.

38. Satellite Dish. This provision states whether or not the tenant will be allowed to place a satellite dish on the building or its roof.

39. Current Tenant List. This provides a list of all the tenants who currently occupy space in the building.

40. Broker Commission. The landlord agrees to pay the broker a commission, and either the rate is given or it is stated that a separate commission agreement will be signed by the landlord and broker.

41. Response Time. This provides the number of days allowed to submit the RFP to the broker.

42. Signature Block and Date. The landlord signs and dates the document.

COMMISSION

Commission is a significant component of the lease transaction. It is essential that both the landlord and the tenant understand the role commission plays in a deal, and the importance of commission to the leasing agent. This appreciation will help the deal to flow more smoothly for all parties involved.

Most landlords agree that a commission is a small price to pay to acquire a tenant—a small cost to do the deal. Yet landlords naturally do not want to pay for a service that has not been performed or a commission that has not been earned. The landlord and leasing agent will consequently want to establish the leasing agent's position in the transaction *before* the prospect is shown the property. This is usually accomplished through the *leasing agreement* or the *registration and commission agreement* between the landlord and the brokerage firm.

When arranging the terms of these agreements, it is important to keep the position of the leasing agent in mind. It is the landlord's goal to develop a compensation program for the brokerage community that will encourage leasing agents to bring prospective tenants to the building, and this requires ensuring a fair commission.

Earning Commission

Almost all leasing agents who work for brokerage firms do not receive a salary, and their compensation comes entirely from the commissions they earn. In addition, leasing agents must pay for nearly all of their business expenses to facilitate a transaction, whether or not the transaction ever develops into an executed lease. Leasing agents are usually the only participants in the lease transaction who do not have a base salary and who will not be paid for their time if the lease transaction is not completed.

When individuals enter the commercial leasing profession, they do not earn any compensation—a commission—for approximately six to 12 months. This is how long it usually takes them to find a client, complete the leasing assignment, finalize a lease transaction, and wait to be paid. Leasing agents are hoping that they will eventually make it through this initial period and will someday earn sufficient commission income to first cover business and living expenses and then to support a comfortable lifestyle.

During the period when leasing agents are not earning any compensation, or when that compensation is not sufficient to cover all their expenses, it is not uncommon for them to rely on savings, a spouse, or parents to pay their bills. Most leasing agents work for three or more years before they believe their annual compensation is commensurate with the time and effort they are spending to build their commercial real estate practice. As a result, few statements are more discouraging and demoralizing to leasing agents than ones such as "We are only a commission away from a deal." Professional and ethical leasing agents place the client's best interests ahead of the commission, and will not recommend or facilitate a transaction just to be paid a commission. They also depend on commissions for their livelihood.

When the lease transaction is complete and a lease is fully executed between the landlord and the tenant, the leasing agent naturally expects to be paid on time per the commission agreement. Landlords would be wise to acknowledge the importance of commissions to leasing agents and encourage them to bring prospective tenants to their building by offering and honoring commission agreements that are fair to all parties involved.

Negotiating a Commission

There are no standard industry commissions, and commission rates and payment schedules are fully negotiable. Commission can range from a few hundred to several hundred thousand dollars, depending on the size of the tenant and the amount of the rent over the term of the lease. The landlord, who typically pays the commission, considers this expense to be the cost of acquiring a tenant and wants to be certain it is fair.

Since commissions are fully negotiable, there are consequently multiple factors that go into determining commission rates and payment schedules. Several of these factors are presented in the bulleted list below.

- **The market conditions for the specific property type.** This will be a strong determining factor for the commission rate agreed to by the landlord and the brokerage firm. For instance, in a strong office building market when vacancy rates are well below 5 percent and rental rates are increasing, landlords can negotiate not to pay commissions on lease renewals. They may also offer a lower commission rate for new leases than they paid just a few years—or even a few months—ago in a weaker market.

- **The size of the prospective tenant.** The commission rate for a 50,000-square-foot supermarket in a shopping center is likely to be less per square foot (or a lower percentage of the base income from the lease) than that of a 2,500-square-foot tenant. The total commission paid for the supermarket lease will be much greater than the commission for the smaller tenant.

- **The difficulty of the leasing assignment.** It is not uncommon for a landlord to offer an incentive commission to get the attention of the leasing community when a space or spaces have been vacant for a long time. The space may be an odd size, such as the "pie-shaped" space in the middle of an "L"-shaped strip shopping center.

- **The availability of a specific leasing agent.** A leasing agent with an outstanding track record may have a full plate of leasing assignments, and will only consider another assignment if the landlord agrees to pay a generous commission.

- **A specific timeframe.** The landlord may have an unusual reason why the property needs to be leased in a specific—usually short—time period. The landlord may need a certain percentage of the building preleased in order to obtain financing to commence construction. Or the landlord may be required to give the building's lender an additional down payment if occupancy or net operating income falls below a predetermined amount. An important tenant in a shopping center may have a *co-tenancy provision* tied to the shopping center's occupancy level, and if the property is close to dropping below that level, the landlord needs to lease additional space in a limited time period. The landlord may also want to sell the building, and a higher occupancy and higher net operating income will generate a greater sales price. Or the property may be on the verge of producing negative cash flow, and the landlord may be close to defaulting on the mortgage if additional gross income is not generated quickly.

- **The broker's fee.** The brokerage company knows its cost to do business and may have a minimum commission rate to take on any assignment.

- **Networking opportunities.** A brokerage firm may accept a lower commission rate than normal in order to establish a relationship with a landlord who is likely to generate additional business.

- **Special circumstances.** A leasing agent may be new to the profession or having a poor year, and consequently needs the business even if the terms are less than ideal.

- **Predetermined limits.** Landlords may have their mind made up to not pay more than a specific commission rate regardless of the circumstances.

In addition to these listed determining factors, there are countless other reasons why commission rates are negotiated to the various levels that are agreed upon by landlords and brokerage firms. Each negotiation depends on the unique circumstances at hand.

Determining Who Pays the Commission

Another negotiable factor is who will pay the leasing agent's commission. Although the custom in the commercial real estate industry has been for the landlord to pay this commission regardless of which party the leasing agent represents, this tradition is slowly changing. There are now times (though they are still in the minority) when the tenant will pay a fee or commission to the tenant rep. Occasionally the letter of engagement between a commercial tenant and the brokerage firm will stipulate that the prospective tenant, and not the landlord, is to pay for the leasing agent's representation.

The situations that lead to the tenant paying the leasing agent a fee or a commission are quite varied. One example of when this might occur is when space in regional and super-regional malls is being leased. Most landlords for these larger malls already have a leasing staff of their own. They know all the national and regional merchants, and may previously have made multiple lease transactions with them; therefore they do not need a leasing agent to find these tenants for them. If, however, a leasing agent *does* present a successful local merchant or restaurant that would be an asset to the tenant mix of the mall, the mall's landlord may or may not agree to pay the leasing agent a commission. If the landlord does not pay the commission, the tenant will.

Another situation in which the tenant pays the leasing agent is when a landlord negotiates to pay a commission rate less than what the leasing agent believes is fair for the time and expertise necessary to complete the deal. In such cases the tenant will often make up the difference. Additionally, the leasing agent may negotiate for the tenant to pay the out-of-pocket travel expenses incurred in a location search that extends outside the area in which the agent normally operates.

A different example of the tenant paying the commission may arise when a retail broker is providing a store development strategy for a certain geographical area. For instance, a retailer may hire a leasing agent to find multiple locations on the West Coast and reimburse her for travel expenses. The tenant may also pay the leasing agent a *retainer* for this analysis and to find space in other retail markets. The specific assignment and compensation will be described in the letter of engagement.

A tenant may also pay the broker a fee to negotiate a lease cancellation. Depending on the market conditions, the broker may negotiate for the landlord to pay the tenant to cancel the lease; likewise, in a weak market, the tenant may need to pay a fee to cancel the lease.

COMMISSION FORMULAS

There are three common commission percentage formulas:

- Commission per square foot;
- Commission with a fixed percentage on the base income; and
- Commission with a declining percentage on the base income.

Not only is the choice of formula negotiated, but the commission percentage within each formula is also negotiated. The following example demonstrates how each formula, as well as a fixed percentage commission, could be calculated.

A tenant is leasing 5,000 square feet in a triple-anchored community shopping center of 200,000 square feet. The lease is for five years with no options. The rent for the first two years is $20 per square foot; for years three and four the rent is $23 per square foot, and the fifth year's rent is $25 per square foot. The tenant has a percentage rent provision of 5 percent, based on a natural *breakpoint*. The lease is triple net. Commissions are typical, negotiated on the base rent or the size of the space and not on the billback charges, the triple net charges, or the percentage rent. These tenant charges can be negotiated to be included in calculating the commission.

An example of the tenant's base charges is shown in Exhibit 4.1. The three common commission percentage formulas (parts *A–C*), along with a

Exhibit 4.1

Sample Tenant's Base Rental Charges

Year 1: 5,000 square feet × $20 = $100,000
Year 2: 5,000 square feet × $20 = $100,000
Year 3: 5,000 square feet × $23 = $115,000
Year 4: 5,000 square feet × $23 = $115,000
Year 5: 5,000 square feet × $25 = $125,000
Total rent: $555,000

formula for an agreed fixed percentage commission (part *D*), are calculated for the situation in Exhibit 4.2.

CO-BROKER COMMISSIONS

It is common in the commercial real estate industry for leasing agents to share their commissions with other leasing agents involved in the transaction. The formula for sharing a commission is negotiable, and it is often calculated through one of the three methods listed below.

1. The most straightforward formula for determining the commission split is for the landlord's leasing agent to share his or her commission with the tenant's leasing agent on an equal, 50-50 basis.

2. Another commission-splitting method is for the tenant's leasing agent to receive a larger portion of the commission. This strategy is designed to encourage tenant leasing agents to present the building to their clients. The listing leasing agent (who represents the landlord) might receive one third of the commission, and the procuring leasing agent (who represents the tenant) might receive two thirds. The split can be any combination of percentages that equal 100 percent.

3. A third popular option is for the landlord to offer a bonus commission to encourage leasing agents to bring prospects to the building. This means that the landlord is paying extra commission. For example, the formula for splitting the commission may be that the listing agent receives 50 percent of the commission and the procuring leasing agent receives 100 percent of the commission. The listing agent's commission ends up being that of a typical commission split, while the tenant's leasing agent receives a full commission.

Most landlords would consider extra commission a small price to pay to lease a difficult space or a space in a soft market. If, for example, a landlord

Exhibit 4.2
Options for Determining the Commission Rate

A. Commission per Square Foot:

Commission of $4 per square foot.
Commission: 5,000 square feet × $4 = $20,000

B. Commission with a Fixed Percentage on the Base Income:

Commission of 5 percent of the base rent over the term of the lease.
Commission: $555,000 base rent × .05 = $27,750

C. Commission with a Declining Percentage on the Base Income:

Commission of 6 percent on the first year's rent, 5 percent on the second year's rent, 4 percent on the third year's rent, 3 percent on the fourth year's rent, and 2 percent on the fifth year's rent.

> *Commission:*
> Year 1—$100,000 × .06 = $6,000
> Year 2—$100,000 × .05 = $5,000
> Year 3—$115,000 × .04 = $4,600
> Year 4—$115,000 × .03 = $3,450
> Year 5—$125,000 × .02 = <u>$3,500</u>
> $21,550

D. Commission as an Agreed Fixed Rate:

Commission shall be $30,000 to lease the 5,000-square-foot space located in the "pie-shaped" space in the middle of the "L" portion of the strip shopping center.

---

pays an additional $10,000 in commission to lease to a 5,000-square-foot tenant, he might be paying out the equivalent of an extra 1.2 months' rent (i.e., the monthly rent for the tenant is $8333.33). However, if the landlord declines to pay the additional commission, and as a result the space is vacant for six more months, he would lose $50,000 in base rent. Assuming the *common area maintenance (CAM) charges* for six months are $12,500, the total lost income for that period would be $62,500. Although the landlord would have saved $10,000 in additional commission, his net loss would be $52,500.

INCENTIVE COMMISSIONS

Incentive commissions are offered to lease difficult spaces—often those that have been vacant for an extended period or that are available in a weak commercial real estate market. A leasing incentive may be offered to lease the last 10 to 15 percent of a building, which is usually the hardest space to lease. Depending on how a building is financed, approximately the last 15 percent of space in a building usually generates the cash flow or profits for the building.

The formulas for incentive commissions are limited only by the imagination of the landlord. A simple incentive is to pay 150 to 200 percent of the commission rate that was offered. Another simple formula is to add one or two dollars per square foot of commission to the current commission rate. Some landlords will offer a one- to three-year lease on a luxury auto, or a trip for two to an exotic location, for leasing a specific space or a minimum amount of space. The incentive can be based on the space leased or on the space leased at a certain rental rate.

As noted in the section above, rent that is lost from a vacant space is never recovered. On the other hand, double commission on a difficult space to lease may seem like a lot (e.g., an additional $20,000 to $30,000, depending on the formula used, for the 5,000-square-foot space in Exhibit 4.2 above), but this cost is usually equal to only about two months' rent. This is one of the reasons why landlords often offer an incentive commission for buildings that might otherwise lease up slowly. It is usually money well spent.

COMMISSION PAYMENT

There are several formulas that can be negotiated for the payment of the commission. Four of the most commonly used formulas are as follows:

1. The commission is paid 50 percent when the landlord and the tenant sign the lease, and 50 percent when the tenant takes occupancy and opens for business.

2. The first half of the commission is paid when the lease is signed, and the second half is paid when the tenant commences paying base rent. If the tenant receives free rent, the second half of the commission may be delayed. Additionally, if the tenant has a weak financial statement, the second half of the commission may be delayed for six to 12 months.

3. The commission is paid in three equal installments: when the lease is signed, when the tenant commences paying base rent, and one year later. If the tenant has a cancellation right, a portion of the commission may be paid after the possibility for cancellation has expired.

4. The commission is paid monthly over the term of the lease. A $6,000 commission for a five-year lease would be paid at the rate of $100 per month.

An accelerated commission payment offer will quickly get the attention of leasing agents. Whatever commission formula is used, the landlord often takes 30 days after a commission is due to pay. During the early 1990s when the office building market was in a depression, with 20-plus percent vacancy rates in many cities and rents that had dropped 25 to 50 percent, some developers offered to pay commissions in full within 48 hours of the lease signing. Since leasing agents are paid only if a lease is executed, such guarantees can be a great encouragement for them to bring tenants to a building.

COMMISSION PAYMENT WHEN THE TENANT VACATES BEFORE THE LEASE EXPIRES

It doesn't happen often, but there are occasions when a tenant vacates the premises and stops paying rent before the lease expires. When this occurs, the question arises as to whether or not the leasing agent or brokerage firm should repay part of the commission (which was paid based on the full term of the lease) earned on the deal. If there is little chance of the landlord recovering the rent and other charges due for the remaining term of the lease, there are various ways that the situation may be addressed.

One option is that the landlord may ask the brokerage firm to repay the unamortized portion of the commission. The brokerage firm, however, may take the position that they filled their responsibility by procuring a tenant, and it was the landlord's responsibility—based on the tenant's financial statement and other factors—to choose whether to accept or reject that tenant. In short, the responsibility of the leasing agent is to procure tenants for the building; the responsibility of the landlord is to decide whether or not to accept that tenant.

If the brokerage firm *does* agree to pay back a portion of the commission, several additional problems may be created. If the commission was shared with another brokerage firm who represented the tenant, it can be difficult to get the second brokerage firm to pay back its portion of the commission. The listing brokerage firm will not pay back the second brokerage firm's portion of the commission. In addition, if the leasing agents involved in the transaction are no longer with the brokerage firm, there is no leverage to get them to pay back a portion of the commission.

An alternative approach is to have the listing brokerage firm re-lease the space at a reduced commission. The question that landlords must consider in this scenario is whether or not the leasing agent will devote sufficient effort to re-lease the space at a reduced commission. Leasing agents may be motivated because they value a relationship with the landlord or feel a responsibility to re-lease the space at a reduced commission rate.

The leasing agreement may also address this situation directly. If it does, it often will state that, if the tenant vacates the premises during the first year of the lease, the brokerage firm will either pay back a portion of the commission or re-lease the space at a reduced rate.

No matter which of the above options is taken, the landlord must focus on re-leasing the space as quickly as possible to reduce the lost income from the vacancy, rather than getting distracted by a disagreement over part of the commission.

FINDING RESOLUTION

When it comes to dealing with questions about commissions, the commercial real estate industry has established procedures to follow. They can be used to determine when a commission is earned, as well as to provide for an understanding of the responsibilities and obligations of each the leasing agent, the landlord, and the tenant. When these procedures are followed, it is unlikely that there will be a misunderstanding between or among the parties to a lease.

The best lease transactions are those in which the landlords think they have received value for the services provided, and the leasing agents believe they have been fairly compensated for their expertise, time, and services. When this occurs, all parties will likely look forward to working with each other on future transactions.

5

Preparing for Negotiations

Knowledge is power in the negotiating process, and one would be well served to be as well prepared as possible when entering into a negotiation. The negotiating process in commercial leasing is one of the most complicated and rewarding aspects of the entire leasing process. As is the case for most of the aspects of commercial property operations, there are very few rules; and the positions of the parties are always in flux, depending on the conditions at the time of the negotiation.

The parties must be as knowledgeable as is practical—not only about their own side of the negotiation, but also concerning the person on the other side of the table. On very large transactions, it is not unusual for leasing agents to do mock negotiations in order to test their positions and responses to various situations. This chapter will outline issues that are critical to any negotiation, from both the landlord's and the tenant's points of view.

THE LANDLORD'S GOALS AND OBJECTIVES

While there is a ring of truth to it, it is overly simplistic to say that the landlord wants the highest rent and best terms available, and will let the rest of the details work themselves out. There are other issues landlords consider when negotiating a lease. It is the responsibility of the landlord to determine the overall tenant mix desired in a property. It is also incumbent upon the leasing agent to provide enough input to the landlord about competitive properties, general market conditions, rent levels, and lease terms, in order to help the landlord reach realistic goals in terms of the tenant mix for any given property.

Landlords must have a clear vision of their goals and objectives for a subject property. This vision must be realistic for the existing marketplace, and must be clearly conveyed to the leasing agents who represent the building. Once the goals have been established, negotiators will then take all of the points into consideration instead of negotiating as if each were a separate item. If goals are not clearly defined, a lack of understanding will make it increasingly more difficult to reach agreement between the parties.

The landlord should have a goal for the target rent and terms for tenant negotiations. For a potential retail tenant, this landlord's goal might be $25 per square foot minimum rent, triple net on the operating expenses, a five-year lease with no options, an improvement allowance of $3 per square foot, and a *percentage rent* provision of 5 percent. These provisions are generally spelled out in a leasing plan for the coming year (Exhibit 5.1). That target may have some negotiating room built in, or it may be the actual deal that the landlord wants to finalize.

Because some tenants may not have clearly defined goals, the landlord should try to understand whatever goals the tenant does have. If specific goals *have* been well established by the prospect, this information can often be used by the landlord to make educated decisions in the negotiating process.

Tenant Mix

No matter the property, the landlord is most interested in the tenant's intended use of the premises. (Use of the premises is covered in more detail in Chapter 12, "Lease Negotiations.") An office building landlord is not likely to want a psychiatrist in the building whose approach is "scream therapy." Or, if the landlords of medical office buildings are targeting only medical professionals, they may decline to accept prospects interested in operating insurance agencies or law firms, simply to maintain consistent tenant use in their buildings.

The shopping center landlord will have a very specific tenant mix in mind for the shopping center and will likely turn away willing tenants if they don't fit into that mix. Industrial properties, on the other hand, have the least concern with tenant mix. This is probably because of the limitations imposed by zoning requirements of local jurisdictions, which automatically influence the mix of most industrial properties. However, the legal use and disposal of hazardous materials by a tenant may concern some landlords.

Credit Rating

The tenant's credit rating (or lack thereof) and financial condition are also important issues in the leasing of space.

Exhibit 5.1

LEASING PLAN: BAYWOOD SHOPPING CENTER

The leasing plan for an existing shopping center is most often associated with the annual budget. Prior to the completion of the budget and leasing plan, a market survey is conducted. That survey will consider the overall demographics and psychographics of the shopping center's trade area, the direction of the economy in that area, and the competitive shopping centers—including their vacancy rates, rental rates, tenant mix, ingress and egress, and overall conditions. Finally, the subject shopping center will be evaluated as to its current position in the marketplace, the overall tenant mix of the shopping center, likely rental rates and terms, and vacancies coming up in the budget year.

From that information, a leasing plan is prepared and becomes the template for the leasing efforts for the coming year. The leasing plan will consider all vacancies that exist or will come up during the year as well as all leases that will expire in the coming year.

SPACE	SQ.FT.	DESIRED USE	RENT/YEAR	TERM	TIs
A3	1,237	Dress store	$36.00	5 yrs	none
B7	4,333	Fast food - Mexican	$32.00	10 yrs	$2.00 sq.ft.
C3	1,866	Sporting goods	$37.20	5 yrs	none
		RENEWALS			
A5	1,250	Baywood Shoes	$40.00	5 yrs	none
A6	2,335	Speedy Print	$42.00	5 yrs	none
C5	4.225	China Feast	$33.00	10 yrs	none

Once this plan is approved by the shopping center landlord, it becomes the leasing plan for the coming year. Unexpected vacancies are evaluated and submitted to the landlord for direction and approval.

Some landlords allow the leasing personnel to commit to such leases if they meet all of the above terms, and most landlords require that they approve each deal even if the deal meets the above criteria.

Some leasing plans will indicate a specific tenant for a space as the number one choice and will then revert to the named use if that tenant is not available.

The landlord provides a very valuable asset to the tenant in exchange for income and, in the case of a retail tenant, a critical element in the synergism of the overall shopping center. The landlord may well contribute to the cost of tenant improvements (TIs) over and above the raw shell of the space and will, in most cases, pay a leasing commission to procure the tenant. For all of these reasons, landlords want to know if tenants have a history of being responsible and paying their bills on time.

This is not to say that the tenants must have perfect credit, but rather that they should have a "good" history of taking care of their financial responsibilities. One of the more difficult questions for a landlord is how to handle the tenant with *no* credit, rather than *bad* credit. This is not an unusual situation for immigrants who want to open up a store or rent an office space, but have not been in the country long enough to establish U.S. credit. It is generally held that a landlord cannot turn down such a tenant prospect for not having credit. Faced with this situation, one would ask for references and try to research the prospective tenant as much as possible. The tenant must live somewhere, and most likely has a car available; those would both be good places to start the search.

If someone has no or poor credit and the landlord leases space to the prospect, it is likely that the landlord will not be interested in providing improvements to the space, and most likely will offer the space in "as is" condition. The landlord will also want to be sure that the tenant has the wherewithal to complete his or her own improvements and operate his or her business successfully. It is not necessary that all, or even most, tenants have an excellent financial net worth, just that they have sufficient assets to do the deal and fulfill their lease obligations.

For example, if a husband and wife are opening a 500-square-foot office as an insurance agency, the required up-front monies and obligations will be fairly modest and the risk to the landlord is minimal. However, if the same couple wants to open a 4,000-square-foot spa and beauty salon, the cost of equipment and hiring personnel will represent a much more substantial investment and operating risk. The landlord will consequently be looking for the tenant to have a greater financial capability to shoulder that burden.

Lease Terms

Tenant rents and terms are based on rents in the marketplace, not the needs of the landlord's pro forma. The position of the landlord and that of the tenant must be taken into account by the other party to reach a lease arrangement that will benefit each.

The length of the lease is an important consideration for the landlord, and will likely be heavily influenced by the market. If a building is newly developed, the lender is likely to prefer tenants with long-term leases to provide assurance that the landlord's loan payments will be made. The length of the lease should also take into consideration the amortization of the landlord's and the tenant's improvements. It takes longer to amortize the fixtures for an ice cream store than it does for a shoe store. A supermarket requires a huge investment in fixtures, and requires a long-term lease to allow the tenant to amortize those costs and establish and capitalize on a good customer base.

The monetary terms of the lease will also be dictated by the local market. As discussed in Chapter 6, "Know the Market Conditions," landlords conduct market surveys to determine rental rates in competitive buildings. They will then compare their building to the competition, and establish competitive rents that will hopefully meet predetermined financial goals. Landlords have a major investment in their properties, and try to lease space at rental rates and terms that will allow for a reasonable return on that investment and their risk. In some development situations where the market will not support the rents to justify the cost of the project, it is not unusual for that project to be scaled down or delayed until market conditions improve.

The landlord's leasing agent typically plays an important role in establishing asking and deal-making rents and lease terms for the property. A good leasing agent will know the existing market, be familiar with the types of deals in the market, and have an educated opinion as to what rent and terms should be under the proposed circumstances. The landlord's property manager should also be providing input as to the proposed rent and terms; but the ultimate decision on the building's asking and deal-making rental rates rests with the landlord.

Rents and terms are always being tested and adjusted as needed. Once the landlord has set the rent and terms for her project—either one under development or an existing building—those terms are then tested in the marketplace. If space rents up rapidly, it is likely that the rents and terms will be increased and tested again. If leasing is going very slowly, the rents and terms may be reduced and tested. Concessions may also be introduced to accelerate improvement in the leasing effort.

Concessions

The value of commercial real estate is determined by the tenants' rents and lease terms (see Chapter 13, "Lease Administration"). If the rental rate is reduced, the value of the building is likely to be reduced as well. Because of this relationship of rents to value, landlords want to keep the rent as high as possible. If the market is indicating lower rents, there is a dilemma. Landlords may be able to resolve this dilemma by offering concessions.

As an example, a landlord wants rents of $25 per square foot for new office space. However, a market survey indicates that the market for similar office space in that area is closer to $23. Knowledgeable tenants are not going to pay the higher rate unless they get something in return, so the landlord turns to concessions to lease up the building.

One prospective tenant is considering a five-year lease on a 3,000-square-foot space. The landlord wants $25 per square foot for this space—$75,000 per year, or a total of $375,000 for five years. The tenant, on the other hand, sees the market at $23 per square foot and expects to pay $69,000 per year, or $345,000 for the five-year period. These two perspectives differ by a total of $30,000.

If the market *capitalization rate* to sell that building is 8 percent, the value of that space in the building at the landlord's rents would be $937,500; from the tenant's calculations, the value would be $862,500, resulting in a $75,000 difference in value. It is important to keep in mind that the landlord's goal is almost always to create maximum value when setting rents.

Cash flow is inevitably a consideration, but long-term value is usually the most common reason for owning commercial real estate.

Taking these factors into consideration, the landlord may offer a building allowance of $30,000 above the standard TIs, while keeping rents at the $25 rental rate, in order to finalize the lease. The tenant will then have the net rental rate that the market indicates; and the landlord will have an additional $75,000 in value, less the $30,000, a concession for a net gain of $45,000.

Tenant improvements are one of the most common lease concessions in commercial real estate. A tenant will nearly always require additional improvements to a space after it is turned over by the landlord. Most often the landlord is able to provide the improvements the tenants wants, but if they are beyond the landlord's standard improvements, additional rent will be charged.

For example, if there is a 2,500-square-foot space in a shopping center with a rental rate of $28 per square foot, the annual rent will be $70,000. If the capitalization rate for that property is 8 percent, the value of that lease is $875,000. However, with a very strong tenant, if the landlord contributes $10 per square foot for TIs, and if the tenant agrees to an additional 12 percent rental rate, the landlord will increase the property's value. The cost of the improvements will be $25,000, and the return on those improvements will be $3,000 per year ($25,000 × .12 = $3,000), capitalized at 8 percent, which will increase the building's value by $37,500. This is well above the amount of the investment that is being repaid. For the purposes of this discussion, we are ignoring the time value of money, common area or *billback* expenses, and some other minor issues in order to make the point that a building's value increases when rents increase, all other things being equal.

Free rent is another common concession. From the landlord's perspective, it does not require cash out of the building owner's account, and it often leads to space being leased that otherwise would be left vacant. In difficult leasing markets, free rent becomes almost a given for all types of commercial buildings.

THE TENANT'S GOALS AND OBJECTIVES

The goals and objectives of the tenant are not directly opposed to those of the landlord, as is often thought. The tenant's general objectives are to find a suitable location in which to conduct business, and to do so at a competitive rental terms. The specificity of these goals varies by tenant.

The retail tenant must be concerned with the ability to generate sufficient sales from a location. If the tenant is a chain store operation, the main motivation may well be to fill in gaps in the trade area, to control or dominate a market, or just to serve a particular area and demographic. Office and industrial tenants generally have a slightly less complicated approach to reaching their goals: the exact building is not as important to them as the general location, the amenities of the building, and the financial terms of the deal. Businesses may not have well-defined goals when they are seeking space. On the other hand, large chains and anchor tenants in shopping centers, and more established office and industrial businesses, have very clear goals.

Tenants who are relocating generally have a fairly good view of the *micromarket,* and most likely will have some target buildings in mind as well as some knowledge of each. These tenants are good prospects to work with in as much as they are already operating, know their space and location requirements, and realize what they would like to change to improve their business operations. Relocation tenants will likely want to look at several alternative buildings and compare each location and the advantages and disadvantages of each building. Some tenants will want a location with low rent, and others will want the newest Class A building in town to project their chosen business image.

The landlord needs to find out as much as possible about the tenant to negotiate the optimum lease terms (see Chapter 6). Rent per square foot is not always the key motivating factor when a tenant chooses a building. An understanding of what drives a particular tenant will assist the landlord in the negotiating process. One tenant may well be motivated by flexible terms, while another tenant may be in a position to grow and consequently motivated by the option to expand. Another tenant may be interested in having the landlord provide all the TIs, even if it means a higher base rental for the space involved.

Lower rent is often not a tenant's main motivator. Many tenants are more concerned with the location as long as the rent "fits" their budget and is competitive in the marketplace. Retail tenants are usually more concerned with their potential sales volume than the rent. They would prefer to have shorter-term leases with multiple renewal options, just in case the location does not produce the expected sales.

Unfortunately, landlords do not want to grant options unless absolutely necessary. They do not want their hands tied in the event that a tenant proves to be troublesome or financially weak, or, if the tenant is a retailer, has merchandise or services that are no longer fashionable. On the other hand, landlords want to keep most of their tenants; so it is unlikely that a landlord will refuse to renew retail tenants' leases if they are generating an acceptable sales volume and complying with their lease. In the case of the office or industrial building, the landlord does not have the tenant's sales to consider, but if the tenant is paying the rent and living up to the lease terms, the landlord is very likely to renew the lease.

CONSIDERING GREEN LEASES

Green leases are becoming an ever more popular trend. They provide a way for landlords and tenants to communicate and meet shared environmental standards, which may include developing a recycling program, improving a building's indoor environment, increasing purchases of environmentally friendly products and materials, improving energy efficiency, and reducing water consumption and waste. Green leases are increasingly being seen as not only a social responsibility, but also as a smart alternative to improve efficiency and reduce costs for the landlord and tenant alike.

Landlords set the framework for their buildings to achieve *ENERGY STAR* and *Leadership in Energy and Environmental Design (LEED)* certifications. The landlord's efforts to green a building and negotiate green leases are often rewarded by an increased ability to attract and retain tenants. Environmentally friendly updates can also mitigate the risk of a building becoming obsolete while simultaneously positioning that building to capture government incentives for green buildings. Landlords also benefit from green leases because they set the foundation for tenant behavior, and can ensure that all tenants take an active role in the property's green efforts.

Green leases are a benefit to tenants as well. They can reduce a tenant's costs by improving efficiency and reducing costs for items like water and energy. The environment is becoming an increasingly important consideration for employees, and environmentally friendly policies often help tenant businesses to attract and retain talent. Research has shown that green leases lead to improved working conditions, advancing productivity, reducing employee absenteeism and turnover, and resulting in higher retail sales for the tenant's business.

Ultimately, green leases offer a win-win situation for landlords and tenants. A wealth of information about green leases and strategies for sustainability in commercial real estate is available from experts like Mychele R. Lord, founder of LORD Green Real Estate Strategies (www.LORDGreen Strategies.com).

THE LANDLORD PREPARES TO NEGOTIATE

Landlords of commercial properties must know more about their property than anyone else. It is critical that they know their property's advantages and disadvantages and how best to address the building's deficiencies when negotiating with prospective tenants.

Almost every commercial project has built-in lease restrictions established by city or county authorities or, in shopping centers, by lease restrictions granted to anchor tenants and occasionally even to large national tenants. Lease restrictions may be that no store can sell liquor, that no delicatessen can be larger than 2,500 square feet, that a theater cannot be within 190 feet of the main entrance to the supermarket, and so forth. Restrictions established by municipalities are usually related to zoning and allowed uses or types of businesses. A landlord must be aware of these limitations at all times. If any of these restrictions become an issue in negotiations, it is much better to quote a restriction beyond the landlord's control than to just say "no."

There are several issues landlords consider when preparing to negotiate a lease. Many are property-type specific. These items, and the property types to which they most commonly apply, are discussed in the sections below.

Shopping Centers

A number of items that the landlords of shopping centers should be knowledgeable about are discussed below.

Tenant Mix.   The landlord of a shopping center should at all times have a target list of the types of tenants desired for the current and future mix of the shopping center, as well as a list of the specific tenants who would be the best choice for any given vacancy. Landlords should know their retail tenants' sales, sales trends over the past few years, merchandise mix, and price points. They should know if each tenant's location is right for the tenant and best for the shopping center's tenant mix and traffic flow.

The specific location of tenants in a shopping center is almost as important as having them in the shopping center in the first place. Destination tenants, such as beauty shops or barber shops, can be located almost anywhere, while impulse tenants such as ice cream and candy stores are most often located in high-traffic areas with good visibility.

The landlord should know how each tenant has contributed to the shopping center or mall over the life of his or her lease, as well as the tenant turnover rate. The landlord needs a complete understanding of the sequence of lease expirations for the next five years. This will provide a guideline for opportunities that arise, such as improving the shopping center's tenant mix, expanding existing tenants, or including new tenants who were previously too large for the available space.

General Sales Data.   A shopping center's sales can be used as a selling tool to attract specific tenants. Landlords should know each tenant's sales history in their shopping center and be prepared to use that information in the leasing effort. Individual tenants' sales are confidential and cannot be discussed. Landlords must be in a position to talk about the shopping center's overall sales record, and prepared to discuss in more general terms the sales of specific lines of merchandise, anchor tenant performance (without giving specific sales figures), and areas of the shopping center that will be impacted by new tenants, remodeling, or expansions.

Landlords should not divulge their tenants' sales. However, success stories may be shared as long as a specific merchant's sales are not revealed. A landlord might indicate that a supermarket tenant's sales are in excess of $800 per square foot, or that the tenant's sales are the highest in that division or store chain. In a regional or super-regional mall, the landlord should know the sales per square foot of all tenants and all categories of merchandise. One can then share that women's wear is averaging over $500 per square foot and has increased sales at the rate of 9.3 percent over the previous year.

Even if a category of merchandise is weak, there is likely to be one merchant doing well. Without mentioning the name of the business, it may be revealed that one merchant is well above the others. It is also satisfactory to share that a given apparel store or food court tenant is the number one producer in that shopping center, as long as the actual sales are not disclosed.

Ingress/Egress.   Traffic flow is critical to the success of any shopping center. If customers cannot get in and out of a location fairly easily, they are likely to go to the next shopping center where ingress and egress are more convenient. Left turn access is a bonus for a shopping center and its tenants. A traffic-light controlled entrance is an even bigger benefit.

The landlord should know the traffic counts on the streets fronting the shopping center. For regional malls it is best to know the traffic count at each entrance, if possible, or at the entrances that support the most traffic in and out of the mall. An excellent tool for showing such information is an aerial photograph with the rates printed for each entrance and street. This makes for a good visual for the leasing agent to use in convincing tenant prospects that this is a good location for their shop.

The Neighborhood and Competitive Properties.   The landlord must have a complete knowledge of the shopping center's trade area and its demographics and psychographics. What is the family profile in the neighborhood? What are their incomes? How many children live there? Is the area blue or white collar? Is housing in the neighborhood mainly apartments, condominiums, or single-family homes? What is the cost of housing? What is the population's education level? Is the population increasing or decreasing?

The area map will show the roads and how easily the shopping center connects with the community at large. Major highways should be identified, as well as major feeder streets that will lead to the shopping center. The area map will further define the property's geographic location by indicating natural physical barriers to the property-such as bodies of water, hills, etc.

It is also important to be in a position to discuss the attitude of the local city or county officials towards business. The property manager should know the cost and requirements to obtain a business license, as well as the process to get building permits for TIs, restaurant or fast food permits, etc.

Landlords should be familiar with each competitive shopping center within the trade area, as well as any shopping centers outside the area that are likely to draw the same customers. They need to know each shopping center's tenant mix, vacancies, asking and deal-making rents, lease terms, likely sales levels, and problems with ingress/egress (if any). Landlords should also know who the anchor tenants are and how well they are faring, the quality of the shopping center's management, the common area costs, whether or not percentage rent provisions are required, any incentives being offered to new tenants, and the general perception of each shopping center. The property's property manager can provide this important information to the landlord.

If any of these shopping centers in the trade area have exceptional features, the landlord should be aware of those features and be prepared either to incorporate such features into his or her own property or to articulate the advantages of his or her shopping center to prospective tenants. It is always best if landlords state these differences in a positive way so that they are not in the position of "knocking" the competition. Instead, landlords should share the benefits of their own shopping center and allow the tenants to draw their own conclusions.

Detailed information should also be gathered for any proposed shopping centers that are likely to compete for the same customers and tenants. The fully informed landlord will know who is planning to develop each new site and the likelihood of that shopping center being completed. Understanding who the developers are and how likely it is that their development will be built allows the landlord to be better prepared to negotiate leases.

Demographics and Psychographics.   The landlord should stay current on the trade area's latest demographics and psychographics. Since many areas are changing rapidly while others are not, a full understanding of the area's customers, their buying habits, and their lifestyles will help landlords in making an impressive presentation to tenant prospects. This will not only help in the negotiating process, but will help the landlord in determining the direction of the shopping center's tenant mix.

Fortunately, advances in technology have made understanding the ever-changing trade area demographics and psychographics easier than ever before. New methods of gathering information, such as the web-based surveys found at Zoomerang (www.zoomerang.com) and Survey Monkey (www.SurveyMonkey.com), may also help a landlord to better understand lifestyle and purchasing habits. Understanding the target consumer as much as possible is a crucial link in developing a story that will attract the right tenants to the property.

The Site Plan.   An accurate *site plan* is a valuable tool in the leasing of any shopping center. Architectural site plans, with the plethora of numbers that appear on them, are not the best site plans to use. Instead, the project architect can prepare a special site plan for leasing purposes, which will emphasize the ingress/egress, parking layout, interior circulation, and location and size of shop spaces. The landlord should avoid putting the names of prospective tenants on this site plan, as a tenant may decide to come into the shopping center because of an indicated tenant and be disappointed if that tenant is no longer in the shopping center.

These leasing site plans will indicate that they are for general purposes only and that the landlord reserves the right to make changes without approval from any tenant. However, great care should be taken to ensure that any changes do not have a negative impact on the shopping center. For example, the addition of too many *pad spaces* or *outlots* has caused problems in some shopping centers by blocking the view of existing tenants, creating traffic jams as a result of fast food drive-up lines, and causing serious parking problems.

Expansion or Upgrade Plans.   A 1950s neighborhood shopping center with a corrugated roof over the walkways will likely have a negative impact on prospective tenants. In general, many older shopping centers become obsolete if they are not updated to reflect the requirements and lifestyle choices of trade area consumers.

Although older shopping centers generally have excess parking, which provides the landlord with options such as expanding *gross leasable area (GLA)* or creating a pad or outlot, a shopping center built in the 1950s to the 1970s can become outdated. One major exception to this impending obsolescence is the "town and country" or "themed" shopping center—an approach that can be timeless if properly maintained. Yet most shopping centers require remodeling and upgrading in order to meet the needs of tenants and be accepted by the shoppers.

If a shopping center is in the process of upgrading or remodeling, those plans and their timetable should be available to tenant prospects. Tenants should be made aware of how the changes will impact the shopping center and whether they will impact lease terms. If there is a special rental program for new tenants who sign up before the work is complete, that plan should be clear and utilized as an effective tool for attracting tenants. However, if landlords are thinking about upgrading or remodeling but are *not* firmly committed, they should wait until plans are finalized to mention them. Another leasing approach is to lease the space at the market rent for the shopping center in the pre-remodeled condition and then, when the remodeling is complete, to increase rent by a few dollars per square foot.

Shopping Center Operations.   For a new shopping center, the landlord should have the plan to manage the shopping center in place. Will the shopping center have on-site management, or will management be from a central office? If it is from a central office, how will problems be handled? Who will the tenant call to discuss problems? How often is management likely to inspect the property? How are the common area billings handled, and what is the current budget? A knowledgeable tenant will want to see—or at least discuss—former billings and increases in the CAM expenses over the past few years, as well as any impending changes that might increase common area costs.

Office Buildings

The following are examples of office building issues that landlords should take into consideration when negotiating a lease.

Building Design.   The design of an office building is a key component in determining the types of tenants who are interested in the space. The *floor plate* is one feature that plays a significant role in determining who these tenants will be. To state it simplistically, large floor plates attract larger tenants and small floor plates attract smaller tenants. The depth from the building core to the curtain wall also determines the size of tenants. Once the floor plate has been established, limitations on the size and shape of individual spaces have also been determined.

Window *mullions* will also have an impact on the size and configuration of the spaces and offices within a building. A law office will often want a large number of private offices, and window mullion spacing is a significant factor in determining the exact sizes of these offices. There are ways of building space that does not match the window mullions, but these layouts are often awkward and more expensive to build than construction that works with the mullion spacing. If a building's floor plate is not a square or rectangle, it can create some space planning challenges.

Site Analysis.   The office building landlord must fully understand the entire building site and how well it works. There are a multitude of questions that may arise concerning the site: Is the landscaping attractive without interfering with tenant operations or security? Are trees and hedges placed and trimmed to minimize any impact on property traffic? Is signage clear and easy to read? Does the building have either the latest in technology or the capabilities for the tenant to add technology within practical limitations?

Are directories well maintained, up-to-date, and clear regarding the locations of building occupants? Are services well located so as not to cause any leasing problems within the building (such as noise or odors)? The office building landlord should be prepared to answer all these questions and more.

Parking.   The landlord should also be prepared to address questions about parking: Is the parking convenient to the building? Is there sufficient parking for building employees and the invitees of the building? If there is paid parking, is the system efficient and are the rates competitive with other buildings in the area? If the parking is decked parking, is it well lighted and brightly painted so as not to be intimidating or difficult to use?

Parking is a major consideration for most office buildings. Some municipalities have a maximum parking ratio for downtown buildings to encourage the use of mass transit by customers and employees. Even when this is not the case, most downtown office buildings have strict parking requirements. Every effort must be made to ensure that parking is secure, is as convenient as possible, and (if it is paid parking) has competitive rates.

Maintenance.   There are many older office buildings that are quite popular and well leased, and generally this is due to a quality maintenance program. An older building can have charm in spite of its age; but if it is not well maintained, it is just an old building. Without good maintenance, the building is likely to have higher tenant turnover, causing rents to drop and eventually leading to a building that is beyond redemption without a major renovation.

There is little excuse for a poorly maintained building. Generally, the tenants are paying for some or all of the upkeep of the building, so funds should be there to keep the building in good condition. Even if the landlord has to make contributions above the income provided by the billbacks, in most cases the resulting increased value of the building will warrant the additional investment.

The major components of an office building are the parking lot, the roof, the heating and ventilating system, the lobby, and the restrooms. If any of these is not well maintained, it will reflect poorly on the building, its tenants, and the leasing effort. Landlords should be able to keep their buildings competitive by inspecting other buildings on a regular basis and making sure that their building does not fall below industry standards. An older, well-maintained building is considerably more attractive than a newer building that is dirty and in need of repairs.

Security.   The issue of security is of importance to office buildings in all locations. Tenants must have a secure environment in which to conduct their business. Fortunately, security is seldom an issue in office buildings.

There are many office buildings that are quite safe and require little or no special security. No matter the location, it is a good idea to walk the building with the local police department and, if possible, your insurance carrier to asses any potential problems. Most office buildings are in locations that do not have security problems. If there *is* an incident in the building, such as a late-night break-in, someone being accosted in the building, or one or more cars being stolen, there may be a need for temporary security or even drive-by security.

Many high-rise and mid-rise office buildings have onsite security. Generally, this type of security is necessary because of the number of people visiting the building rather than any problems with the location. Increased security measures may include a mandatory check-in at the main entrance and limited access to the building.

Medical Office Buildings

Medical office buildings have all of the concerns that office buildings do, plus a few more. The medical office building prospect is typically very interested in the tenant mix and medical specialties in the building. Medical tenants are interested in such amenities as pharmacies, the latest technology, and the ability to adapt the building to their specific needs, such as the ability to use X-ray, CT, and MRI machines.

The location of a medical office building is important to the types of medical professionals it attracts. A building close to a hospital attracts doctors. Dentists and other medical professionals can locate their practice almost anywhere in the city.

Industrial Buildings

Zoning is the big issue for industrial buildings. Industrial building landlords should be fully briefed on their tenants' businesses and make sure that they comply with the zoning restrictions. Additional issues for these landlords to consider include floor loads, clear span ceilings, ceiling heights, utilities, the available labor pool, and transportation systems in the area.

THE TENANT PREPARES TO NEGOTIATE

In the lease negotiation process, the tenant has specific location and lease terms goals and objectives. Tenant interests in lease negotiations can generally be broken down into two categories: those of the retail tenant and those of the office, medical, or industrial tenant. The issues that develop within these two categories of tenants are discussed below.

The Retail Tenant

Retail tenants want the best space that will maximize their sales. A location where the tenant's customer base is represented is necessary for success. Retail tenants are also concerned with the type and quality of shopping center that will make the optimal fit for their business, as well as rent and terms that will allow for a profit. Of course, no one can guarantee tenants that they will earn a profit. But tenants should know what environment is conducive to their success.

One of the major concerns for most retailers is that of the shopping center's tenant mix. Certain apparel stores look for other apparel stores and specific anchor tenants as good co-tenants for cross-shopping. Some will look to the anchor tenants for lines of merchandise that are complimentary to their own. They will also study the customer base to be sure that the age and income levels are compatible with their lines of merchandise. Some fast food tenants will follow other fast food tenants. McDonalds is known for doing substantial market research for its locations and they have a very low failure rate. Because of this, some fast food tenants will wait for McDonalds to choose a location and then go nearby.

All tenants should consider the landlord's terms and conditions and include those numbers into a *pro forma* statement to calculate the likely profit levels they can achieve at that location. If the tenant thinks that sufficient sales can be generated to support the occupancy costs, a lease is likely to be completed. From time to time, in difficult leasing situations, a landlord may offer the lease at either percentage rent only or at a very attractive rent to attract a tenant. However, if the tenant is not confident he or she can generate a specific sales volume needed to generate a profit, even free rent will not be a sufficient inducement.

Retail tenants want a lease term that allows for the amortization of their TIs and other costs of opening a new store, but they are wary of signing a lease term that is too long. The possibilities of the business not doing well, outgrowing the space, or being attracted to a better shopping center being developed nearby are reasons some tenants do not like to enter into long-term leases. Instead, most retail tenants prefer a shorter initial term—usually three to seven years—and would prefer to have but are not likely to get options to control their space should it prove to be a good location. Anchor tenants, including supermarkets, department stores, and drug stores, are more likely to have long-term leases—from 20 to 30 years with multiple five-year options—but they will have the right to sublease or assign the lease should their sales not meet expectations, a better location become available, or their new format not fit their current space.

While it is seldom a provision granted in a retail lease, many tenants will evaluate the shopping center in terms of the possibility for future expansion. This is especially true in regional and super-regional malls. The tenant may take a modest-sized store to test the market and, if it proves successful, may want to expand or move to a larger location in the mall or shopping center. Retailers often format their store sizes after evaluating their sales potential in a prospective shopping center and the demographics and psychographics of customers in its trade area.

Tenants considering a shopping center location will also evaluate landlords to determine if they have experience in shopping center ownership. They will look to the reputation of the developer and the property manager. Shopping centers are one of the few commercial developments where some landlords own several properties and are likely to make multiple deals with tenants. It is therefore incumbent upon the landlords of shopping centers to offer professional, responsive management that will encourage tenants to seek them out for future projects and lease renewals.

Office, Medical Office, and Industrial Tenants

Office tenants look for competitive space in a convenient location for their business. There is seldom only one building that can fill the needs of an office tenant, so choosing one building over another will have little impact on business. It is possible that some businesses are looking for a special tenant mix in an office building—perhaps seeking specifically law offices, insurance companies, stock brokerages, etc.—but in general, office tenants do not have great concerns about the basic tenant mix of the office building.

Office tenants consider the location of a building to be a major concern. They may well choose a location because it is close to people with whom they do business. They may also select a particular building because it is close to the business owner's home. Or they may decide on a location because it is close to shopping and restaurants or proximate to public transportation, the airport, a train station, or rapid transit stations. Medical professionals are concerned with location and co-tenants, while industrial tenants are concerned with location and a building that will accommodate their specific—and sometimes unique—needs.

PREPARING THE TEAM PLAYERS TO NEGOTIATE

Even though there are two parties to a lease arrangement, the team that negotiates the agreement may include several people on both sides. The landlord may be represented by a leasing agent: either an in-house staff member or broker. The property manager may have a role in the negotiation. If the landlord is an institution, there will be an *asset manager* representing the property ownership. Many lease negotiations include legal representation.

The tenant will likely have a leasing agent, possibly have an attorney, and (in the case of larger retail tenants) have store operating personnel.

The Landlord's Leasing Agent

As mentioned previously, the landlord must have full knowledge of the property. In that same vein, the leasing agent must also fully understand the property and the landlord's goals and objectives for the property as well as for the particular negotiation. This agent should have a firm grasp of the overall direction of the property, be familiar with the trade area or the micromarket in which it is located, have researched competitive buildings along with their strengths and weaknesses, and offer a very good read on tenants and what they are looking for in the negotiations.

The leasing agent may have the authority to accept specific terms if they are within preset guidelines from the landlord. It will be the job of this agent to bring to the landlord the various proposals that come out of the negotiations, and to recommend the best course of action if they are not within the initial agreed-upon guidelines.

The Tenant's Leasing Representative

The tenant's in-house leasing representative should be fully aware of the local market conditions, what alternatives may exist to the location under negotiation, the desired economic outcome for the tenant in that location, and the tenant's bottom-line position. The tenant's leasing rep should also know as much about the landlord as possible. As with the landlord's representative, the tenant's agent will most likely not have the authority to accept a deal, but will bring offers back to the tenant with recommendations for consideration.

The Property Manager

The property manager may not always be a party to the negotiations, but should nevertheless have input concerning the desirability of the particular tenant and any potential problems that may arise. The property manager may have known the tenant from another building, and so be familiar with any problems with collections, poor operations, or other issues. These should be explained to the leasing personnel so they can be considered in the negotiations and/or final approval of a tenant.

It is also possible that the tenant may have had issues with a property manager or landlord in another building and is not anxious to deal with those problems again. These discussions should be brought up before the negotiations with the landlord rather than waiting until a lease is signed. It is better to clear up misunderstandings or personality conflicts before a deal is consummated than to wait until they become a problem.

The Asset Manager

An asset manager holds the equivalent position of the landlord. When institutions own properties, the asset manager is assigned to make decisions for the ownership. The main difference between asset managers and individual landlords is that the landlords act on their own behalf, while asset managers act in a *fiduciary* capacity and must make every effort to make prudent decisions for the property. Although they have the same roles, the possible consequences for the two are substantially different. As a result, an entrepreneur landlord is generally more flexible than an asset manager. It is therefore helpful for the tenant representative to know the structure of the property ownership, as it and its representative can play a role in the negotiations outcome.

The Attorney

The attorney also plays an important role in leasing. Typically, attorneys are involved in the transaction to ensure the lease language is in the best interest of the party being represented. Typically, the attorney's role is not to negotiate the business terms of the lease; but there are many attorneys who do negotiate business terms as well as nonmonetary lease provisions.

The landlord or the tenant should make the attorney's role clear, especially if the attorney is present at the negotiations. Most landlords and tenants want only one person negotiating on their behalf, and for that individual to consult with the other interested parties between negotiating sessions. The main job of the attorney is to evaluate the lease language and advise his or her client as to its possible legal and business consequences. The final decision on all issues is still up to the landlord and the tenant.

Construction and/or Operations Personnel

Occasionally, construction or operations personnel may be a party to the negotiations, especially if the building or tenant requirements are complex or expensive. Both sides will want to know what is possible and what is likely to be accomplished within the building's standard allowances and rental structure.

While it is helpful to address these types of issues set before negotiations start, it is often not possible. Still, having all personnel available to participate in the discussions can go a long way towards clearing up potential problems and getting the parties to fully understand the issues and their possible solutions.

NEGOTIATING TIPS

There are several strategies that can improve the lease negotiating process. A few helpful tips are provided below.

Be Prepared

Both the landlord and the tenant should come to the table with as much practical knowledge as possible. The landlord should know who the tenant is. If the tenant has a public company, the available financial and operating information will be useful in understanding the strength of that tenant's position. The tenant, on the other hand, should check out the landlord's experience, management style, and current tenants' satisfaction levels. Tenants will also want to know if the landlord's *common area maintenance (CAM) charges* or billbacks are reasonable for the building and the market.

Each side should also do all that is possible to understand the other side's goals and objectives. It behooves the landlord to find out why tenants are looking for an additional location or moving from an existing space. If tenants have multiple locations, why does this particular location appeal to them? Likewise, tenants should analyze the landlord's building (especially if it is a shopping center) to determine if their business is a desirable fit. Is the available space the best one for the tenant, or is it a compromise because the right space is not available or is beyond the tenant's budget?

In an office setting, the landlord should also ascertain that the tenant fits into the building's tenant mix. Generally, with the exception of specialized buildings, a reasonably quiet tenant with operations that do not disrupt the building's other occupants will most likely be a fit.

Finally, it is a good idea, before negotiations begin, to make sure that the other side has the authority to negotiate and accept compromises. It is quite frustrating to reach agreement on a given point only to be told that the vice president (or anyone else who has to sign off on the decision) could not be convinced.

Consider the Options

Both sides should have a desired financial outcome for the lease negotiations, and both should approach the negotiations with that goal in mind. Generally, if one can explain the reasons behind decisions, they are more easily accepted by others. It is always a good idea to be able to state why certain terms and conditions are necessary, but it is not an absolute requirement. Both parties should also have a fallback position in case the negotiations do not allow for the deal they have in mind. Obviously, one of the fallback positions for either side is to walk away from the negotiations.

A good negotiation is a series of ideas being presented and then accepted, rejected, or compromised. To maintain the pulse of the negotiations, it is a good idea to establish the items that everyone agrees with from the outset, and then to deal with the areas of disagreement. No lease negotiation should be terminated at the early stages until both sides have been able to present their position and discuss the alternatives presented by the other side.

Remaining open to alternative ideas can often be beneficial. A landlord may have a need for a specific base rent and only be able to compromise on the TIs. Or a tenant may be willing to pay for some of the improvements if the landlord provides an option on favorable terms. The deal should be negotiated in its entirety rather than trying to piece together a lease arrangement one point at a time. If landlords get the rent being asked, they may well give on the TIs. However, if the landlord is being asked to compromise without knowing what rent the tenant will offer, it is difficult to reach an agreement.

Keep It Professional

Egos should be kept out of the negotiations. Posturing is not likely to help in the negotiating process, and may well end what could have been a reasonable deal for both parties. It is helpful to keep in mind that one day the landlord may be benefiting from a strong market, but the next time around it may well switch to a tenant's market. For that reason alone, it is a good idea to treat the other side with respect and courtesy. It is not wise to indicate that the other party is being unreasonable by not coming up or down on the rental terms. This may apply to either side, so it is hard to place the blame. One side or the other may have reached the breaking point, and in such a case even a few cents matter a great deal.

If negotiations do fall apart, there is a reasonable chance that the parties may meet again. It is therefore a good idea to end with a handshake and indicate a willingness to make another deal in the future. Closing doors on future connections makes no sense, especially in retail leasing where landlords and tenants make multiple deals.

Everyone who approaches a lease negotiation is interested in walking away with a lease. The exercise is not intended for education, but rather for concluding a satisfactory arrangement—a "win-win" deal. Both sides should be looking for ways to make the negotiations work for both parties. Taking time to understand why the other side has taken a specific position will often lead to an acceptable compromise. A good negotiation generally requires as lot of "what ifs" from both sides before the final arrangements are agreed upon.

Keep Records

Keep a journal record of each negotiation and check it before the next session to see what was covered and where possible problems exist. Quite often a negotiation will take a turn with compromises, but then a break is taken and, when discussions resume, the specifics have been forgotten. Another common problem in prolonged negotiations is that one side may remember only the concessions and not the basic terms of the deal. It is helpful to recap the prior discussions at the start of any new negotiations session.

It is a good idea, after a negotiation session has ended, to send a memo to the other side recapping the day's discussions and the issues that are open for the next session. If there are misunderstandings, this provides an opportunity for them to be addressed so that both sides will be prepared to move forward when the negotiations resume.

Employ Effective Strategies

To begin with, both sides must be aware of the importance of issues and attempt to keep them in perspective when negotiating. It should be noted that all points in a negotiation are not equal. For example, the landlord sets the rents to meet the market, generate income, and create value. The tenant may want the landlord to extend the lease in exchange for a lower rent, but such terms would lock the landlord into a lower rental rate for a longer period of time. Hence the offer is not likely to be accepted, even though it seems reasonable to the tenant.

Be wary of the "Let's split the difference" approach to negotiating. It is too easy for one side or the other to set a ridiculous figure and then offer to split the difference. There is little doubt that some negotiations reach the point that the "split the difference" approach can be a reasonable one, but in general it is not a valid approach to negotiations. Another negotiation ploy is to say something like "I gave you four concessions so you owe me four concessions." Not all concessions are equal.

When one side's negotiations do not seem reasonable, the other side should have no problem pointing out, in a courteous fashion, why that approach will not work. There is nothing wrong with either party explaining why a particular issue is more important to them and provides little room for flexibility. Often the issues can be resolved to the satisfaction of both parties.

Expressing emotions during negotiations seldom leads to a lease deal. This is business—not to be taken personally—and it should be treated as such. A temper tantrum, storming out of a meeting, and name-calling are not good negotiating ploys. If emotions start to build up, it is a good idea to take a break and start again when reason has been restored. It is not likely that the other side is *trying* to incite anger, but sometimes unproductive things are said in the heat of the moment. Anger or an emotional outburst can easily bring negotiations to a halt and make the other party very reluctant to come back to the table.

Choose words carefully in a negotiation. Landlords typically are proud of their buildings and feel they do a good job with ownership and management. If a prospective tenant suggests that everything is not as presented, the landlord is likely to get defensive. On the other side of the coin, most tenants are also proud of their business and reputation. A landlord's suggestion that the tenant is less than the best may bring negotiations to a grinding halt.

Even when nothing negative is intended, both parties should keep in mind that words are powerful and should be used very carefully. This is one of the reasons that it is a good idea to have a leasing agent dealing with another leasing agent: neither of them has a personal interest in the negotiation, and they can therefore be objective. If words are not well chosen, leasing agents are likely to forgive each other; the landlord or tenant may take them much more personally.

It is also important to remember that silence is often a very effective tool. Will Rogers said, "Never miss a chance to shut up." This is often a good negotiating strategy. Just sitting quietly and letting the other side break the silence to start another approach or even offer suggestions or concessions may help move the discussion in a positive direction.

Ultimately, each negotiator must evaluate his or her own techniques and approaches. Following any negotiation, the agent should evaluate what went well, what did not go well, and, more importantly, what can be done to improvement future negotiations. Was the agent too passive, failing to lead the discussion, or aggressive to the point of turning the prospect off to the property? Was the agent unable to answer questions that were asked during the session? Did the prospect become upset during the session and, if so, could this be prevented in the future? There is no single way to negotiate, but agents should evaluate their own approach, try to learn from past negotiations, and refine the process to make future negotiations more productive for all parties involved.

STAGES IN THE LEASING PROCESS

There are several stages in the leasing process, as discussed in the following sections.

Steps for the Landlord and the Tenant

The landlord is almost always leasing a property, even when the building is filled. The process starts with creating interest through brochures, brokers' listings, open houses, booths at trade shows, canvassing, networking in the brokerage community, and general mailings. The next step is negotiating with interested parties. A leasing agent will generally make many contacts for each executed lease, making this a time-consuming process. The next stage is negotiating and finalizing the lease with signatures, and returning the signed document to the tenant. The final stage for the leasing agent is starting all over again by creating interest.

On the flipside of the process, tenants must first study the entire market and identify one or more locations that would work for their needs. The tenant then needs to compare alternative locations and know the market conditions and rents. The next step for the tenant is negotiations—either with one property landlord or with multiple landlords at the same time. For new developments, tenants have to be careful to know that the developer is financially capable of developing the project, or considerable time and effort may be wasted in negotiating a lease that cannot be completed. Once negotiations are complete, the lease must be finalized by obtaining the signatures of both parties and providing a copy to each.

Documents That Begin the Process

Large tenants often start the leasing process with a *request for proposal (RFP)*. Tenants will indicate their needs, generally including the desired area, the size of the building, any special building requirements, and the requested lease term. Landlords or developers will then try to match those requirements and come back to the tenant with a proposal that is as close as possible to the tenant's RFP. Negotiations continue until either the lease is consummated or the parties realize they are unable to reach an agreement.

The next step in the process is the *letter of intent*. This document is generally the result of early negotiations that set the broad terms of a lease agreement while the fine points have yet to be agreed upon. It is commonly used by landlords to generate and demonstrate strong interest in buildings that have not yet been built. A letter of intent has no legal standing in most jurisdictions, but it indicates that the parties are both interested and willing to pursue negotiations. It is a good tool for both the landlord and the tenant to show interest without being bound until all of the terms are negotiated and agreed upon. Some negotiations skip the letter of intent and progress right to a lease draft.

The *work letter* is a more detailed document that generally indicates what the landlord will provide in the way of improvements for the office, retail, or industrial tenant, and what portion of construction will be the tenant's responsibility. The work letter is almost always a very detailed schedule of all the improvements that will be provided by the landlord, with sufficient detail to assure the parties of a clear intent. If the space is taken in "as is" condition or only minor improvements are being provided, a work letter might not be prepared and the information that would be in the work letter is instead inserted in a lease exhibit.

Negotiations

The next step is negotiating the lease itself. These negotiations can be a very time-consuming process and require great attention to detail, especially for major shopping centers and high-rise office buildings that have long and complicated leases. While many lease negotiations last only a few days or weeks, complex lease negotiations can take months to complete.

Both parties must take great care to be sure that all of the terms and conditions of the lease are fully understood before agreeing to them. If there is doubt on either side, the item in question should be discussed until there is proper understanding. Neither side should be reluctant to bring up any issue regarding the lease. Most landlords and tenants are not interested in taking advantage of the other side; they are just trying to protect their interests and must therefore understand what they are agreeing to. There are tens of thousands to millions of dollars involved over the term of a lease, so it is not surprising when the process takes a long time.

Final Approval

The final approval for a lease can take only a few hours, but it may require considerable time as well. Quite often the leasing agents for the landlord and the tenant negotiate the terms, and then the lease must go to their principals for final approval. Generally, when the process has been handled by qualified agents, the final approval is almost certain; but this is not always the case.

In most cases the lease is negotiated, the tenant signs it, and the document is then sent to the landlord for his or her signature. In most states the lease is not legally executed until the landlord has signed it and returned a signed copy to the tenant. It is in the landlord's best interest to evaluate a proposed lease as quickly as practical, sign the lease, and return it to the tenant so that everyone in the process is aware that the lease has been finalized. The old adage "time kills deals" applies to negotiating and executing a lease.

In very rare occasions, the landlord will have difficult space to lease or a highly desirable tenant—conditions that may prompt the landlord to be the first to sign the lease. Generally, when a lease is presigned by the landlord and sent to the tenant for a signature, the tenant is given a specific period of time to sign it before the offer expires. Landlords do not want signed leases out in the marketplace. They want to proceed with other negotiations if a particular deal is not going to be completed.

Tenants will have the same requirements for landlords when the tenant is the first party to sign the lease. The tenant has the same concerns as the landlord in having a signed lease out in the market. It will limit the tenant's options until it is either signed or rejected. In most jurisdictions, if tenants have signed the lease but not received a signed copy back, they are free to cancel the lease at any time prior to receiving the lease signed by the landlord.

QUALIFYING PARTIES AND AVERTING RISK

Because a lease involves substantial financial commitments on both sides, it becomes very important to know that the other party has the financial ability to meet the agreed upon obligations.

What the Landlord Can Do to Minimize Financial Risk

Landlords considering a tenant prospect should ascertain the tenant's credit standing and net worth. In the case of a retail tenant, the landlord also has an interest in the tenant's reputation as a merchant and the tenant's history in the retail business, merchandise, price points, level of service, and projected sales.

A credit check is straightforward and usually very inexpensive. Typically, a landlord is not looking for perfect credit, but wants someone with a good history of paying bills and meeting financial obligations. Credit checks are most often performed after the lease has been agreed upon, but if the lease is very complicated or for a unique space, the credit check may well be done before negotiations begin. This circumvents spending significant amounts of time to finalize complicated arrangements only to discover that the tenant prospect has a poor history of paying his or her bills.

It is also extremely important to get a credit history on the entity actually signing the lease. A husband and wife may well have an excellent credit history but indicate that they want the lease in the name of a family-held corporation. In such a case, the husband and wife's personal credit does not support a family corporation unless they sign a lease *guaranty*. As another example, it is not unusual for national retail tenants to separately incorporate individual stores and, without a corporate guaranty from the parent company, such a lease has no financial backing beyond that of the individual location.

The financial statement of the tenant is another item that is important to the landlord. It is not necessary that all tenant prospects have a high net worth. Many small office space users and small retailers have a limited net worth that is sufficient to support their business. A shoe store of 800 square feet, for example, can be opened with a reasonable fixturization cost. On the other hand, an ice cream parlor or beauty shop requires a fairly large cost in fixtures and build-out, and the landlord would want evidence of a higher net worth to support the lease. Each lease proposal and tenant prospect should be evaluated individually, ensuring that the proper financial tools are in place to meet the obligations of the particular arrangement.

What the Tenant Can Do to Minimize Financial Risk

From the tenant's perspective, it is important to be sure that the landlord has the ability to complete the transaction. An anchor tenant for a neighborhood shopping center is not going to sign a lease with a neophyte developer in the hopes that the developer will be able to complete the shopping center tenant's store and then lease and operate the shopping center in a professional manner.

The tenant should start by checking the landlord's reputation. For a smaller tenant, it might be sufficient to check on the landlord's local reputation to be sure that there are no major problems. Checking with a few of the tenants in one of the landlord's existing buildings is often time well spent. The tenant's leasing agent has resources to check on a landlord's reputation in the industry. If landlords are well-known developers or building owners, it will likely be fairly easy to check their standing in the real estate community.

One of the major areas for a tenant to evaluate is that of the common area costs or pass-through charges. A potential tenant should check the history of these expenses and whether or not they are in line with costs for similar buildings. Discussions with existing tenants may be helpful. Any issues raised by the existing tenants are fair game for a discussion with the landlord. In all commercial properties, the lease language on billback charges is meant to be as broad as possible to encompass every eventuality. For a reasonable landlord who wants to be fair to tenants, such language is not a problem. Unfortunately, some landlords charge expenses to the billback charges that are not allowed in the lease.

If tenants are entering into an especially large transaction, they want assurance the landlord can perform his or her obligations as well. If the landlord is part of a public company, those records are readily available.

Specifics for Retail Tenants

For retail properties, there is an additional concern regarding the landlord's marketing of the property. Generally, malls—as well as lifestyle, specialty, and outlet shopping centers—have a *marketing fund* for marketing, advertising, and promotion. The tenant prospect should check into the existing marketing efforts to see if tenants believe they are effective and, if not, what can be done. Does the landlord contribute to the marketing fund? The tenant should review the past year's marketing program and the current year's marketing plan.

Retail tenants should find out as much as they can about the shopping center's sales. Is the overall shopping center doing well? Are the anchors doing well? Does traffic seem to be strong? The tenant would do well to visit the shopping center at various hours of the day and different days of the week to evaluate the traffic. The tenant prospect should talk with current tenants to get their perceptions of how well they are doing. If they are not doing well, it is important to know what they perceive to be the problem.

A very good resource for researching sales of the different categories of tenants in the different classifications of shopping centers is *Dollars & Cents of Shopping Centers,* copublished by the Urban Land Institute (ULI) and the International Council of Shopping Centers (ICSC). While the sales figures are only averages for all the properties reported, they are still a good indication of typical sales figures in shopping centers. They can provide the tenant and landlord with a good idea of what approximate sales would be for a similar shopping center. The tenant should then be able to extrapolate these figures in analyzing the subject shopping center to help make a leasing decision.

OPTIMIZING YOUR NEGOTIATING POSITION

Lease negotiation is an art, not a science. Depending on the market conditions, either the landlord or the tenant can be at a distinct disadvantage during the process. In a strong landlord market, the tenant will have little room to negotiate because the landlord will have many other options and won't have to work hard or give away concessions to sign leases. In a strong tenant market, however, the landlord will be at a disadvantage and will almost surely be required to make concessions to secure a tenant.

All things considered, the person with the most knowledge of the market and the strongest understanding of the other side will be in the optimal position to take advantage of the existing conditions and secure the best possible deal in the market.

6

Know the Market Conditions

A full understanding of the market in which one operates is essential to making good decisions for both the landlord and the tenant, and this knowledge is crucial to the success of any property.

Real estate is a cyclical industry. All real estate operates in cycles. At one time these cycles were approximately ten years apart. The economy would go through roughly ten years of good growth and then hit a recession, and the real estate markets would follow the same pattern. In more recent years, these cycles seem to be closer to five years in length, and this is likely to change again in the future.

In addition to the cycles of real estate, developers must contend with the development lead time for commercial properties, which can easily run from two to seven years. This means that, at the start of a project, the developer or landlord has no assurance of where the market will be in several years when the project is completed. Yet developers must still make the best possible assumptions and move forward with their project.

Anchor tenants and large chain stores are also dependent on the real estate development market. Although they must project their growth well into the future as landlords do, tenants generally have a shorter timetable to manage their expansion needs.

THRIVING IN CHANGING MARKETS

Most landlords, as long as they are not saddled with excessive debt that limits their leasing options, can work well in either an "up" market (also called a *landlord's market*) or a "down" market (also called a *tenant's market*). Most commercial real estate is a long-term investment and therefore, with the proper guidance from the landlord, is likely to weather either kind of market.

As expected, it is not hard for a landlord to be successful in an "up" market—usually demand is good, rents are increasing, and financing is readily available. In a "down" market, however, rents are either stagnant or decreasing, demand for space is weak or nonexistent, and quite often financing is either very difficult to obtain or too expensive. It is difficult to increase cash flow and value with an existing property in a tenant's market; most landlords are happy to maintain their rents, occupancy, and value during this time, or at the very least to minimize any possible losses until the markets improve.

In either a landlord's market or a tenant's market, it is important to maintain competitive rental rates. If landlords overestimate the value of their space in the marketplace, it is likely to remain vacant. That space may never lease if the rent and terms are excessively high. On the other hand, if landlords price their space below the market rate, that space will likely lease up quickly but they will lose substantial cash flow opportunities, and the building will ultimately lose value.

Tenants have similar market concerns. Even though the tenant's concerns are often more immediate than the landlord's, they are equally important. Every lease proposal should be carefully analyzed and compared by the tenant to the other proposals available in the market. A tenant's final decision often includes factors other than the rental rate and other charges, but the tenant should know exactly what these comparisons are before making a decision.

Comparing Proposals

It is not unusual for a landlord and a tenant to consider more than one proposal. Both will do well to carefully consider the financial impact of the proposals in order to reach a reasonable decision. That is not to say that the financial results will be the most compelling factor, but they are an important element of the decision.

Shopping centers offer a unique situation because the landlord is quite concerned with tenant mix as well as cash flow and value. The first item of importance to the landlord is whether or not the prospective tenant enhances the tenant mix of the shopping center. At one time video game centers, a far cry from what they are today, were potentially not very good tenants for shopping centers because of the unruly teenagers they might attract. Video game center operators would offer rates well above market rents in order to secure locations. In other words, the rent was good, but the tenant was not.

Even if a shopping center does not have percentage rent provisions in its leases, the landlord wants the strongest tenant mix possible to help create the synergism that is critical to a successful shopping center. Once the tenant mix issue has been resolved, the landlord evaluates the financial condition of the tenant and the financial terms of the proposal. If one tenant has much better credit than another, or has a much stronger financial statement, that will weigh heavily on the landlord's final decision. Landlords of very successful shopping centers often look at several proposals and compare them before making a final decision.

Example 1: The Landlord Compares Proposals.   The shopping center is an upscale specialty shopping center, with fashion merchandise and some services. The landlord has an available space of 1,200 square feet and is asking $20 per square foot, against a percentage of sales—most likely 5 percent—and a five-year *triple-net lease.*

A new men's wear store approaches the landlord with an offer (A) to lease the space for $18 per square foot, on a triple net basis, with a five-year lease. The tenant requests a *tenant improvement allowance* of $5 per square foot. This tenant has two other locations and is averaging $450-per-square-foot sales in his other stores.

A local businesswoman also makes an offer (B) for the same space, hoping to open a gift store. It will be her first retail location. She is willing to accept the $20-per-square-foot rent; she would like $2 per square foot in improvements; she will sign a five-year lease on a triple net basis; and she will accept 5 percent of sales as the percentage rent rate. She indicates that her sales will most likely be about $300 per square foot.

The financial terms of (A) are as follows:

Base rent	1,200 sq.ft. × $18	$21,600
Improvements	1,200 × $5 ÷ 5 years	$1,200 per year
Net rent	$21,600 − $1,200	**$20,400**
Percentage rent		
	$21,600 ÷ .05 = $432,000 breakpoint	
	1,200 × $450 = $540,000 estimated sales	
	$540,000 − $432,000 = $108,000	
	5 percent: $108,000 × .05	**$5,400**
Total rent		**$25,800**

The financial terms of (B) are as follows:

Base rent	1,200 sq.ft. × $20	$24,000
Improvements	1,200 × $2 ÷ 5 years	$480 per year
Net rent	$24,000 − $480	**$23,520**
Percentage rent		
	$24,000 ÷ .05 = $480,000 breakpoint	
	1,200 × $300 = $360,000 estimated sales	
	Breakpoint > sales	**$0**
Total rent		**$23,520**

Which proposal presents the better option? The landlord is likely to accept the men's wear store because it has a proven track record of sales. There is no guarantee that the potential percentage rent will be realized but, based on the tenant's past performance, the odds are better than those of the new gift store tenant. If the men's wear proposal were not on the table, the landlord might well accept the gift store—it is also a reasonable proposal and appears to fit the tenant mix of the shopping center.

Example 2: The Tenant Compares Proposals.   Suppose the gift store tenant is considering an option that is identical to the second offer (B) in the previous example. This tenant is also considering another proposal to decide which space is best for her shop. This second proposal (C) is for a space that was a little bigger than she needs. It is for 1,400 square feet, triple net, with $20-per-square-foot rent; but the landlord has agreed to provide a five-year lease and an allowance of $3 per square foot for improvements. The businesswoman estimates her sales at $300 per square foot, and the landlord wants a 6 percent rent provision. The space is in a neighborhood shopping center with a supermarket and mostly service tenants and restaurants.

The financial terms of the first proposal (B) are displayed in Example 1 above.

The economics of the second deal (C) are as follows:

Base rent	1,400 sq.ft. × $20	$28,000
Improvements	1,400 sq.ft. × $3 ÷ 5 years	$840 per year
Net rent	$28,000 − $840	**$27,160**
Percentage rent		
	$28,000 ÷ .06 = $466,667 breakpoint	
	1,400 × $300 = $420,000 estimated sales	
	Breakpoint > sales	**$0**
Total rent		**$27,160**

Which lease would this tenant rather accept? First, the shopping center in the second offer (C) does not provide the best tenant mix for her type of use. If there are no other gift stores within a reasonable driving distance, she may be able to promote her business and be successful without any fashion draw to the shopping center, but this is not her best environment. Second, she is looking at a shop that is larger than she wants, which means more rent, *common area maintenance (CAM)* charges, and utilities (i.e., higher *occupancy costs*).

Since the second shopping center does not provide the ideal location and tenant mix for the gift store owner's business, she is likely to stay with the first offer (B) because the net rent is better and she will not have to take on the burden of an extra 200 square feet.

Selecting Tenants on the Basis of Compatibility

As evidenced in the above proposal comparison examples, tenant mix is an important consideration for shopping center tenants and landlords in any market. It can also be important for office and medical buildings. Tenant compatibility can help these businesses to thrive even in challenging markets. Industrial buildings, on the other hand, are quite often set up for specific types of tenants based on the zoning considerations, so one generally will not find incompatible tenants in the industrial setting.

Compatibility in a shopping center environment is based primarily on three factors. First and foremost is the consideration of merchandise mix; second, with slightly less importance, is that of merchandise price points. A third, much more subtle consideration is the store's operations: the sounds and smells it may create, the customer base, advertising, etc. Leasing agents and landlords must continually evaluate all prospects for their fit into the tenant mix of a shopping center on all three of these points.

Shopping centers are much like department stores: there are many departments, and each has a specialty of its own. The shopping center also targets a specific market segment, which is generally determined by its anchor tenants. If an anchor has an upscale clientele, smaller shops in the same shopping center will also tend to be upscale.

In any given shopping center the range of price points will vary, but they will tend in the direction of the anchor's clientele. In more recent years we have seen discount or off-price merchants become tenants in more upscale shopping centers, but their target market is still the more affluent shopper, albeit at a bargain price. A very low-price jeweler would not likely fit or do well in an upscale shopping center. Conversely, a guild jeweler will not take a location in a shopping center with tenants with low price points.

Compatibility of tenants must also take into consideration the noise levels and/or odors that may come from a particular business. For example, it is usually not a good idea to put a sports bar next to a fashion tenant; the lively atmosphere of the bar might clash with the atmosphere the fashion tenant is trying to create.

One generally does not put a veterinary clinic next to a food store because of the concern of odors. And while many of us consider the smells that come from a bakery to be a pleasant thing, there are merchants (such as fashion designers, shoe store owners, etc.) who would prefer not to have those smells right next door.

A shopping center that positions a new dance studio between a men's wear store and a shoe store may well lose both of the older tenants due to the noise and vibrations coming from the dance studio. And it is generally agreed that a biker bar is not a good tenant in a neighborhood shopping center, whereas a sports bar might work quite well.

Medical office building tenant compatibility is also a consideration. If one has promoted a building as a "medical building," it is not a good idea to lease spaces to other types of tenants, especially if those alternate uses become a dominant part of the tenant mix. It is also not a good idea to put a noisy tenant in most office buildings. One business office building leased space to a psychiatrist whose specialty was "scream therapy," and the tenants on both sides of that office were disturbed.

Often, ground floor tenants in office buildings are more retail- or service-oriented, but their uses should be consistent with the buildings' other occupants. One must also give consideration to the traffic generated by any given use to be sure that one tenant will not tie up the building's parking. Uses that have a heavy stream of traffic may not be good prospects for office buildings with limited parking.

Medical office buildings are particularly sensitive to the mix of the building. Doctors prefer to have a pharmacy and compatible medical specialties in the building, but may not be pleased to see office tenants. Medical professionals want referrals from other medical professionals in the building.

If there is any doubt concerning the acceptability of a given use in a commercial property, it might serve the leasing agent well to discuss that use with a few of the more helpful tenants in the building. It is much easier to say "no" to a tenant before the lease is signed than to deal with angry or upset tenants after the new tenant is in place.

Determining and Establishing Competitive Rates

Because of the importance to landlords of setting competitive rates, one of the most critical questions in the industry is, "How do I get accurate information about rents and terms from competitors?" It is in the best interest of all landlords, leasing agents, and property managers to be aware of market rents and terms, as this allows for more knowledgeable landlords who are able to offer competitive rates and terms. Tenants also need to know market rates in order to negotiate the best lease terms.

The commercial real estate industry is one that has traditionally shared information. As a result, the best way to get information usually is to give information. When calling or visiting a competitor, the best approach is to be honest about who you are and what you are doing. It is helpful to offer similar information regarding your building or to offer the competitor a copy of the market report you are preparing when it is finished. Keep in mind that such a copy should not provide the conclusions reached, but rather should include only the data gathered on competitive properties.

It is important for the person gathering market information to record both the asking rates and the deal-making rates. The *asking rate* is the rent requested and marketed. It is the initial quoted rate for most tenant prospects. The *deal-making rate* is the rental rate for which the space is leased. For example, a landlord may request $30 per square foot (the asking rate) for a space, but the deal ends up at $28.75 per square foot (the deal-making rate).

Another concept to consider is *face rate* versus *effective rent.* The face rate is the rent paid without deduction for concessions, while the effective rent takes into account the free rent and other concessions. For instance, a rental rate at $18 per square foot for five years with six months' free rent has a face rate of $18 and an effective rent of $16.20 per square foot.

To further illustrate this point, a new three-year lease may be executed at the face rate of $25 per square foot, but in order to get that rate the landlord gives the tenant three months' free rent. If the lease is for 1,000 square feet, the rent for that three-year period would be $75,000 at the face rate. However, the allotted free rent will reduce that amount, and the effective rent will end up being $75,000 minus the three months' free rent ($6,250). The net rent is thus $68,750. Dividing this net rent by three years equals $22,917 per year and, when divided by 1,000 square feet, is $22.92 per square foot. If the landlord were unwilling to offer this free rent, however, and were to insist on $25 per foot as the deal-making rate, he would be asking rents approximately 10 percent above the market. This would most likely make it difficult to consummate leases.

THE MARKET SURVEY

The astute landlord and tenant keep abreast of market conditions and try to anticipate the likely impact of these conditions on their lease deals. Conducting a *market survey* is the best way to keep track of this market. Tenants who are knowledgeable about the market conduct a market survey every time they look for space or negotiate a lease renewal. Landlords perform periodic market surveys to stay on top of the market since they often have spaces available or leases up for renewal. This enables both parties to stay on top of a changing market.

The market survey (or market study) is an information-gathering process that helps to establish market conditions and evaluate competitive rates. This survey provides an overview of market conditions and rental rates for buildings in a defined area. It also enables landlords to evaluate their building and compare it to the competition.

The market sets the rent and terms for commercial properties, and the more landlords understand the market, the more likely it is that they will price their space according to the market when establishing their building's rental rates and negotiating leases. An essential element in maximizing the property's income is maintaining the building's rental rates at their market value. To do this, landlords must be knowledgeable about market conditions. This information can be gathered through a market survey. Trends can be identified when the surveys are conducted on a regular basis.

Market surveys are also used in managing and financing the property and in the acquisition process. The surveys enable the landlord to project rental rates, concessions, and lease-up (also known as the building's *absorption rate*), all of which are essential for developing the pro forma for a proposed building or the income components of an existing building's budget. Market surveys are needed when developing or refinancing a building. They are also needed to satisfy the due diligence requirement when analyzing a building for purchase. Accurate information and a correct analysis of the information are essential to meeting the objectives of the market survey.

Determining the Market

The first step in conducting a market survey is to define the area to be surveyed. Determining the boundary of the market for an office building or industrial property, or the trade area of a shopping center, is not difficult when the landlord is active in the area; but when the landlord is not familiar with the area, a more detailed analysis is necessary. It is impossible to place a mileage ring around the property to determine its market area. The boundaries are formed by man-made barriers such as freeways, changes of property use, or the locations of competing buildings. A natural barrier, such as a river, also shapes a market area.

The market's size is another variable in defining its boundary. For instance, the market for a Class A office building in a city's central business district (CBD) may be a half-mile or two miles in each direction, while the market for a regional mall in the same city may cover the entire county. The boundaries of the shopping center's trade area encompass the area in which most of its customers live or work. When determining market rates for a grocery-anchored neighborhood shopping center, the landlord should survey all shopping centers anchored by one or more major tenants and located in the shopping center's trade area. Surveying small, unanchored strip shopping centers or enclosed malls is not necessary because they are not in direct competition with the neighborhood shopping center. If the trade area does not have sufficient competing shopping centers to provide a valid comparison, the landlord should then survey grocery-anchored neighborhood shopping centers in a similar trade area outside the subject shopping center's trade area.

Office buildings are classified as Class A, B, or C buildings and are typically located downtown (in the CBD), in a secondary business district, or in the suburbs. To establish the boundaries of the area to be surveyed, the landlord must first identify the classification of the subject office building and then determine which buildings are its competition.

The method used in determining the area to survey for industrial properties is similar to the method used for office building surveys. Suburban buildings typically do not compete directly with downtown office buildings because most tenants choose among buildings in one particular area.

Information Sources

Almost all of the support information gathered for the market survey will be from secondary sources—in other words, from research that has already been collected into a formal study, often sponsored and delivered through economic development councils, chambers of commerce, the Census Bureau, industry reports, university studies, etc. Secondary sources are those sources that gather information and make it available to industry professionals.

Primary research may be conducted specifically for a subject property—for example, a demographic and psychographic study of consumers who live within a primary trade area. Primary sources are such things as going through a competitive project, finding out rates and terms, and evaluating the property. Both primary and secondary research can contribute to the *market research* that will enable a real estate professional to better understand, competitively position, and successfully lease a subject property.

An effective means for gathering market information is contacting leasing agents and property managers in the marketplace and inquiring about their "asking" and "deal-making" rates, the concessions they make, and their vacancies. Some leasing agents are reluctant to spend time conducting a market survey because they believe their ongoing activities already keep them current on market activity. However, an individual's activities do not give a comprehensive picture of the market. Even though a broker can be current on the activities of one segment of the market, such as high-rise office buildings in the CBD, general assumptions should not be applied to other segments of that market or to other markets.

Economic data for the country, states, counties, and cities are readily available from government sources, the Internet, local newspapers, financial publications and trade journals. As mentioned earlier, most landlords are constantly updating their information. When the time comes to do a formal market survey, landlords should go through the exercise even if they have a good idea of the results—just to be sure that little, if anything, has changed.

Information on the local region and trade area of the property is generally more specialized, but this information is available from demographic and psychographic services that can provide such information as population, incomes, education, spending habits and lifestyle activities. The information can be custom tailored to a zip code, a city, a county, etc. The more detailed the information that one wants, the more the report will cost.

Brokerage firms generally track market data (e.g., vacancy and rental rates) for all areas where they have offices or work. This information is often published quarterly and is mailed to customers or potential customers and most will provide a copy of such analysis upon request. It is good business to keep open lines of communications with all brokers in one's area as they are also good sources of information. If a landlord is willing to share information, the brokers are likely to share the information that they gather as well.

Appraisers are excellent sources of information. When an appraiser calls asking for information on your property it is a good idea to share, as you may well want to ask for information at a later date. Appraisers keep track of rents, terms, values, vacancies, growth areas, problems areas, etc.

Mortgage companies also keep fairly good data on properties, but have less of a reason to share that information than do brokers and appraisers. The acquisition officer of a REIT or an institutional owner is also a good source of information, but not readily available to the general population.

There are several Internet sites that can be quite helpful. CoStar provides a commercial real estate site (www.CoStar.com) supported by major international real estate companies. The site shares information on sales and leasing of commercial properties. LoopNet provides a similar site (www.LoopNet.com), but appears to have a broader scope in that it also encompasses services to the commercial real estate field. Property Line has a site (www.PropertyLine.com) that covers commercial properties for sale or for lease. Many commercial real estate brokerage firms also maintain websites that include valuable market information.

Several brokerage firms publish quarterly market data, including vacancy and rental rates. Daily newspapers often publish articles on the commercial real estate market and market conditions. Additionally, there are several multiple listing sites for commercial properties throughout the United

Exhibit 6.1
Steps for Performing an Effective Market Survey

1. Analyze the national, regional, and trade area economies as they may relate to a shopping center, and the *micromarket* as it may pertain to office buildings, medical buildings, and industrial properties.

2. Analyze the population: its makeup, income, growth (or lack of growth), and any characteristics that may be relevant to the subject property—including job growth in that population, which is important to all commercial properties.

3. Analyze the subject property. Evaluate rents, lease terms, the condition of the property, vacancy factors, tenant mix, trends, sales for retail tenants, and rental collections.

4. Conduct a market survey and analyze the competitive properties on all of the items listed in Step 3.

5. Using all of the gathered information, determine the rental rates for a specific market and building. Price each space within the subject property according to its location and size. The landlord can use this information to develop a recommended course of action for the property to take over the coming year, as well as alternative courses of action.

6. A formal market survey includes the preparation of a written report. This report should include all backup information to support the data presented: photographs of the subject property, photographs of the competitive properties, and charts and graphs to support the conclusions. If a landlord or tenant is seeking only the market rate for a building (or several buildings) when negotiating a lease, a brief summary with a chart listing the rates and features of each building will suffice.

States. Real estate journals are an excellent source of information on the commercial real estate field. Many of the trade journals have monthly articles focusing on specific parts of the country and the state of the various commercial real estate markets.

Global positioning sites are now available to provide much of the same information as demographic companies have in the past, plus they have excellent maps on locations and markets. Google has aerial photos available for almost all sites in the United States.

The Process

A market survey will most likely begin with a review of the macro environment outlining the national, regional, and trade area economies. Key indicators may include unemployment, job growth, housing starts, the average home value, and new home construction. The complete steps for an effective market survey are listed in Exhibit 6.1.

Gathering information about the nation's economic condition and trends is quite easy. There are many sources from which to gather this information. It is not necessary to review a lot of detail; an overview of the economy's health will suffice. Similarly, an economic summary could be obtained for the state. It is important to look for anything that makes the state's economic climate different from that of the rest of the country.

It may be more difficult to define a region and collect specific information for only that area. Regions can be defined by metropolitan areas, submarkets, CBDs, the subject property's trade areas (e.g., a 1-, 3-, or 5-mile radius), and so forth. The region may be as small as a city or a county, or it may be the metropolitan statistical area (MSA) of the Census Bureau. For many retailers, designated market area (DMA) is replacing the MSA because DMA covers television markets.

Again, it is important to look for anything that identifies the strengths or weaknesses of the surrounding area. The closing of a military base in the region could have a significant impact on the area's financial health. The addition of a new, strong employer with a major work center will have a tremendous impact. Is the region attracting new construction and creating jobs and opportunities? Does the business community have confidence in the area?

What to Look For

The market survey evaluates different elements for different types of commercial properties. The differences in market surveys for shopping centers, office and medical buildings, and industrial properties will be discussed later. At this point, all information gathered will have an impact on all types of commercial properties.

The person performing the market survey should look at the population: its size, income levels, sources of income, education levels, ethnic mix, family sizes and makeup, and trends in the population base. This information is easily gathered from secondary sources and can be tailored to fit the specific requirements of a market survey.

The housing market should also be examined to determine if affordable housing is available for the business's workforce. Is the housing market growing or shrinking? Are the housing market values consistent with the needs of the likely work force that will be attracted?

It is also important to look at the infrastructure in and around the property. Are there good roads and freeways? Is there adequate public transportation? Are positive changes either being made or proposed for the area around the subject property?

What is the inventory and condition of competitive or similar properties in the area? Is the market saturated, or is there unmet demand for space? Even if the market appears to have sufficient space, there may well be room for niche space if properly positioned. What new projects are being proposed for the area, and how will those properties impact the subject property?

Part of the landlord's market survey is a complete analysis of the subject property. How old is the property? What is its condition? What are the rent levels, the CAM or billback charges, the main deficiencies, and the main attractions of the property?

Conducting the Survey

Conducting the market survey is not difficult or time-consuming. A landlord or tenant should conduct a market survey when market data is needed for lease negotiations. Landlords conduct (or have their leasing agent or property manager conduct) a market survey when market conditions appear to be changing or when vacancies appear to be increasing.

Depending on the size of the market, the initial survey may take up to two days. Subsequent surveys may take between half a day and a full day. The initial survey takes longer because the boundaries of the market must be defined, competing properties within the boundaries must be located, and the person responsible for leasing each property must be identified and contacted.

Landlord and tenants may conduct their own market surveys. Landlords must be careful not to slant information to fit predetermined goals. This is seldom a deliberate slant; rather, a landlord may simply be very proud of his property and consequently see it in the best possible light. Additionally, there is a tendency to see things that will enforce the desired outcome, and it is easy for someone with personal interest in the survey to unintentionally slant the information in a certain direction.

This situation is the same for tenants—it is difficult to remain objective when personal goals and objectives are at stake. It is quite possible for tenants to become enamored of a specific location due to its proximity to their home or main office, even though that location may not be the best location for their type of business. An objective view from an outside party is often best when making decisions that will impact the property's rental stream and the tenant's occupancy cost.

The most objective market survey is done with no vested interest in the outcome. Generally, a leasing agent knows the market better than most and would be a good candidate to do the survey. The property manager of the building is aware of the building's strengths and weaknesses and is a good candidate to conduct the market survey. There are also other professionals in the industry who conduct market surveys and know how to conduct them on an objective basis. The main reason to have an outside company or individual conduct the market survey is to have an objective analysis of the situation and recommendations based on the *facts,* not the desired outcome.

The Market Survey Form

There are numerous reasons to conduct an informal market survey. However, the landlord should have a more formal survey conducted at least once per year. Very specific information should be gathered and analyzed for this annual survey, often prepared for the landlord's annual budget.

The landlord should develop a market survey form to record the rental information and features of the subject properties and the competition. This market survey form identifies the issues that are likely to be important in comparing the subject property to the competition: things such as location, access, architectural desirability, age, level of maintenance, rental levels, billback requirements, overall management, and any special amenities found in that marketplace.

A standard market survey form is developed for the subject property type. This makes it easier to ensure that all items are covered and that they will be observed in a way that will make it easy to compare the various properties. For shopping centers, for example, one would want the standard form to include items such as tenant mix, anchor tenants, access, visibility, and parking.

Exhibits 6.2, 6.3, and 6.4 are market survey forms for shopping centers, office buildings, and industrial properties, respectively. They request information on location, building features, condition of the property, dealmaking rates, tenant charges, concessions, and vacancies.

Obtaining Survey Information

The best way to locate competing properties is to drive the area within the boundaries of the micromarket or trade area. When landlords locate a competing building, they should inspect it. Competing properties are marked on a map that is updated for subsequent surveys. While inspecting the properties, the landlord or tenant can find the name and phone number of the leasing agent on the directory of the office building or mall or on a sign on the property. With the market area identified and the form in hand, the landlord or tenant is prepared to conduct the survey.

The landlord visits each competing property to learn how it compares with the subject property. The tenant visits all buildings similar to the building(s) being considered. The building's leasing agent can provide the rental data, but only a visual inspection will disclose the building's features and the condition of the property. Office building features such as life safety systems, energy conservation and green building features, and security programs may not be observed during a property inspection. These features are obtained by contacting the building's landlord or leasing agent.

Once the building's features and property conditions are noted, the landlord or tenant calls the building's property manager to review the property's

Exhibit 6.2
Market Survey—Shopping Centers

	CENTER DATA			MAJORS			RENTAL INFORMATION										CONDITION					
CENTER	AGE	NUMBER SHOPS	SOFT	PARKING LOT	MAJORS	VACANCY	ASKING RENTS	DEAL-MAKING RENTS	% TAX	INS	CAM	CPI	HVAC	OTHER	P/L	BLDG	AREA	ACCESS	TENANTS	VISIBILITY	COMMENTS

Exhibit 6.3
Market Survey—Office Buildings

OFFICE BLDG	AGE	STORIES	VACANCY	ASKING RENT	DEAL-MAKING RENT	OPERATING EXPENSES	CPI	OTHER	PARKING	ON-SITE MGT-MAINT	JANITOR	SECUR	ELEV	HVAC/HR	LIFE SAFETY	OTHER

BUILDING DATA — RENTAL INFORMATION — BUILDING SERVICES

Exhibit 6.4

Market Survey—Industrial Properties

Property Date				Majors		Rental Info								
Property	Zoning	Age	Sq. Ft.	No. of Bldgs	Major Tenants	Vacancy	Asking Rates	Deal-Making Rates	Tax	Ins	CAM	CPI	HVAC	Other

Condition			Features								
Parking Lot	Bldg	Area	Access	Type Const	Sprinklers	Util	Ceiling Heights	% Ofc Space	Truck Loading Facilities	Rail Spur	HVAC	Misc

rental information. Most properties do not have onsite management, but the building's directory or a "For Lease" sign may provide information about the management company. If this information is not readily available, the landlord can ask one of the tenants.

The landlord or tenant could acquire the information for the market survey by posing as a prospective tenant, but most landlords, property managers, and leasing agents are willing to share their information. One way to elicit market information from a competitor is for landlords to share specific rental information about their own property. Landlords should be prepared to discuss briefly the size of their building, its location, rental information, and vacancies. They should explain the asking rate and deal-making rate and the concessions necessary to make a deal. For instance: "My building is asking $25.50 per square foot, but we will make a deal at $24 with one month free rent for each year of the lease." Although private information about the property or its tenants is never to be shared, obtaining the deal-making rates is essential. If only the asking rates are requested, the survey data will be distorted, and the conclusion may be incorrect.

Free rent, tenant improvement allowances, and unusual concessions such as moving allowances affect the face rate that is charged. Tenant charges also affect the rental rate. Are the office building operating expenses established from a *base year*? If so, what is the base year? Is a stop clause used? If so, what is the dollar amount of the expense stop? If the property is a shopping center, what are the charges for CAM costs, real estate taxes, insurance, and marketing fund dues? Does the industrial property have a base-year operating expense charge or triple-net pass-through expenses?

The final information to obtain is the vacancy rate or the amount of vacant square footage. For some properties, this information can be obtained by walking the property and examining the vacant space. For instance, in a shopping center the frontage and the side of a vacant space can be paced off to determine its size. For others, such as office buildings, the information must be provided by the landlord, property manager, or leasing agent.

Additional sources of information can be consulted in developing a market survey. Most major commercial brokerage firms produce quarterly or annual market surveys that they release to newspapers and industry journals. The leading commercial brokerage firms often hold annual breakfast or luncheon meetings to report on the market in their areas. Several Institute of Real Estate Management (IREM) chapters around the country hold market forecast mini-seminars. The real estate or business sections of local business magazines and newspapers frequently report on the real estate market.

Applying Survey Information

Market research is a dynamic and evolving process that establishes the understanding from which professionals make informed decisions and forecast into the future. After all the market information has been obtained and entered into the market survey form, the landlord can compare the subject property with the competition, determine the property's position in the market, establish its market rental rates and concessions (if necessary), price each space accordingly, and project the property's lease-up. When competitive properties are compared to the subject property, the analysis produces the market rent and terms, leasing targets, and major work, if any, to be done on the property to make it more competitive.

The tenant can gather similar information and conclusions by conducting a market survey. This is valuable information for selecting buildings as possible business locations and negotiating a lease or a lease renewal.

THE MARKET SURVEY AND PROPERTY TYPES

As well as analyzing the overall financial markets and the *macromarkets,* landlords conduct portions of the market study that are tailored to their specific property type. The subject property's micromarket or trade area is analyzed by evaluating the competition. The economic condition of the area, growth or lack thereof, competition, and alternative buildings with similar available space must be considered for each type of property, as outlined in the sections below.

The Shopping Center Market Survey

The shopping center market survey is more complex than the market survey for any other property type. To begin with, it must consider the economic conditions of the trade area to determine if the area is dependent on a single industry (e.g., the auto or aerospace industry) and determine the economic health of the trade area. The survey must also consider the region in which the shopping center operates to understand its macro environment. And, in addition to all of the other items that should be considered, the retail property landlord looks at the sales figures of the property's existing tenants to evaluate the rental rate potential for the shopping center. The tenant does not have access to the shopping center's sales figures, but a retailer can inquire after other retailers concerning their performance.

The landlord and tenant also pay close attention to vacancy factors in the local market and what they mean to the landlord's property. Is the vacancy factor increasing or decreasing? Have vacancies been on the market for a long period of time, or do they lease up quickly? Are rents and terms increasing or decreasing, and what does that mean for the subject property? Are there any new shopping centers being proposed for the trade area that will impact existing properties?

The size of the trade area being surveyed will vary based on the type of shopping center or retail property and its location. In downtown New York or San Francisco, the trade area for a retail property may be only a few blocks. The neighborhood shopping center landlord, on the other hand, looks at other neighborhood shopping centers within a two- to five-mile area.

Each size and type of shopping center operates in a unique market that defines the likely customers for that shopping center as well as their buying strength. The shopping center landlord must consider who the competition is and where they are located in relation to the subject property. It is helpful to understand the typical trade areas for various types of shopping centers before discussing the market survey, and so the customer draw for each is discussed below.

The Convenience Shopping Center.   The convenience shopping center is typically a very small shopping center of 5,000 to 30,000 square feet, possibly anchored by a convenience market plus several small local stores providing services or goods to the immediate area. Its draw can be from only a few blocks to one or two miles.

The Neighborhood Shopping Center.   The neighborhood shopping center is typically anchored by a supermarket and/or drug store. In the past it provided mostly services, but in recent years has been occupied by apparel stores, shoe stores, etc. to serve the needs of the busy workingwoman. This type of shopping center is typically between 30,000 and 150,000 square feet, and its drawing range is from 2.5 to five miles depending on the location of other neighborhood shopping centers.

The Community Shopping Center.   Generally, the community shopping center is anchored by a junior department store, discount stores, and specialty stores, and may include a supermarket and/or drugstore as well as a good assortment of fashion stores drawn by the anchor. This type of shopping center will also have a good range of services, and typically ranges from 150,000 to 400,000 square feet. It will draw from about two to seven miles, again depending on where the competition is located.

The Regional Mall.   The regional mall is generally anchored by two or more department stores; has a tenant mix of fashion stores, jewelry and gift stores, limited service tenants, and restaurants; and often includes a movie theater. The main themes are fashion and the "full shopping experience." This type of mall ranges between about 700,000 and one million square feet, and draws traffic from five to seven miles depending on the location of competitive malls. The original regional malls were built as open-air shopping centers. Later they were almost exclusively enclosed, but since the late 1990s the development of open-air malls has been revived.

The Super-Regional Mall. These malls are generally anchored by at least three and as many as seven department stores. Super-regional malls have a very broad mix of fashion, jewelry, gifts, and entertainment, a good selection of restaurants, and a high level of ambience. These malls are one million square feet or more, and draw from seven miles up to 25 miles depending on the competition. In rural areas the trade area for regional and super-regional malls can include an entire county and even most of the state.

The Specialty Shopping Center. The specialty shopping center can easily be confused with entertainment and lifestyle shopping centers, but there is a distinct difference. The specialty shopping center draws a wide range of customers, but often is anchored with restaurants, specialty shops (such as apparel and gift shops), and galleries that appeal specifically to the tourist. Property of this nature often features "experience" in the form of entertainment and physical amenities—lush landscaping, carousels, fountains, and outdoor dining and gathering places.

The Lifestyle Shopping Center. The lifestyle shopping center was first developed in the early 1990s but is one of the fastest-growing types of shopping centers. Originally, lifestyle shopping centers had no traditional anchors (e.g., a department store or an upscale supermarket); rather, the shopping center itself, its upscale tenant mix, and its ambience were the major draw. The "second generation" of lifestyle shopping centers added department stores and upscale grocery stores to their tenant mix.

The lifestyle shopping center has many larger national book and apparel stores, upscale national and local apparel stores, jewelers, home decorator shops, kitchen shops, shoe stores, and sit-down restaurants. It is an open-air shopping center, with a very high level of ambience that emulates the town square of times gone by. The lifestyle shopping center is generally found in more affluent areas and will draw from upwards of 20 miles.

The Entertainment Center. Entertainment centers have similarities to lifestyle shopping centers, but they have an added element of entertainment—theaters, game rooms, live theater, and IMAX theaters. They may not have the upscale elements of a lifestyle shopping center. It is sometimes hard to distinguish between an entertainment center and a lifestyle center. The draw for an entertainment center is much like that of a lifestyle center: around 20 miles, depending on where the next competitive shopping center is located.

The Outlet Shopping Center. The outlet shopping center was one of the dominant shopping centers developed in the 1980s and early 1990s. The tenant mix of outlet shopping centers now includes upscale merchants.

The Power Shopping Center. The power shopping center comprises mainly large box stores, such as Lowe's, Best Buy, Circuit City, Marshalls, Kohl's, and any other large, price-conscious merchants. It has limited small shop space. This type of shopping center is often found on the outskirts of a major city, and will draw from upward of 25 to 30 miles depending on where the next one is located.

The Office and Medical Office Building Market Survey

The survey for office and medical office buildings encompasses all of the general market survey items mentioned above. As with all other types of properties, the landlords of these properties try to find out what buildings are being proposed in the area and to determine what such development may mean to their building. Yet competition in office and medical office buildings is much different than in shopping centers, and this is reflected in the market survey. The tenant for these buildings is interested in current rents and market conditions.

The Office Building Market Survey. Generally, office buildings will compete within their class and their specific area of town, generally referred to as the *micromarket*. For example, downtown Class A buildings generally compete with other downtown Class A buildings. These lines of competition are not all that clear, however, because the lower end of one class of office buildings can easily compete with the upper end of the next class (e.g., the lower end of Class A buildings competing with the upper end of Class B buildings).

If the rents and terms of a Class A building are dropped to that of a Class B building, the two quickly become direct competition and market rents are lowered for both classifications of buildings. This often occurs when the market is soft and rents are declining for one or more classifications of buildings with rents and terms that are very competitive with the next class of building. The market survey examines the subject building's location relative to the competition, architecture, parking availability, management, billback charges, and building features and amenities.

Another area of the micromarket that the landlord and tenant should try to understand is that of the sublet market. Quite often, especially in difficult markets, the sublet market is quite active and can be tough competition for the landlord trying to lease space at market rates. Tenants with financial troubles may well sublet their space (at lower rents) to relieve themselves of the burden of all or a portion of the rent and other charges, and this may provide direct competition for landlords in the area, providing a great opportunity for tenants to lease space below the market rate.

Office Building Absorption Rates.   The office building market is also analyzed on the basis of *absorption rates.* While the market survey must cover many other aspects of the market, the area of absorption rates is an important one. Absorption rates affect the market and rental rates.

If a market would have two million square feet of office space available, and in the previous year 500,000 square feet had been absorbed (leased), that market would be said to have a three-year supply remaining if nothing else changes. A three-year supply is a lot of space to lease up, so it would not be likely that any new buildings would enter the market unless they were already in development and it was not practical to stop the development process. On the other hand, if there were a 1-million-square-foot supply and in the last year 850,000 square feet had been leased, it would likely be a landlord's market and developers would be looking to add space.

The office building landlord examines absorption rates for the relevant micromarkets to see how much space has been leased in the last quarter and in the last year. That amount is then compared to the amount of space available in the entire market to determine if space is leasing at a faster or slower rate in the micromarket. This will let the landlord know how many years of inventory are available in that particular market at any given time.

Absorption rates do not apply to retail space, although one might hear them quoted as a factor in the market. Shopping center space is much different than office space in that the demand is created by the buying power of the public. A market could well be saturated with mall space and still have a need for a supermarket-anchored neighborhood shopping center. Likewise, a lifestyle shopping center that is strategically located may thrive in a market that is already saturated with shopping center space but ready for a new and exciting shopping venue.

The Medical Office Building Market Survey.   The market survey for a medical office building is similar to that for a traditional office building. However, there are some differences that are worth noting. Because medical office buildings are so specialized, the landlord should first determine the overall demand for medical office space in a particular micromarket. This will reveal if there is still unmet demand or if the market is already saturated.

The status and location of existing space is a central issue for medical office buildings. If that space is old and unattractive, or is poorly located, it will not attract medical professionals who prefer newer medical office buildings that are close to a hospital. Proximity to hospitals is critical for many medical specialties. Newer medical office buildings provide the opportunity to meet the most current technology demands of the medical profession while, most likely, offering more attractive, efficient space in the process.

The Industrial Building Market Survey

Industrial building tenants are interested in such things as the size of a building, its location, the area's labor market, and truck, shipping, rail, and air transportation. They care about housing availability and its cost for their employees, and these elements should be reflected in the landlord's market survey for industrial buildings. Industrial tenants will also be interested in the workforce union situation and "right to work" issues. Local taxation on goods in process will be of interest to manufacturers, as will the attitude of the local community towards industrial uses in and around the area. These are critical factors for industrial tenants selecting where to locate their business.

THE TENANT'S MARKET SURVEY ISSUES

Market surveys are helpful for tenants as well as landlords. The survey information that is gathered informs tenants about what is available and how it best suits their specific needs. The tenant uses the same sort of information as does the landlord, and will also want to understand the building's trade area or *micromarket*. Tenants will use this market information to understand what options may be available and which locations may be best for their business.

It is as important for the tenant to do a market survey as it is for the landlord. A tenant may lease a space because the rent and terms appear to be attractive, only to find out that the space was below market for any number of negative reasons. The building may be old, maintenance may be poor, management may not be responsive, the area may be declining, and so forth. The more tenants know about a prospective area, the better they can make the best decision about where to locate to maximize their operations and profits.

The astute tenant wants to know everything that the landlord wants to know, but usually has the disadvantage of not being in the real estate business and not being familiar with conducting market surveys. Large retail chains and anchor stores often conduct market surveys using in-house personnel or brokers, and assemble excellent market information. Smaller tenants and even some chains may use outside consultants who specialize in the retail market survey. A good market survey provides invaluable information for negotiating a lease, but it is not a tool to which smaller merchants commonly have access.

Obviously, rent and terms are a major consideration for all tenants. In addition, they want to find out as much as possible about a prospective landlord from the survey. Tenants do not want to get involved in a property if the landlord will have a difficult time leasing up the space or keeping the building properly maintained. For example, anchor tenants are typically very careful about going into new developments, and are concerned with the developer's reputation, relevant experience, and ability to complete the development. A prospective tenant should look at the proposed management structure to be sure that those involved are experienced and responsive to tenant needs, and should not hesitate to talk with existing tenants to see if they are satisfied with the management team.

Shopping center tenants look to the tenant mix to be sure that the traffic generated within a shopping center will support their business. Discount merchants will not want to be in a higher-end shopping center, and vice versa. Tenants usually produce a *pro forma* to determine their likely sales, and then evaluate those sales against the rent and charges for a particular shopping center.

An office building tenant typically has a bit more flexibility, since one specific office location is generally not that much better than another. There are exceptions: Some office buildings have a theme to their tenant mix, being tenanted mainly by lawyers, or by publishers, or by insurance companies, etc. But other than those specialized buildings, most buildings within the same general area and building classification will meet the tenant's needs. So the tenant focuses on finding an attractive and convenient building, competitive rent and terms, and responsive management.

A medical office building tenant, on the other hand, will be interested in modern technology, proximity to a hospital, the availability of other specialists and services (such as a pharmacy), potential referrals from other medical professionals in the building, and the convenience of the building for that tenant's particular needs. Management of a medical building is a specialty, and the astute tenant prospect will investigate the landlord's experience with and understanding of such buildings.

The market survey for an industrial tenant will focus on location— including proximity to transportation—and a compatible labor pool. If the tenant needs a highly specialized building, there may be only one or two in the market. Tenants may need a build-to-suit building in order to meet their needs.

USING THE MARKET SURVEY
TO ESTABLISH RENTS

A market survey is used to determine the overall rental rate for a specific building and to evaluate and price the various spaces in the building according to each space size, desirability, location, and sometimes the type of tenant for the space. The methodology is different for each type of property.

Shopping Center Rents

Anchor tenant rents are almost always based on the value of the building, the value of the land, and a modest return on that cost. If the tenant is highly desired, the landlord may offer the tenant very favorable terms and hope to increase rents for other spaces as a result of the traffic draw of that tenant. Many retailers are attracted to a shopping center by the anchor tenant or other strong and popular retailers.

In a neighborhood shopping center, rents are often the highest for spaces immediately adjacent to the anchor store entrances and for end-cap spaces. These tenants have the highest natural traffic past their doors and excellent visibility, and they pay a premium for that location. Very small shops, between 500 and 1,000 square feet, will pay a premium because they are more expensive to build per square foot and generally tend to be well located. Shops that do not face the same street as the anchors are likely to command a lesser rent and also have higher turnover. Pad and outlot tenants will pay a premium because of their prominent location within the shopping center, and those rents can easily be double that of a typical in-line space.

Regional and super-regional malls have a slightly different pattern, but the theory is the same. The anchor tenants may well own their spaces, or they may pay minimal rent. Stores immediately adjacent to the anchors and close to major entrances, as well as small stores located on and near the central court, pay a premium. Food court tenants pay some of the highest rental rates, but also tend to generate some of the highest sales per square foot.

High-volume, recognized national tenants will generally get better rental rates than less successful and local merchants with similar uses. This applies unless a local merchant has a recognized draw in the marketplace. Tenants in all other shop spaces will pay approximately the average rental rate for the shopping center, with some adjustments for store size and location.

Office Building Rents

Office building rents are a little easier to understand and set than are shopping center rents. For the most part, office space within smaller buildings is pretty much equal; but there are some exceptions. Full-floor tenants generally get a better rate than other tenants, as do those who lease multiple floors. And there may be basement office space that goes for a lower rate.

For an office building in the downtown retail core of a city, the ground floor is generally the most expensive space in the building. Additionally, any floor or portion of a floor with a good view will bring a higher rent. In mid- and high-rise buildings, rents are often priced per floor or per every five floors: the higher the floor, the higher the rent. Penthouse space is almost always leased at a premium rent. Any office building with a decent view from the penthouse floor will be able to command a top rent for that location, and sometimes is leased to a restaurant.

The Office Building Sublet Market

Landlords in the office market do their best to minimize sublet space in their buildings for many reasons. The main reason is that landlords do not want existing tenants competing with them in the leasing of space. They do not want tenants profiting from the landlord's real estate. The sublet market is a difficult one to track, but it is important for the landlord to know what is happening in that market and to realize that space may be available in the landlord's own building at rates below those being quoted by the building's leasing agents. The availability of sublet space will have a negative impact on the absorption rates in a given market and give the appearance of a weaker market than what really exists.

A strong sublet market comes about in one of two ways. The most common is a recession in which tenants must divest themselves of expenses, one method of which is to sublet space. The other way that strong sublet markets come about is that, in a very strong office market with rising rents, many tenants perceive an opportunity to move to cheaper locations and sublet their existing space for a profit. Landlords will want to include a *right to recapture provision* in tenants' leases. Tenants, on the other hand, will resist that language, feeling that they have taken on the obligation for the space and that the landlord loses nothing if they profit from it.

An astute tenant can benefit from the sublet market. Sublet rent is generally lower than market rent, and quite often the space is already fully built out and ready for move-in. The main issue that a tenant faces in the sublet market is that of the lease term. One who sublets is often limited to the time left on the original tenant's lease, not knowing if the lease will be renewed. However, sublet tenants may well be taking space that would go vacant if they were not available to take it over, so they are not without a strong negotiating position for an extension, especially if the leasing market is not strong.

Industrial Building Rents

More often than not, industrial space is turned over to the tenant as a raw shell and the tenant provides the improvements. The pro forma rent for this space when it is developed is based on the cost of the shell plus the land and site improvements, as well as a reasonable market return on that space, subject to the micromarket rents in the area. If the space has improvements, those costs are included in determining the rent. The rent the landlord is able to achieve is the market rent, regardless of the cost to build the building and improvements. Incubator space is a little more expensive to build and has higher rents. In a *planned unit development (PUD),* those spaces that are the closest to transportation and services will require a higher rental rate, and those with fewer conveniences will rent at a lower rate. Because very large industrial buildings are less expensive to build, rents in these buildings tend to be less per square foot.

LEASING IN A LANDLORD'S MARKET

As mentioned in the beginning of this chapter, a *landlord's market* is one in which demand is stronger than supply, vacancies are few, and rents are rising. These markets come in cycles and are often reflective of the overall economic conditions in the country as well as the immediate area. The other side of the landlord's market is the *tenant's market,* in which vacancies are fairly high, supply exceeds demand, and rents are either falling or staying flat or level.

Landlords want to lease as much space as possible during an "up" market, and to sign tenants up for longer-term leases to lock in the good rent and terms. During this type of market, landlords are likely to test the market with higher quoted rents on each new lease to see where the market will "top out." The landlord is less likely to grant concessions during this type of market and will most likely be a little more particular concerning the financial strength of each tenant prospect.

Landlords may take the opportunity of a strong market to provide a higher level of finish for all types of commercial properties with a commensurate return on investment (ROI), thereby increasing the value of these buildings. Both parties can benefit from such an approach. In a landlord's market, there is no free rent and the asking rent is often the deal-making rent.

Occasionally, a retail tenant is in a position to negotiate a lease on very favorable terms. The landlord may give a retail tenant who generates excellent sales and traffic a lower minimum rent as an inducement to enter into a lease. These types of deal most often require the tenant to pay for CAM charges.

LEASING IN A TENANT'S MARKET

Given the cyclical nature of the commercial real estate market, there will be times when the market favors the tenants. Generally, the cycles change slowly and the market evolves from a strong landlord's market to a strong tenant's market over a period of five to ten years.

In a tenant's market, the tenant is in a very good negotiating position. Landlords have vacant space and few prospects. They often start offering incentives to prospective tenants. These incentives may be free rent, overstandard improvements, moving expenses paid by the landlord, and, in an extreme situation, buying out the tenant's existing lease (if the move is from one building to another).

Additionally, landlords are likely to offer incentives to the brokerage community to get the attention of leasing agents. It is not unusual for a landlord to offer a double commission to lease space in a weak market or in a building with leasing problems.

During the tenant's market, tenants should shop carefully to find the best deal in the marketplace that still meets most of their needs. A bargain is not a bargain if the tenant gives up too much in the way of location, building standards, convenience, or image just for lower rent. The tenant should consider a longer-term lease at this time to lock in the lower rental rates and good lease terms. One of the major considerations for the tenant under these circumstances is that of flexibility. Tenants may prefer a shorter lease term for the flexibility to relocate as their business space and location needs change. The final decision will be a tradeoff, with attractive long-term rental rates weighing against future conveniences and flexibility.

The concession preferred by tenants varies with each tenant's specific situation. Some tenants prefer free rent, some want a lower rent over the term of the lease, and still others prefer elaborate tenant improvements (TIs).

Tenants will also ask for options at favorable terms in a tenant's market. Instead of taking a five-year lease with no options, a tenant may ask for a three-year lease with two three-year options and a fixed rent. This is designed to secure the best terms possible and still have the ability to get out of the lease if the tenant's space needs change or if another location is best for the tenant.

In a tenant's market, office tenants often negotiate moving costs, including the cost of new business cards, stationery, phone systems, etc. Any cost that the tenant will be faced with for relocation is fair game for negotiations.

By studying the market, landlords and tenants have a better chance of negotiating the best possible lease deal. If both the landlord and the tenant are sincere about entering into a lease with one another, and both are fully aware of the market conditions, it is likely they will be able to reach a deal that will be a win-win situation.

7

Tenants Maximizing
Their Potential in
Commercial Properties

This chapter is designed to present issues mainly from the tenant's perspective. It explains how tenants can maximize business, which also indirectly (and sometimes directly) benefits their landlord.

The landlord–tenant relationship should never be an adversarial one. If the landlord and tenant each want what is best for themselves, then they want what is best for the other party. Of course, each will do his or her best to maximize the economic terms of any lease arrangement or to protect his or her own interests in problems that may arise, but both should be looking for the "win-win" solutions to problems and their overall relationship.

In order to maximize the benefits of the landlord–tenant relationship, the tenant should approach it as partnering with the landlord to improve one another's business. This is why it should be clear that, although this chapter concentrates on the tenant's ability to maximize his or her own potential in the relationship, the landlord will be doing the same and trying to make sure that the tenant is thriving.

The very first step in a good landlord–tenant relationship is having a positive attitude from the outset. The tenant should enter into negotiations for a new space with the thought that the landlord and the tenant should work together to contribute to each other's success. Naturally, the landlord should adopt a similarly positive attitude with any new tenant.

A good relationship starts with the tenant asking questions. In any negotiation, both parties have the ability to walk away if their leasing objectives are not met. Even when problems arise during the negotiating process and lease preparation, the landlord and the tenant should give each other the benefit of the doubt that any misunderstanding can be resolved. Any item in question should be pursued as an error or mistake rather than as a deliberate misinforming or an attempt to take advantage of the tenant. Once again, landlords should also be displaying this same charitable attitude during the negotiations.

The more informed tenants are about selecting a location and operating their business in that location, the greater the likelihood those tenants will meet or exceed their business plans. Different types of commercial properties require different information, which will be discussed in the context of each property type below.

THE RETAIL TENANT

There are several key elements that a retail tenant must consider in order to maximize profits and maintain a positive landlord–tenant relationship.

Location and Tenant Mix

The retail tenant has many issues to resolve when locating and negotiating a lease in the right location. Retailers' first priority is finding the best location for their product and services. There are several issues retailers must consider when determining which shopping center or retail location will be best for their business.

The type and design of the shopping center also must be consistent with the retail tenant's operation. The image of the off-price or outlet merchant is one of organization, depth of merchandise, and reasonable prices. Such tenants desire a well-designed and -maintained shopping center, but they do not want fancy and complicated architecture. One of their concerns is their occupancy cost, and an elaborate shopping center costs more to build, has higher rents, and costs more to operate. On the other hand, a high-end merchant does not want a sterile, unattractive shopping center as its setting. The design must be consistent with the tenant's desired image.

Retail tenants need to have a complete understanding of who their customers are and how that relates to a given shopping center or retail location. A good shopping center for a retailer may be one in which the tenant is the only one offering a specific line of merchandise or performing a certain service. Or the tenant may prefer to be one of several merchants selling the same type of merchandise: Fashion stores often like other fashion stores as co-tenants. Shoe stores prefer to be located by other shoe tenants. And specialty food stores—except for supermarkets—most often like other food stores as co-tenants. The tenant must be able to determine the best mix for the success of his or her business.

Additionally, the tenant's location within the shopping center may be a very important factor. The astute tenant often wants to be positioned between anchor tenants to maximize foot traffic. However, these spaces accordingly tend to have higher asking rents than spaces around the side of the shopping center. And it is important to keep in mind that a small shop right at the entry point of the shopping center, even if it is not between the anchors, may well be the shopping center's best location. In a mall setting, most tenants want to be near an anchor with merchandise that will attract their same customer base, while also being near similar merchandise stores for easy cross-shopping. Tenants should generally avoid storefronts that face the side of a shopping center or are located down a blind hallway unless they do not need visibility and traffic flow. These locations generally have much lower rents, but that is because they are much less desirable.

Tenants should also be aware of their potential neighbors, and would be wise to pass on a location with neighboring businesses that do not complement their business and attract similar customers. It is not likely that a landlord will grant a tenant the right to approve his or her neighbors, so the tenant should do as much research as possible concerning all existing and potential neighbors. For example, any *pad space* or *outlot* locations that are reserved for future construction may eventually limit or destroy the tenant's visibility from the parking lot or street. Certain neighboring tenants may be noisy, such as a karate studio, dance studio, or sports bar. Other stores may emit odors detrimental to the tenant's business. Nail and hair salons, veterinarians, and pet shops often deal with odor problems, but these usually can be resolved with adequate ventilation. Even some food operations emit odors that are not conducive to high-end jewelers or fashion stores.

Marketing Efforts

Signage must be adequate and visible for the retail tenant. Restrictive signage can inhibit a tenant's sales, and may be an adequate reason to reject a location. Newer shopping centers tend to have much more limited signage allowances than those of the past. It is possible that a competitive shopping center down the street has a 30-foot-high pylon sign with many tenants listed on it while a proposed shopping center has no such sign. A general rule of thumb is that the tenant must be able to put up adequate signage for customers to find the store. People in the shopping center's other stores should be able to see all the tenants' signs, prompting them to return to shop there.

The astute tenant will also ask about the requirements of *marketing funds.* Enclosed malls, lifestyle centers, outlet malls, and specialty shopping centers typically have a marketing fund to promote and market the shopping center and its tenants. Most merchants will have their own marketing efforts, but the shopping center is likely to be stronger if it also has a collective marketing effort.

In past years, the merchants' association was the most common marketing format for shopping centers. All shopping center merchants were required to join the association and pay dues at a prescribed rate; and the landlord would contribute 20 to 25 percent of the budget and oversee the shopping center's marketing effort. This method was not very effective because many merchants had different needs regarding marketing, making it difficult to get them all to agree on one approach. Merchant meetings often were not effective. Very few shopping centers still use the merchants' association approach today, but there are a few that remain in older shopping centers.

The most effective marketing effort for shopping centers today is the marketing fund. With this approach, each merchant is required to contribute to the fund and the landlord administers the program. Quite often landlords will name an advisory committee to discuss marketing plans and make recommendations, but those merchants do not have a vote in the final outcome. The landlord may make a financial contribution, but the fund is operated by the landlord on behalf of the tenants. National retailers prefer the marketing fund over the merchants' association because it is professionally operated by trained shopping center marketing personnel, and their store managers do not have to spend time serving on committees or as an officer of the merchants' association.

One exception to the marketing fund's contribution requirements is that anchor tenants generally do not contribute to the shopping center's marketing efforts. This is because they have very expensive and effective marketing programs of their own, and it is very difficult to coordinate those chain-wide efforts with each shopping center in which they are located.

However, anchor tenants do advertise heavily and thus draw the bulk of traffic to the shopping center, making it attractive for the smaller shops to locate there. As long as these anchor tenants are generating good sales volume and promoting the other stores in the shopping center, they are an asset to all involved and should not be criticized because their lease arrangements appear to be more favorable.

If there is a marketing fund, each merchant will do well to be as involved as possible and to help guide the program towards advertising efforts that will benefit his or her own business as well as the center. Even if the merchant has his or her own marketing program, every effort should be made to work and cooperate with the landlord-sponsored efforts. In order to maximize these efforts, it is incumbent upon the landlord to present the shopping center's marketing plans well in advance so tenants can properly plan and coordinate their efforts. Merchants who do not cooperate with the landlord's overall marketing efforts quickly appear uncooperative and seem to have no interest in what the landlord is trying to do—market the shopping center to the benefit of all the tenants. The shopping center's marketing director will appreciate suggestions to improve the marketing efforts.

Common Area Charges

The operations of a shopping center are complex and expensive. It is a good idea for the landlord to send an explanatory letter to every new tenant, elucidating the charges and how they are calculated. The tenant should be given a complete explanation of the common area expenses and how they will be billed within the shopping center. While a good explanation of the charges from the landlord is essential to a good negotiation, the tenant is well served to seek counsel from an outside expert to determine if the common area maintenance (CAM) charges are similar to those of other shopping centers and the CAM lease provision is fair to the tenant. (CAM and other pass-through charges are discussed in more detail in Chapter 12, "Negotiating the Lease.")

If at any point tenants feel they have not been properly billed or that there are errors in the CAM or other pass-through charges, those tenants should go directly to their landlord (or the landlord's property manager) for clarification. A polite question will almost always be met with a reasonable response. Tenants are entitled to an explanation of the charges and how they were calculated, and a polite but persistent approach will usually elicit the desired result.

Rules and Regulations

Complying with the rules and regulations of the shopping center will go a long way towards maintaining a good landlord–tenant relationship. *Rules and regulations* are considered an evolving document, and are attached to the lease. Some shopping center landlords incorporate the rules and regulations within the lease provisions. Abiding by the lease provisions prevents conflicts with the landlord. Often, those who do not comply are local store managers and small tenants who either are not familiar with the lease or don't understand the importance of complying (or the ramifications of not complying) with the lease.

All of the lease provisions, rules, and regulations are there to ensure that the shopping center is operated effectively and efficiently for the benefit of all the tenants. If a tenant parks his or her car right in front of the store, other tenants may feel they should be able to do the same. When this occurs, the best customer parking stalls are eliminated. If one tenant puts up paper advertising signs in the windows, other merchants feel they should also be able to put up similar signs. These paper signs give the shopping center a disorderly appearance. These situations then become a management problem for the landlord, and tenants who violate the lease provisions are looked at in disfavor by the landlord. This may be taken into consideration when the tenant's lease is up for renewal.

Reminding other tenants of the need to follow the rules can be a big help to everyone involved. Some tenants want to impress and please other tenants more than they want to please the landlord.

Managing Disputes

Every merchant should show a positive attitude to the shopping public, fellow merchants, and the shopping center's management. When a tenant has a legitimate problem with the landlord, it should be discussed in private with the management of the shopping center rather than with a group of disgruntled merchants. Conversely, if the landlord has an issue with a tenant, it also should be discussed in private with that tenant. Obviously, if an unfavorable situation persists and management does not appear to be working on it, or has no interest in resolving the problem, then the tenant should go directly to the landlord.

Working Together

Finally, each tenant in a shopping center can have an impact on the other tenants and the shopping center as a whole. A shopping center is like a department store to the public. Each department or tenant brings customers to the department store or shopping center, and an opportunity exists for cross-shopping within the department store or within the shopping center. Conversely, if one tenant fails to open on time and a customer comes running into the shopping center on the way to work only to find that shop closed, the customer will likely have a poor image of the shopping center. If a store is poorly stocked or the display is always dusty, or the clerks are rude or (worse yet!) almost nonexistent, this will reflect on the image of the shopping center as a whole. It is incumbent upon all tenants to make sure their store is maintained at a high level to reflect positively on the whole shopping center and to make the shopping experience a good one for every customer. The beauty of this approach is that it is also good for the tenants' businesses.

Merchants should make every effort to maximize their sales. While that may seem to be an obvious goal for all merchants, there may be opportunities cooperating with the shopping center management, coordinating sales and promotions with the shopping center's marketing director, anchor tenant and other tenants that are overlooked.

It is helpful for good relations to be established throughout a shopping center. The tenant should make sure to get to know the shopping center manager, and, if there are any on-site personnel, the accounting personnel, marketing staff, and other individuals involved in the operations of the shopping center. This is not to say that the tenant must go to lunch with the staff or have coffee with them on a regular basis, but keeping in touch and sharing problems, concerns, and, yes, even successes will go a long way towards maintaining a positive and cooperative landlord–tenant relationship.

It is also helpful for the merchant to get to know the managers of the anchor stores. These managers are almost always willing to share their marketing calendar with interested smaller merchants in order to coordinate their advertising and maximize their sales. It will also improve relationships within the shopping center if anchor store managers are aware that other employees, managers, and owners of other shops are shopping at their stores.

A successful merchant consistently looks for ways to cross-merchandise with other merchants in the shopping center. Often the landlord can help to facilitate this cross-merchandising by making suggestions to the tenants involved. There are unlimited opportunities to cross-merchandise with other stores. A dress store can set up a display in a shoe store and vice versa. A men's wear store can exchange displays with a sporting goods store and a music store can exchange displays with a bookstore. There is no end to the cross-merchandising that can be accomplished in a shopping center when most—if not all—of the merchants are working together.

Vacancies hurt everyone involved in a shopping center, and so the astute merchant will be on the lookout for merchants to fill vacancies within the shopping center. Existing merchants want the cross-traffic generated by all of the other shops in the shopping center. If vacancies persist, customers may feel that the shopping center is not doing well, and tenant prospects will wonder why a space has been vacant for so long. Landlords cannot pay a commission to an unlicensed entity (i.e., most merchants), but most landlords will show their appreciation for a successful referral. Even if the landlord does not demonstrate gratitude, the tenant will benefit from helping to fill a vacancy in the shopping center with a merchant who will advertise and attract shoppers and contributing to the shopping center's success.

Customers like to shop in a successful atmosphere, and merchants like to "stay and play" in a flourishing environment. The goal of the tenants and the shopping center management should be to maximize every tenant's sales and have each tenant paying percentage rent in addition to the minimum rent. When this happens the tenants' sales are exceptional, the stores are very profitable, and the landlord generates additional income. There is no better win-win situation in a shopping center, mall, or other type of retail property.

THE OFFICE OR MEDICAL OFFICE
BUILDING TENANT

The office or medical office building tenant searches for a location that meets one or several important issues—not necessarily the location with the lowest rent. Proximity to one's home or one's business base is a strong incentive for choosing a specific location. Co-tenants who are likely to do cross-business or provide referrals are also a strong incentive.

Generating Business from Other Tenants

To improve relations in the building, many office and medical office buildings have events during some of the holiday seasons, and some have events two to three times a year with no holiday involved. These gatherings are meant to provide an opportunity for everyone to get to know everyone else in the building, enabling them to work together for a better building. Each tenant should make a point of getting involved in these programs and in working with management to make them as successful as possible. The more the tenants get to know each other, the more likely there can be cross-business.

If the landlord does not create a building directory, a tenant in the building should put together a list of each tenant in the building and what they do, and distribute it to each business to encourage cross-business. Some tenants may opt out of such a directory, but most would be happy to know what others do and to circulate their own information.

Being the Best Possible Tenant

Once the lease has been agreed upon, the tenant should make every effort to understand and comply fully with all the building's rules and regulations. In an office or medical office building setting, a tenant who does not follow the rules of the building or does not pay the rent on time may be considered a problem tenant. A tenant who parks in customer parking or leaves trash in the hallways also will be considered a problem tenant by building management. This could have a negative impact on landlord–tenant relationship during the lease term and especially at lease renewal time.

If someone on the building staff is not performing up to standards, the issue should be brought to the building's management's attention. However, this should be done in a polite and proactive manner rather than through accusations or frustration. The tenant should make a point of meeting and maintaining an open dialog with the property manager, engineer, security chief, maintenance chief, and all the building's staff. The tenant should also have a designated employee who is the point of contact with building management and who the building management can count on to communicate and cooperate in solving any mutual problems during the lease term.

Resolving Conflicts

As mentioned above, it is a good idea for tenants to get to know the others in their building and to establish a dialog with them. It is much easier to resolve a problem with an adjacent tenant if one begins the discussion on good terms. Noise, trash, and parking problems can usually be resolved easily if the parties involved sit down and "chat" about the situation. If this approach does not work, the next step is for the tenant to talk to the building manager. The best approach, however, is for the tenant to talk with the other party to see if they can resolve the issue on their own. If they cannot, *then* going to management makes sense.

There is usually an opportunity for medical professionals to provide and receive referrals from other medical professionals in the building. The medical community is a closer community than the general business community, so a medical professional may already know some of the other professionals in the building. Medical professionals and their office manager should introduce themselves to the other tenants in the medical office building. The building's property manager may be able to assist in providing these introductions. The office manager should get to know the building's property manager and staff, for there will be many times when the office manager needs the assistance of the building staff for maintenance and other issues. The building's property manager needs to be aware of the special needs of the tenants' patients. The office manager should have a working knowledge of the lease and the building's rules and regulations so issues that arise can be discussed and resolved quickly.

THE INDUSTRIAL TENANT

Depending on the size of the industrial building or park, industrial tenants may be able to develop cross-business and referrals from the other tenants. It is best for each tenant to get to know the other tenants and discuss each other's business and type of customers. Industrial buildings are considered the least complicated type of building to manage. However, there are a few issues the landlord and tenants may need to work on together to assist the tenants with their operations while maintaining the overall operations of the industrial park.

The industrial property tenant is generally much more interested in the function of the building than in its aesthetics. Industrial tenants usually do not have scores of customers visiting them on a daily basis, so their concerns are usually centered on the most efficient means to operate within their premises. In attempting to operate as efficiently as possible, a unique set of problems may arise. Exterior storage can become a problem with industrial tenants and should be avoided unless the landlord's complete approval has been obtained in advance. Where trucks are parked and for how long can be an issue with neighboring tenants and the building's property management.

These and any other issues that can create conflicts should be discussed during lease negotiations. If issues that can cause difficulty between the tenant and the landlord are not anticipated until after the lease is executed or after the tenant opens for business, they should be discussed as soon as possible with the building's property manager. If problems do arise, as with other property types, an established line of positive communication between the tenant and landlord will lead to a resolution of the issue.

THE MIXED-USE DEVELOPMENT TENANT

Everything that has been said about tenants in shopping centers and office buildings holds true for tenants in a mixed-use development. Furthermore, mixed-use developments may provide additional sources of business when they include condominiums and hotels. The astute landlord of a mixed-use development creates venues for businesses to reach out to other tenants and residents in the building to generate business. There are many opportunities to market directly to the other businesses and the residents in the building.

Mixed-use developments are often large projects, and the property management staff usually sends a newsletter periodically to everyone in the building. Tenants should provide the property management staff with information about their business (e.g., sales, new merchandise, or services offered) that can be included in the newsletter. The property management staff may include promotional materials provided by tenants along with the newsletter. The property management staff also is likely to have signs around the property promoting and directing customers to each tenant. They may give each business and resident a welcome kit that includes coupons from other businesses in the mixed-use development. The tenants should always be thinking about how to reach out to the other businesses and the hundreds of residents in the building.

A mixed-use development is a complicated building to manage and operate. Different uses in the building have different work and life schedules. Noise, orders, and deliveries that are normal in single-use buildings can cause problems in a mixed-use building. The property management staff devotes several hours to carefully drafting the building's rules and regulations so each tenant and resident has the least possible disruption and benefits from the best environment in which to live, work, or operate a

business. It is incumbent upon all parties to adhere to the rules and regulations, since the potential for infringement on another's territory is magnified
in the mixed-use environment.

TENANTS EVALUATING ALTERNATIVE LOCATIONS

Depending on the property type, there are many options for tenants to
consider when evaluating alternative locations.

Options for Retail Tenants

Retail tenants have many choices regarding where to locate their business.
Some locations are very expensive, but may still be the best location due
to co-tenants and the *demographics* and *psychographics* of the trade area.
It is helpful and possibly essential to the success of a retailer to look at the
ten different types of shopping centers discussed in Chapter 6, "Know the
Market Conditions." This will ensure that the retailer is located in the type
of shopping center that is best for the business. In years past, it was much
easier to classify shopping centers based on their size and anchor tenants,
but the traditional merchandise staples for each type of shopping center
have changed along with the changing demographics, making shopping
center classifications more blurred.

When retail tenants are considering where to locate, they will want to
consider which type of shopping center best fits the merchandise they sell.
For example, a high-end jeweler is not likely to want to move into a "big
box" shopping center, because most of the other merchants are discount
merchants and may not draw the high-end type of customers for which the
jeweler is looking.

In addition to making sure that other co-tenants will enhance their
drawing power, retail tenants also want to evaluate anchor stores for compatibility. In all but the specialty shopping center, anchor tenants set the
tone for the shopping center and quite often are the major reason why certain merchants choose to locate there. Anchor tenants typically do considerable research before moving into a location; they select locations where the
population has income and buying habits consistent with their department
store merchandise.

Each tenant should also do a demographic and psychographic study of
the trade area in question to determine who the likely customers are and
to study their buying habits. It is not enough to understand the total family income; the tenant also needs to know how that money is earned and
how it is spent. A blue-collar family with an income of $70,000 per year

will spend their money differently than a white-collar family in the same income level.

Before entering into a lease, tenants should try to determine the most likely sales levels that they will generate from the specific location. There are information sources to determine what the average customer spends for almost any commodity. Tenants use this information and multiply it times the population within the trade area of the selected shopping center, producing the approximate available sales for that type of merchandise in the area.

After determining the available sales, the tenant must consider who is in the market selling the same types of merchandise and estimate those sales. If the existing sales in the marketplace equal or exceed the sales potential, then the location is probably not a good choice for the tenant's business. However, if the existing sales do not exceed the sales potential (and this is generally the case), there is likely room for another store. Additionally, if tenants feel they can be competitive by doing a better job of selling than those already in the marketplace, they may enter the market even if it appears that sales are already at the maximum.

Once tenants have decided on the likely volume that can be generated in a specific location, the applicable rent and charges should be analyzed to see if the location will support their business. It should be noted that it generally takes one to two years for the tenant to be profitable. The tenant consequently should have the resources to support the business until sales reach the necessary level to make a profit.

One option for a tenant location is the freestanding location, or *pad space*. These locations have high visibility and often very easy access, but their rent is higher than in-line locations at the same shopping center. If the tenant can anticipate sufficient sales volume to support the high-end location, it is a good alternative in spite of higher rent and expenses.

There are three types of pad tenant transactions, depending on which one the developers choose. The most common pad deal is the ground lease. The tenants lease the land on a long-term basis and then build their own building. Some pads are sold to the tenant or an investor and will have operating covenants with the remainder of the shopping center. The third type of deal is a build-to-suit lease, in which the landlord provides the pad and the building and leases it to the tenant for a specified period of time.

Retailers located in many good neighborhoods or street locations can generate sales that are the same or better than they would be in a shopping center. The advantage to a good street location is there are no CAM costs and no mandatory store hours, enabling retailers to set their own hours and better control their labor costs. Not all streets are good retailing locations, and tenants may be tempted to take a street location for the lower costs; but they should first project their sales forecasts to be sure that adequate sales potential exists for that location.

Options for Office Tenants

Office tenants have many more locations to consider because their business is seldom location dependent. Office locations include very small garden-style office buildings, to mid-rise office buildings with modern amenities, to Class A high-rise office buildings that offer prestige and services (e.g., the services of restaurants, banks, and retailers) that are a benefit to the tenants in the building. The Class A office building is the most expensive space per square foot.

Many businesses do not need to be located in the most expensive building, and a Class B building may be right for them. If companies are image conscious, their leaders are likely to pay extra to be in one of the best buildings in the area. Many tenants—even high-profile companies—have additional, less expensive, backroom accounting operations in suburban locations that they use as "working" locations. Customers are not likely to come calling at these low-profile locations, and the company's name may not even be on the building.

When looking for a new location, the tenant should look at the *floor plate* to be sure that the desired size of space is available. It is also important to avoid an odd configuration of space that may make the office layout difficult and inefficient. This usually results in more space and higher rent than is necessary. Tenants should also shop around to be sure that they are getting the optimally sized space. For example, if a tenant only needs 1,500 square feet of office space, that tenant does not want to end up taking 2,000 square feet just because it is the only space available and increasing his occupancy cost by a third.

The tenant should compare all the possibilities to be sure that the rates are competitive. If one building is quoting on rentable square footage and another is quoting on usable square footage, the tenant will want to adjust them to the same formula to make an accurate comparison. An example of comparing rentable and usable square footage is provided in Chapter 10, "Financial Issues."

Medical office tenants are generally most interested in location, co-tenancy, and the availability of the latest technical equipment. They desire co-tenants with the potential for referrals, as well as supporting specialty co-tenants who will fit well with their own practice's area of expertise. Additionally, the medical office building tenant prospect may need to be located near a hospital. Such locations are generally more expensive but are worth the extra expense if the doctors are required to be at the hospital on a regular basis.

Existing medical office building tenants can be of help to their landlord by staying on the lookout for other medical office tenants who may be looking to relocate. If they pass along suitable recommendations to the landlord and aid in the process of finding additional co-tenants for the building, all parties involved will benefit. The existing tenant's position will be strengthened by the addition of other quality tenants to the building.

Tenants should take advantage of every opportunity to generate business in the building in which they are located. They also should develop a good rapport with the building's property management staff and the landlord. It is in the best interest of each tenant to be considered an asset to the building. Being an asset does not mean giving in to the landlord when the tenant is right on an issue, but it does mean making every effort to have a mutually beneficial relationship.

Commercial leases are long-term arrangements; and even when a lease is only for three to five years, both sides benefit from a cooperative relationship. It is incumbent upon the landlord and the tenant to do everything possible to make their relationship a win-win situation. Both should make it their personal responsibility to create that positive atmosphere and to do everything they can to make each other as profitable as possible.

8

Profiting from a
Commercial Location

The layout and design of commercial properties should be executed with
the tenant's operations in mind at all times. There are few existing properties that tenants would call perfect, but most commercial buildings are
designed with the tenant's business in mind. There are buildings that have
so many built-in problems that leasing and retaining tenants become a
challenge. A landlord's most effective leasing tool is a well-designed, well-
maintained, and well-managed property. While there are many quality architectural firms for all types of commercial buildings, it is still a good idea
to have property managers—and even a few tenants—look over plans for
a building and discuss how to minimize problems once the building is
operational.

Tenants should be familiar with the operations of the type of commercial building they occupy. The operations of the building have a direct
impact on their occupancy costs. More important, the operations of the
building may impact their business operations. The operations of a shopping center, from leasing to maintenance of the common areas, may have
a direct impact on the retailer's sales and profits. It is wise for tenants to
discuss the operations of commercial buildings with their leasing agents
and the building's property manager. There are several publications in the
real estate industry that discuss best practices for managing and leasing
commercial properties. The Institute of Real Estate Management (IREM) has
published *Managing and Leasing Commercial Properties, Shopping Center
Management and Leasing,* and *Office Building Management.* These publi-

cations provide tenants with an understanding of what they should expect from the management of a building.

DEVELOPMENT CHALLENGES

Over the years, there have been many mishaps in the layout and design of commercial properties. Examples include a 17-story office building designed with only one janitor sink in the building. Another building was designed to have ficus trees on each interior landing but provided no light or water access to care for them. One shopping center with 900 front feet of sidewalk had no hose bibs to clean the walks; another was designed to have Christmas decorations on each light pole but supplied no outlets to plug them in. These are operational issues, but the greatest challenge is when the building has faulty designs that do not meet the needs of most of the targeted tenants. Many more shopping centers have had back corner shops with no visibility and no place for a tenant's sign. Trash doors have been installed in such a way that the trash bins couldn't be moved. Office suites have been positioned adjacent to elevators or heating and air conditioning plants so noisy that the suites were unusable.

The list goes on and on. Generally, these mistakes come from an inexperienced landlord trying to maximize income and value by creating as much space as possible on the site, but they usually end up being expensive problems that make the building difficult to lease.

No matter what type of commercial property is being developed, the landlord should retain an architect who is knowledgeable and experienced in that property type. The design should be carefully reviewed to minimize problems. No property is likely to be perfect, but every effort should be made to eliminate any deficiencies that might reduce the rental income or turn off prospective tenants.

Even buildings that have been up and operating for years can have old problems corrected to enhance the property's value, make it easier to lease, and command higher rents. If the property is in a good location, any reasonable amount of money spent on resolving building problems will likely provide a good return in the long run.

It should also be noted that modern, clean, and well-operated properties make it easier for tenants to attract and keep good employees. It is depressing for workers to have to work in space that is poorly lit, has poor HVAC, or has problems with the plumbing or electrical systems. The morale of a tenant's employees often weighs heavily on the tenant's decision to lease a new space.

Effective property operations start with planning and documentation. All plot plans, space layouts, and *floor plates* should be as accurate as possible. With today's *computer-aided design (CAD)* programs, there is little excuse for large discrepancies between the plot plans and the actual square footage. Any vacant pads or outlots should be clearly shown on all plot plans, and the leasing personnel and/or landlord should be able to discuss building sizes and heights for these sites so that the tenant will be able to foresee any visibility problems.

While most leases have a provision allowing the landlord to make changes at will, there are limitations to how far he or she can go with changes—especially if they adversely impact any tenant. It is better to lose a tenant in the negotiating process than it is to have them move into a space only to decide that the leasing agent, landlord, or documentation has misled them. If poor planning negatively impacts commercial tenant operations, the property's leasing and renewal efforts will in turn suffer.

TENANT IMPROVEMENTS

Tenant improvements (TIs) are an area of concern for both the landlord and the tenant. In a landlord's perfect world, the tenant would pay for and complete all his or her own TI needs beyond the shell of the building and the landlord would have no concern with them. In the real world, however, the landlord must take an interest in TIs to ensure that local codes are followed and the building is not damaged in the process. Additionally, in many cases market conditions will dictate that the landlord provides some level of improvements in order to attract tenants.

The landlord's major concern when agreeing to provide TIs is the tenant's financial viability. If a vacant unit is leased on an "as is" basis, the risks are that it may become vacant again or that the tenant may do excessive damage. On the other hand, when a landlord makes an investment in TIs, the cost of the TIs is usually completely lost if the tenant fails and vacates the property. Because of this risk, the landlord should require a business plan and both financial and credit checks from a new tenant before making a reasoned decision about proceeding with TIs.

The landlord must also be careful about determining exactly who the tenant is under these circumstances. If the tenant is a subsidiary of a major corporation but is signing the lease under a separate corporate name or a *limited liability company (LLC)*, the landlord could have little or no protection if the tenant defaults. If the tenant is a desired tenant for the building, but the tenant's past performance or credit is not solid, the landlord may ask for a personal guarantee or a guarantee from another entity. The landlord may also choose to offer future rental credits, or initial free rent, to tenants paying for their TIs, understanding that those with poor histories or limited credit may not be able to front these improvement costs.

Tenant Improvements in Shopping Centers

In neighborhood shopping centers and convenience shopping centers, it is common for the landlord to provide the tenant with what is called a *vanilla shell* from which the tenant builds out the premises. The vanilla shell will generally consist of a slab floor, store front and door, rear door, drop ceiling and light fixtures, one bathroom fully equipped, painted walls, and an air conditioning system and electrical distribution. In order to encourage a strong tenant to sign a lease, the landlord may agree to provide extra improvements either for an additional return via increased rent or for no additional charge.

The landlord should carefully define any additional improvements so there is no confusion. For example, if the agreement calls for carpet, it should also state the cost or allowance for the carpet. Generally, TIs provided by the landlord are set forth in an exhibit to the lease that lists everything the landlord will provide, and indicates that everything else will be the tenant's responsibility.

From the tenant's point of view, each should make sure that the desired quality is met and that the timing of the improvements is satisfactory. It is expensive for tenants to provide improvements over and above landlord allowances, so the tenant is going to try to get the space with as many improvements included as possible. The tenant is also going to want assurances that the landlord's work will not get in the way of the tenant's work.

In larger shopping centers such as regional malls, super-regional malls, and power shopping centers, it is more typical for the landlord to provide the shell of the building and for tenants to provide and pay for their own improvements. In strip shopping centers the landlord usually leases space in a vanilla shell condition or in "as is" condition. In each of these cases, the landlord must make sure that all improvements meet local codes and do not represent any hazards to the building or its neighbors. The landlord also wants assurances that the improvements will be done in a timely manner so that the tenant will open for business as quickly as possible—certainly no later than the agreed upon date—and that all improvements will be paid for in a timely fashion so as not to result in a *lien* being placed on the shopping center.

Most large chain stores and anchor tenants have their own construction crews that are quite adept at building out spaces—generally at more competitive rates than the landlord is able to offer. Occasionally the landlord will provide a "turnkey" store for the tenant. This means that the landlord will not only provide the shell of the building, but also will provide all of the interior tenant requirements such as floor coverings, fixtures, special décor, and possibly even signage. A turnkey store is very rare and is generally provided only as a last resort when a certain tenant is badly needed to attract other desirable retailers to the property. However, there are many success stories of a landlord reaching out for such a tenant and consequently finding the catalyst to lease the rest of the property.

When tenants have their own contractors, the landlord should provide rules and regulations for conducting the work. There may be concerns about noise and the disruption of adjacent tenants. On-site materials and temporary utilities during construction will have to be considered. And there will almost always be issues about blocking other tenants' operations while installing underground utilities, awnings, rear storage, etc. These matters should be resolved with proper rules and regulations, regular inspections, and coordination with the tenants and their contractors.

Many tenants open their first store in the area within a shopping center. It is in the best interest of both the landlord and the tenant to get the store open for business as soon as possible, and so the landlord should help the tenant with a list of recommended local contractors if needed. If the tenant needs assistance obtaining building or health department permits, the landlord should help with the process. The landlord will also benefit from monitoring the tenant's work to be sure that it is in accordance with the agreements and likely to be completed on time.

Tenant Improvements in Office and Medical Office Buildings

Office and medical office buildings typically provide a standard TI package for tenants, and any additional improvements are negotiated items. In a landlord's market, the tenant will pay for additional improvement costs; while in a tenant's market, the landlord may pay for those same charges in order to induce the tenant to sign a lease. In either case, the landlord prefers to install the additional improvements to maintain the integrity of the building systems.

If tenants insist on doing their own improvements, the landlord should approve the contractor, insist on building permits, and oversee the work while it is underway. Air conditioning systems, electrical systems, plumbing systems, roof penetrations, and any floor penetrations need special consideration. Just as with shopping center improvements, the office or medical office building landlord has a set of rules and regulations for the tenant's contractors to be sure that the job is done to code and with minimum disruption of the building's other tenants. If the tenant needs to penetrate the roof membrane, the landlord should insist that his or her own contractors either perform the task or inspect the work that is done to ensure that it is completed properly and the roof will not leak.

When the landlord contracts for the TIs, the tenant will want a walk-through inspection with the landlord's representative to be sure that all of the agreed upon construction and improvement items are completed and in accordance with the agreements. Any items discovered during this walk through should be taken care of by the landlord as quickly as possible. Any items that the landlord is providing for the tenant for an additional fee should be listed in writing along with the corresponding prices to avoid any misunderstandings. If there are any supervision or construction management fees to be charged to the tenant, they should be revealed prior to the start of the work.

Tenant Improvements in Industrial Properties

With the exception of incubator spaces in industrial properties, most industrial buildings are turned over to the tenant as shell buildings and the tenant provides his or her own improvements. The incubator tenant generally gets a raw *shell space* with floor, walls, bathroom, front and back doors, and most likely an HVAC system. If a tenant wants the landlord to provide additional improvements, they are handled much like those in a shopping center. All of the same concerns regarding rules and regulations, building permits, and minimal disruptions to adjacent tenants apply.

Rules and Regulations for Tenant Improvement Work

As touched upon in the sections above, the main reasons for rules and regulations in TI work are to be sure that the adjacent tenants are not disturbed, the building's systems are not damaged, the operations of the building are not disturbed, and the work is completed according to plans and within city and county guidelines. Typical rules include the following:

1. The tenant may not make any alterations or improvements without the landlord's prior written permission.
2. All requests for additions or alterations must be in writing and must be accompanied by a drawing showing what is to be done.
3. All work must be performed with the proper building permit issued by the local authority.
4. All work must be done between the hours set by the landlord.
5. The landlord must preapprove any onsite staging.
6. Any core drilling must be preapproved by the landlord and done within specified hours.
7. Any penetrations of the roof must be either done by the landlord's contractor or supervised by the landlord's contractor.
8. Any deliveries are to be done during specified hours, at a place designated by the landlord.
9. Materials and/or trucks are not to block any tenant entrances, tenant storefronts, or prime parking spaces.

10. When elevators are involved, all deliveries must be assigned elevator times.

11. All contractors must carry evidence of liability insurance and a bond if working in a tenant's space, and they must name the landlord and the landlord's property management firm as additional insureds.

12. All work must be done by licensed contractors.

13. Contractors are to be liable to the building for utility costs during construction.

14. The tenant is responsible for all costs and will prevent any *liens* against the building and/or will immediately satisfy any liens that are filed.

15. The tenant is to maintain entrances to the construction site or staging area in a clean and safe manner at all times during the entire term of the construction project.

16. The tenant is responsible for any construction barricades and/or safety devices for the protection of the public during construction.

17. The landlord and tenant are to have final inspection of all work, and the landlord is to issue written approval when the job has been completed satisfactorily.

18. The landlord is to be provided with a certificate of occupancy issued by the municipality.

The rules should be shown to the tenant during lease negotiations; he or she will need time to look them over to be sure there are no likely conflicts with the work that has to be done. Some work, such as using a crane to put an air conditioner on the roof, is disruptive but the problems can be minimized with cooperation.

Other critical issues for the tenant include any limitations on the contractor's work schedule. Restricted working hours, special hours required for core drilling or other noisy operations such as jackhammer work, inconvenient areas for staging, and limitations on deliveries are all matters of concern. If such limitations cause the contractor to work overtime, the tenant will want to work out better conditions with the landlord to minimize extra costs if possible.

Lease Commencement and Tenant Improvements

One of the major issues to be resolved in connection with TIs is that of the lease and rent commencement dates. Typically, the landlord and tenant will estimate the construction time needed and agree that the lease will start (1) on the date of opening; (2) on the date of certificate of occupancy; or

(3) at a specified point—60 days, for example—after the signing of the lease. If the build-out is for a restaurant, the days for construction may well be 120 or 180 days; however, the time allowed should be commensurate with the job being done. For carpeting and painting, most would allow no more than 30 days.

Even with specific dates set for completion, both the landlord and tenant should monitor the construction closely to be sure that it is progressing satisfactorily. It is not beneficial for either the landlord or the tenant to have construction run over schedule. In these cases, either the tenant will have to pay rent on nonproductive space or the landlord will have to waive rent because construction has not been completed.

The tenant wants to negotiate a sufficient timetable for the completion of any work that must be done. If the scheduled improvements of the premises are completed in time to allow the tenant to open sooner than expected, he or she will want free rent until the official start date. Some landlords feel this is a good incentive to get the tenant to open as soon as possible, while others feel that rent should be paid as soon as the tenant is open for business.

A variation to this approach is for the tenant to start paying rent as soon as the lease is signed, even while construction is underway. This generally only happens when a site is in great demand and a tenant wants to secure the location from competitors.

Improvements under an Existing Lease

It is not at all unusual for existing tenants to want to make changes or improvements to their space during the lease term. A good commercial lease will require the tenant to seek landlord approval prior to making these alterations. It is a good idea to get all such requests in writing, including the full scope of what the tenant wants to do.

The initial discussions do not need to have architectural drawings— either a narrative or hand drawings that show the scope of the work will suffice. Unless the work is very complicated or involves the building's major systems, a simple drawing should be sufficient for the landlord to evaluate what the tenant wants to do. Once the landlord and tenant are in agreement, then more detailed drawings can be made and added to the discussion. The final plan is ultimately still subject to the landlord's final approval before construction may commence.

If the local city or county requires plans for the project, the landlord should also require these plans. Likewise, if the city or county requires a permit, so should the landlord. And, with the exception of improvements such as changing the carpeting or painting the walls, the landlord should not allow any changes or additions to the premises without a building permit.

Just as the landlord would have oversight of new construction, he or she also should have oversight of all additions and changes. It would be preferable for the landlord to do all improvements to the building; but since this is not always practical, supervision must suffice.

If a tenant asks to install improvements that are not likely to be of interest to future tenants, the landlord should require that the tenant agree to remove such improvements and restore the premises to their original condition at the end of the lease term, as requested. Such items as fish tanks, built-in desks, overhead wiring, and tenant signs can prove costly to remove after the tenant has vacated the premises.

SHOPPING CENTER ISSUES

Most shopping centers are open seven days a week, and many are open 24 hours a day. They frequently have tremendous foot traffic. The tenant's success in these shopping centers often depends somewhat on the quality of the landlord's original planning, leasing, and operations.

Building Layout

One of the first issues that the shopping center landlord addresses is that of the shopping center's layout. The desire to maximize a site's square footage often leads the landlord to build space that is hard to see and difficult to access. This space is often inferior, but it is reasoned that it will be leased at lower terms and therefore not be wasted. However, in reality this space is often only good for tenants who do not rely at all on foot traffic. Any other type of retail operation is likely to fail in such a location. Examples of these commonly encountered layout problems are identified below.

Retailers should be able to evaluate shopping centers and the available spaces in which they are considering leasing space. Signing a lease in a poorly designed or leased and managed shopping center may make it difficult for the retailer to achieve projected sales and profits.

Spaces That Are Too Deep.   In the past, tenants tended to take very large spaces that made their shops very deep. In more recent years, however, tenants have largely downsized to become more efficient. The very deep spaces that are left can become a leasing problem. Quite often landlords have to cut down on the store's depth, leasing out only the front 60 to 80 feet. Some will then put storage behind that space or try to fit in another store that faces a different direction.

Shoe stores in the 1950s took up as much as 7,000 square feet. Today they are more in the area of 2,000 square feet. The larger, older store spaces left over became quite difficult to lease, especially in neighborhood shopping centers. Popularly priced fashion tenants sometimes consider neighborhood and community strip shopping centers. Some of these larger stores are now right for the larger spaces that were difficult to lease, but others are still too large for the majority of tenants.

L-Shaped Spaces. L-shaped spaces can be very difficult to lease. Quite often the L-shaped store is the result of splitting up a very large space with a much smaller space at the front corner. Generally, the smaller front shop will command a much higher rent than the L-shaped portion, but that revenue may well be lost due to the difficulty of leasing an oddly shaped store.

Unanchored Spaces. Small shops will likely do better if they are placed between anchors. However, in an effort to maximize the *gross leasable area (GLA)* of a shopping center, landlords will often add space with little or no anchor tenant support. In a major mall, this unanchored space may be an unanchored wing of the mall. In a neighborhood center, it is often a row of shops facing a side area of the center with no visibility from the anchor stores. The anchors generate the traffic for the center and the small shops must be placed to take advantage of the traffic.

Spaces with poor visibility are a problem because they do not provide the necessary foot traffic, making it difficult for most merchants to survive. While one solution to this lack of visibility is to charge a lesser rent for these spaces, tenants often do not do well in such locations, causing high turnover rates and making it difficult to attract new tenants regardless of the rates. In general, tenants who generate their own traffic are more likely to succeed in unanchored spaces but still prefer shopping centers with anchor tenants nearby. Extra signage can also help the issue of poor visibility; but these are always going to be substandard spaces unless the situation is corrected.

Malls without anchors were originally a problem to be overcome in almost every instance. However, although many unanchored malls still do not fare well, the lifestyle shopping center has managed to overcome not having a major anchor (like a department store) and instead has several smaller anchors. Lifestyle shopping centers generally have many strong national tenants and a high level of ambience, and perform well in spite of not having major anchor tenants.

Second-Floor Office Spaces. Second-level office space has not worked well in most shopping centers. The occupants of this space must compete with retail customers for parking, and in most markets the locations are not considered to be the best for office space. However, recently lifestyle shopping centers and some regional and super-regional malls have begun to include more mixed-use components, and we are therefore likely to see more office towers, hotels, apartments, and condominiums added to shopping centers in the future. Despite these additions, the purely second-floor offices are still likely to run into problems.

Malls That Are Too Wide.   Malls that are too wide are an especially difficult problem to solve. When the customer cannot easily shop or see both sides of a mall, the desired synergism is usually lacking. Some possible solutions include adding kiosks to the mall, moving out shop fronts to make the area between stores smaller, including children's play areas, and incorporating larger seating areas to give the sense of intimacy, but these solutions are all likely to be very expensive but necessary.

Pie-Shaped Spaces.   One generally sees pie-shaped retail spaces where two strip buildings come together to form an open, pie-shaped piece of land. Landlords see this open area as an opportunity to lease more space, but these oddly shaped spaces cause leasing problems because they offer limited frontage, a wide back area, and very little room for signs and overall store visibility.

Parking

Parking requirements are a critical element for most shopping centers. Some anchor shopping center tenants may place a requirement in their lease for the property to have a minimum number of parking stalls available. Anchor tenants in shopping centers want to be certain that there will always be sufficient parking for their customers. The city also requires minimum parking ratios for shopping centers, and anchor tenants may negotiate lease provisions that require landlords to provide a minimum number of parking stalls. The agreement may state, for example, that the shopping center will have a parking ratio of at least five stalls per 1,000 square feet of GLA, or that the shopping center will never have fewer than 490 parking stalls and that no more than 30 percent of them will be for compact cars.

Shopping centers need good *ingress* and *egress,* but also good circulation and convenient parking for all stores. Most cities and most anchor tenants will have parking requirements that ensure sufficient parking spaces in shopping centers, but they seldom address circulation.

A shopping center can be at a disadvantage if the customers cannot easily access it. The minimum level of parking required by most communities and anchor tenants is likely to provide adequate parking. However, very busy shopping centers need to find additional ways to make parking convenient for all of their customers, or risk losing them to competitors in more convenient locations.

Additionally, tenants are concerned that prime parking will be used for long-term parking by office employees or theater patrons. Most shopping centers require employees to park in a specified area of the shopping center to maximize customer convenience, and tenants want assurance these areas are well lighted and safe. Leasing agents should be fully aware of how the shopping center will be operated and in a position to discuss parking issues with prospective tenants.

Hours of Operation

Hours of operation are important to both the landlord and the tenant. Some tenants will argue that their goods and services do not lend themselves to the shopping center hours, but the concern is with the customer who will want to be able to rely on the minimum hours for all the shopping center's uses.

Office buildings usually keep the following hours: 7:00 or 8:00 a.m. until 6:00 p.m. on weekdays; 8:00 a.m. to noon or 2:00 p.m. on Saturdays; and the building is closed on Sundays and holidays. The hours of a medical office building are usually extended beyond the hours of a typical office building. It is not uncommon for medical groups to see patients during the evening and on weekends. Urgent care facilities in medical office buildings may operate 24 hours a day.

Hours of operation are extremely important for retail properties. Hours should be established so that anchor stores are open for the full duration of a shopping center's hours. Uniform hours need to be established for neighborhood and strip shopping centers. Enclosed malls have specific hours that tenants must be open and, unless tenants have an outside entrance to their premises from the parking lot, they cannot remain open after the mall closes. An exception is made for theaters and other entertainment uses.

In general, malls are extending their hours by opening earlier and staying open later on the weekends. Strip shopping centers, restaurants, supermarkets, and drug stores have hours that extend well beyond the shopping center's minimum hours; and smaller merchants should be free to stay open as long as they wish past the minimum hours. Pad and outlot tenants may also stay open for extended hours. A few non-retail tenants, such as medical, office, and government tenants, are usually granted the right to maintain negotiated hours. Service businesses, such as real estate offices or insurance agencies, may negotiate not to remain open in the evenings or on Sundays.

Age

Obsolescence is quite common in shopping centers built in the 1950s and 1960s. Store fronts become outdated, lighting shows its age, landscaping gets old and rangy, and signage becomes antiquated. As more and more new centers come to an area, the existing establishments appear increasingly older by comparison.

The shopping center industry has indeed matured. Older, dated shopping centers require investments by the landlord for improvements and building updates if they are to offer the best shopping environment for tenants and customers. Because so much public infrastructure exists at these well located sites, many shopping centers are being redeveloped—some into mixed-use projects.

Signage

Tenants in all property types may have logos and readily identifiable signs that are important to their advertising. However, shopping centers have by far the most complex needs and detailed regulations regarding signage.

Signage is one of the more important elements for the retail tenant. Tenants all want a big sign on the street with their name on it. However, cities and landlords have concluded that this is not in the best interest of either the community or the property, so large pylon signs are seldom approved in newer properties.

A landlord's sign criteria are created within the limits of city or county guidelines. Sign criteria have become much more relaxed in recent years in an effort to allow the tenant freedom in creating a retail identity; however, the shopping center's guidelines must still be followed. The lease guidelines may address hours signs, credit card logos, and slogans to maintain uniformity within the property. It is essential that the landlord approve all signs prior to installation.

Sometimes a tenant's sign will not be in conformity with the signage criteria. The landlord does not want to make an exception that will cause existing and future tenants to request similar exceptions; this would make the sign criteria meaningless. In such situations the property manager and the tenant must come together to work out a solution.

Tenants in shopping centers want identity and exposure to people walking or driving by their stores, and the landlord wants to control the appearance of the shopping center to prevent it from becoming gaudy or offensive. To address both parties' desires and concerns, the landlord will develop signage criteria that limit the types and sizes of tenants' signs, while still allowing them to have signage that is representative of their business, easy to read, and visible. Sign criteria should take into account any local laws that may govern the issues of size, materials, and positioning for display.

Each individual tenant is therefore allowed a sign with strict guidelines. The sign criteria may well limit the tenant's sign to being 75 percent of the width of the storefront, no more than 18 to 24 inches high, backlit, free of animation, and preapproved by the landlord.

The most common type of sign in today's shopping centers is the monument sign, which is replacing the older, larger (often 30 feet high) pedestal sign. Monument signs are generally situated on the ground and will have four to six of the largest merchants named along with the shopping center name. These signs are likely to be placed at the major entrance(s) of a shopping center. Major regional and super-regional malls have their sign on the façade of the building and may also have monument signs at major entrances.

Tenant Mix and Synergism

The use provisions in each tenant's lease are critical for balancing the tenant mix in a shopping center. Tenants want the broadest lease language to allow them the most flexibility, but the landlord must control the uses that are allowed. This regulation prevents unfair competition and ensures that the shopping center offers the broadest mix of goods and services possible in the given market. An exclusivity lease provision or limitations on the ability of other stores to sell certain merchandise should be clearly stated prior to the tenant signing a lease. The store's merchandise lines should be clearly understood by both the landlord and the tenant.

Tenant mix and synergism are very important in any shopping center. Landlords should take time during the negotiations process to orient the prospective tenant to the anchor tenants and their niche in the marketplace. Tenants should be encouraged to analyze their own merchandise mix and coordinate it, as best they can, with the anchor tenants and other tenants to maximize the merchandise available to the shopper. In order to optimize the synergism among various merchants, the landlord should also emphasize the importance of the merchant being part of the shopping center's marketing and promotional efforts, if they exist, and adhering to the shopping center's hours for the shopper's convenience.

Retailers should carefully evaluate the tenant mix of the shopping centers in which they are considering leasing space. They should first visit the anchor tenants to determine if their customer draw includes the same customers. Then they should evaluate the shop tenants to determine if their businesses are compatible and if they share the same customers. Retailers want to benefit from customers cross-shopping in the shopping centers.

Common Area Maintenance

Common area maintenance and administration also can be a major concern among landlords and tenants. Landlords want lease provisions that allow them to do whatever it takes to maintain the property in a clean and safe manner. While tenants also want cleanliness and safety, they are concerned with writing a "blank check" to the landlord to get the job done. Landlords must therefore try to get the broadest lease language possible to ensure that all shopping center maintenance costs are reimbursed by the tenants. They must then administer common area maintenance in a fair, competitive, and cost-effective manner.

There are a variety of issues involved with common area maintenance in a shopping center. Great care should be taken with landscaping to be sure that large bushes or monument signs do not obscure lines of sight. Pedestrian walkways should be carefully delineated, and cart corrals and planters should be well marked to prevent accidents in the parking areas.

Trash removal and exterior storage are important issues in shopping center operations, and are generally addressed either in the basic lease or in the rules and regulations. Because trash removal can be a problem, most shopping centers prefer to have a shopping-center–wide program. Anchor tenants seldom take part in such programs, but all small merchants are required to subscribe to the service. These billings are charged separately when all the tenants are not part of the shopping-center–wide trash removal program. If all the tenants are in the program, then the cost can be billed in the shopping center's common area maintenance (CAM) charges.

When there is a mandatory program for trash removal, the landlord must be sure that the locations are convenient and that the rates for that service are competitive. Tenants will most likely be satisfied to have the trash removal under the landlord's control, but they will want assurances that the locations are convenient, sites are well maintained, and prices are competitive.

Good communication from the landlord will go a long way towards maintaining a good relationship with the tenant, even when costs are higher than either would desire. It is often helpful for the landlord to advise tenants in regard to what is being accomplished and what still needs to be done in the common areas. For example, if there is a heavy snowfall, the landlord has no choice but to deal with the accumulation and provide a convenient place for the shoppers and maximum benefits to the tenants. This is likely to be expensive, but keeping the tenants informed about the process will go a long way towards maintaining the relationship. A landlord may feel that good communication with tenants regarding common area maintenance is not that important; however, some tenant prospects talk with existing tenants about the shopping center before signing a lease, and any bad relationships are bound to emerge in those discussions.

OFFICE BUILDING ISSUES

Office building tenants face fewer issues than retail tenants, but they still have concerns regarding the operations of the building and how they can impact their business. They need to be aware of how the landlord perceives them and how this can impact their leasing and lease renewals. Since management has a big impact on leasing, and especially on re-leasing, the building manager should be professional and responsive to the tenants' requests and needs. It is in the office building landlord's best interest to remove or mitigate all problems within his or her control to make the leasing process easier and to improve the chances that existing tenants will renew their lease. If the management is offsite, it takes greater effort to be responsive to tenant needs. A regular visit by the property manager to the tenants can go a long way towards maintaining good relationships.

Operations and Amenities

The landlord must take into consideration the kinds of features and services an office building has to offer. Operational concerns for tenants include the building's hours of operation, the hours of the HVAC system and the costs, calculations for after-hours HVAC use, and janitorial service. If tenants need overstandard utilities, they want to know if these utilities are available, what they will cost, and how those charges will be calculated and billed.

Bay depth, floor plates, and window *mullion* spacing will also have an impact on the types of tenants that the building attracts. A landlord can do little about an existing building's features, but he or she can maximize the space within those limitations and market the space to tenants who will be comfortable with the building's configuration.

In addition, office tenants are very interested in building amenities. Those amenities may include an onsite first-class restaurant, a bank or savings and loan on the ground floor, retail shops on the ground floor, and services such as cleaners and concession or snack shops. For smaller tenants, a building conference room can be a huge benefit. Some tenants want covered parking for their executives. Smaller tenants may request access to administrative services on an as-needed basis.

Appearance

The overall appearance of the building is also a feature that has an impact on leasing. Most Class A office buildings do not have appearance problems; however, smaller garden-style and low-rise office buildings can be out of harmony with their surroundings or may use inexpensive or lower-quality materials, amenities, and landscaping. These buildings with appearance problems are more difficult to lease.

As far as the building's interior appearance is concerned, the lobby provides the tenant's or customer's first impression of the building. This initial encounter should be a very positive one. That is not to say the lobby must be overly large or dramatic, but it should be consistent with the area and the types of occupancies expected in the building. It should also be maintained at the highest level so as to consistently present a positive experience. Elevators are equally important to the tenant's overall experience, because the building's customers and employees spend a lot of time in them. They should be modern, clean, well maintained, and responsive to the needs of the building.

Location and Access

An office building's location can affect operations. It is not uncommon for the prime office area of a city to change, leaving what was once the best area as a second or third choice. Naturally there is little that landlords can do about their building's location, but they can make up for a poor location with good maintenance, the proper amenities, and competitive rental rates.

Access can be a problem in any location. It is especially frustrating for tenants and their customers to have a building that is quite easy to see, but difficult to access. Directional signage can be of some help, but tenants are not going to be anxious to lease space in a building that is difficult to find and access.

Parking

In addition to easy access, convenient parking is also a concern for all types of office buildings. Tenants want sufficient parking for their employees and convenient parking for their clients and customers. They also want competitive parking charges, and for underground and deck parking to be well lighted and clearly designated to make it easy to find one's automobile.

In major metropolitan areas, most mid-rise and high-rise office buildings have either underground or multiple-deck parking. Most garden-style and low-rise buildings have surface parking. There also must be controls on employee parking and the parking areas for visitors, which generally mean that employee parking is farther from the building while visitors have reserved spaces closer to the entrances. In some cases, there is covered parking reserved for those willing to pay an extra fee.

Some cities require office buildings to have a minimum number of parking spaces, which helps to guarantee that there will be adequate parking available, while other cities limit the number of parking stalls to encourage people to take public transportation.

Green Buildings

It is becoming much more common for office tenant prospects to inquire about the availability of green programs within a building, including recycling, energy saving measures, transportation management plans, green development practices, etc. The environmental movement has also impacted company values and may drive a tenant's ultimate location to a sustainable green site. Many tenants are interested in being good corporate citizens and want a building that will support that position.

Technology

A few years back the *smart building* became a part of the mix of office buildings, but currently it still comprises a very small portion of these buildings. Internet access in office buildings has become an indispensible business element. High-speed access is essential and is expected by even the smallest office users. Fortunately, the retrofitting of an office building for high-speed Internet is not a prohibitive venture.

In addition to Internet access, many tenants need other high-tech services such as satellite dishes, multicomputer networks, high-speed data transmission, and computer rooms with special wiring and air conditioning capabilities. An office building landlord must decide who the customers will be for his or her space and then be sure that the building has been fitted with the necessary services to appeal to these tenants.

Security

Security needs in office buildings vary depending on the location of the building and the building's size. Security is important to all office building tenants, but in varying degrees. The typical garden-style office building tenant is generally concerned that his or her employees are safe where they park, in the building, and on its grounds. If there are any security issues, the building is likely to have either an onsite security guard or a drive-by service.

Mid-rise and garden-style office buildings may have tenants who require a security screening system for all employees and invitees. Many office buildings with governmental offices require such security, as do buildings with art galleries, jewelry wholesalers, and financial services tenants. The level of security provided by the building will attract certain tenants who are willing to pay additional charges for these services as long as they are competitive.

Adequate parking lot lighting is also an essential feature that promotes safety in office buildings. All landlords and property managers should be aware of the importance of well-lighted pathways and parking areas in deterring misdemeanors in their buildings and minimizing liability if crime should occur.

Floor Loads

Floor loads can limit the types of tenants a building can attract. On the other hand, to design and engineer a building to handle the heaviest of floor loads just to have the capability of handling different types of tenants is not practical. The landlord must decide on the desired types of tenants in advance and then design the building accordingly.

General office floor loads run in the area of 100 pounds per square foot. If the building is likely to have medical labs, heavy office storage, or law libraries, the floor loads should be approximately 150 pounds per square foot. Engineering and construction for these heavier loads can be quite expensive. It may be practical to design an office building that has the capability to handle heavier loads on only the bottom two or three floors.

Building Names and Signage

Tenants in office buildings typically have signage on the building's directory and in the entrance to their premises. The building may have signage criteria and a process for approval that are similar to those of retail properties.

It is not unusual to see a large office building with several different company signs prominently displayed. Now and then, very strong tenants will agree to lease space in mid- or high-rise buildings—usually Class A buildings—that they want named after them, and will negotiate for the exclusive right to have their name on the building. This right generally includes permission to install a fairly large sign on the side of the building. The landlord should carefully consider whether or not the naming of the building after a specific tenant will create any future leasing problems or limit the likely tenant prospect pool. If the tenant has a prominent name or brand in the market, such naming can have a very positive impact on the building.

Tenant signs and identification are important to the tenant. Signs and directory listings should be taken care of as quickly as possible for new tenants. The most effective approach for creating and installing acceptable signs is for the office building to have a standard sign package available for all tenants. Tenants are provided with signage criteria and submit their desired wording, in writing, to the landlord, who then has the signs made and installed. (Signage is discussed in more detail in Chapter 3, "Prospecting.")

The Load Factor

The *load factor* of an office building has a considerable impact on the tenant's *occupancy cost*. The load factor is the relationship between the building's gross footage and its *usable area*. Higher load factors are created when a building is very inefficient, with overly wide corridors, very large atriums, and/or numerous work and storage areas. If a building has 100,000 square feet of *gross area* and 90,000 square feet of usable space, the load factor for that building is 10 percent. For every 1,000 square feet of usable space, the tenant will pay rent on 1,100 square feet to cover the load factor. It is not unusual for an experienced tenant to ask to be shown how the load factor was calculated and/or have the numbers verified by an engineer or space planner.

It is generally held that tenants resist the load factor when it approaches

17 to 18 percent. In buildings in which the load factor exceeds this threshold and leasing is adversely affected, landlords may arbitrarily reduce the load factor to a lower level. The best approach for the landlord, if he or she is involved in the building development, is to limit the load factor as much as possible while making sure that the building is attractive and efficient. One seldom sees a load factor in garden-style or low-rise office buildings.

Building Operating Expenses

Maintenance and operating expenses are of concern to all tenants. A building's operating expenses should be reflective of its maintenance levels. Most tenants are quite willing to pay the *billbacks* if the building is well maintained at all times. They want to perceive value, not necessarily the lowest price for services. Even if the management is located offsite, a building should be maintained in first-class condition at all times.

Lobbies, elevators, and other high-traffic areas should always look good and be functional in order to make a good impression on tenants and customers. Building corridors should also be bright and well maintained. Their condition will have a strong impact on tenant perceptions of the building. Restrooms are another important element of a successful office building. They should be modern, very well maintained, and sufficient in number to service the entire building.

Incorporating Retail Tenants

Retail tenants are not all that common in office buildings. Some mixed-use projects contain offices, retail spaces, hotels, and even condominiums, but the typical office building does not have much retail space. Office buildings in the retail core will have retail on the ground floor. A high-rise office building might have a restaurant in the penthouse.

Generally, if there are enough retail tenants in an office building, they will have their own common area allocations that are completely different from those of the office tenants. Retail tenants clean their own stores and generally provide their own utilities, wet trash removal, and all interior maintenance. There are, however, several issues that a landlord must deal with if harmony is to be maintained between retail and office tenants occupying the same building.

One of the major issues that must be addressed is that of odors. Many retail operations produce odors—some pleasant and some not so pleasant—but almost all retail odors are unwelcome in an office environment. Hair salons and nail salons can have distinctly unpleasant odors. Restaurants have both cooking odors and waste odors. And a coffee shop or bakery may have very pleasant odors, but these generally are not considered favorably when they permeate an office building.

All of these odors can be controlled with a good ventilation system. Such a system should be designed and installed by the landlord or, at the very least, approved by the landlord to be certain it is strong enough to remove the odors. The landlord should also make sure that the ventilation system is well placed, insuring that odors will not return to the building once they have been redirected.

A second concern that goes along with retail tenants in an office building is that of noise. Most offices are fairly quiet operations, and nearby noise can be quite bothersome. Along with noise there are also often vibrations that can cause as much discomfort as the sounds themselves. Even some restaurants have loud background music that can be troublesome. Noisy air conditioning or refrigeration equipment placed near an office tenant space can also be the source of problems. Masking noise is not difficult if it is considered during the construction of the building or the tenant's space.

Deliveries and waste removal for retail tenants are also potential problems in the office building. Ideally, retail tenants should have their own rear entries so that deliveries do not have to be made through the building's lobby. These rear entrances are also very useful in the removal of waste from retail establishments. Wet garbage and grease removal are special considerations. The building should have provisions for the sanitary storage of both items until they are properly picked up and removed. However, many buildings are not designed for rear entrances and, in these situations, the property manager establishes rules for when deliveries may be made and how trash is to be removed.

Signage and access are two additional concerns. Retailers in office buildings frequently have internal signage that is consistent with the building's image, but some may not have street signage. If retail tenants are on the street, they will have signage on the street; but for retail tenants in the building the landlord may need to provide directional signage and additional signage on the building's directory and in the lobby. Whatever the situation may be, retail tenants need adequate signage to support their business. Also, if retail tenants located within the building are open beyond the building's standard hours, their customers need access to them. The best example of this is a restaurant located above the ground floor.

MEDICAL OFFICE BUILDING ISSUES

Although some office buildings have a few medical tenants, the discussion here concerns medical office buildings. Medical office buildings are more expensive to build and operate than office buildings, and they present a unique set of concerns.

To begin with, medical equipment can present some challenges. If the building has a lab or MRI or CT scan unit, the floor loads have to be much higher than they would be for a typical office building. The plumbing and electrical systems also must have a very high capacity due to the type of equipment that is used. Vacuum systems and compressed air systems are needed in some medical and dental suites, and many medical offices today have in-house X-ray equipment that makes shielding necessary. And emergency generators are a major incentive for a medical office building because they can prevent the disruption of medical procedures if a blackout hits the area.

The division of space presents another important concern for medical office building landlords and tenants. In order to avoid odor transfer, the exhaust or ventilation system has to have the capacity for high turnover and distinct separation between adjacent spaces. Insulation between adjacent spaces—and even within various operations sharing the same space—must be adequate to avoid noises and conversations carrying from one room or space to the next. Special accommodations may also have to be made for vibrating equipment and its possible impact on adjacent spaces.

Another critical issue for medical office buildings is that of sanitation. The standards of cleanliness are much more stringent in medical office buildings than in office buildings, and janitorial services need to be of a higher level to meet the needs of the medical profession. In addition, medical waste must be properly disposed of and removed from the building.

There may be special security issues. Most medical tenants have drugs onsite and, while they are responsible for keeping those secure, the landlord is responsible for the security of the building.

In addition, parking presents unique challenges for medical office buildings. Parking for doctors should be accommodated; many doctors have to make hospital calls and then return to the office, and they do not want to spend time hunting for parking spots. They are therefore likely to have assigned spaces, often quite close to one of the building's entrances. Medical office buildings must also supply adequate parking facilities for patients coming to the premises. Easy drop-off for patients is a major need, and there are generally two or three spaces reserved for exactly that purpose near the building's main entrance or the entrance closest to the elevators. These spaces must be monitored to ensure they are not used for longer-term parking.

INDUSTRIAL PROPERTY ISSUES

Industrial properties have evolved from dingy, out-of-the-way locations to major planned developments with attractive landscaping, signage, and amenities. The potential tenants are different for each type of industrial property, and landlords must ascertain each tenant's space and operational requirements and whether the tenant's business meets the zoning classification for the property.

Industrial Categories and Zoning

There are property classifications that guide where the landlord might find prospective tenants for a particular property. The *Urban Land Institute (ULI)* classifies industrial properties into six different categories, listed below.

1. *Warehouse distribution.* This is a very large category that encompasses the regional warehouse, bulk warehouse, and rack-supported warehouse, as well as heavy distribution and refrigerated distribution.

2. *Manufacturing.* This is the second largest classification, and it covers manufacturing, assembly, and general repair-related processes.

3. *FLEX.* This third-largest classification covers the areas of research and development (R&D) and the office showroom.

4. *Multitenant.* These properties are generally smaller in size, with an upper limit of 120,000 square feet. They are often configured in either an "L" or a "U" shape, and they have multiple tenants with square footages generally ranging between 5,000 and 15,000 square feet.

5. *Freight forwarding.* This classification covers all areas of transportation, including road, rail, water, and air. The category has two subcategories: intramodal (or truck-to-truck) transportation; and intermodal transportation, which involves both airplanes and trucks.

6. *Data switch center.* This is the newest category, and encompasses two different facility types: the data warehouse and the switch center (where calls and data are routed). While both of these facilities are quite similar, the data warehouse has a much higher power need.

In addition to the industry categories, almost every city has very specialized zoning requirements for each industrial use category. For example, one Midwestern city has only two zoning classifications: "light industrial," which covers the areas of wholesale operations, light manufacturing, repair shops, etc.; and "heavy industrial," which covers heavy manufacturing, recycling centers, junkyards, and so forth. Another city has three classifications: "industrial park" for all light industrial uses; "garden industrial" for larger, heavier industrial uses; and "planned commercial park," for projects in excess of 25 acres and that are master planned. Some municipalities have six or more industrial classifications. Each of these categories has very specific tenant requirements, and the landlord needs to be sure that the zoning is appropriate for the tenant's use.

Location and Access

Location is as critical to industrial tenants as it is to tenants in all other types of commercial properties. Industrial tenants often care about the convenience of freeway access, rail access, air transportation for shipping and executive travel, seaports, and the location of suppliers with whom they work on a regular basis.

The labor and housing markets are also of concern to most industrial tenants. A ready labor supply is especially vital for assembly plants and data and shipping points. The availability of skilled workers at reasonable costs is an important factor in the location of an industrial tenant. Additionally, housing costs can have a sizeable impact on where a tenant locates. For example, some computer manufacturing firms moved out of the San Francisco Bay Area due to high housing and labor costs.

For those industrial tenants involved in the manufacturing and warehousing of goods, ingress and egress will be two further issues of importance. Most of these uses have goods delivered and shipped out in large trucks, and they require easy access to the property. It is up to the tenant to lease a sufficient parcel to handle the necessary trucks onsite, but it is up to the landlord to ensure that the roads within the property are properly designed to handle these large trucks.

Chemicals

Environmental considerations are very important for the industrial sector. This is especially true for tenants involved in manufacturing processes. All chemicals must be handled and disposed of according to the applicable laws and regulations.

The landlord should make sure that the tenant is aware of and prepared to meet all environmental requirements. It is not unusual for the landlord to conduct occasional environmental audits of tenants with industrial uses that might raise chemical concerns and to require copies of any reports tenants are required to submit to the state or other municipalities. Such industries as plating, auto parts manufacturing, cleaning solvent production, and jewelry manufacturing are all problematic uses if the chemicals are not used and disposed of properly.

Floor Loads and Clear Heights

Floor loads and *clear heights* are also important for accommodating a wide range of industrial uses. Manufacturing locations, storage warehouses, and computer centers often have very heavy equipment and extremely concentrated stored items with tremendous weights. Larger industrial buildings should consequently be designed and built to handle heavier floor loads. Floor load needs between 150 and 250 pounds per square foot are not unusual for these larger industrial buildings.

Manufacturing and storage uses may require very high, clear-height ceilings. These allow tenants the most flexibility in designing the interior for their specific use. A ceiling that is too low or has many columns may make the building unsuitable for many tenants. It is essential that landlords are aware of these tenant needs so as not to limit the range of prospective industrial tenants who are interested in a property.

Storage

A major issue in industrial parks is that of exterior storage. Most industrial tenants are likely to have enough space and storage room for their operations at the outset; however, as the business grows there is a tendency to try to create storage in the parking lot. Some industrial businesses will try to park fully loaded long-haul truck units onsite, claiming that the stored items are about to be unloaded. This can be unsightly as well as cause maintenance problems if the parking lot is asphalt.

The landlord must have good lease language to prevent such actions and have management supervision to detect such lease violations. It is in the best interest of both the landlord and the tenant to keep the property visually attractive and in good repair.

Mini-storage or self-storage facilities have become an important part of industrial properties. They allow for the inexpensive storage of business records, excess home furniture, store fixtures, etc. These storage facilities are fairly inexpensive to build and operate, and they can use oddly shaped properties. Additionally, they often provide the buffer between heavier industrial uses and office or residential uses.

The main issue for tenants of mini-storage units is that of security. In the past it was not unusual for mini-storage facilities to have 24/7 monitoring by onsite property managers, but that strategy did not work well. Today the most common security system involves a locked outer gate with electronic access by a coded card. This system records anyone who comes in or out, providing the landlords with fairly good knowledge of who may be in the facility. During daytime hours, storage facilities typically are staffed by individuals who can handle both the renting and the maintenance. Additionally, properties are fenced to prevent unlawful access.

Security

As with all other commercial properties, security is an added concern for industrial properties. If the building is a freestanding, triple-net-leased property, security is up to the tenant. However, in multitenant properties, exterior security is typically the landlord's responsibility. A security assessment should be made of the property and any problem areas addressed to provide the safest environment possible within reasonable limits. An evaluation of the property by the landlord's insurance company and the local police department should reveal any security concerns as well as the best approach to eliminating or minimizing them. However, most industrial properties do not have security problems.

In conclusion, the location, design, amenities, features, and management of a commercial building have a direct bearing on the landlord's ability to lease the space. Every effort should be made to make the building tenant-friendly and to keep the building operations as efficient as is practical. Tenants need to understand the operations of the types of buildings they occupy. Their goal is to select the best building for their operations and be able to negotiate the best lease terms based on the building's strengths and weaknesses.

9

Defining the Premises

In commercial leases, the square footage of the premises and the overall property are components used to establish the rents and the common area maintenance (CAM) charges and/or billback expenses. It is therefore important to both the landlord and the tenant that square footage measurements are correct. Because so many of the financial terms in a lease depend on ascertaining the correct square footage, it is in the best interest of both parties to obtain accurate figures. Proper measurements benefit both parties: for the landlord, they mean income, which translates into cash flow and ultimately into value; for the tenant, they mean occupancy costs that are accurately calculated.

When cases of inaccurate measurements have been carried to the courts, the landlord often has been faulted for any significant errors, because it is his or her job to "get it right." With the introduction of computer-aided design (CAD) it is possible to get extremely accurate measurements on all commercial spaces. There is no excuse for the landlord to wonder if all the space is included in the square footage, or for the tenant being concerned about paying for more space than what is stated in the lease. The use of CAD programs is essential for new construction. However, the use of such programs is also a good idea for existing buildings to guarantee that spaces are being properly represented.

Commercial lease language often will indicate that the landlord and the tenant agree that the space is an approximate number of square feet. The purpose of this language is to prevent disagreements at a later date over the square footage. However, if the landlord measures the space inaccurately and overstates the area by a large margin, the tenant may challenge the square footage.

MEASURING OFFICE AND
MEDICAL OFFICE BUILDING SPACE

The Building Owners and Managers Association (BOMA) International is the recognized authority for measuring space in office buildings. *Standard Method for Measuring Floor Area in Office Buildings,* a BOMA International publication dated June 7, 1996, sets out the industry-accepted methods of measuring all office spaces. The following subsections are adapted from that text.

Measuring Gross Building Area

Gross building area is not to be used for leasing purposes except when an entire building is leased to a single tenant. This area is computed by measuring to the outside finished surface of permanent outer building walls, without any deductions. All enclosed floors of the building, including basements, garages, mechanical equipment floors, penthouses, and the like, are calculated. Gross building area is sometimes referred to as *construction area.*

Floor Usable Area

Floor usable area is computed by measuring the area enclosed between the finished surface of the office area side of corridors and the dominant portion and/or major vertical penetrations. Building common areas are considered to be part of floor usable area, and no deduction is made for columns and projections necessary to the building. Where alcoves, recessed entrances, or similar deviation from the corridor line are present, floor usable area is computed as if the deviation were not present.

Floor Rentable Area

Floor rentable area is the result of subtracting from the gross measured area of a floor the area of the major vertical penetrations on that same floor. No deduction is made for columns and projections necessary to the building. Spaces outside the exterior walls, such as balconies, terraces, or corridors, are excluded. Building rentable area is equal to the sum of all floor rentable areas.

Rentable versus Usable Area
of an Office Building

The *rentable area* of an office building typically includes space available for tenants' exclusive use as well as identified common areas, while the *usable area* is the area to which the tenant actually can have exclusive use. However, the landlord must realize a return on the entire building, and consequently the *rentable/usable ratio* has become standard for office and medical office buildings. In simple terms, the rentable/usable ratio is the relationship between the actual space that the tenant will be able to use exclusively and the entire building's area including all common areas (or the *gross area*).

If the gross area of a building is 200,000 square feet and the usable area is 180,000 square feet, the rentable/usable ratio will be 1.11. For every square foot of usable space that the tenant leases, he or she will pay rent on 1.11 times that space to include the rentable area. If the tenant leases 2,500 square feet of usable space, rent will be paid on 2,775 square feet of space. It is important for the tenant to understand this ratio and then use it to compare rental rates on spaces different buildings in the marketplace to determine which spaces are competitive.

Measuring Usable Area

The *usable area* of an office area, store area, or building common area shall be computed by measuring the area enclosed by: the finished surface of the office side of corridor and other permanent walls; the dominant portion or a major vertical penetration; and the center of partitions that separate the area being measured from adjoining office areas, store areas, and/or building common areas. As with floor usable area, no deductions are made for columns and projections that are necessary to the building. A floor's usable area is equal to the sum of all the usable areas on that same floor. Where alcoves, recessed entrances, or similar deviations from the corridor line are present, usable area is computed as if the deviation were not present.

Measuring Building Common Area

A building's *common area* comprises areas that provide services to building tenants but are not included in any specific tenant's office or store area. If a shared conference area were available to all tenants in the building and not rented to one specific tenant, that portion of the building would be a component of its common area. This area would be similar to any usable area of the building in the method of its measurement, but would be part of the building's common area rather than its usable area.

MEASURING RETAIL SPACE

As of this writing, there is no industry standard for measuring shopping center space. It is usually agreed that retail space should be measured to the outside of any outer wall, to the centerline of any *demising wall,* and across the major portion of any storefront regardless of indentations for the front door. Tenants should fully discuss this issue with retail landlords to be sure that they understand the method of arriving at the square footage and that they are satisfied that they are getting the space for which they are paying. Additionally, tenants should get confirmation regarding their portion of the building and how it is calculated, in order to be satisfied that they are paying their fair share of the *pass-through charges.*

As with office buildings, BOMA International has defined the most commonly accepted standards for store area measurements in the retail industry. As for all other commercial properties, a triple-net building's area is measured to the outside of all exterior walls, and there are no deductions made for common areas in multitenant buildings.

For individual stores, BOMA guidelines state: "The number of square feet in a ground floor store area shall be computed by measuring from the building line in the case of street frontages, and from the inner surface of other outer building walls and from the inner surface of corridor and other permanent partitions and to the center of partitions that separate the premises from adjoining shop areas. No deductions shall be made for vestibules inside the building line or for columns or projections necessary to the building. No addition should be made for bay windows extending outside the building line."

In many areas of the United States, the standard area measurement is obtained by measuring to the outside of all outside walls and to the centerline of any demising walls, with no deductions for supporting posts, entrances, or showcases. Mezzanines are seldom used to arrive at full square footages. Where basements exist, they are usually treated separately from the ground floor space, and this additional area may be included at a lesser rent.

When leasing retail space, it is always a good idea for the landlord to explain to the tenant how the measurements are made. It is difficult for a tenant to make certain measurements—to measure to the centerline of a demising wall, for example—and therefore he or she will almost always come up with less square footage than will the landlord.

Leasing agents may disclaim responsibility for the landlord's square footage measurements; they are not responsible for measuring the space. That responsibility falls to the landlord, but the tenant should still make some attempt to verify that the space measurement is accurate. Some landlords will round up for their own benefit and to make calculations easier.

However, most landlords are honest and only want accurate figures and calculations.

Square footage is almost always verified with an *estoppel* certificate when the property is either financed or sold. The estoppel is an agreement concerning the square footage, rents, and general terms of the property. Should a tenant challenge the square footage after an estoppel has been executed, he or she is placed in a difficult position since an agreement has already been reached on the matter. If the square footage is wrong, however, the landlord should be willing to adjust it even if the tenant has already signed an estoppel.

MEASURING INDUSTRIAL SPACE

The following subsections provide the basics for measuring space in industrial buildings. For a more in-depth analysis, the reader is directed to the book *Standard Methods for Measuring Floor Area in Industrial Buildings*, published by BOMA International and the Society of Industrial and Office REALTORS (SIOR).

General Guidelines—Exterior Wall Methodology

Exterior wall methodology is the most common approach to measuring space in industrial properties. When using this method to measure industrial building space, the rentable area in single-occupancy buildings is the same as the gross building area, or the area between the exterior walls on all four sides extending from the ground to the roofline. In multiple-occupancy buildings, the rentable area is the area reserved for the exclusive use of the tenant plus a proportionate share of the building's common area.

The full floor area of a one-story building is measured by determining the area enclosed by the *measure line*, which follows the line of all the building's exterior walls at floor level. If there are multiple stories, this measure is repeated for each additional full floor. For multistory, multiple-occupancy buildings, the area occupied by major vertical penetrations is also subtracted from each level's full floor area to determine the rentable area. The major vertical penetrations are measured with their enclosing walls.

If there are multiple tenants in the building, each tenant's full floor area—as well as the common area—is measured to the measure line for exterior walls, to the centerline of the demising wall for walls shared with another tenant or a common area, and to the exterior face of the enclosing wall for walls shared with major vertical penetrations or the floor's common area. For multistory buildings, floor common areas are measured as a tenant's area.

Rentable mezzanines are measured to the measure line on the side where the mezzanine is erected along the face of an exterior wall, to the end limits of the mezzanine floor on the interior sides or the centerline of the demising wall when sharing a wall with an office space or another tenant's area, and to the exterior face of the wall enclosing a floor's common area. In a multitenant building, the area of the rentable mezzanine is added to each tenant's area on the basis of exclusive occupancy.

Rentable stand-alone mezzanines are measured to the end limits of their floor, such limits not running along the face of an exterior wall. This area is also added to each tenant's area on the basis of occupancy in a multitenant building.

Gross building area of a one-story building is the sum of the ground level full floor area plus the total area of rentable mezzanines plus the total area of rentable stand-alone mezzanines. To find the gross building area for multistory buildings, the full floor area of each additional floor must be added to the calculation. In either case, the gross building area is also the rentable area.

Each tenant's rentable area is the sum of that tenant's full floor area, plus the tenant's area of rentable mezzanine, plus the tenant's area of rentable stand-alone mezzanine, plus the tenant's proportionate share of the common area.

General Guidelines—Drip Line Methodology

An alternative method for measuring industrial space is known as *drip line methodology*. It is not nearly as common as exterior wall methodology, but is worth mentioning because it may be found in some areas.

The full floor area of a one-story building is measured by determining the area enclosed by the measure line, which follows the most exterior drip line at the floor-level perimeter of the building's roof system. For multitenant, multistory buildings, the area occupied by vertical penetrations—measured with their enclosing walls or the measure line—is subtracted from the full floor area for each floor, and this measure is repeated for each additional full floor to find the floor rentable area.

If there are multiple tenants, the tenant's area is measured to the exterior face of walls enclosing a major vertical penetration, to the measure line in the case of the exterior wall, and to the centerline of the demising wall when sharing a wall with another tenant's area or a building common area.

In multistory buildings, the tenant's area on each full floor is measured to the exterior face of the walls enclosing a floor common area. Floor common areas are measured to the measure line in the case of the exterior walls and to the exterior face of the other walls enclosing them. Building common areas are measured as a tenant's area.

Building common area is measured without its enclosing walls when it shares a wall with a major vertical penetration, to the measure line in the case of an exterior wall, and to the centerline of the demising wall in the case of a wall that is shared with another tenant's area or a building common area.

Rentable mezzanines are measured to the measure line on the side where the mezzanine is erected along the face of an exterior wall, and to the end limits of the mezzanine floor on the interior sides or the centerline of the demising wall when sharing a wall with another tenant's area, an office area, or to the exterior face of the wall enclosing the floor common area. In a multitenant building, the area of rentable mezzanine is added to each tenant's area on the basis of exclusive occupancy.

Rentable stand-alone mezzanines are measured to the end limits of their floor, such limits not running along the face of an exterior wall. In one-story, multitenant buildings, the area of rentable stand-alone mezzanine is added to each tenant's area on the basis of occupancy.

Gross building area of a building is the sum of the ground level full floor area, plus the full floor area of any additional floors, plus the total area of rentable mezzanines, plus the total area of rentable stand-alone mezzanines. The gross building area is also the building's rentable area.

If the building has multiple tenants, each tenant's rentable area is the sum of that tenant's area on the full floor (or several full floors), plus that tenant's proportionate share of the floor common area on that floor (or floors), plus that tenant's area of rentable mezzanine, plus that tenant's area of rentable stand-alone mezzanine, plus that tenant's proportionate share of the building common area.

Working through Complications

It is easy to see that the measurement of space in an industrial building can become quite complex and lead to disagreements between landlord and tenant. The use of a CAD system should minimize these potential problems, but the landlord and tenant should work towards a mutual understanding at the outset of the relationship. It should also be noted that measuring space to the drip line is seldom used. Many consider this method unfair to the tenant because the measurements encompass space that is not readily usable by the tenant.

DETERMINING SPACE MEASUREMENTS FOR THE LEASE DOCUMENT

Every lease should have an exhibit that shows either the entire project (when practical) or an adequate portion of the project (e.g., the full floor of an office building or a shopping center wing) with the space delineated to show its exact location. Crosshatching the specific location in red often makes it easily visible and will show up on a copy of the site plan.

Additionally, an exhibit showing the actual leased space is another good tool to define what is being leased. This requires a drawing, which can be done either by the property's architect or by someone in the office tracing an existing drawing to identify the space.

SPACE PLANNING

Space planning is an important component of the leasing process. The space planner, who acts as a valuable leasing tool for the landlord by helping tenants to understand their space needs, is most often paid by the landlord. Sophisticated tenants quite often have their own space planners and have a good idea of what they need before they start the leasing process. However, smaller or independent tenants generally have less understanding of their real space needs, and assistance from the landlord can help finalize a lease.

The space planner's job is to work with tenants to produce viable space plans for their occupancy in the building, keeping within the financial constraints of the landlord's and each tenant's willingness to spend additional funds. Quite often the space planner will have several typical floor plans to start the discussions and then will make adjustments based on the tenant's needs and budget considerations. The cost for an effective space planner is money well spent if it assists prospects in reaching conclusions about their space needs in the building.

Very large office buildings may have a space planner on staff, at least during the most critical portion of the building's lease-up. The alternative is to use a space planner on a consulting basis, in which case the space planner is usually compensated per square foot of the space plan. The space planner is not there to do a build-out drawing for the tenant, but it is not unusual for a very helpful and effective space planner to be retained by the tenant to finish the job. The space planner should be fully aware of the building, the standard tenant improvement (TI) package, and any available upgrades. A good space planner is aware of which improvements are likely to increase the construction budget substantially.

Space planning is more common with office and medical office buildings than with shopping center and industrial buildings. However, there are some considerations for these types of properties as well, and they are discussed below.

Shopping Center Space Planning

For retail locations, the landlord has little to do with the tenant's space planning. The landlord/developer must initially decide on the types of tenants likely to be attracted to the shopping center, and accordingly provide spaces in appropriate shapes and sizes. In larger shopping centers, it is often possible to build out large sections of the shopping center with back walls and post and beam construction inside, but without demising walls until some leases are signed. The landlord then has the flexibility to finish the space to a specific tenant's needs. In many strip shopping centers, the space is demised based on the anticipated size of the shop tenant. This expedites the build-out of the tenant's premises but may limit the size of space some tenants lease.

Anchor tenants are usually very specific about their needs, and the landlord will have little input outside of keeping the exterior design consistent with the rest of the shopping center. Build-to-suit and *pad* tenants also do most of their own space planning, but are subject to the exterior of the building being compatible with the balance of the shopping center.

If landlords need to split existing spaces, they must be sure that the remaining space is still a viable unit and likely to be leased without too much extra effort or reduced rent. Creating pie-shaped spaces, dog-legged spaces, or hard-to-see spaces is not good planning, as these tend to be difficult to lease. Yet sometimes this is unavoidable because of the size and configuration of the land being developed. Too often, the answer to leasing difficult spaces is to lower the rent, causing the value of the entire shopping center to decrease.

One of the major considerations for shopping center landlords is to prevent less experienced tenants from taking space that is much too large for them simply because it is the only space available. Few small or local merchants really know their optimum space size, so it is up to the landlord to help. The landlord tries to maximize the shopping center's sales per square foot, and keeping tenants in properly sized spaces is a major step in that direction.

Dollars & Cents of Shopping Centers, copublished biannually by the Urban Land Institute (ULI) and the International Council of Shopping Centers (ICSC), provides information on the typical sizes of almost every retailer. Within these parameters, the landlord should be able to work with prospects to help determine the best space size for their business without adding unnecessary space that will generate superfluous rent and other charges.

Strip shopping centers and neighborhood shopping centers most often lease their spaces in *vanilla shell* condition. This means that the landlord provides the walls, one restroom, the drop ceiling, the heat pump, air conditioning, the storefront, and the electrical distribution system. Malls and lifestyle shopping centers are most often leased with the landlord providing only the demising walls, the roof, and utilities brought to the lease line. Generally, a smaller local tenant is not experienced in building out the premises, whereas a tenant leasing space in a large regional or super-regional center often has an organization that can take care of any construction involved.

Industrial Property Space Planning

Most large industrial tenants know their needs and are likely to look for space with those needs in mind, with little help from the landlord. Incubator space is often already built out, and there is little for the tenant to do but use it "as is" or look for something else that meets the operation's needs. However, many industrial properties now include the headquarters and other offices of major manufacturers, so office space needs may be a consideration as well. Towards that end, an industrial landlord may choose to have a space planner available to help tenants work out office arrangements.

ZONING AND PERMITS

It is up to landlords to fully understand the zoning for their commercial properties and to make sure that their tenants' use of the premises is within those regulations. If there is any doubt, the landlord should check the zoning before entering into a lease.

The landlord also should be aware of what the permitting process requires for various types of use. Restaurants have building permit issues, but also health department issues. Medical offices and labs have similar permitting requirements. Uses such as beauty salons, jewelry manufacturing, and cleaning establishments may have special permitting requirements. The landlord should be aware of these requirements and be in a position to help tenants work their way through them.

It can be argued that the landlord really has no responsibility to get a tenant's building and occupancy permits, but, in most cases, until tenants open for business there is no rent or income for the building. The property's property manager should be available to assist the tenant whenever possible. Tenants want confirmation that their use is within the zoning limitations and general requirements of a specific location. A retail location may well be zoned for an office use, but the covenants, conditions, and restrictions (CC&Rs) of the shopping center may prohibit this use.

LANDLORD-PROVIDED IMPROVEMENTS

Landlords prefer to lease commercial space in "as is" condition. However, in most office and medical office lease deals the landlord provides tenant improvements (TIs). Typically, once a tenant has vacated the premises, the landlord will remove any fixtures and improvements that have been left behind, clean the premises to "broom clean" condition, and deliver the premises to the new tenant. The landlord should be aware that a past tenant has not left behind personal property such as sign cans, phone systems, etc. The new tenant may come in and assume he has the right to use these items only to have the former tenant come back to claim them.

If the new tenant is able to negotiate additional improvements to be provided by the landlord, the landlord should draw up a lease exhibit indicating exactly what is to be provided and that any additional work will be at the tenant's expense. The landlord should either set a dollar limit on the improvements or indicate the exact amount and grade of carpet, the particular number and quality of light fixtures, the specific number and quality of doors, and so forth. It is in both the landlord's and tenant's interest to fully understand what is being provided. It is also good business for both parties to have a walkthrough as soon as the new tenant takes over the premises so that completed work can be inspected, necessary repairs or corrections can be agreed upon, and a timeframe for these improvements can be established.

In office and medical office buildings, tenants naturally will want to receive the maximum amount of improvements from the landlord, but this is determined by the market and the competition in the marketplace, the strength of the tenant, and the vacancy factor in the building in question. Office space is commonly leased in one of three ways. A full *turnkey operation* can be provided by the landlord, but this is likely reserved for only the strongest and largest of tenants; however, if a smaller but financially strong tenant is willing to pay a return on the cost of the extra improvements, it is likely that such a lease can be negotiated. The second level of improvements is an agreed upon tenant allowance, such as $40 per square foot of usable area. The third level of improvements is paint and carpet only. And, finally, the space can be leased in "as is" condition, with the tenant paying for all improvements.

If the premises is being taken over by the tenant in "as is" condition, this usually means that the landlord will not paint the walls or replace carpeting, but that the basic building systems are in good condition and that air conditioning, electrical, and plumbing systems are functioning properly. There are no rules as to what is "acceptable" condition for the handing over of leased property, but the parties should both be fully aware of and agree to the conditions to avoid future conflicts.

LANDLORD LEASING DOCUMENTS

Leasing documentation is especially critical for properties that have yet to be built. All of the original documentation should be as accurate as possible. The property site plan should be accurate to the best of everyone's ability. There are always circumstances that require last-minute changes, but those can be dealt with on a one-on-one basis with the tenant.

Most site plans have a disclaimer that they are only for general layouts, building positioning, etc. and that the landlord has the right to make changes without notifying tenants. However, some changes in the site plan can have a major impact on tenants: In a shopping center, adding a pad or *outlot* in the parking lot may have a great impact on the street visibility of some tenants in the strip space behind the pad building. Obstructing a second floor office tenant's view with a parking structure after the lease is signed will likely create problems. Eliminating parking or reducing the parking ratio for an office building after leases have been signed will be problematic. These significant changes should be disclosed to tenants in advance to minimize complications.

The construction exhibits are a critical leasing item to both parties and should be very specific regarding what is *building standard,* to be provided by the landlord, and what is to be provided by the tenant. Language should be very specific for the benefit of both parties.

Additionally, the timelines for TIs should be very detailed concerning what is to be done and when. If there will be interface between the tenant's contractors and the building contractors, the specifics of those relationships should be established and specific construction timelines set up. It is very expensive for either party if the other does not perform as agreed.

Once the lease has been negotiated, the landlord should prepare the proper number of copies and submit them immediately to the tenant for review and comment. Time is critical in any leasing situation, and wasted time may mean that the tenant changes his or her mind or is contacted by a competitor with a better deal.

BILLBACK ISSUES

One of the major landlord and tenant considerations is that of billback items. Since landlords usually pass these charges on to their tenants, some landlords may not pay enough attention to the impact of these charges on the tenants. The large majority of landlords, however, are quite conscientious about billbacks; but tenants must also be diligent in making sure that they understand the billbacks and how they will be calculated and billed to them.

It is not all that unusual today for tenants to hire outside consultants to review common area charges and challenge those billings. For this reason alone, landlords should be especially careful in the administration of the entire billback program.

Shopping Center Billbacks

There are several general methods used for charging shopping center common area billbacks among tenants. A small shopping center often has only one common area budget, and that budget will be allocated based on either pro rata square footage or pro rata leased square footage (discussed in more detail in Chapter 10, "Financial Issues"). Both are fairly straightforward. There may be anchor tenants involved who are responsible for their own roofs, exterior walls, trash removal, and insurance, so the anchor tenants and other tenants may have two different allocations. The landlord should always be able to show how each allocation is calculated and how he or she arrives at each tenant's share.

An enclosed mall may have an entirely different setup for distributing common area costs. Normally, there is one overall common area budget for the exterior or parking lot area of the mall and all tenants—including the anchors—contribute to these expenses. A second budget exists for the mall common areas, and the anchor tenants usually do *not* contribute to this budget even though they have fronts on the mall, because they feel they do not benefit from the mall being there. Some anchors do make a token payment to the mall expenses, but they seldom pay their pro rata share. All the other tenants who face the mall pay for the common area expenses.

A separate budget often exists for the food court and is shared only by food court tenants. Food court tenants share a dining area, trash removal facilities, and employees to bus and clean the food court. These tenants also must pay their share of the mall and exterior common area costs, so their share of the expenses can be quite high. However, because there is a shared dining area, the food court tenants lease smaller spaces. These are also some of the highest grossing tenants in most malls, so the costs should not be onerous.

If there are shopping center tenants who provide some of their own services, confusion may arise when calculating common area billbacks. It is not unusual for a few tenants to provide their own insurance coverage, some to provide their own trash removal services, and many to have their own separate water meters. This will result in a different set of expense pools for each of those items.

A tenant may be required to pay, for example, 5.42 percent of the overall common area expenses. However, because two other tenants provide their own trash removal and consequently make the pool of tenants contributing to the shopping center's trash removal service smaller, this same tenant must pay 7.2 percent of the shopping center's trash removal costs. Some shopping centers have as many as eight or nine separate expense pools, and there is nothing wrong with this arrangement as long as the landlord is able to properly explain the situation and accurately calculate the tenants' expenses for each pool, and the tenants understand and agree with the allocations.

Office Building Billbacks

Office building tenants should familiarize themselves with load factors and comparisons of rent charges.

Load Factors.   Office and medical office building tenants will also pay their share of the building operating costs, taxes, and insurance premiums. An issue for office and medical tenants is that of rentable area versus usable area. Most office buildings have large atriums, big entrances, elevator lobbies, etc., and the landlord must receive compensation for these common areas. This is accounted for in the leasing process by adding a *load factor* to each tenant's rent charges.

The load factor is calculated by dividing the building's total common area by its total usable area. For example, if a building has 20,000 square feet of atriums and lobbies and 120,000 square feet of space to be rented to individual tenants, the building is said to have a load factor of 16.67 percent (20,000 ÷ 120,000). For every square foot of usable space a tenant rents in this building, a factor of 16.67 percent of that footage will be added to the tenant's rent. So if the tenant leases a usable area of 1,600 square feet, he or she will end up paying rent and charges on 1,867 square feet (1,600 × .1667 + 1,600).

Tenants therefore will ultimately pay rent and charges on the building's common area space as well as on the space intended for their exclusive use, hence the term *rentable area*. Various buildings have different load factors. It is up to the tenant to evaluate each location to decide if the building's load factor seems reasonable and if the common area space is worth the additional charge.

Comparing Rent Charges.   In order to compare competitive leasing proposals, it is helpful for the tenant to calculate all spaces in usable footage and then make the comparisons. Available spaces in the following three example buildings are used to illustrate this point.

- **Building A** has 1,250 square feet of usable space. There is no load factor, and the rent per square foot is $25.00. The total rent is $31,250 per year.

- **Building B** has 1,200 square feet of available space, with a load factor of 13.5 percent. The total rentable area is 1,362 square feet, at $22.50 per square foot. The effective usable rent is therefore $25.54 per square foot, or $30,645 per year.

- **Building C** has an available space of 1,400 square feet, with a load factor of 12 percent. The rentable area is 1,568 square feet, with a quoted rate of $21.00 per square foot. This translates to a usable rent of $23.52 per square foot, or $32,928 per year.

Although Building C offers the best price per square foot of usable area, it is also the largest space. If the tenant does not need this much space, the spaces in Buildings A and B offer a lower total yearly rent. The tenant must also look at the billback charges as they will be applied to the rentable area; this additional factor can add substantial costs to the total charges.

Industrial Property Billbacks

Industrial tenants often have fairly straightforward common area billback expenses, and these billbacks almost always appear in a single budget. Industrial tenants typically pay their pro rata share of expenses based on leasable space. There can be some exceptions, but they are rare. Landlords should be able to properly explain any exceptions to prospects so there is full agreement on the charges.

COMPLYING WITH ADA REQUIREMENTS

Compliance with the *Americans with Disabilities Act (ADA)* requirements cannot be ignored. ADA is a federal act with governing rules and regulations, and the penalty of noncompliance can be severe, including civil and criminal penalties. Tenants should investigate the condition of the premises relative to ADA compliance prior to signing the lease, as those requirements could easily fall on tenants after they have committed to the lease.

The major question that arises is who will provide and pay for ADA compliance items. The landlord typically is responsible for overall building requirements, while the tenant pays for items that are user-specific and within the confines of the leased space. It is not likely that the landlord will have any interest in paying to bring tenant fixtures or equipment to ADA compliance. However, there is nothing to stop the parties from negotiating another arrangement that is satisfactory to both sides.

The physical space is especially critical to the tenant's needs, and he or she should spend sufficient time evaluating it to ensure compliance with all laws, zoning requirements, and local rules. The tenant should resist the urge to take a space simply because the rent and charges are lower than elsewhere. In the end, a less expensive space may not serve the tenant's business needs as well as a higher-priced space.

10

Financial Issues

The commercial property lease is a financial instrument. The property's cash flow and ultimate value are established through the terms of the lease. The landlord walks a fine line between having a vacant unit and maximizing the financial terms of a lease. It is important for the landlord to maximize the financial terms of each by knowing the market conditions while creating the best tenant mix for the property. In the long term, this will maximize the value of the property and provide tenants with the best environment in which to operate their business.

Because commercial leases are for extended periods, the negotiated terms become much more consequential for both the landlord and the tenant. With a month-to-month lease, the landlord can change the terms to meet market conditions every 30 days if desired. A month-to-month lease has a downside, though: the landlord and the tenant may cancel the lease with 30 days' notice. On the other hand, a lease with a major retail tenant that has a 25-year term, with five options of five years each, provides little or no opportunity for the landlord to adjust the rents to market conditions. The tradeoff for the landlord is that the development has a major tenant. If the development is a shopping center, the major tenant is critical to the development of the project. From the tenant's perspective, the long-term lease provides the opportunity to build a long-term business with a known and controlled occupancy cost for many decades.

Tenants, on the other hand, must negotiate a lease term that ensures that their business will not be disrupted with an unexpected relocation if their lease is not renewed, while also allowing the ability to relocate when their business either outgrows their space or another location becomes better suited for their business. The tenant must carefully analyze the right lease length to meet the above-mentioned concerns. The tenant does not want to be saddled with an onerous lease—especially if the economy is headed for a downturn. Both sides of any negotiation should keep the other party's position in mind, and both should work towards a win-win deal.

RENTAL INCOME

The value of a building can exceed its actual cost to develop and its replacement cost by the value of its leases. In essence, the value of a building is based on its income stream. It is the rental and miscellaneous income minus the operating expenses of the building that create the value in commercial properties. Value is established by capitalizing the net operating income (NOI) by a capitalization rate (*cap rate*), usually determined by the marketplace. Landlords always try to optimize their building's value, even when they have no intention of selling or refinancing the building.

Tenants, on the other hand, look for the best financial deal they can make, while simultaneously seeking the best retail space, office location, or industrial site to meet their business needs. While it is necessary for there to be a meeting of minds to complete a lease arrangement, both sides look at different factors in reaching this decision.

The Landlord's Effective Rent

All commercial building landlords develop a budget for their buildings, while developers prepare a *pro forma* for their development. Leasing is an important component of a building's budget and a proposed development's pro forma. The budget and pro forma should include a deal-making rent for all of the vacant and anticipated vacant spaces in the property. The deal-making rate is used because the asking rent is seldom realized. Landlords may be required to offer concessions to lease space within a reasonable timeframe.

It is important for landlords to fully understand the financial implications of each lease. This is not to say that any lease that does not meet the pro forma will be rejected, but landlords must understand the net effect of each lease on meeting all of their obligations and objectives. Often the landlord focuses on just the rental rate and concessions. The landlord needs to consider how the monetary and nonmonetary lease provisions impact the building's operations and affect its value. Lease provisions are discussed from both the landlord's and the tenant's perspectives in Chapter 12, "Negotiating the Lease."

One of the means to evaluate a lease deal is calculating its effective rent. The *effective rent* is the total net rent received over the lease term when divided by the number of months in the term. A simple example is a three-year lease, with three months free rent, for a space of 2,000 square feet at a rental rate of $26 per square foot:

Lease term: 3 years (3 months free rent)
Base rent: $26 per square foot
Space: 2,000 square feet

Annual asking rent: 2,000 square feet × $26 = $52,000
Total asking rent (3 years): 3 × $52,000 = $156,000
Monthly base rent: $52,000 ÷ 12 = $4,333.33
3 months free rent: $4,333.33 × 3 months = $13,000
Total rent due: $156,000 − $13,000 free rent = $143,000
Effective rent: $143,000 ÷ 36 months = $3,972.22

In this example, the effective monthly rent brings down the monthly asking rent from $4,333.33 to $3,972.22. Put another way, it takes $361.11 per month to cover the free rent concession in this lease. The effective average rental rate over the three years is $3,972.22 ($143,000 ÷ 36 months ÷ 2,000 square feet = $1.99 per square foot).

The Tenant's Effective Rent

Although the rental terms of a lease are the same for the landlord and the tenant, the tenant looks at the negotiation from a slightly different perspective. The tenant's calculation will take into account any building common area maintenance (CAM) charges or billbacks when arriving at the tenant effective rent.

For the same example given above, assuming that the building's annual billbacks are $6 per square foot, the tenant's side of the ledger would be as follows:

Monthly asking rent: $4,333.33
Free rent reduction: $361.11
Annual billbacks or CAM charges: $6 per square foot
Monthly billbacks or CAM charges: $0.50 per square foot (2,000
   square feet × $0.50 = $1,000 per month)
Tenant effective rent: $4,333.33 − $361.11 + 1,000 = $4,972.72

Both sides must look carefully at the net effect of each lease proposal on themselves and the other party to understand fully how the agreement impacts the parties to the lease.

Occupancy Costs

The landlord and the tenant also look at occupancy costs from a slightly different point of view. For the landlord, the tenant's occupancy costs are those that are billed by the landlord—such as base rent, percentage rent, and common area or billback charges. All other tenant costs would be required in any property, so they are not the landlord's direct concern.

The tenant, however, considers occupancy costs to include the base rent, any percentage rent, and common area or billback charges, *as well as* any *key money* paid and the *amortization* of improvements for that particular location.

Percentage Rent

The concept of percentage rent is well established, and it is accepted by most retail tenants. The reasoning behind percentage rent is that the landlord has built a retailing environment that is stronger than that of comparable stores in freestanding locations, and consequently the landlord wants to share in the tenant's success in that location. Most retail tenants have no quarrel with this approach, but want to be sure they can make a reasonable profit within the structure of the lease.

In theory, both landlord and tenant are doing well if the tenant is paying percentage rent. At the point that most percentage rents become effective, the tenant's sales are at a fairly high level and occupancy costs are at the lowest as a percentage of their sales, even though they are paying additional rent to the landlord.

However, some shopping center landlords—especially those with many small, local merchants—have elected to forego any attempt to get percentage rent provisions. Instead, they just negotiate the highest possible minimum rents for the marketplace with annual rental increases. They reason rents are so high the typical small merchant's sales are not likely to exceed the level to pay percentage rent, so it is not worth the trouble to negotiate and administer percentage rent. However, the landlord never knows when a tenant—especially the owner of a restaurant or jewelry store—may do exceptionally well and generate sales that would exceed a percentage rent breakpoint for paying percentage rent. It is best for the landlord to negotiate for market rent, annual rental increases, and a percentage rent lease provision. The market conditions and the negotiating strength of the landlord and the tenant will determine the outcome of the negotiations.

With percentage rent, tenants typically pay either the greater of their base or minimum rent or a percent of their sales. Many smaller merchants are under the mistaken impression that most arrangements include base rent plus a percentage of all of their sales, and such an arrangement could increase the occupancy cost more than the tenant can afford.

Exhibit 10.1
Typical Percentage Rents

Supermarket	1–2 percent (usually closer to 1 percent)
Restaurant	5–6 percent
Fast food	5–8 percent (usually closer to 5 percent)
Variety store	3 percent
Women's ready-to-wear	5–6 percent
Men's wear	5–6 percent
Shoes	5 percent
Electronics	3 percent
Hardware	4 percent
Sporting goods	5 percent
Cards and gifts	6 percent
Jewelry	6 percent
Drug store/pharmacy	2.5 percent
Fabric store	5 percent
Pet shop	6 percent
Hair salon	6 percent
Dry cleaner/laundry	7–7.5 percent
Nail salon	6 percent
Department store	2 percent

Percentage rent rates vary depending on the type of retailer or service tenant. They vary by business type, and a range of acceptable rates makes the selected percentage fully negotiable. The percentages are based on the tenant's profit margins and have evolved over the years to fairly standard percentages. *Dollars & Cents of Shopping Centers,* which is copublished every two years by the Urban Land Institute (ULI) and the International Council of Shopping Centers (ICSC), lists the median percentage rate and the lower and upper deciles for each tenant category; it is the best source on percentage rent rates for various tenant types.

Examples of typical percentages are displayed in Exhibit 10.1. Big box and discount stores and other anchor tenants have low percentage rates. Fashion, jewelry, and gift stores have higher percentage rates, and service tenants have the highest percentage rates.

Breakpoints.   The point at which a merchant starts paying a percentage of their gross sales as percentage rent is called the *breakpoint.* The breakpoint can be either natural or artificial. The *natural breakpoint* is determined by dividing the base or *minimum rent* by the percentage rent rate. If, for example, the rent is $2,400 per month and the percentage rent rate is 6 percent, the natural breakpoint is $2,400 ÷ 0.06, or $40,000 per month and $480,000 per year. Another way of stating this is that the minimum rent of $2,400 covers the first $40,000 per month of sales. The tenant pays a percentage of all sales above $40,000 per month. The tenant's percentage rent is annualized. If the tenant's annual sales are less than $480,000, any percentage rent paid during the year is refunded to the tenant.

The *artificial breakpoint* is a negotiated figure. Quite often, anchor tenants will do internal calculations to determine the gross sales figure at which they hit profitability for a given location. They will then negotiate an artificial breakpoint, without reference to the natural breakpoint. The artificial breakpoint is often negotiated up or down based on additional contributions made by either the tenant or the landlord to construction, tenant improvements (TIs), etc. Retailers with high sales per square foot and who are strong traffic draws are in a good position to negotiate an artificial breakpoint above the natural breakpoint.

There are several common circumstances in which tenants choose to negotiate higher breakpoints. When the premises are in poor condition but the landlord has no money to invest in improvements, the tenant may agree to do the improvements and increase the breakpoint to a figure that allows recovery from the extra costs. Very successful retailers or restaurants usually have the negotiating strength to negotiate higher breakpoints. And, if the shopping center is having occupancy problems, the landlord may agree to artificially high breakpoint to entice the tenant to enter into the lease.

Landlords also have several reasons for negotiating artificially low breakpoints. When a tenant has negotiated a below-market rent, the landlord may ask for a lower breakpoint in order to recover more quickly if the tenant does well. If a shopping center's sales are substantially higher than national averages, the landlord will want the opportunity to collect additional rent and have it paid sooner. Similarly, landlords who have contributed to their tenants' improvements will want to have the opportunity to recapture their TI costs by collecting additional percentage rent. This can be accomplished by using an artificially low breakpoint.

Here is an example of the impact an artificially low and an artificially high breakpoint can have on the percentage rent a tenant owes. In the scenario, the natural breakpoint is $500,000, the tenant's sales are $600,000, and the percentage rate is 6 percent.

> Percentage rent owed with a natural breakpoint: **$6,000**
> ($600,000 − $500,000 = $100,000 × .06)
> Percentage rent owed with an artificially low breakpoint of
> $400,000: **$12,000**
> ($600,000 − $400,000 = $200,000 × .06)
> Percentage rent owed with an artificially high breakpoint of
> $600,000: **None**
> ($600,000 − $600,000 = 0)

Deducting Expenses.   Anchor tenants have been able, at times, to negotiate the right to deduct certain expenses from any percentage rent due.

Although, in reality, these two elements have nothing to do with each other, some tenants in strong negotiating positions have been able to prevail in this matter. The most commonly deducted items are real estate taxes and insurance premiums—both fairly substantial expenses. For example, a tenant might originally owe $56,000 in percentage rent for a given year. However, this tenant is allowed to subtract the $32,000 already paid in taxes and insurance premiums for that same year from percentage rent owed, thus reducing the percentage rent payable to $24,000.

In these rare situations, the right to deduct expenses is usually limited to a single year. However, some tenants in very strong negotiating positions manage to negotiate a cumulative arrangement that allows taxes and insurance paid at *any* time during the lease to be deductible from any percentage rent paid during the lease term. If the taxes and insurance payments for a year exceed the percentage rent owed for that year, the balance not recaptured from percentage rent is carried forward and applied to percentage rent owned in subsequent years. Few tenants are able to negotiate a recapture from percentage rent.

Using Annual versus Monthly Sales.   The typical percentage rent provision calls for tenants to report monthly sales. Because collecting sales reports and percentage rent can be more difficult than collecting minimum rent, many leases provide for a monetary penalty or fee if tenants do not submit sales reports on time. However, most tenants pay percentage rent monthly, when their sales exceed their breakpoint, and at the end of the year the sales are annualized. If the tenants' sales do not exceed their annual breakpoint, any percentage rent paid is refunded.

A store could easily pay much more in percentage rent if sales were calculated on a stand-alone monthly basis rather than averaged annually. Even if a store does not reach its annual breakpoint with high sales, it could still be required to pay a monthly percentage rate (commonly for those with holidays or significant promotions) that would be returned at the year's end.

To illustrate this point, suppose there is a candy store that is 1,200 square feet. The annual rental rate for this space is $24,000 with a percentage rent of 6 percent. This tenant's monthly sales for a year-long period are as follows:

January:	$14,762
February:	$45,677
March:	$17,251
April:	$18,202
May:	$37,666
June:	$16,434
July:	$17,223
August:	$18,335

September:	$19,678
October:	$42,337
November:	$23,556
December:	$55,778
Total:	**$326,889**

The natural breakpoint for this tenant is calculated by dividing the percentage rent of 6 percent into the annual rent of $24,000, for an annual breakpoint of $400,000. On that basis, the tenant would not owe any percentage rent for this year. However, if the calculations were done on a *monthly* basis, the monthly breakpoint would be $33,333, which is calculated by dividing the monthly rent of $2,000 by the percentage rate of .06. The candy store tenant would then owe the following percentage rents for the months with sales above the breakpoint:

February (Valentine's Day):	$45,677 – $33,333 = 12,344 × .06 = $740.64
May (Mother's Day):	$37,666 – $33,333 = 4,333 × .06 = $259.98
October (Halloween):	$42,337 – $33,333 = 9,004 × .06 = $540.24
December (Christmas):	$55,778 – $33,333 = 22,445 × .06 = $1,346.70

By calculating percentage rent on a monthly basis, this tenant ends up paying almost $3,000 more in rent. This is unfair to the tenant. Annual adjustments are the most equitable approach to percentage rent payment.

Percentage Rent Refunds.   Ultimately, and unless the lease states otherwise, annual sales determine whether or not a tenant pays percentage rent or receives a refund of percentage rent paid during the year. If the tenant does pay percentage rent based on monthly calculations, but annual sales ultimately are not sufficient to mandate percentage rent payment, the landlord is obliged to refund the excess percentage rent to the tenant after the first of the year.

The tenant should negotiate the timeframe for calculating and paying any refund. The landlord would like to have two to four months to determine if a refund is owed, while the tenant wants the landlord to make this determination within a month of the December sales report submission—typically by the end of February. The second issue to negotiate is how is the overpayment of percentage rent is refunded to the tenant. Many landlords prefer to credit any overpayment towards the tenant's future rent payments, while others will send the tenant a check for the overpayment amount.

Declining Percentage Rents.   Some high-volume tenants negotiate a *declining percentage rent*. Such a deal is executed under the theory that good sales volume is due mostly to the tenant's own efforts but also partly to the quality of the landlord's shopping center. Consequently, once the high-volume merchant reaches an exceedingly high sales volume, the percentage rate applied to additional sales is lowered. The landlord, on the other hand, still wants to be reasonably certain that a particular tenant will meet the required sales volume before agreeing to this declining percentage rate, to ensure that the deal will be profitable for both parties.

Supermarkets are more likely than most tenants to use the declining percentage rate approach. A typical percentage rent provision for a supermarket has a 1.25 percent rate applied to sales above the breakpoint. Assuming that a supermarket has a minimum rental of $160,000 and a 1.25 percent rental rate, the natural breakpoint for the market would be $12.8 million. If the supermarket generated sales of $25 million, the tenant would owe the landlord the base rent of $160,000 in addition to percentage rent of $152,500, for a total rental of $312,500.

However, if the tenant is in a strong negotiating position and expects to generate high sales, that tenant might be able to negotiate a declining percentage rate to reduce the amount of percentage rent owed. For instance, this could include a 1.25 percent rental rate for gross sales above the breakpoint ($12,800,000), up to 15,000,000; a 1-percent rate for the next five million dollars in sales; and 0.75 percent for all sales above the 20-million-dollar level. The total rent for this supermarket with $25,000,000 in gross sales would then be calculated as follows:

Base rent:	$160,000
1.25 percent of $2,200,000:	$27,500
1.00 percent of 5,000,000:	$50,000
.75 percent of 5,000,000:	$37,500
Total rent:	**$275,000**

By using a declining percentage rent in this example, the tenant saves $37,500, and the landlord still receives $115,000 in percentage rent.

THE IMPORTANCE OF SALES REPORTS

Sales reports are important in determining if a tenant owes any percentage rent. They have other significant benefits as well. By tracking tenant sales over a period of years, the landlord can track how well tenants are doing by comparing their sales figures to either the sales reported in *Dollars & Cents of Shopping Centers* or those of other tenants in the same category within the shopping center.

Generally, tenant sales are recorded on a spreadsheet that shows sales from the month the tenant opened for business to the current month's sales. By looking back over this period of time, the landlord can evaluate how well the tenant is performing. This is especially helpful when working with a tenant on a lease renewal, and is one issue landlords use when evaluating whether or not to offer a merchant a lease renewal.

In addition to determining how well tenants are doing, sales reports are also used to calculate what percent the tenants' rents and other charges are to their sales. To calculate this percentage, landlords compare a tenant's costs—for items such as rent, billbacks, and the marketing fund dues—to the tenant's sales.

It is generally accepted that this percentage for a merchant should not be more than two to three times the tenant's percentage rent rate. Obviously, when a merchant has just started a new business or opened a new store, the tenant's occupancy cost as a percentage of sales will be high; but once the merchant is established, the occupancy cost should fall into the acceptable range. If a tenant has a percentage rent of 5 percent, the expected occupancy cost should be in the range of 10 to 15 percent of sales. If the occupancy cost is below that figure, it is assumed that the tenant is doing well; if the occupancy cost is above that figure, the landlord should do further analysis to determine whether there is a problem or the tenant is still in the growing curve.

In larger shopping centers, with several tenants in some categories of merchandise, landlords compare tenants' sales within categories such as men's wear, women's wear, shoes, restaurants, food court, etc. The various merchants' sales are listed in their category and, using disguised identities, tenants are shown their sales per square foot and the percentage of increase or decrease for the current month and year to date in comparison with the other tenants in their category. These reports are given to each merchant to demonstrate how each is doing with respect to the rest of the shopping center's tenants; they are a good starting point from which the landlord can discuss tenant concerns and provide suggestions for improving sales.

THE LEASE FORM

The party that supplies the lease form usually starts off in a stronger negotiating position, since the other party is negotiating from someone else's document. Landlords prefer to use their own lease forms. The use of a single form for all the tenants allows for an easier negotiation and administration of the completed lease. A standard lease is much easier for the landlord to negotiate, as he is familiar with the agreement and the reasons behind all of the provisions. When using a tenant lease, it is a good idea for the landlord to use the services of an attorney and or a commercial leasing agent who is familiar with lease documents to monitor any changes and the impact of some provisions on the property, as well as the landlord's rights and obligations from legal and operational perspectives.

Most tenants will accept the landlord's lease form, but there are exceptions. Anchor tenants in shopping centers almost always have a lease form of their own, and they insist on its use. Many larger national retail tenants also have their own lease forms that they make every effort to use. However, they will use the landlord's form if required to—and then engage in extensive negotiations so that it often ends up looking more like their own form after the negotiations are complete.

Office building tenants usually use the landlord's lease form. However, many governmental agencies insist on using their own form. Quite often, ground floor retail, banks, and savings and loan offices may request to use their lease form. The lease modifications required for these types of uses are usually substantial. The work involved in either converting the landlord's lease form or modifying the tenant's form to meet the situation is substantial. Again, the use of legal counsel is advised for both parties to the lease.

Industrial tenants usually use the landlord's lease form. Very few industrial tenants have enough locations to have their own lease document. However, there are a few very large users who may insist on their own forms. This is often the price of landing a large tenant. Even if the industrial tenant is substantial, the landlord should still make sure that tenant is financially sound before offering substantial concessions and using an unknown lease format.

Industrial *incubator tenants* use the landlord's lease form. As long as the landlord has prepared a reasonable document that is not onerous, it is usually accepted with few, if any, modifications.

One of the more complicated lease forms is used for tenant build-outs or build-to-suits. The basic lease document is similar for these situations, but the exhibits are generally much more complicated. It is critical for the landlord to be very specific about what is to be provided and what the tenant is to provide. This applies equally to the tenant in these situations. It is not good business to indicate that the landlord will provide "turnkey" improvements without defining exactly what is to be provided. The landlord must have protection against cost overruns, and the tenants must have protections that they will get what was agreed.

Landlords should take great care to consider what a tenant is asking for before agreeing to provide it. The landlord must know the exact cost before committing to the improvements. In many cases, a build-to-suit will have a specific dollar figure allotted for total costs and an increased rental factor if the costs exceed that figure. Some build-to-suit leases will have what is called an *upset figure*. For example, the lease might include a provision that says the landlord has the right to cancel the lease or have the tenant pay the difference if construction estimate costs exceed a specific amount (e.g., $500,000).

LEASE LENGTH

The length of a lease is an important factor for both the landlord and the tenant. Landlords have often indicated that "short leases make for good tenants," meaning that poor tenants can quickly be replaced if a short-term lease is in place. In reality, the situation is much more complicated than this implies. On newly developed properties, lenders often want the initial lease terms to be at least five years. Because of the cost for TIs, many office landlords prefer five- to seven-year leases. Tenants frequently choose longer terms in order to amortize their fixturization and improvement costs. The average lease length also varies by property type, as detailed below. As a rule of thumb, most commercial leases for local tenants under 5,000 square feet are three to five years.

Shopping Center Lease Terms

Anchor tenants will always insist on long-term leases. The typical supermarket and drugstore lease has an initial term of 20 to 25 years, and department store tenants often prefer 30-year leases. These tenants usually have multiple five-year renewal options. Supermarket tenants prefer 20-year leases, with eight five-year renewal options.

Some retail anchor tenants prefer to own their own sites. They enter into a common area agreement for the design, layout, and operations of the shopping center. The landlord benefits from not having to own this tenant space or be concerned with the lower rate of return that is likely with the smaller tenants. However, the downside is that the anchor can go *dark,* leaving the landlord with no control over which tenant will occupy the space. Also, when the landlord wants to sell the shopping center, buyers may prefer to acquire the anchor tenant's space to control the use of the space. The anchor tenant is usually a credit tenant, and this strengthens the credit rating of the shopping center being acquired.

National chain stores, such as 30,000-square-foot bookstores or clothing stores, have 20- to 25-year terms and options. The smaller national chain store tenants are likely to have shorter-term leases, in the range of seven to 11 years, and usually without options. Local, independent retailers typically enter into three- to five-year leases without options.

Pad or outlot tenants—such as restaurants, banks, and fast food tenants—usually have a 10- to 25-year ground lease with a few options.

Temporary tenants have become a surprisingly large source of income for regional and community malls. A mall with a good temporary tenant program (also known as a specialty leasing program) can generate more than $2 million in annual rent. Temporary tenants can occupy several types of spaces: kiosks, carts, retail merchandising units (RMUs), wall shops, spaces under the stairs in two-level malls, vacant stores, carts, and areas in the parking lot. Temporary tenants generally have occupancy terms from one week to one month, and some go up to one year.

The temporary tenant usually enters into a licensing agreement rather than a lease. A license agreement provides the tenant with fewer rights than a lease.

Incubator tenants in shopping centers are similar to temporary tenants, but they are usually trying out their concept in the shopping center or mall with the idea that they will become permanent tenants if they do well. They may lease the front one-third to one-half of a space. The duration of these "trial" arrangements can range from just a few months during a season to a full year. Most often an incubator tenant has a special lease arrangement for this trial period, and has agreed to terms for a permanent lease if they achieve or exceed a targeted sales volume. In a soft real estate market or a shopping center or mall with a vacancy problem, incubator tenants can be a good way to fill vacancies.

Office Buildings

Lease terms in office buildings vary with the size and type of the building. Class A office buildings usually have longer-term leases, in the range of five to seven plus years. These terms are intended to allow adequate time for the amortization of TIs, which can be quite substantial in a Class A buildings. The landlord does not want to pay frequently for additional TIs. In mid-rise, low-rise, and garden-style office buildings, the leases are usually in the range of three to five years. Ground floor retail tenants and restaurants require longer-term leases, from 20 to 25 years and possibly with options.

Medical office buildings typically have leases with durations of five to ten years—again because of the need for more TIs and a higher tenant fixturization cost. Medical office building tenants are stable; they choose their locations carefully, not wanting to disturb their patient and referral base. Because of the expense to build out medical office space, medical professionals seldom relocate to another building. Pharmacies in medical office buildings normally need longer-term leases.

Industrial Buildings

Very large industrial tenants who require a significant amount of TIs usually want longer-term leases in order to amortize their improvements. Almost all other industrial uses are leases in the range of five to ten years. Incubator tenant leases are in the range of one to three years.

COMPARING OFFICE BUILDING LEASE PROPOSALS

Office and medical office building space measurements have become quite sophisticated over the years. Improvements in this area have been geared towards providing the landlord with rent on almost all of the space in the building while also being fair to the tenant in how the space is measured.

The concept of charging rent in office buildings on the *rentable area* has become the industry standard. Today's landlords and most tenants understand the rentable and usable concepts. Landlords use the rentable/usable method of measuring space to be competitive in their rental structures. When most or all landlords are using the same method to measure space, they can make a fair comparison of various lease proposals.

Rentable versus Usable Floor Area

Office and medical office space needs to be measured carefully. Office and medical office buildings are the only buildings that have both a usable and a rentable factor for measuring space, and it is critical for both the landlord and the tenant to fully understand and be able to explain this concept.

The Building Owners and Managers Association (BOMA) International's method for measuring usable and rentable square feet is the industry standard. The floor usable area of an office building is defined by BOMA International as the result of subtracting the area occupied by major vertical penetrations on each floor from the measured gross area of that same floor. No deduction is made for columns and projections necessary to the building. Spaces outside the exterior walls, such as balconies, terraces, or corridors, are excluded. The building area equals the sum of the floor usable area of all floors.

Rentable area, as defined by BOMA, is computed by measuring the area enclosed between the finished surface of the office area side of corridors and dominant portions of the permanent outer building walls and/or major vertical penetrations. Building common areas are considered to be part of rentable area. No deduction is made for columns and projections necessary to the building. Where alcoves, recessed entrances, or similar deviations from the corridor line are present, rentable area is computed as if the deviation were not present.

Most office and medical office buildings have leases based on rentable square footage, which takes into consideration the tenant's portion of the building's common area. Obviously, an office building with large, towering atriums and seating areas will have a higher common area factor and more rentable area than a building with limited common space. When a tenant is looking at space for lease in an office or medical office building, he or she should be aware of the rentable/usable ratio and evaluate the rent and charges with this knowledge in mind.

The percentage of rentable space to the usable space is called the *load factor.* The usable square feet in a tenant's premises are increased by the load factor. If the load factor is 12 percent, it increases the usable square feet by 12 percent. Twelve percent is "loaded" onto the tenant's usable square footage. Load factors above 15 percent are considered high, and if a load factor is too high the building is not as competitive. In this case, the landlord may arbitrarily reduce a building with a 20 percent load factor to 15 percent to be competitive.

Proposal Comparison Example

To help demonstrate how the concept of rentable area versus usable area works, two different office building proposals are presented below. While there may be many other factors in determining which is the best building for the tenant, this example compares these buildings on the basis of the rental rate alone. The assumptions will be made for 1,000 square feet of usable space in each building. The calculations are shown below.

Building A is a 75,000-square-foot building with a load factor of 11 percent. The annual rent is $26 per square foot of rentable space.
Rentable square feet: 1,000 square feet + 1,000 × 0.11 (load factor) = 1,110
Annual rent: 1,110 × $26 = **$28,860**

Building B is an 80,000-square-foot building and does not have a load factor. The annual rent is $27 per square foot.
Rentable square feet: 1,000 square feet (no load factor)
Annual rent: 1,000 × $27 = **$27,000**

Building B is the better deal for the tenant based only on rent. The tenant would get 1,000 square feet of usable space in either building, but would have a slightly lower rent in Building B because there is no load factor.

INFLATION PROTECTION

It has been argued that a triple-net lease is all that a commercial landlord needs to be protected against inflation. This is simply not the case. Triple-net provisions protect the landlord against increased operating expenses, but do nothing to protect the value of the rental income. One dollar today will most likely be worth less next year. While this may not be a lot to be concerned with on a one-year basis, over a period of five years the erosion could be 15 to 35 percent, and in years past it has been even more.

If landlords rewrote each lease on an annual basis, rents could be increased to the inflation rate and there would be no problem. However, leases are written for longer periods of time, so landlords negotiate an inflation rent adjustment. There are two ways to accomplish this protection. The landlord can choose to use the *consumer price index (CPI)* or a negotiated fixed rental increase. In a good market, increases are normally made on an annual basis and occur on the anniversary of the lease commencement.

Whether the price increase is based on the CPI or on a negotiated amount, these increases are seen in virtually every type of commercial lease. They are, however, much more common for smaller tenants than for either anchor tenants or strong national tenants. Retail anchor tenants may allow for rent increases every five years over the term of the lease. Their position is that percentage rent provisions fulfill the same purpose, providing that the tenant prospers during the lease term and pays percentage rent. Even if the lease has a percentage rent provision, the landlord should make every effort to negotiate periodical rent increases during the course of longer-term leases.

Consumer Price Index Increases

The CPI is a monthly measure of changes in the prices of goods and services consumed by urban families and individuals, compiled by the Bureau of Labor Statistics. It has been chosen as the vehicle for rental increases because it is out of the control of any individual and, as best it can, it measures price increases in goods and services. There are several choices to be made when choosing which index to use. Most commercial leases use the CPI for metropolitan areas. All items are indexed to the nearest geographical area that is published for the property's population area.

It is also a good idea to use the index for three months prior to the increase date. For example, if the increase is to go into effect on January 1, using the October index will ensure that the appropriate information is available in time to calculate the increase and apply it on the effective date. As long as the chosen index remains the same throughout the term of the lease, the figures should not vary greatly from month to month.

Experienced tenants may ask for a maximum increase on the CPI. If that is granted, the landlord will negotiate a minimum increase. If the tenant asks for a maximum 5 percent increase, for example, the landlord may agree to this maximum as long as the tenant accepts a 3 percent minimum increase. This protects both parties in the event of no inflation or runaway inflation.

Negotiated Increases

Some strong national retail tenants will not allow for an annual CPI increase, but will allow for some limited increases—such as 2 percent per year allocated every five years. On long-term leases, some tenants in strong negotiating positions will agree to a 2 percent annual increase and have their rent adjusted to the full CPI at the end of every five-year period.

In many cases, the easiest strategy for determining rent increases is to use a negotiated increase rather than the CPI. This negotiated increase can occur every year, every five years, or with any other frequency. It is not unusual for a lease to have a defined rent for the first year, and for the base rent to increase each year by either a percentage of the rent or a specific monetary amount. The rent may be $20 per square foot for the first year, $21 for the second year, $22 for the third year, and so forth. This becomes a known factor for both landlord and tenant, and there is no concern with indexes and calculations.

LEASE CONCESSIONS

While landlords do not like to provide lease concessions, they often do for one of two different reasons. The most common reason is that it is a *tenant's market,* and therefore it is necessary to grant concessions to do deals. Concessions might also be granted when the landlord is asking very high rents and, in order to achieve those rents, concessions must be given.

Because the value of all commercial buildings is established by the value of their leases, it is important to maintain base rents at the highest possible level. If there was no concern about value, there would be little reason to hold the rents at a high level and make concessions to bring down the effective rent.

For example, assume the market rent for office space of 2,000 square feet is $22 per square foot. The landlord wants to lease this space at $23 per square foot because the building is the newest in the area and should have high appeal. In order to be competitive, however, the landlord decides to offer free rent that would bring the tenant's *net cost* down to the market rate of $22.

If the market indicates a cap rate of 8 percent for selling or financing the building, then at $22 per square foot triple-net, the value of the space is $275 per square foot; at $23, the value becomes $287.50 per square foot. If we assume a one-year lease, this difference in value for the 2,000-square-foot space is $25,000. If the free rent concession cost the landlord $5,000, it is a worthwhile deal for the landlord as well as a benefit for the tenant. This is a simple example demonstrating why it is sometimes in the landlord's best interest to provide concessions to improve the value of the building.

In a tenant's market, the concession may be necessary to fill space. Sometimes it is necessary to give concessions that provide an effective rent below the landlord's breakeven rental rate. Collecting some rent and billback charges is better than collecting nothing. A building with a large vacancy can have a negative impact on the existing tenants and tenant prospects. This is magnified in the shopping center situation, as there is no way to mask vacancies. Each vacancy in a shopping center means fewer shoppers, and all the tenants feel the effects.

Free Rent

Concessions can take many forms, depending on the needs of the landlord and the tenant and what the market dictates. Free rent is a common concession that appeals to both the landlord and the tenant. Free rent granted by a landlord is often considered to be a no-cost item because the property was already vacant and not producing any rent. If the lease was not completed, the space would have remained vacant and no rent would have been collected.

The big decision for the landlord is whether to give free rent including billback or common area charges, or just free minimum rent. Obviously, the best position for the landlord is to grant free base rent, but insist on receiving billback payments on the theory that they are out-of-pocket expenses and should be recovered. The tenant is likely to negotiate for no tenant charges paid during the free rent period. The additional tenant charges (e.g., billback expenses, CAM charges) are often overlooked when negotiating free rent and become a disputed issue when the tenant takes occupancy. When negotiating free rent, be sure each party knows what is included and excluded.

The granting of too much free rent at the commencement of a lease can become a problem: the tenant may get used to not paying rent and not budget rent for when it is due. Some landlords try to spread out multiple months of free rent over a longer period of time to avoid this reluctance. If three months of free base rent are required to make the deal, the landlord may try to make these "free" months the first, sixth, and twelfth months of the lease, or the first month for the first three years of the lease. The ability to spread out free rent will depend on what other landlords are doing in that market and the landlord's goals and objectives for the property. Some landlords prefer to "burn off" the free rent during the beginning of the lease. Free rent will also be considered when the landlord calculates net effective rent.

Early Occupancy

Early occupancy is mostly found in shopping centers, where tenants may negotiate to open without paying rate until a specific date if they complete building out their improvements before that date. This is an incentive for tenants to work hard to get their store open as soon as possible. The sooner a retailer opens, the better it is for all the tenants in the shopping center.

Early occupancy is also found in office building, industrial building, and even medical office building leases. Generally, the rental commencement date is agreed upon and, if the tenant can open and operate prior to that date, there is no additional charge. Many landlords do not agree with giving a tenant early occupancy and expect the tenant's rent to commence when the tenant opens for business if that date precedes the agreed upon date. The two determining factors for whether a landlord provides early occupancy are the market conditions and the landlord's philosophy.

Overstandard Tenant Improvements

Overstandard TIs may be found in all types of properties, but they are most often found in office buildings. In a new building, there is commonly a predetermined level of TIs for all space in the building based on the building's pro forma. If tenants want upgrades or additional improvements, they are usually at the tenant's expense. However, in a tenant's market or in the case of very strong tenants, tenants may negotiate for the landlord to provide these additional improvements at no extra charge. Overstandard improvements can be an asset to the building, but a costly asset.

Moving Costs

A concession sometimes seen during a strong tenant's market is for the landlord to pay the tenant's moving costs. Moving costs as a concession are more common in office buildings where one building's location is often as good as the next, so this added incentive may be the deciding factor in signing a lease. This concession often includes the cost of the physical move as well as new business stationary, new business cards, relocated telephones, etc. It is a good idea for the landlord to get a fairly accurate estimate of the cost of the move prior to making this commitment.

Special Requests

Tenants may have specific requests that can assist in finalizing lease negotiations. Landlords will benefit from listening to those needs and trying to meet them whenever financially possible. However, caution must still be taken. One concession that did not work well for landlords in the past—and is seldom seen—is the cash-up-front arrangement. In this arrangement, landlords provided substantial cash up front to tenants as lease incentives, only to have the tenants disappear before paying any rent. Though this concession is rarely found today, landlords are cautioned against making any such arrangements unless they are certain that the tenant is viable and will be available to fulfill the lease obligations.

PASS-THROUGH CHARGES

Pass-through charges, or billbacks, can be the source of more contention between a landlord and tenant than just about anything else in their relationship. They have the potential to be a source of disagreement between the two parties to a lease: Landlords want the right to charge their tenants with all of the costs that the tenants would face if they owned the building. Tenants, on the other hand, have little or no control over these billbacks and are concerned that their landlord might not control their costs or might charge expenses to the pass-through charges that are not part of the cost to operate the building or were not agreed on as pass-through charges.

Over the years there have been many attempts by both parties to resolve these issues. One of the more common resolutions is for the tenant to negotiate a cap, or a maximum cost, for a given expense or (more likely) for all the expenses. The cap may state, for example, that the item in question cannot be increased more than 3 percent in any given year. Or it may state that CAM charges cannot exceed $6.75 per square foot per year. In this case, the limit might increase by a percentage every year to offset inflation.

Another way for the tenants to control pass-through charges is to exclude certain items. Obviously, tenants will exclude any expense that they incur on their own, such as trash removal, utilities, insurance, etc. In addition, it is not unusual for some anchor tenants to attempt to negotiate exemption from their shopping center's security costs. They might also exclude charges like the resealing of parking lots from their billback expenses.

As mentioned previously, anchor tenants in shopping centers may occasionally negotiate the right to deduct real estate taxes and insurance premiums from percentage rent that they owe. From the landlord's point of view, this is not a valid approach; but a strong tenant may still be able to demand and receive this concession.

Regardless of the particulars of a lease, it is in the best interest of both parties to be sure that the lease language is clear concerning the allowable pass-through charges and how these charges will be calculated. The clearer the language, the less likely that issues will arise in the future.

Shopping Center Common Area Costs

The pass-through charges for shopping centers are separated into several categories and billed separately. Taxes are also billed separately because some tenants may be on separate tax parcels (e.g., an anchor tenant and a pad tenant). The rest of the shopping center is probably on one tax parcel, and tenants are billed their pro rata share of the tax bill for this parcel. Insurance is also billed separately. The anchor tenants and the pad tenants usually have their own building insurance policy, and the rest of the shopping center is insured by the landlord. Tenants are billed their pro rata share of the cost of that policy. The landlord insures the common areas, and this expense should be included in the common area maintenance expenses so all the tenants pay their pro rata share of common area insurance.

Not all tenants pay their pro rata CAM share, because certain items can be negotiated out of tenants' leases. This is potentially problematic when a major tenant occupies a certain amount of the shopping center's leasable area (e.g., 32 percent) but negotiates to pay a smaller share of the CAM costs (e.g., 25 percent). The shopping center landlord must either pay the difference (7 percent in this example) or, if the other tenant leases permit, pass that cost along to the remaining tenants. Such lease arrangements are rare in strip shopping centers and must be fully spelled out in the lease negotiations and lease document if they are to be enforceable. Anchor tenants on malls usually negotiate not to pay for mall common area maintenance but will pay for parking lot and exterior common area maintenance.

It is also not uncommon for fast-food tenants to be required to pay a premium on common area costs due to the nature of their operations. This premium is generally stated as a higher percentage of CAM costs (e.g., the fast-food operator who occupies 2.7 percent of the center may actually pay 3.6 percent of the costs). The excess amount should be credited against the expense balance of the other tenants, as they are presumably paying the higher maintenance costs within their allocations.

Shopping centers' common areas can be costly to maintain. Enclosed malls are visited by hundreds and thousands of shoppers daily and are costly and complex to operate. Maintaining a mall with shoppers of all ages around and providing security, indoor lighting, air conditioning, and, in many cases, food courts take the skills of a dedicated management team. The lease should be clear and specific, spelling out as many of the common area items as possible, with the caveat that common area maintenance will include—and not be limited to—the mentioned items. New issues are inevitably encountered that need to be taken care of with the common area maintenance budget.

While the discussion should stay focused on leasing rather than on management, it is a good idea to be able to discuss past CAM charges in an existing property to show prospective tenants cost trend lines. For a new property, the estimates for common area expenses should be as realistic as possible. Landlords should be quite willing to show the tenants how these costs were determined.

One of the most contentious areas of common area provisions is that of administrative or supervision fees and/or management fees. The administrative fee is a CAM charge that is a percentage of the CAM budget and covers the management of the common areas. The management fee is typically a percentage of the shopping center gross income and is passed on to the tenants as part of the common area expenses. Up until the 1980s, the industry standard was to charge an administrative fee but not the management fee to

CAM. That changed in the 1980s when landlords replaced the administrative fee with the management fee. The management fee is much greater than the administrative fee.

A few landlords charge both the administrative fee and the management fee to CAM. Most leases are carefully worded to convey the landlord's intent in this regard, and this usually results in few problems. However, some older leases have language that is unclear about what fees will be included, and some landlords have been known to interpret this language in a very broad context that causes problems with the tenant. Landlords and tenants can agree to almost anything they choose, but the agreement should be between two parties who are fully informed regarding the terms and conditions.

In recent years, some shopping center landlords have introduced a flat CAM rate in an attempt to end problems with year-end adjustments and disputes over increasing CAM costs. Flat CAM rates have two basic approaches. The first approach is for the landlord to estimate the CAM charges for the coming year and provide the tenant with those figures. The tenant will then pay a monthly fee towards CAM costs, and there will be no year-end adjustment. In this scenario, both parties are relying on the budget being fairly accurate. The landlord does not want any great additional expenses, and the tenant does not want the actual expenses to be considerably less than what is being paid. If the CAM expenses are lower than the agreed flat CAM rate, the landlord keeps the difference; but if the CAM expenses exceed the agreed flat CAM rate, the landlord cannot bill the difference to the tenants.

The second approach is to have a flat CAM rate for all of the CAM expenses except for very volatile items such as real estate taxes, insurance, and, in some areas, snow removal. The CAM costs are estimated along with the uncontrollable expenses, but at year-end only the uncontrollable expenses are adjusted. This approach can work favorably for both the landlord and the tenant, providing the original estimates are realistic for the shopping center.

Office Building Billbacks

The billbacks for office buildings have not changed dramatically over the past several years. There are no differences between office buildings and medical office buildings, except that medical office buildings are more expensive to maintain. Pass-through charges for office and medical office buildings include all the costs to operate the building, including the building's management fee, and are billed as one charge. Real estate taxes are included as a line item in the office and medical office building operating expenses that are passed through to the tenants. All maintenance, taxes, insurance, and on-site maintenance and maintenance personnel are a standard part of the office building's billback equation; the only question is how these charges will be billed.

For many years, the use of a *base year* was the most common method for billing office pass-through charges. As tenants found problems with this approach, however, the industry changed to a *stop provision*. The stop-provision approach is quite similar to the base-year system, except that the stop provision sets a dollar figure as the base. This figure is meant to represent the cost of operating the building during the initial year of the lease.

In a soft leasing market, tenants may be able to negotiate the base year to a later year in the lease or the stop clause to a higher figure. For instance, a tenant who occupied the premises in 2005 may have negotiated for 2006 to be the base year. That tenant would have started paying operating expenses in 2007. On the other hand, if the market is strong, landlords may negotiate for the base year to be the year before the tenant takes occupancy. The tenant would then pay pass-through or billback charges during the first year of occupancy.

Another approach is the stop-expense method, in which the landlord pays the operating expenses to a predetermined dollar amount per square foot, and the tenants pay everything above that amount. Obviously, tenants want to be certain that the figure used is a fair representation of the expected costs of operating the building. For example, a tenant with 8,000 square feet in a building with a $7 "stop" and operating expenses of $7.25 would pay $2,000 in billback or pass-through charges. (The tenant pays $0.25 per square foot on 8,000 square feet.) The main difference between a base-year provision and a stop-expense provision is that the base year is defined by a certain year and the stop expense by a predetermined dollar amount. The end result is much the same.

Exceptions exist in office building billbacks as well as shopping center common areas. Some tenants negotiate for a cap on the amount of the annual base year increases. Some have annual base year increases, but certain items may be excluded or capped. Usually only very large tenants are able to negotiate these exceptions unless the market is a strong tenant market. Landlords prefer a "fully net" or "triple-net" provision for billing pass-through charges, but the market does not accept this method of pass-through charges in most areas of the country. Single-tenant industrial and retail buildings and many shopping centers use a triple-net lease.

Gross-Up Expenses for Office Buildings

The full *gross up* explanation appears in Chapter 12. However, it is important to remember that the concept of *gross up* involves determining what the actual costs would be to operate a fully occupied building. A successful gross-up approach, however, creates more balance and benefits both the landlord and the tenant.

Industrial Building Billbacks

Industrial property billbacks are most similar to those of shopping centers. They are typically a triple-net lease, also referred to as a *fully net lease,* meaning that all of the building's operating costs are part of the tenant's pass-through charges. These expenses generally run much lower than those for shopping centers because industrial buildings have fewer amenities, are seldom open 24 hours a day, have fewer common areas and have much less traffic.

There are several types of industrial properties, and the method of billing industrial pass-through charges will vary for single- or multi-tenant buildings, multi-tenant industrial parks, and business parks. Industrial properties are usually on triple-net leases but some use a base year to bill tenants for the pass-through charges.

THE NET LEASE

It is not uncommon to hear words like *net lease, triple-net lease,* and *fully net lease* used in the leasing of commercial properties, and yet people often have different understandings of what these terms actually mean. Consequently, their use poses potential problems. It is critical to define exactly what is meant for each specific lease rather than leaving the definitions up to interpretation.

Commercial leases were all *gross leases* until about 50 years ago. The basic rental would be a fixed amount, and within that rental structure the landlord would pay all of the building's operating expenses, including taxes, insurance, and maintenance. An easy way to remember these three gross lease items is the acronym TIM (taxes, insurance, and maintenance).

One problem that soon presented itself with this structure, however, was that the real estate taxes could increase far beyond the rental amount, making the lease financially unprofitable for the landlord. Because of this, taxes were the first item to be separated from the base rental. Instead of using the gross lease structure, tenants would pay a base rental in addition to their share of the real estate taxes. This is a *single-net lease.*

Insurance premiums also became problematic. As with taxes, landlords soon extracted these charges from the basic rental structure so that tenants would still pay their share of the insurance on the building. A *double-net lease* is one in which the tenant pays base rent, taxes, and insurance. Maintenance was the final item to be separated from the basic rental, completing the structure for a triple-net lease. In a *triple-net lease,* the tenant pays base rent, taxes, insurance, and maintenance.

Both the landlord and the tenant should be involved in a very careful and complete discussion about what is included in the lease's common area and/or billback provisions. There should be clear understanding on both sides about what is included in pass-through charges and how they will be calculated. It is much better to spend a little more time in the negotiating process than to wait until the first year-end adjustment to have a major disagreement arise. Both parties should be aware of regional jargon and be sure to define all terms that are not clear.

PAD OR OUTLOT NEGOTIATIONS

Pad or outlot sites are highly sought after in shopping centers and occasionally in office buildings. They are seldom found in industrial parks, but could potentially work well there as well. Pad spaces are typically occupied by restaurants, fast food tenants, banks, savings and loan offices, or promotional retailers who can afford higher occupancy costs in return for the location's high visibility.

Most pads are on the street perimeter of a shopping center, providing excellent visibility and access from main roads. For this reason, these sites are generally valued around one-and-a-half to two times the value of an average tenant space in the shopping center.

There are three types of pad deals: the ground lease, build-to-suit, or sale of the site. A separate parcel is created for each pad so they can be sold or developed separately from the rest of the shopping center.

Developers who choose to use the ground lease are careful to select strong tenants with obvious financial strength to both build out the location and effectively operate the store. The landlord also wants to be protected against the lessee taking out a mortgage to build the store and then defaulting on the loan, so the parcel usually cannot be encumbered. The ground lease tenant generally pays a base return on the site: usually the value of the land times a rate of return around 12 to 13 percent, on a fully net (also known as triple-net) basis. Additionally, the site may be part of the declarations of *easements* and agreements for the entire site, which will control the architecture, ingress and egress, and distribution of the common area operating costs. The ground lease is the most common pad deal.

The choice to develop the site, or use a build-to-suit arrangement, is quite similar to the ground lease. The exception is that either the landlord will actually develop the building *or* the tenant will develop the building, sell it back to the landlord, and then lease back the building and land. Again, the lease will be a triple-net (fully net) lease and subject to the declarations and common area contributions. These leases are long-term leases in order to give both parties a chance to recover the cost to build the building.

The third option is the outright sale of the pad or outlot, using the selling price that is determined by the local market and the desirability of the particular location. Because the outlot is one of a property's most valuable parcels, there is often a temptation to procure an early return through this sale. However, even though the site is still subject to the declarations, the landlord nevertheless loses some control over the site if the pad is sold. Most developers prefer the ground lease and then the build-to-suit lease; the least preferred pad deal is the sale of the pad. Developers and landlords like the long-term income stream for a credit tenant.

SUBLETTING AND ASSIGNMENT

Most landlords do not favor their tenants subletting or assigning their leases, because a *sublet* or *assignment* provides competition to the landlord—quite often at rates below market rents. However, from the tenant's perspective, these options can be very appealing. Subletting or assignment may provide the means to shed the obligation of a long-term lease or reduce expenses if financial difficulties arise or a space is no longer needed.

Lease agreements are usually very clear about the terms and criteria that will be acceptable for the landlord's approval of a *sublease* or an assignment. Most courts have held that the landlord cannot prohibit subleasing or assigning but can set forth reasonable requirements for the granting an approval. Landlords generally have a lease provision regarding subletting and/or assignment, and charge a fee for the handling of the transaction. (Assignments are discussed in more detail in Chapter 12.)

In office buildings or industrial buildings, landlords are most concerned with the financial strength of tenants. They are also concerned with the new tenant's use and parking requirements. For example, a landlord might be concerned if an insurance company's financial processing office wants to sublease to an employment agency. This change could dramatically increase the number of employees in the space and impact parking.

In retail properties, landlords are not only interested in the financial statements of the proposed sub-lessees or assignees; they are also interested in the tenants' experience and expertise in operating the business. For example, a landlord with a McDonald's tenant will likely have no interest in seeing that space assigned to a smaller, independent operator with less financial strength.

One of the ways that landlords protect their position is to require that the original tenants are not released from their responsibilities under the lease. In a sublet situation, the original tenant is always liable on the lease and may even continue to act as a middleman between the landlord and the sub-lessee. In an assignment, the new tenant takes the place of the original tenant and deals directly with the landlord. If the assignee defaults, however, the landlord will look to the original tenant to fulfill the lease terms if the assignment is without release. If the assignment is with release, the assignor is not liable for any of the assignee's lease defaults.

The lease term is another important issue in subleases and assignments. If the sub-lessee takes less time than the lease term, the landlord needs assurance that the original tenant will be around to fulfill the obligation. On the other hand, if the sub-lessee or assignee wants a longer lease term, it is usually a good idea to negotiate those terms at the outset rather than waiting for the lease to expire. If, however, the market is getting stronger and demand is good, some landlords may want to wait and see how well a given sub-lessee or assignee does closer to the lease expiration date. This can cause problems for sub-lessees, who may want assurances that they will be allowed to operate for a given period of time in order to amortize the cost of purchasing the business and the cost for new improvements or equipment.

KEY MONEY

The payment of key money (see Chapter 12) is not common in the industry, but it may take place when a new tenant is willing to pay for a previous tenant's improvements or a great location. Very strong regional malls, super-regional malls, and outstanding street retail locations have been able to get key money because of the strength of their location or prior improvements.

Some tenants also try to procure key money from a subtenant or assignee. This may happen if they are subletting or assigning space at a phenomenal location or if the rent is well below the market rate.

11

Lease Renewals

The lease renewal is one of the most important transactions in commercial real estate, and yet it often does not get the attention it deserves from the landlord or the tenant. Both parties frequently leave the renewal until the last minute, taking for granted the other side's desire to extend the lease agreement. Each party often assumes that the only necessity is for both parties to agree on the new rental rate. The consequences for this lack of foresight are often severe.

The party desiring a lease renewal often pays a high price when the other party chooses not to renew. For tenants, the result can be major disruptions to their business, including severely impacted cash flow and profits. For landlords, some of their building's gross income is lost and, if the vacating tenant occupies a large space, the building's cash flow may become negative. A recent study of mid-sized office buildings shows that, on average, the cost of a renewal lease is less than half the cost of a new lease.

PLANNING AHEAD

Instead of anticipating a casual meeting to discuss a lease renewal with the other party to the lease, both the landlord and the tenant should approach the lease renewal with the same diligence they used in planning for and negotiating the original lease. To avoid possible negative outcomes that may accompany poor planning, the landlord and tenant should decide well in advance of the lease expiration date whether or not they want to negotiate a renewal. Renewal discussions should commence at least six months prior to the lease expiration for anchor tenants, and for large national tenants renewal discussions should start one to two years prior to the lease expiration. This gives both parties a chance to find out the desires of the other and to make plans accordingly.

If both parties agree to renew the lease, the transaction itself should be completed months before the lease expires. If the landlord decides not to renew the lease for a given tenant, that tenant should be notified as soon as possible to allow for other arrangements to be made. Likewise, if the tenant decides not to pursue the renewal, the landlord should be given adequate notice.

Landlords should include lease renewals when developing a building's marketing and leasing plans. Likewise, tenants should include lease renewal analyses in both their short- and long-term business plans, and as part of their growth strategies.

Both the landlord and the tenant should prepare themselves by remaining aware of market conditions during the entire lease term. Too often tenants sign a lease and then stop paying attention to market conditions. After a few years, they are shocked with the increases and are frustrated that their business may be threatened by increased costs. Most landlords keep up on market conditions, and it is to their advantage to discuss these changes with their tenants during the lease term to keep them aware of the market.

Ideally, both the landlord and tenant should conduct (or have conducted for them) a market survey to assist in determining the relative strengths and weakness of each party's negotiating position. Knowing the cost to relocate and the cost to replace a tenant is an important component in the negotiating process as well as the final decision of whether to renew a lease. The landlord and the tenant may use commercial real estate professionals to provide them with important market information. These professionals are usually skilled negotiators, and their recommendations can improve their client's negotiating position, resulting in the best possible deal.

EVALUATING LEASE RENEWALS

Each party should consider the available alternatives when deciding whether or not to renew a lease. The other side's perspective on the relationship and reasons for electing to renew or not should also be taken into consideration. Often, the analysis used in deciding to enter into the original lease can be used to evaluate the renewal decision.

The Landlord's Decision to Renew

Prior to meeting with a tenant about a lease renewal, the landlord must determine whether or not to offer that tenant the opportunity to renew. The lease renewal is the least costly deal a landlord is likely to make, but there are still many factors that go into this decision. The ten issues listed below are items landlords frequently consider during lease renewal deliberations.

1. *Market conditions.* In a *landlord's market,* landlords evaluating lease renewals are able to use more stringent criteria to evaluate factors like tenant financial statements and net worth. In a *tenant's market,* on the other hand, landlords may have to lower these standards in order to keep space occupied and generate gross income. Landlords must consider other space options in the market available to the tenant.

2. *Tenant use.* Landlords consider whether or not a tenant's use is still compatible with the building's other uses. For example, retail landlords attempting to change their merchandise focus or the price points of their shopping center may choose to replace a particular tenant.

3. *Tenant mix.* Landlords of shopping centers, office and medical office buildings, and occasionally even industrial parks need to be aware of the tenant mix of businesses or services in their building. Tenant mix is one of the major considerations in a retail property landlord's lease renewal decision. Landlords want tenants who contribute to the synergism of the tenant mix and meet the needs of the shopping center's customers. If a different use or tenant would be a stronger prospect for the future of the property, the landlord may want to make the change.

4. *Financial performance.* Landlords who want to increase their building's value seek tenants who are credit worthy. All things being equal, a building with credit-worthy tenants will almost always sell at a lower *cap rate* and generate a higher selling price than will one with tenants who are not credit worthy.

5. *Lease requirements and violations.* No landlord wants tenants who continually violate provisions in their lease. Late rent payment is the obvious lease violation, but there are others that discourage landlords from offering lease renewals. For example, tenants in shopping centers who do not maintain required minimum store hours, allow their employees to park in prime customer spaces, do not keep their

merchandise fresh, or fail to keep their store well stocked are not prime candidates for lease renewal.

6. *Occupancy.* If properties have high vacancy rates or several tenants with leases expiring during the same year, their landlords are more likely to be willing to renew a tenant's lease, likely on terms favorable to the tenant.

7. *Cost.* Landlords consider the cost of *not* renewing a tenant's lease.

8. *Time.* The time it will take to find replacement tenants is an important factor. How long will the space remain vacant if the lease is not renewed? Rent lost due to a vacancy can never be recaptured.

9. *Co-tenancy.* Landlords must weigh the impact that vacancies may have on existing tenants. Although co-tenancy may be relevant to office and medical office buildings, it is primarily a shopping center issue.

10. *Sales performance.* Retail property landlords prefer to have retail tenants with good customer draw, who will pay percentage rent in addition to their base rent. These tenants are evaluated on past sales performance. Landlords look for sales levels that exceed those of similar tenants. Tenant sales are also compared with national averages found in *Dollars & Cents of Shopping Centers,* copublished biannually by the Urban Land Institute (ULI) and the International Council of Shopping Centers (ICSC).

Renewing the lease of a tenant who is paying percentage rent is a more complicated task than a straightforward renewal. The landlord wants to bring the rent up to the current market rate, but also tries to increase the base rent to cover the existing base rent plus percentage rent being paid. The tenant will usually accept bringing the rent to the market rate, but will be reluctant to see all of the percentage rent converted to minimum rent— just in case the market has a downturn and the tenant's sales decline. This issue is often overlooked when renewing the lease with a tenant who has been paying percentage rent.

The Tenant's Decision to Renew

A lease renewal can have many advantages for the tenant as well as for the landlord. A renewed lease guarantees a known, proven location and eliminates the disruption and cost of a move. It also means that the tenant's customers are not inconvenienced when discovering the tenant has relocated. Retail customers may not follow a merchant to another location.

However, the choice to renew a lease is also a complicated decision from the tenant's perspective. As for landlords, there are multiple issues that contribute to the tenant's ultimate decision. Listed below are several factors that tenants often consider when determining whether or not to negotiate a lease renewal.

1. *Lease terms.* Tenants want to know if there are buildings with better lease terms available. If the market is weak, tenants may be offered attractive lease terms and paid moving expenses to relocate. This is especially true for office tenants, whose businesses often can be located in any building within a micromarket. Also during a soft market, rents for Class A buildings may be reduced significantly, allowing tenants in Class B buildings to upgrade their space and location to a Class A building without paying much higher rents. If a tenant's lease is expiring within a year, there are leasing agents who are more than willing to study the market and determine the best deals available for that tenant.

2. *Location.* There may be space that is better located for the tenant's business. This is especially important to retail tenants because their location is likely to affect their sales. Location is important to the operations of other tenants as well because it potentially means better access to freeways or public transportation, close proximity to government facilities, or being near an important customer.

3. *Space needs.* Tenants consider if they need more space or, on the flipside, if they can operate just as efficiently in less space and lower their occupancy costs.

4. *Landlord performance.* The landlord's performance is another issue to consider. Tenants want landlords who have lived up to their lease obligations and kept their property well maintained. It is also important that the landlord is concerned with the individual tenant's operations and success.

5. *Tenant mix.* Tenants are concerned with the other types of businesses in their building, which can affect traffic flow, customer draw, and the location's general environment. If there is a nearby business that is detrimental to the tenant's operations or image, that tenant may seriously consider moving. On the other hand, tenants are also eager to remain in a building with tenants who contribute to their success.

6. *Cost.* The cost to *not* renew the lease must be considered. Tenants consider the costs involved in a move, including lost sales during the move; additional advertising for the new location; changing telephone systems, letterhead, and business cards; possible double rent

while making the transition; moving costs; and even the potential for losing employees.

7. *Time.* Tenants consider the downtime involved in a move. How long will it take to make the transfer and get the new location up and running?

For both the landlord and the tenant, understanding the other party's evaluation criteria is also critical. Understanding the other party's perspective and knowing the market conditions are two of the most important components of developing a successful strategy to negotiate the terms of a lease renewal.

THE COST OF NOT RENEWING A LEASE

If the lease is not renewed, it may create a challenge for both the landlord and the tenant. Knowing the costs of not renewing the lease is therefore important for both parties. There are both direct and non-direct monetary costs to be considered.

The Landlord's Costs

The landlord has many costs to consider when not renewing a lease.

Direct Monetary Costs.   There are many direct monetary costs that landlords must face when a lease is not renewed. The most obvious of these is the loss of base rent, since new leases usually require vacancy prior to the lease's commencement. There is also the loss of percentage rent, or *overage* rent, paid by some retailers and service tenants.

An often overlooked cost is the loss of the building's *pass-through charges.* These charges, shared by most tenants per their lease arrangements, are an income component in the landlord's operating budget and cash flow. If free rent is negotiated with a new tenant, another issue to resolve is whether or not pass-through charges will be reimbursed during the free rent period. This is an issue that is often poorly documented in a lease and can lead to disputes between the landlord and the tenant.

Another cost is that of TI expenses to rebuild the premises for a replacement tenant. New leases generally require more improvements than renewals. Retail and industrial properties are often re-leased in "as is" condition, but if the market is soft the replacement tenant may be offered a tenant improvement (TI) allowance. Landlords of office and medical office buildings, on the other hand, almost always provide improvements for new tenants. In a soft market these costs will be greater—easily in the tens or hundreds of thousands of dollars. A related cost to consider is the downtime as TIs are being constructed.

The cost of concessions for a new lease is also a factor. These are limited only by the imagination of the tenant and the landlord, and can include lower rent; reduced, capped, or eliminated pass-through expenses; free or reduced parking rates; overstandard TIs; reimbursed moving expenses and relocation notifications; new signage; gifts; and any other negotiated concessions.

The final direct monetary cost for not renewing a lease is the commission paid to the leasing agent for a replacement tenant. In a soft market, the landlord may pay a double commission to get the space leased. On the other hand, the commission for a lease renewal—if required at all—is usually considerably less than that for a new lease.

Non-Direct Monetary Costs.   The non-direct monetary costs for landlords when tenants do not renew their lease are also significant. The impact to the building and the other tenants is a major consideration.

Specific tenants often provide services that attract and retain other tenants (e.g., a restaurant or bank in an office building), and the loss of these key tenants may have a negative impact on the leasing of other space in the building. For example, a stock brokerage firm can be important to an office building's image. In a medical office building, a pharmacy is a significant addition, and some medical practices are an important source of referral business to other medical professionals. A shopping center is impacted when tenants with good customer draw decide not to renew their lease. Too many vacancies in a shopping center can create a negative perception in its customers' minds. The non-direct cost of these tenants not renewing their leases may be that other tenants decide to leave as well and the building's tenant mix is weakened.

In addition to the concern about losing the existing tenant, there may also be the unknown factor of whether or not the replacement tenant will be a good tenant and live up to the landlord's expectations.

There are two other costs to not renewing a tenant that seldom come into play; however, when they do, they can be very costly for the landlord. The first is that, if the landlord were to sell the building, vacancies could impact the building's selling price and how long it takes to sell. The second is that, occasionally, a building's lender will require the landlord to pay down a portion of the loan if the building's occupancy, gross income, or *net operating income (NOI)* falls below a predetermined amount.

Example: The Landlord's Cost to Replace a Tenant.   Here is an example of the landlord's total cost to replace a hypothetical 5,000-square-foot office building tenant. If the vacating tenant occupied 10,000 or 20,000 square feet instead, the cost to replace the tenant would be two or four times these amounts.

The cost of losing this tenant is based on the following assumptions:

- The new tenant will sign a four-year lease.
- The building's base rent is $30 per square foot, with a dollar-per-square-foot increase beginning the third year.
- The vacating tenant has a base year for pass-through operating expenses, and the tenant's costs are $3 per square foot.
- The new tenant will have its base year be the year the lease is executed.
- There is one month of free rent for every two years of the lease.
- For the new tenant, TIs are $25 per square foot. The tenant renewal would have received $5 per square foot in TIs.
- It is estimated that it will take six months to find a replacement tenant and two months to construct the TIs.
- Commission is 6 percent of the base rent for a new tenant; the property management company would have received a 3 percent commission for the vacating tenant's lease renewal.

The cost to replace the tenant is then as follows:

- Loss of rent for ten months (six months to find and enter into a lease with a replacement tenant, two months to build out the premises, and two months of free rent): $110,000
  - Base rent: $100,000 ($30 per square foot × 5,000 square feet ÷ 12 × 8)
  - Pass-through expenses: $10,000 ($3 per square foot × 5,000 square feet ÷ 12 × 8)
- Tenant improvements: $125,000 (5,000 square feet × $25 per square foot)
- Total commission: $36,600
  - Year one rent: $150,000 × 6% = $9,000
  - Year two rent: $150,000 × 6% = $9,000
  - Year three rent: $155,000 × 6% = $9,300
  - Year four rent: $155,000 × 6% = $9,300

Total cost to replace the tenant: $271,600

The cost to renew the existing tenant would have been:

- Tenant improvements: $25,000 (5,000 square feet x $5 per square foot)
- Commission: $18,300
  - Year one rent: $150,000 × 3% = $4,500
  - Year two rent: $150,000 × 3% = $4,500

○ Year three rent: $155,000 × 3% = $4,650
○ Year four rent: $155,000 × 3% = $4,650

Total cost to renew the tenant: $43,300

Cost difference between renewing and replacing this tenant:
$271,600 − $43,300 = **$228,300**

In this example, the landlord is spending $228,300 more to replace the tenant than he would have spent to renew that vacating tenant's lease.

The Tenant's Costs

Although the landlord's cost of not renewing a lease can be significant, the tenant's cost of not doing so can be much greater. A tenant's entire business may suffer if the lease renewal decision is not handled with foresight.

If location is important to the tenant's business, relocating to a less desirable location can have a tremendous impact on its success and profits, as well as daily operations. Retail and service customers are not likely to patronize a business that relocates far away, and they can sometimes even be deterred by a move of just a few blocks. The tenant who relocates may also lose the customer draw provided by an anchor tenant or other key tenants in the area. For instance, a dry cleaner who is adjacent to a supermarket in a shopping center is likely to lose many customers in the process of moving a few blocks away to an small, unanchored strip shopping center. Will the customer base need to be rebuilt after the move? The tenant must consider whether or not a different location will impact employee retention or make it more difficult to recruit the best employees.

Another cost for the tenant not renewing a lease is the moving expense. This includes the cost of the physical move, the costs to connect computers and other equipment, and the cost to notify customers of the new location. Another relocating cost is printing new letterhead, business cards, and other marketing materials.

Finally, the tenant should consider the cost of building out the premises in a new location. Even if the new landlord is contributing to the TIs, this contribution may not cover all the build-out costs. This can be a significant cost for any business—and especially for medical professionals and other tenants with high fixturization costs.

Although it still may be worthwhile for a tenant to not renew a lease and move to a new location, these additional costs must be considered carefully in order to reach an informed decision about the lease renewal.

DOCUMENTING THE LEASE RENEWAL

When the landlord and tenant do agree to renew the lease, they must document this agreement. Documenting a lease renewal can be a complicated process. It is best for the landlord to draft a new lease, but this does not always take place.

The easiest (though not the most effective) way to proceed is often for the landlord to prepare a *lease extension agreement* and have it signed by the tenant. The tenant is not likely to offer much resistance to this approach. This lease extension, though usually initiated by the landlord, is often beneficial to the tenant alone. Yet it continues to be used by landlords because it is a simple and quick way to prepare the lease renewal document.

When the landlord provides the tenant with a lease addendum to extend the existing lease, it will state the terms of the lease extension. These may include the updated rent amount, possible changes to the pass-through operating expenses for office and medical office buildings, and the period for which the lease is extended. However, the lease that is being extended is usually at least three years old—and often older than five years. It is not a state-of-the-art document, and may not include the latest lease provisions that protect the landlord.

Another frequently encountered problem with the lease addendum is that, after stating the changes in terms such as rent and expiration date, landlords often make a blanket statement that all other terms and conditions remain in full effect. Such catch-all phrases can be problematic: if the landlord provided free rent, TIs, or other concessions in the original lease, the tenant could argue that those original terms should be repeated.

For example, a certain institutional landlord of high-rise office buildings in the Midwest extended a tenant's lease with an addendum that employed the phrase "all other terms and conditions shall be the same." One week after the lease renewal was executed, the tenant called the landlord asking for the same six months of free rent and $20-per-square-foot TIs that he received in the original lease. The landlord stated that he had never intended to provide these concessions a second time; they were never discussed and were not part of the negotiations. The tenant, however, said that his intentions in the negotiations were to receive these concessions; otherwise he would never have agreed to the lease addendum. The addendum's wording, being vaguely inclusive, meant that the landlord had to provide the tenant with these concessions even though that was not his original intent.

If the landlord does choose to extend a lease through the use of an addendum, phrases such as "all other terms and conditions shall remain the same" should never be used. If confusion is to be avoided, the addendum must state that no concessions offered in the original or subsequent renewals will be provided to the tenant during the new lease term.

Although the landlord is well advised to avoid using a lease addendum, it is usually in the tenant's best interest to renew a lease using a lease addendum—unless it is onerous or the tenant wants certain provisions to be renegotiated or eliminated. If the original lease is on the tenant's lease form, however, then it is likely that the tenant will be the one to prepare the lease addendum. Just as for the landlord, in this case it is in the tenants' best interest to use their most recent lease form instead of an addendum when preparing the lease extension.

OPTIONS TO RENEW

The option to renew is often a difficult consideration for landlords. It has been argued that, as long as rent is negotiated at the market rate, landlords should be willing to grant options to renew. However, there are more issues involved in this decision than rent alone. If, for example, a tenant proves to be troublesome, or if a retail tenant has lower sales volumes than other comparable merchants, the landlord may want to bring in another tenant even if it is at a lower rental rate. Or it may be in the landlord's best interest to remove an existing tenant to allow a neighboring tenant to expand. Options to renew restrict these and other choices.

When there is an option to renew in the lease, the tenant can choose whether or not to extend the lease and the landlord must accept the decision. Options favor the tenant. The tenant has the right to decide whether or not to renew the lease, and the landlord must accept the tenant's decision.

Negotiating Issues

Even though many landlords do not like to grant tenants the option to renew, some tenants will receive renewal options because of their strong negotiating position. Tenants with higher fixturization costs, such as restaurants, need longer-term leases with options to amortize their fixturization cost over several years. In a weak market, landlords may be required to offer options to other tenants.

When an option is offered to a tenant, several issues need to be considered. These include setting the option rent at the current market rent, mandating 180 days' advance written notice to exercise the option, requiring that the tenant not be in default at the time of the option notice, and cancelling the option if the tenant has ever been in default. In the case of retail tenants, landlords may specify that tenant sales must have reached a predetermined level in order to exercise the option. Accordingly, landlords generally monitor lease renewals and options six months prior to their effective dates to be sure that notices are timely and that all required conditions have been met.

Proper Notice

One of the requirements for the tenant to exercise the option to renew is to notify the landlord in writing during a prescribed period before the lease expires. Usually this must be done between 90 and 180 days before the expiration. Sometimes the lease will also require that the notification is not too far in advance. For instance, some tenants cannot notify the landlord of their intent to renew a lease more that 180 days in advance of the expiration date.

If the tenant occupies a significant amount of space in the building, the time requirements are often extended several months. It is not uncommon for anchor tenants in shopping centers or major tenants in office buildings to exercise their option to renew a lease one to two years before it expires.

There is some disagreement in the commercial property management industry concerning whether or not a landlord should notify tenants when their renewal option notification date is approaching. If landlords do not want a particular tenant to renew the lease on pre-agreed terms, they may hope that the tenant misses the required notification period. Some choose to wait several days after the deadline has expired, and then notify the tenant that this notification period has passed. They then negotiate the lease on terms that are more landlord-friendly, or may choose not to renew the lease at all.

Although some landlords maintain that tenants bear the responsibility of remembering when to renew the lease, this strategy does little to help landlord–tenant relations. Another thing to consider is that good tenants may simply forget the deadline because they are so busy running their store or office. It may not be in either party's interest for the landlord to punish these tenants for an oversight.

No matter what position landlords take on the renewal option notice issue, it is a good idea for tenants to have a mechanism to remind them of the time period to extend their lease. In the past, this was often accomplished through the use of a *tickler file*. Today, several software programs will inform the tenant when to notify the landlord to extend the lease.

TENANT RETENTION

Directly related to the lease renewal, tenant retention is a major landlord concern for several reasons. In addition to the added costs of finding a new tenant when an existing tenant decides to leave, high tenant turnover is not good for the image of any commercial property. This is most obvious in shopping centers, where vacant stores are quite visible to tenants, prospects, and the shopping center's customers.

Tenants are a building's most important asset. They provide the income that pays for the building operations and debt service and provides the cash flow and return on investment (ROI). An income-producing commercial building is almost always valued based on its income stream or net operating income (NOI), and this is dependent upon the tenants' rents and other charges.

Tenant Retention Programs

During the devastated office building market that lasted from the mid-1980s to the late 1990s, landlords realized that a tenant retention program is essential to minimizing the cost associated with tenant turnover and maximizing a building's income and value. Astute landlords, regardless of the size of their buildings, have their property manager develop and implement a tenant retention program. Landlords of larger buildings have even more opportunities for tenant-retention activities.

Treating tenants as the valuable asset they are is the foundation of a tenant retention program. The first (and many believe the best) step towards tenant retention is to fulfill every lease obligation promptly. The landlord should provide tenants with everything for which they negotiated. The landlord also needs to accurately bill tenants for their rent and pass-through charges. Tenants lose confidence in landlords who bill them incorrectly, causing mistrust to develop. If tenants discover that a landlord has charged expenses that are not appropriate for the building's pass-through expenses, they are less likely to renew their lease when the time arrives.

The Property Manager's Role

The property manager is typically the one who develops and implements the tenant retention program for the landlord. A successful tenant retention program requires the property manager to be responsive to tenant requests and maintenance calls. The building should be maintained in the same or better condition than when the tenant moved in.

The property manager also is advised to have regular—and usually short—visits with each tenant. These visits should commence with the start of a new lease and continue during the entire lease term, and are intended to maintain a dialogue between the property manager and the tenant. They act as a tool to keep the property manager up-to-date on how tenants are doing and how they feel about the property. These visits are also a good opportunity for the property manager to keep tenants apprised of market conditions and changes taking place within the property. This approach minimizes surprises for both the property manager and the tenant when renewal lease negotiations commence. This also enables the property manager to be aware of and promptly address any concerns the tenant may have, preventing these issues from becoming recurring problems.

Improvements

As another step towards retaining tenants, the landlord can make improvements to the building to make it more appealing—upgrading the office building lobby, halls, and restrooms; modernizing the elevators and mechanical systems; and adding amenities (e.g., a conference room, an exercise room, a covered outdoor area, and a lunchroom with vending machines). Improving the building's tenant mix with tenants who provide services for office building tenants or provide strong customer draw for retail tenants is an important benefit for tenants. Additionally, green features are becoming an increasingly attractive incentive for tenants, and achieving a *Leadership in Energy and Environmental Design (LEED)* certification is important to many tenants.

There are also tenant and community programs that the landlord can pursue to make the building feel like a good place to work. Depending on the type of building, these can include a tenant appreciation picnic on-site, holiday activities, and decorations in the building's lobby throughout the year. Luncheon speakers on entertaining or educational topics can be provided during the lunch period for the tenants' employees. Community activities, such as food drives, blood drives, and toy collections during the holidays, show tenants and their employees that the landlord is an active community citizen. A newsletter sent to the tenants' employees with helpful hints, introductions of new tenants, profiles of existing tenants, and upcoming building activities can prevent the building from developing an institutional feeling.

Landlords should at all times treat tenants like they are trying to win their renewal decision. They should treat tenants with respect, provide all services that are required under the lease, and make the tenant experience in the building as pleasant as possible.

LANDLORD RETENTION PROGRAMS

Although tenant retention programs are fairly common, seldom do tenants think of establishing landlord retention programs. It is difficult to find articles, newsletters, or book chapters on the subject of the landlord retention program. However, when tenants realize the cost of relocating and the importance of their premises and location to their operations and success, they may decide to develop and implement a strategy for retaining their landlord. Landlord retention programs focus on tenants convincing their landlord that they are an asset to the building and should have the opportunity to renew their lease.

As with the tenant, the landlord's primary concern is receiving what was negotiated in the lease. The landlord does not want tenants who create problems, and wants the rent to be paid in full and on time. Landlords also expect tenants to fulfill all of their lease obligations in a timely manner. If a tenant has cash flow problems and is unable to make rent payments on time, the landlord expects that tenant to notify the building's property manager as soon as possible so the situation can be resolved.

Another step towards landlord retention is for the tenant to bring all legitimate issues and concerns to the attention of the landlord or property manager. No one wants to hear petty complaints on a regular basis. And, although the landlord is not a partner in the tenant's business, the tenant should view the landlord as having an important role in the business's success.

THE LEASING AGENT'S ROLE IN LEASE RENEWALS

Leasing agents do not typically get involved in lease renewals. However, if the real estate market is soft (a tenant's market), leasing agents may contact tenants to ask if they want to be represented when they negotiate a lease renewal. Leasing agents may offer to provide the tenant with a market survey and alternative buildings for their consideration.

It is usually in the tenant's best interest to be represented by a leasing agent when renewing a lease. The leasing agent provides market knowledge, presents alternative locations, and prepares a comparison of the advantages and disadvantages of renewing the lease and relocating. However, unless the leasing agent is paid by the tenant, the leasing agent may not earn a commission if that tenant renews the current lease instead of relocating to another building. This situation may discourage leasing agents from encouraging tenants to renew their lease, even it is the best deal and location.

Landlords, on the other hand, usually prefer not to deal with leasing agents when negotiating a renewal. If the market is strong, landlords often will not pay a commission to a leasing agent who represents a current tenant even if that tenant chooses to renew the lease. However, landlords know that during a weak commercial real estate market—or when a building has a vacancy problem—they may have to pay this renewal commission to be competitive and to retain tenants. Though a landlord prefers not to pay an outside leasing agent a commission for a lease renewal, the negotiated commission is often part of the cost to renew.

Few landlords will negotiate a lease renewal directly with the tenant; the exception is landlords of small buildings who may negotiate their own lease renewals. Instead, landlords often choose to have the building's property manager negotiate lease renewals with tenants or the tenants' leasing agents. This approach works well because the property manager has developed a working relationship with the tenant, knows the market and the alternative buildings to which the tenant might relocate, and is loyal to the landlord. Occasionally renewing leases is part of the management's responsibility, and there is not additional compensation paid to the property management company for this activity. Typically property managers are compensated for the additional responsibility of renewing leases.

Just like the commission for a new tenant, the commission paid for a lease renewal is negotiable. The landlord may pay the leasing agent half of whatever commission rate is paid for a new tenant. The rationale behind this is that a renewal takes less time than finding a new tenant and negotiating the lease; accordingly, the leasing commission is less. In a soft market, however, a leasing agent may be able to negotiate a higher commission; a landlord may pay a leasing broker up to a full commission for renewing a current tenant's lease.

During a strong market, on the other hand, the landlord may refuse to pay the leasing agent any commission at all. In this case, the leasing agent must be paid by the tenant. This is one of the reasons many leasing agents do not solicit tenants to renew their lease in a strong market. Consequently, when the market becomes a landlord's market and the landlord will not pay the leasing agent's commission, it may be wise for the tenant to offer to provide compensation in order to receive the benefits of the leasing agent's knowledge of the market, recommendations, and negotiating skills.

When leasing agents represent tenants for the lease renewal process, they can also provide valuable market information. Seldom are tenants aware of the rental rates in the area, and they are almost never aware of space that is available in the building's micromarket or *trade area*. The leasing agent is able to conduct a market survey to provide market rental rates and concessions—if they are being offered—for buildings in the location(s) to which the tenant will consider moving. For each micromarket or trade area, there is a range of market rental rates for each classification of building.

The leasing agent can help the tenant by developing a comparison report on alternative buildings for the tenant. The leasing agent can also inform the tenant of the landlord's cost to find and negotiate a replacement tenant. The tenant may use this information in developing a strategy to negotiate the lease renewal.

LEASE RENEWAL TERMS

If a lease renewal is being considered, market research should be done by both parties in advance and plenty of time should be allowed to attend to the details of a renewal negotiation.

Rental Rates

The rental rate is an obvious term that needs to be agreed upon for the lease renewal. Most tenants will end up paying the market rate for their space in a lease renewal. The market survey can be used to determine market rates and negotiating the rental rates of a lease renewal.

A "strong" tenant or a large government tenant may negotiate to pay 95 percent of the market rate. These "strong" tenants are almost always credit worthy. They often take large space in office or industrial buildings;

in retail operations, a strong retail tenant produces sales well above the national average, provides significant customer draw, and brings other retailers to the shopping center. Strong tenants are likely to have negotiating power with their landlord.

In a soft market, landlords may be willing or even required to lower base rents to retain tenants. They may offer to renew tenant leases ahead of time at favorable rates. Landlords benefit from knowing that tenants will not relocate at the end of the lease, leaving them to incur the high cost of finding a replacement tenant in an unfavorable market. Agreeing to an early lease renewal can also benefit the tenant if favorable lease terms are negotiated, such as a lower rental rate on the remaining term of the existing lease and favorable terms during the renewal period.

Pass-Through Charges

Another monetary issue to negotiate for the lease renewal is that of pass-through charges. Pass-through costs almost always increase every year that the building's operating expenses increase. For office and medical office buildings, determining what base year to use when calculating these charges for the tenant is significant. The landlord prefers to use the base year already in place, which is usually the year the tenant moved into the building or the year after that move. The tenant, on the other hand, desires a new base year to be established—usually the current year, or the year the lease renewal goes into effect.

The monetary difference between these base year approaches can be considerable. If, for example, the tenant is paying $4 per square foot for pass-through charges *above* the original base year, changing that base year to the year the renewal is signed will cost the landlord—and save the tenant—$4 per square foot for each year of the lease renewal. If the tenant occupies 5,000 square feet, this amounts to $20,000 for one year and $100,000 for a five-year lease.

Lease Length

The length of the renewal lease term is another item that must be negotiated. The renewal term is usually the same length as the original lease, but it can be negotiated for any length.

If the parties cannot agree to a lease renewal term and neither party wants the lease to terminate, the lease may be allowed to continue on a *month-to-month tenancy*. This has advantages and disadvantages for the landlord, and especially for the tenant. When the lease is renewed from month to month, the landlord and the tenant have additional time to negotiate a longer lease.

If the lease is allowed to continue on a month-to-month basis, the tenant has additional time to consider alternative locations. However, the downside is that this tenant is also playing a very risky negotiations game, because the landlord can also choose not to continue the lease at any time. The landlord needs only to provide 30 days' notice that the tenant must vacate. This is problematic for the tenant because it is almost impossible to find another location and coordinate and implement a move within 30 days.

If the tenant prefers to renew the lease, it is not beneficial to allow the lease to expire and continue on a month-to-month term. An alternative to this approach is to renew the lease for a short term, such as one or two years. This will provide the landlord and the tenant with time to consider their other options or finalize a longer-term lease. Additionally, if the lease renewal process is started well in advance, the negotiations can be finalized before the original lease expires, negating the need for a month-to-month arrangement while allowing adequate time for more permanent arrangements to be made.

It is always in the interest of both the landlord and the tenant to plan ahead and be prepared for lease renewal negotiations. Both parties should be aware of the market conditions, the other party's position, and available alternatives when considering the terms of a potential lease renewal. This will allow them to achieve the most beneficial lease terms possible.

12

Negotiating the Lease

A successful negotiation of the lease is one of the most important responsibilities for both parties involved in the process. The results of a lease
negotiation have long-term effects on the landlord's property as well as
the tenant's business. The ideal outcome of lease negotiations is a win-win
situation for each party, which occurs when each party achieves its desired
outcome.

The person (or persons) responsible for negotiating the lease on behalf
of the landlord must understand how each lease provision impacts the cash
flow and value of the property, as well as its tenant mix and daily operations. The person (or persons) negotiating the lease on behalf of the tenant
must understand how each lease provision impacts the operations and the
profitability of the tenant's business. Since the landlord and the tenant are
obligated to fulfill their responsibilities described in the lease, they both
should understand their rights and obligations in the lease they are signing
and how the lease impacts them.

With a thorough understanding of the lease document, the leasing agent,
property manager, attorney, landlord, and tenant can negotiate each provision to achieve the best possible deal. The lease document is a lengthy and,
for some people, an intimidating document; yet reading the lease reveals
that most of the provisions are relatively easy to understand. Those provisions that may seem a little complicated can be explained by an attorney,
or by an experienced leasing agent or property manager.

This chapter is designed as a reference for both landlords and tenants,
as well as the professionals negotiating on their behalf. The general lease

form is discussed, along with its required components; this is followed by an extensive review of specific lease provisions. The landlord's and the tenant's positions are presented, and in some cases there is a discussion on how the provision impacts the landlord's property and/or the tenant's business. When both parties to the lease negotiations understand the other party's point of view, they are more likely to work towards a successful compromise that will meet the concerns of both.

THE LEASE FORM

The party whose lease form is chosen starts the negotiations by presenting their side of each issue. This is often a negotiating advantage. Each party would be wise to insist that their lease form is used. In practice, however, the landlord's lease form is used almost all the time. Most tenants do not have a lease form and it is usually too costly for them to have one drafted. Even if they did, the landlord might resist accepting it.

Anchor retail tenants and governmental agencies are exceptions to the general trend and will typically insist on using their own lease form. Some national shop retail tenants and a few large office users also will attempt to have their lease form used. In these situations, the negotiating strength of the landlord will determine if the landlord's lease form or the tenant's lease form is chosen.

A landlord will often tell a tenant that the lease form is a "standard lease." In fact, the lease may be that landlord's own standard lease, but there is no industry "standard lease." Regardless of whose lease form is used, every provision can be negotiated to the satisfaction of both parties. The outcome of the negotiations will depend on each party's negotiating strength, skill and understanding of the lease, prioritization of that transaction, and attitude towards negotiating the lease. When all the parties to the lease negotiations work towards a win-win situation together, the results almost always end with an executed lease.

THE COMPONENTS OF A LEASE

No matter which lease form is used, to be valid it must include six required components that are described and defined in very specific language. These required components are: (1) the parties to the lease; (2) a description of the leased premises; (3) the term (or duration) of the lease; (4) the consideration of the rent and charges paid to the landlord by the tenant and the use of the premises by the tenant; (5) a description of the tenant's use of the premises; and (6) the rights and obligations of both parties. These components may appear in a different order, but they must all be present for the lease to be valid. The first five components are typically found on the first page or two, and the sixth requirement is covered throughout the rest of the lease.

The initial pages of the lease provide a summary of the basic lease terms and a listing of the parties to the lease. They also contain a description of the permitted use, the duration of the lease term with its commencement and expiration dates, the amount of minimum rent as well as rent escalations or increases, and when the first payment is to be made (the rent commencement date). If appropriate, the percentage rent rate, the proration basis for the tenant's pass-through charges (itemized for operating expenses and common area maintenance), and the amount of the security deposit will also be included. If the lease requires a *guarantor,* the name and address of that party are also included. The remainder of the lease gives a detailed description of the rights and obligations of each party.

The following discussion in this chapter includes many of the lease provisions commonly used in a commercial lease, as well as the landlord's and tenant's perspectives on those provisions where applicable. Some of the provisions discussed are found only in leases for retail tenants. The table of contents is followed by an alphabetical listing and discussion of the specific provisions; and reviews of the *substantial completion letter* and lease exhibits conclude the chapter.

Table of Contents

The lease is a substantial document, typically in length between 15 and 30 pages. Some landlords will use a lease that is over 50 pages. The lease contains a table of contents for quick reference, which identifies the pages on which specific lease provisions appear. The precedent is for the pages to be numbered with lowercase Roman numerals.

Acceptance of Keys

This provision states that if the tenant gives the keys for the premises to the landlord or the landlord's representative, the lease is not thereby cancelled. This is to prevent a tenant from claiming that, because the keys to the premises were given to the property manager or to maintenance personnel, the premises were surrendered to and accepted by the landlord, and the tenant is no longer obligated to fulfill the terms and obligations of the lease.

Acceptance of Premises

Tenants have a specific time period, usually no more than one week after the premises are turned over to them, to notify the landlord in writing of any construction defects. If the tenant does not notify the landlord within the specified time period, that tenant has accepted the premises by default.

Tenants may negotiate for a longer notification time period. They want an unlimited time period to notify their landlord of any structural or unobservable defects. Tenants also want the landlord to correct any defects that are found as soon as possible. To avoid a conflict, the tenant and landlord should complete a checklist upon move-in and move-out, itemizing defects in the premises.

Advertising

Shopping center landlords want all their tenants to advertise and promote their businesses in order to maximize sales potential. There are several benefits to the tenant and the landlord when the tenant's sales are strong. First, better sales mean a more financially sound business. Second, there is a relationship between sales and the rent a retailer can (and will) pay. Retailers want their rent to be within a percentage range of their sales, and higher sales mean they can afford more rent. Third, the greater the retailer's sales, the greater the opportunity for that tenant to pay percentage rent. An advertising provision is seldom used in strip shopping center leases, but it is often used in leases for regional malls as well as lifestyle, entertainment, outlet, and specialty shopping centers.

Originally, this advertising provision required tenants to spend a minimum percentage of their gross sales on advertising (usually 2 percent) and to provide evidence of that expenditure. But monitoring the amount a tenant spends on advertising is difficult for the landlord, and a dispute can arise over what constitutes advertising.

As an alternative, the provision may require the tenant to advertise in a minimum number of the shopping center's advertising tabloids. If the tenant does not advertise a minimum number of times, the landlord may place an ad giving the tenant's name and address, and the tenant will be responsible for reimbursing the landlord for the cost of the ad. Tenants will negotiate for a minimum number of tabloids to advertise in, based on their advertising and merchandise plan.

Alterations

The landlords of office and medical office buildings almost always coordinate the construction of their tenants' alterations. They want to maintain the integrity of their building's mechanical, electrical, and structural systems. They also want to ensure that all work in the building is of the same standards. If major tenants in an office or medical office building insist on performing their own alterations, the landlord will place stringent requirements on the tenants and the contractors doing the work.

On the other hand, landlords of industrial properties will often allow all of their tenants to perform their own alterations. And tenants in shopping centers are responsible for coordinating and contracting for the improve-ments to their premises.

The lease should state whether or not the tenant may construct any improvements to the premises. If the tenant is given permission to do so, the landlord will review and approve in writing any plans for alterations, additions, or other improvements. The landlord will require tenants to abide by the building's rules and regulations: acquiring all necessary building permits; obtaining a bond equal to or exceeding the cost of the alterations; possibly using union labor; designating when construction may occur, when the elevators may be used, how materials may be delivered to the premises, the location of construction staging areas, and how common area carpeting and wall coverings are to be protected; and ensuring that no mechanic's *liens* will be placed on the property. The contractor will be required to maintain specific insurance coverage as well as "additional insured" status for the landlord and the property management company.

Tenants are usually prohibited from doing work on the roof without the landlord's prior written approval and supervision by the landlord's rep-resentative. Landlords will also restrict tenants from core drilling or other construction activities that may be disruptive to other tenants, their visitors, and customers during normal business hours. Additionally, depending on whether the alterations add value for re-leasing the premises, landlords may stipulate that the leased premises be restored to original condition at the tenant's sole expense when the premises are vacated or the lease expires. The cost to remove wiring and cabling can be expensive, and the landlord will usually require the tenant to remove all wiring before vacating the premises.

Office and medical office building tenants may believe that they can construct alterations at a more cost-effective price than the landlord, and will want to negotiate the right to construct either all improvements or just the nonstructural alterations. Some tenants negotiate the right to make nonstructural changes and enhancements—up to a certain dollar amount—without the landlord's approval. These improvements may include replacing the flooring, installing new wall covering, painting, installing cabinets, etc.

In all cases, the tenant should negotiate so that the costs of the land-lord's alterations are at fair market price. The fee that the landlord adds to supervise the work should also be reasonable, and it is a percentage of the alteration costs or as a fixed fee.

Arbitration

There are some landlord–tenant conflicts that may be settled faster through *arbitration* than by going to court. If the landlord and the tenant do not agree on certain issues, such as the market rent for an option period, they may submit the issue for arbitration. The arbitration provision provides an alternative to going to court to settle a dispute.

This provision states which issues will be arbitrated and which will not. Landlords prefer to deal with monetary default through the legal system; however, many nonmonetary default issues may be better handled through arbitration, with people who understand real estate. There is little to negotiate in this provision other than which issues will be arbitrated and which method of arbitration will be used.

Typical Arbitration.   The typical arbitration provision states that each party will choose an arbitrator, the two arbitrators will choose a third arbitrator, and the three will decide the issue. The lease should state the minimum qualifications of the arbitrators, such as five years' commercial real estate experience in the area in which the property is located. The arbitrators have a specific time to rule on the dispute. Either each party pays for their arbitrator and they split the cost of the third arbitrator, or the losing party pays for the entire arbitration cost.

Baseball Arbitration.   Another approach is referred to as the *baseball arbitration* method if the dispute is over the rent for an option. The landlord presents a rental rate and the tenant either accepts or rejects the rate. If tenants reject the rate, they present a countered rate. If the parties do not agree on the rental rate they select either one arbitrator or they each select one and the two arbitrators select a third arbitrator. The arbitrators decide which rate is the closest to the market rate, and that rate becomes the rent for the option period.

This approach encourages each party to study the market and submit a rate close to or at the market rental rate, rather than understating or overstating their opinion of the market rental rate. It also prevents the arbitrators from splitting the difference between what the landlord and the tenant believe the market rental rate to be.

Assignment

The *assignment* provision is important to tenants because they often cannot sell their business unless the landlord agrees to the lease assignment. Landlords prefer to have the right, at their discretion, to approve tenant requests to assign or sublet a space. They run credit checks, background checks, etc. on the tenant signing the lease, and they would want any tenant taking over that business to be just as financially sound and desirable. The courts may require that this approval process be reasonable. The landlord may place requirements on the *assignee,* such as: having the same (or greater) net worth as the assignor, occupying the premises with the same use (for minimum impact to the tenant mix), and having reasonable experience operating the business.

The tenant will first negotiate for the absolute right to assign its lease; if that cannot be negotiated, then the tenant will negotiate less stringent approval criteria for the assignee. The landlord will require the tenant to pay a fee for the landlord's time and the expense of having an attorney review the assignment. The tenant needs to be sure that this fee is a reasonable charge. The tenant also needs to carefully read the landlord's consent to assignment form to be sure the landlord is not taking a percentage of the business's sale price or making other onerous requirements.

The landlord who approves an assignment will want the assignment "without release"—meaning that the *assignor* (the tenant assigning the lease) must fulfill the obligations of the lease if the assignee defaults. Under an assignment without release, the landlord can collect from the assignor if the assignee doesn't pay the full rent. If the assignee is a retailer or operates a restaurant or service business, and closes that business, under the continuous operations provision the landlord may require the assignor to step in to operate the business. This is an obvious hardship, especially if the assignor has moved on to another business or retired.

The assignor usually does not want to be required to operate the business if the assignee vacates the premises, and may negotiate that the continuous operations provision does not apply to the assignor. An assignment "with release" frees the assignor from all future obligations of the lease. If the assignee defaults, the landlord cannot look to the assignor to cure this default. The tenant will negotiate for an assignment with release, especially if the assignee has a better net worth than the assignor.

If the issue of assignment with or without release must be negotiated, the tenant may offer an alternative that requires the assignor to guarantee the performance of the assignee for a limited time (e.g., for the first few years of the remaining term of the lease). If the assignee does not default in any obligation during the specified time period, the assignor is then released of all obligations under the lease. Default of a lease is usually nonpayment of rent. Another criterion that may release the assignor from the obligation is whether or not the assignee's retail sales exceed a predetermined level.

Attorneys' Fees

All leases typically provide that the prevailing party in any legal action concerning the lease is entitled to reimbursement of reasonable legal fees.

Auction and Sale

This provision applies to shopping centers, other retail properties, and office buildings with a retail component. Because "going-out-of-business" signs, sales, or auctions can give the impression that the property type itself is failing, landlords include in the lease a provision stating that the tenant may not conduct a bankruptcy or going-out-of-business sale or auction—or post signs announcing such activities—without the prior written consent of the landlord.

This can be a difficult provision for tenants to negotiate. Landlords are wary about leasing to tenants who are concerned with a possible bankruptcy sale. Tenants may instead negotiate for specific types of sales in addition to the standard sales, such as annual "blow out" sales, anniversary sales, and so forth.

Auditing Rights

The tenant is given the right to audit the common area maintenance (CAM) charges and other pass-through charges, such as real estate taxes and insurance. Because the landlord incurs expenses on behalf of the tenants, it is only fair that they have the right to audit the landlord's pass-through charges and review the invoices. The landlord should place the following ten restrictions on that right:

1. The audit must commence within 90 days of the date the tenant receives the year-end adjustments.
2. The tenant can only audit the period of the most recent year-end adjustments.
3. The audit will be conducted in the place where the landlord maintains the financial records and during normal business hours.
4. The results of the audit will be kept confidential.
5. The auditor will not be paid a contingent fee.
6. The auditor will be a certified public accountant (CPA).
7. The landlord will receive a copy of the audit.
8. The tenant must not be in default of the lease during the audit.
9. If the landlord disagrees with the results of the audit, another CPA who is mutually selected by the landlord and the tenant will conduct the audit and those results will be binding.
10. The tenant may not withhold rent or other payments during the audit.

There are several issues listed above that the tenant may negotiate out of the audit provision, especially items five and six, as many tenant audit firms do not comply with these points. The tenant also negotiates for the right to audit all prior years' charges. Just as the retail tenant pays for the landlord's sales audit if the tenant's sales are overstated or understated by 2 percent or more, the tenant will want the landlord to pay for the cost of the audit if it is proved that the landlord overcharged the tenant by more than 2 percent of the actual costs.

Authority of Signatory

Each party should establish the authority of the individuals who represent the landlord and the tenant. An entrepreneur signs the lease for a business as its owner. In the case of a *corporation,* an officer of the company may be a signatory on behalf of the corporation. However, the authority of that officer to commit the corporation to the lease should be officially documented. It is common for the landlord to require a corporate resolution authorizing the corporate officer to sign the lease. The tenant may require the same of the landlord. The corporate resolution should be appended to the lease as an exhibit.

Cancellation

There are many situations for which a cancellation provision may be negotiated. If the right to cancel is given, both the landlord and the tenant should be able to cancel. Some retail tenants request this cancellation right. The provision allows the tenant the right to cancel the lease if the retailer's sales do not exceed a specific sales volume. This right should not be easily given, but may be a consideration for the landlord to attract strong tenants for a successful tenant mix or in leasing a troubled shopping center.

In the rare situation in which this concession must be granted, the landlord should place restrictions on the cancellation right. The sales level a retail tenant needs to achieve to void the landlord's cancellation right should be reasonable, and attainable under the existing circumstances. Restrictions may include the tenant being open for business for a minimum of two calendar years (including two Christmas seasons), and preferably three or four calendar years.

Landlords should limit the right to cancel to a one-time right rather than an ongoing right, and should negotiate a mutual right of cancellation for both landlord and tenant. If there are unamortized tenant improvements (TIs) or leasing commissions at the time of cancellation, the tenant should be obligated to pay those as a condition of the cancellation. After the tenant notifies the landlord of an intent to cancel the lease, the tenant should be required to remain open for an additional four to six months. This period provides the landlord with time to re-lease the space.

If a shopping center is having leasing challenges, tenants will argue that they are taking a big risk to sign the lease. Opening and promoting a store in a shopping center is a huge investment, and if a store that is successful at other shopping centers is unable to succeed at that particular location, the tenant may want to cancel the lease early. Since tenants invest tens to hundreds of thousands of dollars in opening a store, they do not want any cancellation penalty. The tenant may also want to cancel the lease if one or more anchor tenants in the shopping center close their stores. This is called a *co-tenancy provision.*

Medical professionals may negotiate for the right to have the lease cancelled if the firm's principals die or become disabled. In such circumstances, it is likely the practice is sold and another medical professional assumes the lease. If patients are transferred to the acquiring professional's place of business, that professional will not want to assume the lease with the purchase of the practice. The landlord may negotiate for the tenant or the tenant's estate to pay for the unamortized portion of any TIs and commissions, the commission to re-lease the premises, and a cancellation penalty. The landlord may also require the tenant to have a life insurance policy with all or some of the proceeds going to the landlord to pay the above-mentioned costs. More often, when the medical practice is sold the buyer continues to operate the practice in the existing premises.

Commission

A landlord does not want to pay a commission that was not earned nor agreed upon to a leasing agent. Occasionally, more than one broker or leasing agent may claim to represent the same tenant. A dispute can arise if it is unclear who represents the tenant, and the landlord may be forced to pay two commissions and/or incur legal expenses to settle the dispute. To protect the landlord against this possibility and to protect the tenant from paying an extra commission, the lease should clearly identify who is responsible for payment of the commission and which leasing agent is entitled to the commission.

The lease provides a blank space for the name of the tenant's broker and requires the tenant to represent and warrant that no other broker is authorized to represent the tenant. Some states require leasing agents and property managers to inform the parties to the lease which entity they represent. Such a statement can be included in this provision.

The landlord usually pays commissions. The tenant wants the lease to state that the tenant has no responsibility or liability to pay any commission. Traditionally, the landlord pays a commission to the tenant's leasing agent; but this is slowly changing. Some tenants will pay a fee to their leasing agent or pay a fee if the landlord will not pay a commission. The lease indicates to the tenant whether or not the landlord will pay a commission to the tenant's leasing agent.

Common Area Maintenance and
Pass-Through Charges

Pass-through and CAM charges include several expense categories—maintenance, utilities, insurance, real estate taxes, security, management fees, etc. The method of billing these charges to tenants varies depending on the type of property and the type of lease; the amount depends on whether the tenant's lease employs a base year, uses a stop provision, or is a triple-net lease. Net leases, as well as the methods for billing expenses to tenants in different property types, are discussed in detail in Chapter 10, "Financial Issues."

Lease Language.   Landlords do not want the lease to limit the expenses included in pass-through charges by stating that the tenant will pay "the following list of expenses." The tenant may interpret this to mean that any expenses incurred but not listed cannot be billed, and landlords want to make sure they have the right to pass through to the tenant all the legitimate expenses of maintaining and operating the premises. Landlords therefore want the lease to state the basic pass-through expenses while allowing for additional expenses as needed. Representative lease language might be "the pass-through expenses or the common area maintenance expenses shall include but are not limited to the following list"; and the provision could include an itemized list of specific expenses of the pass-through and CAM charges, as well as mentioning "such other necessary and/or related expenses as may be incurred."

Tenants naturally do not want their pass-through expenses to include items that they believe are not operational expenses, such as commissions, costs to resolve tenant disputes, and TIs. They will also negotiate for exclusions from pass-through charges for: art work in the common areas; interest or penalties for late payments; charitable and political contributions; expenses arising out of latent building defects; costs not attributable to the operations of the building; *reserves* for bad debt; expenses for services not offered to the lessee; costs for overstandard services provided to any tenant; depreciation; mortgage payments; expenses related to vacant spaces; attorneys' fees related to enforcing the lease; and so forth. Landlords will accept these exclusions.

One exclusion that is often negotiated is the cost of capital improvements. The landlord wants to include capital improvements to upgrade the common areas—such new carpeting in the hallways—in the pass-through charges. The landlord also wants to pass through to the tenants the cost for energy-saving equipment or other equipment that will reduce the building's operating costs. If the landlord cannot recapture these costs, and the savings benefit only the tenants, there is limited or no incentive for the landlord to incur these expenses. Tenants may negotiate for the cost of the equipment to be amortized over its useful life, while the landlord might counter by financing the cost of the equipment and including the payment in the pass-through charges.

Leased or Leasable Square Footage.   The formula for determining each tenant's pro rata share of the CAM and pass-through expenses can be based on "leasable square footage" or on "leased square footage." In the leasable square footage formula, the tenant's pro rata share is the percent that tenant's premises are to the entire square footage of the building. This is by far the most common formula used for calculating common area and pass-through charges.

The leased square footage formula, on the other hand, measures the tenant's pro rata share against only the percentage of the space that actually is leased. When the formula for measuring space is based on leased space, the numerator is still the square footage of the tenant's premises, but the denominator is the gross leasable area (GLA) of the leased spaces only:

Square Footage of Tenant's Space ÷ GLA of Leased Spaces = Tenant's Pro Rata Share

Consequently, the denominator changes every time a space is vacated or leased. As the amount of leased space decreases, the tenant's pro rata share gets larger. If half of a shopping center were vacant, a tenant's pro rata share would be double what it would be using the leasable square footage formula.

As an example to demonstrate the practical difference between these two formulas, consider a tenant who leases a 2,000-square-foot space in a shopping center. The GLA of the shopping center is 100,000 square feet, and the shopping center is only 80 percent occupied. Based on leasable square footage, this tenant would have a pro rata share of 2 percent (2,000 ÷ 100,000 = .02). However, using the leased space formula, this same tenant would be responsible for 2.5 percent of the charges (2,000 ÷ 80,000 = .025). With pass-through charges totaling $300,000 in the shopping center, the tenant's pro rata share would be $6,000 at the 2 percent rate ($300,000 × .02) and $7,500—a significantly higher amount—at the 2.5 rate ($300,000 × .025).

The landlord's theory behind using leased square footage is the merchants in the shopping center are benefiting from the maintenance of the common areas, and therefore they should pay the total costs. However, merchants do not believe they should be charged for the costs attributed to vacant spaces. Tenants believe they are being unfairly penalized by having to pay a higher percentage of tenant charges simply because the landlord is unable to lease the vacant space. Experienced tenants will not accept the "leased area" concept, and the "leasable area" concept is standard in the industry.

Management Fee or Administrative Fee.   The building's management fee was a pass-through charge for office buildings, medical office buildings, and industrial buildings well before the shopping center industry began including it as a CAM expense in the late 1980s. Prior to this time, shopping center landlords charged only an administrative fee for the costs to manage the common areas.

The management fee, which is usually based on a percentage of the property's collected income, is much greater than an administrative fee, which is a percentage (usually 10 to 15 percent) of the CAM expenses. Anchor retail tenants would negotiate for an administrative fee of 5 percent or less, and seldom accept the management fee as a pass-through expense. Most other shopping center tenants, however, are not in a strong enough position to negotiate eliminating the management fee from the CAM expenses.

Some landlords are very aggressive and still attempt to negotiate both a management fee and an administrative fee. Tenants need to keep in mind that these two fees are for the same service. They need to carefully read this lease provision and negotiate one of those fees out of the CAM charges, or they may be surprised to discover that they have agreed to be charged twice for the same service. In such a situation, the landlord might take the position that the tenant agreed to the two charges when signing the lease, and insist that the terms of the lease be followed.

When the management fee is agreed to as a pass-through charge, the tenant should negotiate a cap on the fee. The cap can be based on an agreed percentage of the building's gross income or a fixed dollar amount. This provision may state that the fee will be based on industry standards, but in a dispute neither party may agree to what that industry standard is.

Caps on Pass-Through Charges.   Tenants are advised to place some restraint on the landlord's pass-through spending to operate the building, and may negotiate for a cap on the pass-through charges. A cap places a limit on the amount of the charges or on their annual increase. Landlords will resist caps, because they believe that they operate their building efficiently and there are several expenses over which they have little or no control. If a cap is negotiated, the landlord may agree to cap the controllable charges to a specific percentage increase each year, such as 5 percent, but not to cap the uncontrollable charges—such as real estate taxes, insurance, utilities, snow removal, etc. The tenant also may negotiate to cap the amount of spending allowed on capital improvements.

Pass-Through Operating Expense Accounting.   The pass-through provision gives the landlord the right to estimate pass-through charges for the coming year. The tenant pays one-twelfth of the estimate each month. The provision also obligates the landlord to provide the tenant with a year-end adjustment for these estimated expenses by a specific date. The industry standard is to provide the tenants with a reconciliation of the prior year charges by the end of March. However, the landlord may prefer an open date, and some landlords wait until after the summer to account for the prior year's pass-through charges. Tenants desire an earlier deadline, and may negotiate that they have no obligation to make up for any underpayment of the actual charges if the landlord does not provide them with a reconciliation of the charges by a specific date.

Fixed CAM Charges.   Some shopping center landlords bill tenants a flat CAM charge and do not make adjustments for the actual CAM expenses. This can eliminate any disputes over the charges, and guarantees a known cost for tenants. Yet it is risky for both the landlord and tenant because the expenses may exceed the flat charge or be overstated. When negotiating a flat rate, the prior year's CAM charges should be used as a base to determine the coming year's CAM expenses. These expenses need to be carefully reviewed to determine if there are any unusually high or low expenses—such as an abnormal snow fall—that might distort the figures.

If a shopping center is being developed, each party can conduct a survey of CAM expenses for similar shopping centers in the area. Usually there is an annual percentage increase to the flat CAM charge. The landlord may negotiate for a percentage increase to the controllable charges but no cap for those that cannot be controlled.

Open and Enclosed Mall CAM Charges.   The terms *mall* and *strip shopping center* are often used interchangeably, but there is a difference between these types of shopping centers. A *strip center* is a row of stores facing a parking lot or the street. A mall is a shopping center with two rows of stores facing each other with a walkway between them. A mall has two and possibly three CAM budgets, each with a separate charge to the tenants—one for the parking lot and exterior areas, another for the mall area common areas, and the third for the food court if applicable. This permits the separation of pass-through expenses for tenant billings.

Tenants who do not front on the mall, such as pad or outlot tenants, pay their pro rata shares of the parking lot and exterior CAM expenses, but they are not billed for the mall CAM expenses. Only food court tenants pay towards the food court budget. Tenants on the mall pay both the parking lot and exterior CAM and the mall area CAM charges, though anchor tenants often negotiate exemptions from paying the mall area CAM expenses. These anchor tenants may state that they do not need the mall's common area because they have entrances to their store from the parking lot, and they are able to negotiate because the developer knows they are crucial to the mall's success.

When an anchor is exempted from paying mall area CAM expenses, the landlord wants the shop tenants to pick up the remaining CAM costs. Each shop tenant's proration is then based on the GLA of the tenant's premises divided by the total square footage of all shop space for stores that front on the mall, excluding the square footage of the anchors. (The store areas of shops in a satellite building and/or pad tenants are not included.)

GLA of Tenant's Space ÷ GLA of Shop Space with Mall Frontage =
Tenant's Pro Rata Share

Thus, if a mall has 800,000 square feet of GLA, of which shop tenants occupy 200,000 square feet, anchor tenants have 575,000 square feet, and pad tenants occupy 25,000 square feet, the denominator for the shop tenants' proration formula would be 200,000 square feet. A shop tenant in a 2,000-square-foot space would pay 1 percent of the mall CAM costs (2,000 square feet ÷ 200,000 square feet = .01). However, the denominator for parking lot and exterior CAM for all tenants would be 800,000 square feet, and the same shop would pay one-fourth of 1 percent as its share of those costs (2,000 square feet ÷ 800,000 square feet = .0025).

The tenant should negotiate the size of anchor tenants who are excluded from paying mall area CAM charges. Sometimes anchors will pay a small contribution towards the mall area's CAM, and the other tenants will negotiate to have these funds credited against their pro rata CAM charges.

CAM and Operating Expense Pass-Through Insurance.   The cost of insurance for office buildings and industrial properties is included in the operating expenses that are billed to the tenants. For shopping centers, the insurance included in CAM charges is for property damage to the common areas and for liability coverage if someone is injured in those areas. This portion of the insurance premium is excluded from the building insurance expense that is billed separately to the tenants. The premiums are divided this way because some tenants—i.e., those in freestanding buildings and sometimes the anchor tenants—are responsible for providing their own *fire insurance, extended coverage insurance,* and *liability insurance.*

For example, the landlord would not include a freestanding restaurant in the insurance coverage for the buildings in a shopping center, and the restaurant's square footage would be excluded from the denominator used in calculating the other tenants' pro rata shares of the building insurance expense. However, the restaurant tenant would still be obligated to pay a pro rata share of the common area maintenance expenses, including the liability and property damage insurance coverage on the common areas. By allocating part of the premium for the insurance on the whole shopping center as a CAM expense, the landlord ensures that those tenants who pay for maintenance of the common area also pay to insure it. The same situation prevails when anchor tenants own and insure their building but pay a pro rata share of CAM expenses, which include insurance for the common area.

Maintenance Reserves.   The maintenance reserves provision allows the landlord to charge for a reserve for major maintenance needs that may arise in the future. For instance, if a parking lot needs to be resurfaced in three years, the landlord may bill tenants their pro rata share of the cost monthly for the next 36 months. Major tenants do not pay towards this maintenance reserve but pay their pro rata obligation when the expense is incurred. Office and medical office building landlords may use maintenance reserves to replace items such as *heating, ventilating, and air-conditioning (HVAC) system* equipment or carpet in the common area. This allows the landlord to collect in advance for major maintenance instead of either billing the tenants one large amount in the year the expense is incurred or billing the tenants over three to five years following the year when the expense is incurred.

Tenants want to be certain that the landlord uses the reserves for their intended purpose. This can be an issue when a property is sold and either the seller keeps the reserves or the buyer transfers the reserves to a personal account. If tenants agree to a maintenance reserve, they should require the landlord to place those funds in a separate trust account and provide all tenants with an annual accounting of the maintenance reserves.

Common Area Billings.   Common area costs are billed monthly, and they are based on an annual budget developed for the calendar year. Consequently, the tenants pay one-twelfth of the budget each month. At the end of the year, the budget is adjusted to actual costs. If the actual costs exceed the budget, the tenants are billed for their pro rata share of this overage. If the budget is less than the actual costs, the tenants are either given a credit towards the next rent payment or a check for their pro rata share of the savings.

Some anchor tenants will not pay their share of common area expenses based on an estimated budget, and will pay only for actual expenses. They require the landlord to provide copies of invoices with their billings. Anchor tenant leases may provide them with the right to approve the common area maintenance budget within a specific date and require the property manager to obtain a minimum of three bids on all maintenance jobs that exceed a certain dollar amount. The anchor tenants also may attempt to negotiate the exclusion of certain expenses, such as the cost of security, from their pro rata share of the CAM charges. The landlord will negotiate for no exclusions—especially security costs—from their share of the expenses.

Gross Up Operating Expenses.   The operating expenses charged to a tenant are based on the method for billing pass-through expenses that is agreed upon in the lease. The gross-up provision allows the landlord to *gross up* operating expenses that are affected by the building occupancy, which may include utilities, service contracts, janitorial costs, management fees, and property taxes.

It is common to gross up operating expenses in office and medical office buildings, but the concept is often misunderstood. Some tenants believe that the landlord is padding expenses when the building's pass-through charges are grossed up, although the purpose of grossing up the operating expenses is to have the tenants pay their fair pro rata share. Contained in the bulleted list below is an example of why gross up is a fair approach.

Gross Up:
- The example office building is 100,000 square feet.
- A tenant occupies 10,000 square feet in that building.
- The tenant pays a 10 percent pro rata share of the operating expenses.
- Janitorial costs are $1 per square foot.
- The cost for janitorial services at 100 percent building occupancy would be $100,000.
- The cost for janitorial services for the 10,000-square-foot tenant would be $10,000 (10,000 square feet × $1 per square foot).
- The building is only 50 percent occupied.
- The cost for janitorial services for the half-occupied building is $50,000 (50,000 square feet × $1 per square foot).
- If the tenant is charged his pro rata share of 10 percent, the charge is only $5,000 ($50,000 × .10) for janitorial services, while the actual cost to clean the tenant's premises is $10,000.
- When operating expenses are grossed up to 100 percent occupancy, the cost for janitorial services is stated at $100,000 (100,000 square feet × $1 per square foot) and the tenant is billed $10,000 (10,000 square feet × $1), which is the actual janitorial cost for the tenant's space regardless of the building's occupancy level.

A gross up benefits tenants who have a base-year lease. Since these tenants pay their share of the increases after the base year, they benefit from higher operating expenses during that base year. Since they must pay their pro rata share of operating expenses above the base-year expenses, higher operating expenses during the base year mean less of an increase in operating expenses for the following years.

Tenants will want the operating expenses grossed up to 100 percent occupancy during their base year when they have a base year operating expense pass-through provision, meaning that tenants pay their pro rate share of all expenses above their base year, which is usually the year they take occupancy of their premises. If the building is not fully assessed for real estate taxes because it is new, the tax assessment for the first year may be based on a partially built building and the real estate taxes will need to be grossed up. If the building has low occupancy, a tax appeal may earn a lower assessment; again, the real estate taxes will need to be grossed up.

If the tenant's lease is not a base-year lease, the tenant may negotiate for the gross up to be at 95 percent building occupancy since a building is seldom fully occupied at all times and a 5 percent vacancy factor is the standard vacancy rate used for a building's pro forma. However, the difference between 95 and 100 percent is nominal. It is easier and there is less chance of a mathematical error if 100 percent is used.

Higher base year operating expenses benefit tenants with a base-year lease, but they also benefit landlords who use other methods of billing operating expenses. The purpose of this provision should not be to bill the tenant for the maximum tenant charges allowed, but to charge tenants for their fair share of the building operation costs.

BOMA International has published a book describing the gross-up process in more detail: *How to Adjust Operating Expenses for Occupancy Changes in Office Buildings: The "Gross-Up" Process.*

Compliance with Governmental Requirements

The landlord places the burden on tenants for compliance with governmental regulations that affect their occupancy. If a tenant does not comply, the landlord retains the right to perform the work needed for compliance and bill the tenant.

Tenants will negotiate that the building meets all governmental regulations when they take occupancy; if not, the landlord will promptly bring the building up to compliance at no cost to the tenants. The cost of future governmental regulations is a negotiable issue.

Condemnation and Eminent Domain

This provision addresses the government's right to take property for public use upon the payment of just compensation. Such a provision cancels the lease if all the premises are taken by *eminent domain.* In case of a partial taking, the landlord and the tenant have a right to cancel the lease if more than a specific percentage (e.g., 20 percent of the premises or common area) is taken. Tenants should determine what percentage of their property's parking lot and other common areas can be taken without impacting their business. If more than that portion is taken, they will want the right to cancel their lease.

The landlord is given all rights to the entire damages awarded or the total payment through eminent domain. The tenant is allowed to claim from the condemning authority all compensation that may be recoverable because of loss incurred in damage to the tenant's business or the removal of merchandise, furniture, trade fixtures, or equipment.

Continuous Operation

An issue related to store hours and critical to the synergy of a shopping center is uniform hours of operation in all the stores. The *continuous operation* provision requires tenants to maintain store hours as designated by the landlord and prohibits them from closing their store for any length of time. It also requires the tenant to keep in stock, on the premises, a full and ample line of merchandise; to maintain an adequate sales force; and to occupy and use the entire premises.

Shopping centers and other retail properties are the only property types that routinely require this provision. Retail landlords require tenants to remain open because of each business's importance to the synergy of the property's tenant mix. More tenants being open means greater choices for shoppers and a greater opportunity for the landlord to collect percentage rent.

A penalty needs to be negotiated for violations of continuous operation. The landlord may want the right to cancel the lease, while the tenant may prefer a monetary penalty. Anchor tenants seldom agree to a continuous operation provision.

Co-Tenancy

A co-tenancy provision provides a right to one tenant based on another tenant's cessation of operations. Through this provision, tenants may ask to pay only percentage rent or to cancel the lease entirely if a named co-tenant leaves or occupancy falls below a specific percentage. From a landlord's perspective, this provision can have a domino effect on losing tenants and should be avoided. From a tenant's perspective, key tenants may be an important customer draw and, if they vacate, any resulting decline in sales and profits needs to be mitigated.

If a co-tenancy is granted, the landlord negotiates for a time period (e.g., six months to one year) to replace the vacating tenant before other tenants may cancel their lease. An alternative to allowing tenants to close their store and cancel the lease is to allow them to pay reduced rent—or percentage rent and tenant charges only—until the space is re-leased. Another option requires tenants to show proof of declining sales (e.g., 10 percent or more) before they can exercise their co-tenancy provision rights.

This provision was common in the 1970s and early 1980s, but was then almost unheard of for the next 15 years. Today, co-tenancy rights are seldom included in a tenant's lease—especially an anchor tenant's lease. Exceptions include some of the major tenants in lifestyle shopping centers. Because there are no traditional anchors in most lifestyle centers, many of the stronger, national tenants negotiate for the right to cancel their lease if specific tenants vacate the shopping center. The landlord will attempt to resist the request for a co-tenancy provision; however, if an important tenant is in the balance, the landlord may not have a choice and consequently will provide a co-tenancy provision.

A co-tenancy provision could be tied to the occupancy of a shopping center. If occupancy falls below an agreed percentage (e.g., 70 percent) tenants with co-tenancy provisions may exercise their co-tenancy rights. Under these conditions, a decline in the shopping center's occupancy rate may cause significant pressure on the landlord to retain tenants who are having rent payment problems or whose leases landlord would prefer not to renew. Seldom do landlords agree to a co-tenancy provision.

Default By the Landlord

Tenants negotiate for the right to cure a landlord's default. Often this default has to do with the landlord not maintaining the building. Tenants want the right to subtract from their rental payments any costs they incur to cure a landlord default. They may also negotiate the right to cancel the lease if the landlord's default impacts their business. The landlord wants sufficient time to cure a default and will resist giving tenants the to right to cancel their lease.

Default By the Tenant

There are two types of defaults: monetary and nonmonetary. The lease states what comprises a monetary default (e.g., not paying rent and other charges) as well as what timeframe the tenant has to cure the default.

A nonmonetary default—such as a retail tenant not maintaining the mall's hours or not submitting sales reports to the landlord—may require a different time period, depending on the type of nonmonetary default to cure. The time to cure a monetary default may be only a few days, while the period needed to cure a nonmonetary default may be a week or a month.

If the tenant does not cure a nonmonetary default in the allowed time period, and if the landlord can cure it on behalf of the tenant (e.g., repairs to the building or premises that are the tenant's responsibility), the landlord wants the right to cure the default and charge the tenant for that cost. The tenant negotiates for a cure period that is as long as possible, as well as for what remedies the landlord may execute in the case of a default.

Description of the Leased Premises

Each party wants to be sure that the other party has no doubt about which space they are negotiating for, and so the lease must include a readily identifiable description of the leased premises. This explanation may take several different forms, such as a street address, a description of the space covered by the lease, and the legal description of the property. Attached to the lease is either a *site plan* (for a shopping center or single-tenant industrial building) or a *floor plan* (for an office building, medical office building, or multi-tenant industrial property) with the space outlined and crosshatched.

The size of the space is usually stated in this provision. Space measurement is discussed in detail in Chapter 9, "Defining the Premises." Regardless of the method agreed to by the landlord and the tenant to measure the space, the square footage may be off by a few feet. The landlord prefers that the lease states the space is "deemed" to be a specific square footage. If both parties agree to this wording, they are agreeing to the size of the space regardless of its actual size. Tenants prefer that the exact square footage is stated in the lease, but this may be difficult since the results may change by a few feet every time the space is measured. As a result, tenants may agree that the space is "approximately 'X' square feet."

Entry By the Landlord

The landlord must retain the right to enter office and medical office buildings at all reasonable times to inspect and provide essential services and clean the premises. For retail stores, retailers maintain and clean their premises, and most landlords do not want the right to enter a tenant's space because of concerns regarding lost or stolen merchandise. They generally advise retail tenants to change the locks upon occupying the premises, and landlord entry in the case of an emergency would be by force.

The Estoppel Certificate

An estoppel certificate is needed whenever a landlord refinances or sells a property. A prospective buyer of income-producing property or a lender who is financing (or refinancing) a property will want to know each tenant's lease status and to verify the information provided by the landlord.

The lease includes a provision that requires the tenant to execute an *estoppel certificate*—a statement by the tenant of the status of the lease—at the landlord's request. The landlord will require the tenant to sign the estoppel with a short time period, usually 10 to 14 days. If the tenant does not respond to this request, the landlord is empowered to act as the tenant's attorney-in-fact in executing the estoppel certificate.

Estoppel certificates include the following information: the term of the lease, the expiration date, the amount of rent per the lease, the amount of the security deposit, any delinquent or prepaid rent, what options exist, whether or not all the landlord's work has been performed, landlord or tenant defaults, and any lease modifications. They also state that the lease is in full force and effect, and should include the date to which rents and other charges have been paid. The intent of the estoppel is to cut off any tenant's claims regarding the above issues. However, tenants do use estoppels as leverage for claims or outstanding issues with landlords.

Tenants may negotiate for additional time to allow their attorney to review the estoppel. Many lenders and buyers of property, as well as national tenants, request to use their own estoppel form instead of the landlord's. It is not always practical for the landlord to agree to this in advance, because a future lender or buyer may require a specific form.

Exclusive Use

An *exclusive use provision* grants the tenant the sole right to sell a specific product or provide a specific service. Because the *exclusive* prevents the landlord from bringing in other tenants with similar product lines, landlords are understandably reluctant to grant this provision. Exclusives are found mainly in retail properties, but they are occasionally an issue when leasing office and medical office buildings as well.

In malls as well as in lifestyle, entertainment, and outlet shopping centers, most uses must be duplicated to provide consumers with a wide variety of merchandise, opportunities for comparison shopping, and entertainment. In neighborhood, community, and specialty shopping centers, many uses can be duplicated without harm to any of the merchants.

From a landlord's perspective, exclusives place a limitation on their ability to lease a shopping center or other type of building by excluding tenants who provide the same merchandise or services as the tenant with the exclusive. Exclusives also put an administrative burden on landlords and property management companies and, if violated, create liability. Even if landlords do not intend to duplicate a use, it is best for them not to grant an exclusive, as it could undermine their efforts to create the optimum tenant mix.

A tenant may negotiate an exclusive for a multitude of reasons. The tenant may not want competition or may be trying to exclude a particular business from entering the location. Or the tenant may provide a service that requires expensive equipment (such as a medical group that purchases MRI equipment) and want the opportunity for increased referral business to pay for and earn an acceptable return on the cost and operations of the equipment.

The general rule, for the landlord, is to avoid exclusives. There are, however, a few exceptions when a landlord may agree that an exclusive is warranted. If necessary, the landlord may be able to grant an exclusive that will be less burdensome while still accomplishing the tenant's objectives. When exclusives must be granted, the following should be included in the provision:

- *Exclusives should not apply to anchor tenants, their assignees, or their sub-lessees.* Anchor tenant use provisions have few, if any, restrictions. Anchor tenants add new lines of merchandise during their lease term, and some of that merchandise may conflict with another tenant's exclusive.

• *They should not apply to any existing tenants, their assignees, or their sub-lessees.* The use provisions of existing tenants may not prohibit them from selling a product that a new tenant has an exclusive right to sell.

• *Exclusives should not be transferrable to a tenant's assignee or sub-lessee.* The tenant who is granted an exclusive should not be allowed to transfer this right to others.

• *Extensive limitation on the product sold or service provided should be applied.* For example, an exclusive use to operate a hair salon should not include the exclusive right to sell beauty products, because several other types of stores sell such products.

• *Exclusives should exclude the incidental sale of the product by other tenants.*

• *They may be limited to a particular area.* For example, an exclusive might apply only to the north wing of a shopping center.

• *They may be contingent on the payment of percentage rent.* For instance, if tenants do not pay percentage rent by the third calendar year of the lease, their exclusive rights are forfeited.

• *Exclusives may be offered for a specific period.* They might apply only to the first year of operations, providing tenants a chance to start their business without direct competition in the shopping center or building.

• *Specific damages if the exclusive is violated must be included.* This is very important for landlords. If specific damages are not included in the lease, the tenant may claim millions of dollars in loss of business, loss of income, and loss of the value of the business. The provision should state that the tenant is not entitled to any monetary damages. The tenant may have the right to cancel the lease or have the minimum rent eliminated; the tenant would then pay only percentage rent along with the other tenant charges, or the tenant's minimum rent may be reduced.

Expansion Rights

The expansion rights provision is often referred to as "the first right of refusal." Though it may seem like a fair request by the tenant, it can be problematic for the landlord. The landlord wants to remain able to lease the space to another tenant—possibly one who will occupy a large amount of space in the building. A problem could arise if the landlord forgets the tenant's right and leases the space to another tenant.

If this provision is granted, it is usually to a large space use and often a national tenant. If this lease provision must be given, the landlord is advised to place obligations and restrictions on the expansion right, such as the following:

- Designate the exact space for which the tenant has the first right of refusal.
- Increase the rent on the additional space to market rate.
- Stipulate that tenants have a limited timeframe after availability is announced to notify the landlord of their intent to take the space.
- Require that the tenant must lease the space within a specific period.
- State that the tenant must not be in default.
- Provide the tenant with a one-time right.
- Stipulate who pays for the TIs.
- Set forth the expiration date.
- If tenants exercise this right, given them a limited time to sign the lease for the new space.

Tenants are also advised to negotiate the restrictions listed above, attempting to remove them entirely or at least to make the provision less onerous.

Failure to Deliver the Premises

In rare instances, the landlord may not be able to deliver the premises to a tenant on the agreed upon lease commencement date. This may be due to a setback in the construction of a new building, a delay in the move-out of an existing tenant, a holdup with building out the TIs, or *force majeure.*

Because landlords do not want to lose new tenants in these cases, they will insert the following stipulations into the lease: (1) the lease remains in force under such circumstances; (2) the landlord cannot be held liable for any loss or damage; (3) the minimum rent and all tenant charges are waived until such time as the landlord delivers possession of the premises to the tenant; and (4) in the case of shopping center property, tenants may extend the allotted time (usually 60 days) to fixturize their premises. In negotiating the lease term, either party may request that any delay in possession will extend the term of the lease for an amount of time equal to the period of delay.

A delay in the move-in date can cause havoc to a tenant's business. Some retailers will only open a new store during specific periods of the year, and typically avoid "blackout periods" (e.g., November, December, or January). If a window of opportunity is missed, the retailer may not open for three or more months. Under such circumstances, retailers negotiate for their lease commencement to be deferred to a specific date. Tenants may insist that, if the delay extends beyond a certain number of months, they have the right to cancel the lease.

When tenants give notice to their current landlord that they will not renew their lease, only to find out that their new space will not be ready for occupancy as planned, they may be left with nowhere to go when their lease expires. If the current landlord has not yet re-leased their space, the lease may be allowed to continue on a month-to-month term; however, the tenant is then at the landlord's mercy. In such situations, landlords often charge 150 percent of the tenant's last month's rent—or even more.

Tenants may negotiate for their new landlord to pay a penalty if the premises are not ready on the agreed date. This penalty could be tied to the additional rent these tenants will have to pay in their current building, or to the cost of finding a temporary location. Seldom is the space not ready when a landlord commits to a date; however, when this does occur, the disruption places financial and operational hardships on the tenant, and that tenant will want to be compensated.

Floor Area—Definition of Measurement

As discussed in Chapter 9, the office building and the industrial property industries have published standard methods for measuring space, and leases will often refer to these standards. The shopping center industry does not yet have a standard method for measuring tenant premises, and so the *floor area* provision defines the method to be used for measurements. Tenants are advised to read carefully the method used for measuring space in the building. They should always negotiate for the right to measure the space and adjust past and future rents to the correct amount of space if necessary.

Force Majeure

The force majeure provision relieves landlords of liability or responsibility if they are delayed or hindered in, or prevented from, performing any act or obligation required by the lease because of strikes, lockouts, "acts of God," riots, failure of power, governmental laws or regulations, war, or other causes beyond their reasonable control. Any obligation so delayed is extended for a period equivalent to the period of the delay. The most likely delay on the landlord's part arises during construction of the building or TIs. Tenants should also negotiate for similar force majeure rights.

Go-Dark Provision

Major tenants will request a go-dark provision. This provision allows the tenant to close operations while continuing to pay rent (*go dark*). The tenant's position is that, as long as the landlord receives rent payments in accordance with the lease, the tenant should have the right to close the store. The landlord may argue that a major tenant has been given concessions—perhaps a prominent location, a long-term lease, an attractive rental rate, etc.—because of that tenant's drawing power. If this tenant's store closes, the shopping center may be devastated, the rest of the tenants will suffer, and the landlord will not receive the benefits for the above-stated concessions.

The go-dark provision may be a determining factor in whether or not a lender will finance or refinance the property. If landlords must give a tenant a go-dark provision, they will negotiate for the following: required advance notice, reimbursement of unamortized TIs and commission, and the right to recapture the premises and terminate the lease if the tenant goes dark.

Tenants, on the other hand, may not want the landlord to cancel the lease if they go dark. For anchor tenants, often the rent they pay is substantially below the market rate, allowing them to sublease the space at market rent and earn a profit. Tenants may offer the landlord a *buy-out* based on the present value of the lease. For a large tenant, this buy-out can be in the hundreds of thousands of dollars.

Green Standards

If a green lease is pursued, the lease may include a section that identifies all the environmental standards and goals that have been agreed upon by the landlord and tenant. These green standards may be provided as a stand-alone document, or they may be included as a lease exhibit. See Chapter 5, "Preparing for Negotiations," for more information about green leases.

Guaranty

When the tenant entering into a lease has a weak financial statement, the landlord will want an additional guarantee that rent will be paid and other lease requirements will be honored. If a corporation entering into the lease does not have a strong financial statement, the landlord may require the owners of the corporation to guarantee the lease. If the lease is with a sole proprietorship or a partnership, the landlord may require that the lease is personally guaranteed by the sole proprietorship or partners. If the sole proprietorship or partners do not have a sufficient net worth, the landlord may require a third-party guarantee. A lease *guaranty* is generally attached as a separate document (exhibit) to the lease.

Tenants want to minimize their financial obligation to the landlord and will negotiate to eliminate the guaranty. They might agree to accept a guaranty only if their net worth falls below a predetermined amount. Retail tenants may negotiate to be relieved of their guaranty as long as their sales are above a predetermined amount.

If a lease guaranty is necessary, tenants may negotiate several changes to the guaranty to minimize their financial risk. Tenants may propose to limit the guaranty to the first year or two of the lease. The landlord may agree to this request but make it contingent upon the rent and other charges being paid on time during that period. The tenant may then request one late payment (of no more than a few days) just in case a rent check is not delivered on time or an accounting error occurs.

Hazardous Substances

Cleaning up a hazardous spill is very costly. In addition, a buyer may delay or cancel the purchase of a property, or a lender may delay or cancel the financing or refinancing of a property, if a hazardous substance is present. However, some tenants must use hazardous materials in the operation of their business—photo processors, dry cleaners, automobile repair shops, and service stations are obvious examples—and their activities must be monitored. Many medical professionals handle hazardous medical waste. The landlord's main concerns in regards to hazardous materials are illegal use, disposal, and who pays for governmental fines.

Beginning in the 1980s, a hazardous substances provision was added to commercial leases to prohibit tenants from illegally using or disposing of hazardous substances in or on the premises or the common areas of the property. The tenant is required to:

- Comply with all governmental regulations regarding hazardous substances.
- Allow the landlord to inspect the premises.
- Pay for all cleanup costs, fees, and penalties imposed by any governmental authority.

If the tenant is a medical professional, that tenant will also be required to contract with a certified and licensed medical waste removal company.

The tenant negotiates for the landlord to certify that the property has no known hazardous waste and, if it does, that the tenant is not responsible for its cleanup and relevant penalties.

Holdover

The holdover provision has important economic implications for both parties. Any *holdover tenancy* after the expiration or termination of a lease is construed to be a *month-to-month tenancy* subject to all the terms and conditions set forth in the lease. However, the minimum rent is increased for the holdover period—usually to 1.5 times the minimum rent due for the last month of the lease term. This increase is used as a motivating factor to get the tenant to vacate when the lease expires. The greater the rent increase during the holdover period, the greater the likelihood that the tenant will either agree to a lease renewal or vacate the premises.

The landlord may even negotiate for a holdover rent of two to four times the last month's rent to motivate the departure of a tenant. This is especially helpful when the premises are already leased to another tenant who expects to take occupancy by a specific date. The tenant may also lose all other concessions, such as a cap on pass-through charges, and be liable for any damages the landlord suffers from the holdover. These damages may include the penalty the landlord must pay to the tenant who has leased the space but cannot move in on the agreed date.

Tenants often hold over because the space they are moving into is not yet ready. It is to their benefit to negotiate for rent to increase only a nominal amount during the holdover period, for no changes to be made to the lease, and for no penalty to be charged.

Hours of Operation

Though tenants usually have building access 24 hours a day, the hours of operation vary depending on the type of property and need to be clearly stated. The HVAC (heating, ventilating, and air conditioning) is operated during building hours stated in the lease, and the tenant is charged for any after-hours HVAC use. Individual tenants may open earlier and stay open later than the core hours, and must negotiate for HVAC during these hours (see "Hours of Operation" in Chapter 8 for more detail).

HVAC Hours

Typical hours for HVAC service are the typical office hours of operation (outlined above). These hours change slightly depending on the area of the country and the building's tenant profile. If the lease does not state the hours during which the building will provide heating, ventilating, and air-conditioning, a tenant can demand HVAC at any time of the day and night, even during the weekend. For example, an accounting firm stays open late into the night and on weekends during tax season, and needs HVAC service during those hours. Since the lease does not state the hours for HVAC, the landlord is required to provide this service after hours and account for the expense as an operating expense paid by all the tenants.

To accommodate the needs of firms with long hours and weekend operations, the lease may provide for after-hours (after the building's stated hours of service) HVAC for a charge. This charge is based on the cost of energy, the use of the equipment, and the rate of an on-duty building maintenance engineer, if one is required. After-hours HVAC income is credited towards the building's operating pass-through expenses. The amount of the charge is not stated in the lease, because it will vary as utility rates change and labor costs increase. Some HVAC systems can monitor a tenant's use of HVAC during non-standard building hours.

HVAC Maintenance

This provision applies to retail and industrial properties. Tenants were originally responsible for maintaining the HVAC units in their premises, but improper maintenance and costly repairs led to a requirement that tenants submit copies of their maintenance contracts to the landlord. The situation was aggravated by the use of different contractors, inconsistencies in the quality of service and specifications in maintenance contracts, and the added problem of damage to the roof by contractors on it to service the units.

The updated HVAC maintenance provision gives the landlord the right to maintain the HVAC unit and makes the tenant responsible for the cost of preventive maintenance, repairs, and replacements. Because all work is contracted to one company, the property manager is usually able to negotiate a discounted service price. This ensures that HVAC units will be serviced properly and will be in good condition at the expiration of the tenant's lease. An efficiently run HVAC unit and a discounted service fee also result in direct savings for the tenant, and the life of the equipment is prolonged. The provision also ensures that only one service contractor has access to the roof, where HVAC units are usually located, decreasing the likelihood that the maintenance contractors will damage the roof through excessive foot traffic or leaving materials on the roof.

Tenants want this provision to state that the price of the service is at the market rate, and may want to negotiate who is responsible for the cost of major repairs and equipment replacement. They also may require that the equipment is inspected by a certified contractor, all necessary repairs are made, and faulty equipment is replaced before they assume responsibility for servicing and maintaining the equipment. Additionally, tenants may negotiate out of being responsible for replacing equipment, especially if the unit is an older unit or a major replacement is needed during the last year of their lease.

If tenants install a supplemental HVAC unit, the landlord will want them to pay for the unit and be responsible for the maintenance, repairs, and replacement of the unit.

Insurance—Building

Insurance is included as a line item in the operating expense budget of office and medical office buildings. Insurance typically is billed separately to tenants in shopping centers and free-standing industrial properties. Building insurance is not included in a shopping center's CAM charges because anchor and pad tenants are usually responsible for insuring their space, while the landlord provides the insurance for the other portions of the shopping center.

When the landlord insures a building, tenants are responsible for reimbursing the landlord's cost to insure the property. The landlord does not want to limit the type or amount of insurance coverage that may be necessary. The lease may state that "insurance shall include all insurance premiums for fire, liability, rent loss, flood, earthquake, and any other insurance or *endorsement,* which may include an 'all risk' endorsement or any other insurance that the landlord or landlord's lender deems necessary." Some anchor tenants in shopping centers and industrial tenants in free-standing buildings may attempt to have specific coverage, such as earthquake and loss of rent insurance, excluded from their share of the insurance cost. They also may negotiate to cap the amount of liability insurance coverage. Though non-anchor tenants do not have the negotiating strength to obtain these exclusions, they may still attempt to place limitations on the type and limits of insurance coverage for which they agree to reimburse the landlord.

The lease will also state that if the tenant's business causes the building's insurance premium to increase, the tenant will pay the increase.

Insurance—Tenant

The landlord wants to be certain that if any of a tenant's inventory, fixtures, or equipment is damaged, stolen, or destroyed, that tenant will have the funds to replace those items, continue to operate the business, and pay rent. The *insurance provision* states that the tenant must carry insurance on the furniture, fixtures, equipment, and inventory of the business. In a shopping center or ground floor retail space in an office building, the tenant may be required to have plate glass coverage. The lease mandates that the tenant have a minimum amount of liability insurance; usually the amount is between one and two million dollars. The tenant is also required to have *business interruption insurance.*

The tenant must provide the landlord with evidence of such insurance and include the landlord (and the landlord's property management company) as a named insured on the policies. The landlord often agrees to this provision if the tenant's net worth remains above a specific amount. The lease should also allow the landlord to provide coverage if the tenant does not obtain the required insurance, and to be reimbursed by the tenant for the cost.

The tenant should review carefully the type and limits of insurance coverage. Some landlords require tenants to have insurance coverage that is neither standard for their use nor common in the industry.

Janitorial Services

The landlord typically provides janitorial service for office and medical office buildings. The lease should state the frequency of janitorial service, list the days this service will be provided, and state that the landlord will determine janitorial specifications. The tenant may request that the janitorial specifications are an exhibit to the lease and that the landlord not be allowed to change the specifications without the tenant's approval.

Key Money

A seldom-used lease provision that benefits the landlord is the *key money* provision. Under this provision, the tenant pays the landlord a fee—usually a substantial amount—for the right to lease space in a property. This provision is most often seen in retail properties, and might be used for a new shopping center expected to be a great success or for an existing retail property that is already extremely successful or in a phenomenal location.

Landlords are rarely able to charge this fee. If the premises are in a highly desirable location, tenants assigning their lease to another tenant may be able to negotiate for key money from that tenant (the assignee).

Landlord's and Tenant's Work

The lease usually includes a provision that states the condition of the premises when the landlord delivers them to the tenants, and that the tenants agree to accept the premises subject to completion of any landlord's work. The landlord's and tenant's work exhibit describes any landlord's work to be completed as well as specifying what work the tenant will provide for the premises.

Late Charge

The lease gives the landlord the right to charge a *late fee* if the tenant does not pay rent by a predetermined date. If a tenant does not pay the rent on time, the landlord has two primary means of recourse: to give the tenant a formal notice of default or to assess a late charge.

Tenants negotiate for the landlord to give them written notice that the rent has not been received and to grant a grace period before the late charge is assessed. Tenants don't want to be assessed a late charge in the case of an accounting error or a late mail delivery. Landlords, on the other hand, don't think they should have to remind tenants to pay their rent on time and prefer that a late charge automatically be applied if the rent is not received on the date it is due. Because most commercial tenants pay their rent by mail, landlords often give a three- to five-day grace period before the late charge is assessed.

The amount of the late charge should be stated (e.g., 12 percent of the amount past due); in no event should the percentage rate be more than the legal maximum allowed. If the landlord uses the services of an attorney to collect delinquent rent, the attorney's fees should be a tenant expense in accordance with the terms of the lease.

Lease Commencement versus Rental Commencement

It is not unusual for the lease and the rent to commence on different dates. For example, the lease may begin while a retail tenant is installing fixtures and merchandise, but the rent payments start at a later date.

Landlords want their tenants to abide by the terms and conditions of the lease (such as tenant's insurance and parking provisions) while building out their premises or moving in. It is to the landlord's advantage for both the lease and rent to commence as soon as possible, potentially as soon as the TIs have been substantially completed by the landlord. Tenants benefit when rent commences after they have opened for business.

Liens and Encumbrances

If the tenant does not pay a contractor for TIs or maintenance, that contractor may place a lien on the leased premises or the property. Such an encumbrance can delay or prevent the sale or refinancing of the property. To protect the landlord's interests, the liens and encumbrances provision requires the tenant to keep the premises and the property free from any liens arising from work performed or contracted by the tenant. It also gives the landlord the right to require the tenant to obtain payment or *performance bonds* in an amount equal to 1.5 times the total estimated cost of work, materials, labor, and supplies. The tenant negotiates to be free from acquiring such performance bonds. Lien rights for the landlord and tenant vary from state to state.

Maintenance of the Tenant's Premises

This provision varies depending on whether or not the landlord is responsible for maintaining the tenant's premises. The lease states which repair and maintenance items are the landlord's responsibility, and which items are the tenant's responsibility.

It is common in office and medical office buildings for the landlord to maintain the tenant's premises. The cost of the maintenance, including janitorial service, is included in the building's pass-through operating expenses.

Leases for these buildings may exclude specific maintenance, such as cleaning the carpet and window coverings. Tenants may negotiate the number of times a week janitorial service is provided and the level of service. An exhibit containing janitorial specifications from the agreement between the landlord and the janitorial company may be included in the lease.

In shopping centers and most industrial buildings, tenants are responsible for all repairs and maintenance to their premises. The tenant is usually responsible for all maintenance inside the leased premises, and the landlord performs all maintenance outside those premises. The landlord typically maintains the exterior walls, roof, foundation, structural portions of the building, and common area. The cost of repairing and maintaining these areas is usually included in the CAM charges.

If the tenant is responsible for but fails to maintain the premises, the landlord, after providing written notice to the tenant, has the option of performing the necessary work and charging the cost to the tenant. Tenants are expected to repay the landlord promptly, or risk being placed in default. Tenants negotiate for a reasonable time period to contract for the repairs after receiving written notice from the landlord.

Marketing Fund or Merchants' Association

This lease provision applies only to shopping centers and major retail properties and may require tenants to support the *marketing fund* or, much less commonly, the *merchants' association*. The provision states the minimum payment required, usually based on the tenant's square footage, and provides for an annual increase in funding.

The landlord negotiates for tenants to be required to contribute to this fund, and will make participation mandatory. Anchor tenants may reject mandatory participation, but will often agree to contribute to the funding efforts. Tenants negotiate whether they must pay dues and, if so, the amount of annual fees, how increases are determined, and the amount that the landlord must contribute to the fund. Landlords often give between 20 and 25 percent of combined tenant contributions.

Marketing funds, which replaced the merchants' association, are typical in malls and lifestyle, entertainment, outlet, and specialty shopping centers. They typically do not exist in neighborhood and community strip shopping centers and power shopping centers.

In shopping centers where marketing funds exist, tenants are required to pay a grand opening assessment, which is usually a dollar amount per square foot. Tenants who open for business within a year of the grand opening are also assessed grand opening dues to offset the shopping center's initial marketing efforts. Tenants should negotiate these charges and the amount of the landlord's contribution.

Medical Waste

Medical waste can be classified as hazardous materials (see "Hazardous Substances" above). If present, the lease must outline how medical waste will be disposed of and stipulate that the tenant is liable for any damages or fines resulting from its use, storage, or disposal.

Most Favored Tenant

The most favored tenant provision derives its name and function from the "favored nation" trade advantages that one country gives another. It is a provision that is neither well known nor often used in the industry, though it does appear in shopping centers, office buildings, and medical office buildings.

This provision grants a tenant all the concessions that other tenants have or will be granted. For example, if one tenant has a cap on real estate taxes and another does not pay CAM charges, a tenant whose lease includes a most favored tenant provision is automatically granted both those concessions.

Tenants whose leases are negotiated early in a building's lease-up period may seek "most favored tenant" status. If they are told they are receiving the best deal any tenant will be offered, a most favored tenant provision can guarantee this statement.

Landlords want to avoid granting this provision, which may appear in tenant-generated lease forms. Occasionally, national shop tenants will include this provision in their standard lease form, usually towards the end of the lease. However, the tenant will usually delete it at the landlord's insistence.

Options

Options usually provide benefits for tenants and potential obligations for landlords. Although some landlords and leasing agents offer options freely, most landlords are understandably reluctant to grant them. Tenants, on the other hand, want to negotiate for as many options as possible. Several types of options can be incorporated into a lease, and they are usually granted by the landlord as specific concessions when necessary. The option(s) granted in a particular lease may relate to the lease term (extension or renewal of the lease), the premises (expansion of the tenant's space), or the lease itself (cancellation by the tenant).

Option to Extend. An option to extend grants the tenant the right to extend the lease term. Most landlords prefer not to grant this option because many factors can work to their detriment during the term of the lease, making an extension of the lease unfavorable. If, for example, rent is not paid on time, a retail tenant's sales are low, or a tenant causes problems for building management, the landlord wants to be able to allow the lease to terminate at its expiration.

The tenant should always negotiate for a renewal option. The option doesn't cost the tenant anything, and it provides the possibility of remaining in the premises beyond the lease expiration. If rent during the option period is pre-negotiated, the renewal rental rate may be lower than the market rental rate. If the pre-negotiated rental rate is higher than the market rate, the tenant could renegotiate for a lower renewal rate. Landlords are likely to agree to lower the rate, or they will be left with a vacancy.

If the landlord must grant an option to extend the lease, it should be contingent on several criteria, including the following:

1. The tenant must not be in default of the lease on the date the option is exercised and when the option period commences.

2. The tenant must provide notice that this option will be exercised within a specific timeframe—e.g., no later than 120 days and no sooner than 180 days before the lease expires.

3. The option right will be canceled if the tenant has a number of defaults or a major default, or if the lease has been assigned.

4. If possible, the option is contingent on the retail tenant paying percentage rent or exceeding a specific sales volume during the last two years of the lease.

The tenant may counter these requests as follows:

1. The tenant must have a reasonable time to cure a default before losing the right to extend the lease.

2. The time period to exercise the renewal option may be extended, and the tenant is granted a grace period.

3. Minor defaults do not void the option, the tenant will have reasonable time to cure the default, and the option is assignable with the lease (which is often necessary to sell the business).

4. If the tenant has a percentage rent provision, the option is not contingent on the tenant paying percentage rent. If the base rent is high, it may not be possible for the tenant's sales to exceed the *breakpoint* to pay percentage rent. If this issue becomes a deal breaker (though it is unlikely), the tenant may agree to lose this option if sales do not exceed a predetermined level that the tenant believes is easily achievable.

The rent for the option period can be stated as a predetermined amount, adjusted to market rate, or stated as an increase based on the consumer price index (CPI). The landlord wants it to be no less than the rate paid during the last month of the prior lease term. If the rent is to be based on the current market rate, and that market rate is less than what the tenant is already paying, setting such a minimum protects the landlord from undue financial loss. However, the tenant still is likely to renegotiate the rent down to the market rate in these situations.

If the rent in the option period is based on market rent, this provision should describe other comparable buildings as well as the size and location of the premises within the buildings that will be used to determine this amount. This protects both the landlord and the tenant from an unnecessary dispute and possible arbitration.

Option to Expand.   An option to expand the tenant's leased space may be related to specific space designated on the site plan (for a shopping center or an industrial park) or the floor plan (for an office building or medical office building). The right to expand to additional space gives the tenant flexibility in growing its business. However, this provision becomes an obstacle for landlords if they have other tenants in mind for the space into which the tenant has the right to expand.

If landlords must offer this concession, they prefer to grant a *first right of refusal* to lease additional (usually contiguous) space, based on the lease terms they would offer to another prospective tenant for that space. Tenants are given a limited time (usually three to five days) to accept their landlord's offer. Anchor tenants usually negotiate for a longer period to respond.

Alternatively, some landlords offer a *first right to negotiate,* which gives the tenant the opportunity to negotiate for additional space before the landlord negotiates with any other prospective tenant. If the landlord offers this provision, it should state that, if the landlord and tenant are unable to agree on the terms of the lease for the additional space within a specific time period (e.g., ten days), the landlord may negotiate and enter into a lease with another tenant. The landlord may provide this concession for a limited period, such as during the first two years of the lease.

Neither of these "first right" provisions is common in shopping center leases, but they frequently are found in office and medical office building leases.

Option to Cancel.   See "Cancellation" above.

Option to Purchase the Property.   This provision gives the tenant the option to purchase the property. The price may be fixed, based on a formula, or determined by an appraisal. There are several issues to negotiate if the tenant receives this option: how an appraiser will be selected; whether this provision allows the first right of refusal or the first right to negotiate; how this right can be fortified; and when this right can be exercised. The tenant has a limited timeframe in which to notify the landlord and execute the sale.

Options Allowing the Landlord to Terminate the Lease.   It may be appropriate for a lease to include options that favor the landlord. In retail leases, the landlord may negotiate for the right to terminate the lease if the tenant does not achieve predetermined sales objectives—which may be stated as total dollars or dollars per square foot—within a certain period. The lease may also be cancelable if the tenant has not generated overage rent within a prescribed period, but seldom will a tenant agree to this provision.

Overstandard Utilities

The landlord must have the right to charge the tenant for the consumption of utilities in excess of the standard amount consumed by the typical tenant. Some medical groups or physicians may have equipment that consumes excessive amounts of electricity. In a shopping center, hair salons, restaurants, and Laundromats may consume excessive water. These tenants should be charged for their overstandard consumption if the water service is on a master meter. If possible, it is helpful to have a separate meter or submeter for their utility consumption. If this is not practical, the lease should allow a charge for excessive utilities that are consumed.

Tenants want to be sure they are being charged fairly for their consumption of overstandard utilities. They may negotiate for a formula to be used in these calculations. They also want the additional amount paid to be credited to the overall utility charges.

Parking

The parking provision is important to shopping centers and other retail properties. Convenient parking is an important criterion for a successful shopping center. Parking stalls closest to the stores turn over eight or more times a day—i.e., eight or more customers may use each of those well-located stalls every day. Consequently, when a tenant's employee parks all day in one of those stalls, many customers are deprived of this convenience.

The landlord often requires tenant employees to park in a designated area. This prohibits their use of prime customer parking areas and grants the landlord the right to fine tenants and/or tow employee cars for parking in the nonemployee parking spots. The fine (usually $50 to $100 per violation) is assessed to the tenant instead of the employee because the tenant is the party to the lease. Tenants do not object to this provision because it is good for their business. However, they may negotiate to receive at least one warning before such a fine is issued.

Parties

It is important to know exactly who the tenant is—e.g., a corporation, a partnership, a *limited liability company (LLC),* a married couple, or an individual. If the lease is with a general partnership, all of the partners should sign it. If the tenant is a married individual, it is usually best to obtain each partner's signature. If only one of them signs, it is wise to obtain the advice of an attorney regarding spousal obligations.

The landlord may want proof that the person signing the lease for a partnership or corporation is authorized to enter into the lease on behalf of that entity. The tenant may want similar proof that the landlord's representative is authorized to enter into the lease on behalf of the landlord. It should be noted that, in most states, minors may void a lease at their option, so it is important to proceed cautiously if the prospect's age is in question. The landlord may not have the option to cancel a lease with a minor.

Percentage Rent

Retail tenants and some service tenants usually have a percentage rent provision in their lease. The typical retail lease provides for the tenant to pay either the minimum rent or a percentage of sales—whichever is greater. This provision requires tenants to submit monthly sales reports and an annual statement of sales signed by an officer of their company.

Most leases have a fixed percentage rate for the entire term of the lease. Some landlords with older leases receive a substantial amount of percentage rent from their tenants, whereas leases executed in the past five years have high breakpoints that mean tenants seldom achieve the sales volume to pay percentage rent. There is always the possibility a tenant may do exceptionally well and pay percentage rent. The percentage rate used for calculating whether a tenant owes percentage rent is based on the type of business and its profit margins.

Percentage rent is discussed in more detail in Chapter 10, "Financial Issues."

Quiet Enjoyment

This is one of the provisions in a landlord lease that directly benefits the tenant. It states: "Tenant shall have and quietly enjoy the premises during the term of the lease, provided that Tenant fully complies with and promptly performs all of the terms, covenants, and conditions of the lease." The tenant may want to negotiate to ensure that minor defaults do not void this provision.

Radius

To protect the opportunity to collect percentage rent and avoid diverting sales, retail landlords prohibit their tenants from opening another store nearby. The *radius provision* prohibits the tenant from opening a similar store within a specified distance, e.g., three to five miles for a strip shopping center and five to 15 miles for a regional mall. If the tenant opens a store within the radius restriction, that tenant may be required to add the sales from the new store to those of its store in the shopping center when calculating percentage rent. Another reason for the radius provision is to protect the traffic flow to the shopping center.

Tenants will usually accept this provision but negotiate the radius distance. They also do not want the landlord to have the right to cancel the lease if they open a nearby store, and consequently bargain for a lesser penalty for violations. It also may be arranged that tenants are not in default of their lease if they acquire another business or chain store with a store within the specified radius.

Recapturing the Premises

Many landlords object to a tenant earning a profit on their space because they assumed the original risk in developing or purchasing the building, and they are the ones who sustain losses during a soft market. The landlord's right to recapture allows the landlord to take back space that the tenant wants to sublet or assign.

This *right to recapture provision* came about in the early 1980s. In the mid-1970s, the office building market was soft in most areas of the country, so tenants were able to negotiate long-term leases on very favorable terms. When the office market firmed up in the early 1980s, and rents more than doubled, some tenants sublet or assigned part or all of their space at a considerably higher rent than they were paying, realizing substantial profits.

This provision may apply to shopping centers as well as office buildings. Anchor tenants who close their store in a shopping center might assign the lease. Since they are usually paying much less than market rent for the space, such an assignment or a sublet could yield a substantial profit.

Rather than recapturing the premises, the landlord might allow the tenant to sublet or assign the space, provided that the profit is paid back to the landlord. One drawback this creates is that the tenant may not be willing to charge higher rent without benefiting from the increase. An alternative is for the landlord and the tenant to share the increased rent. If they do split the profit, it will be after deducting the costs to re-lease the space, including commissions, advertising fees, attorneys' costs, and TIs.

Reconstruction

After a major loss, the landlord generally reserves the right to cancel leases and not rebuild if the loss exceeds a certain percentage of the property. That percentage is determined on a project-by-project basis, but it is important that the specified percentage remain the same for all leases within a given property.

Tenants want the right to cancel their lease if the damaged or destroyed portion of the property impacts their business. Landlords prefer to allow this only if there has been a substantial impact to a tenant's business. Tenants also want to negotiate the length of time the landlord has to reconstruct the building before the tenant may cancel the lease. There should also be a guarantee that the building will be reconstructed to standards that are the same as or better than those in place before the damage.

Recycling

If the management of the building implements a recycling program, either voluntary or as required by the local municipality, tenants are required to participate fully in the program. A recycling program may be part of a green building program, and may reduce waste pickup and building operating costs. Depending on the market for recycled materials, selling these materials may earn a profit that can be credited to the building's pass-through charges. Tenants may negotiate to share in any savings generated from the recycling program.

Relocation

The relocation provision grants the landlord the right to relocate a tenant's premises. It is common in office buildings but not often found in shopping center leases. Office building landlords don't want a tenant who occupies a smaller space to prevent a much larger tenant from moving into the building. The relocation provision therefore allows the landlord to relocate the tenant to comparable space at the landlord's cost.

This provision is usually omitted from shopping center leases for several reasons: the importance of a specific location to a merchant in a shopping center, the differences in the rental rates for particular locations, and the costs of relocation. Many retail tenants do not accept a relocation provision because the location of their space is critical to their business. However, relocation may be an important consideration in leases with temporary or seasonal tenants, for tenants located next to another tenant with the right to expand, for combining spaces to attract larger tenants, or in allowing the flexibility to recapture space when expanding or remodeling a shopping center.

If retail or office tenants accept a relocation provision, they want to guarantee that they will not be moved to a less desirable space, or that in such an occurrence rent will be adjusted accordingly. Retail tenants may negotiate to limit relocation to a particular area in the shopping center. Landlords should agree to pay for moving costs as well as for building out the new space to the tenant's existing specifications. All tenants are advised to negotiate for the landlord to pay for *all* relocation costs, including the cost to connect computers, new letterhead, relocation notices, etc. Tenants may also ask for their rent to be abated during the move, and possibly for a couple days after the move, so that they have time to organize their business.

Rent (Base or Minimum)

The rent provision states that the tenant will pay to the landlord, without notice or demand and without any deductions, a fixed annual minimum rent. This will be paid in monthly installments during the term of the lease, either on or before the first day of each month. If the lease commences on a date other than the first of the month, the monthly minimum rent is prorated for the first month, based on a 30-day month. The minimum rent is usually the starting point for lease negotiations between the landlord and the tenant.

If free rent is given to the tenant, the lease must be very specific as to whether or not all other charges (e.g., building operating expenses, pass-through and CAM charges, taxes, insurance) are also free during that period. The best way to prevent any misunderstanding is to state the date on which each of these charges will commence.

All rents and tenant charges, except percentage rent, are due and payable monthly concurrent with the payment of minimum rent. Percentage rent is usually paid at the end of the month based on the prior month's sales. Collectively, these payments are defined by the landlord as the tenant's *occupancy cost*.

Minimum Rent Adjustment.   This is one of the most negotiated lease provisions. The three related issues to negotiate are: (1) the method used to increase the rent; (2) the amount of each increase; and (3) the frequency of the increases. Landlords want rent adjusted annually, while tenants negotiate for a flat rate during the entire term of the lease.

Market conditions are the determining factor in rent increases. This is another reason why landlords—and especially tenants—should conduct (or have conducted for them) a market survey before they negotiate a lease. This survey will provide not only market rental rates but also market rent steps and building pass-through charges.

Rent Adjustment Documentation.   Rent increases may be stated as part of the minimum rent provision or in a separate provision. Regardless of its presentation, the provision for increased rent includes several blanks for listing the adjusted (stepped-up) annual and monthly rental rates and the periods they cover. The specific increases may be an agreed upon fixed amount (e.g., $1.00 per square foot per year) or a percentage increase.

Cost of Living Adjustment.   Another approach—one that both landlords and tenants believe to be fair—is based on the rise in the cost of living (i.e., the inflation rate measured in the CPI). The increase in minimum rent is based on the percentage increase in the CPI from one period to another. Landlords want this *cost of living adjustment (COLA)* to be made annually, while tenants negotiate for longer periods (usually two to three years) between adjustments.

Landlords generally believe that an annual CPI rent adjustment protects the property's value from inflation and increased operating expenses that are not reimbursed by the tenants. However, retail tenants are usually concerned that the CPI increase may exceed the increase in their sales, and all tenants need to keep their rent increases to a manageable level. For these reasons, the minimum rent adjustment based on the CPI is negotiable.

In the early 1980s, the CPI increased more than 10 percent each year. To prevent double-digit minimum rent percentage increases in situations such as this, tenants attempt to negotiate a ceiling or cap on the CPI increase. For example, a tenant might agree to an annual CPI adjustment of no more than 5 percent. In conceding to a CPI cap, the landlord will want to be ensured of receiving no less than an agreed upon minimum increase, and therefore will negotiate for a floor to the CPI. Thus, if the tenant requests a 5 percent ceiling, the landlord may insist on a 3 percent floor. The lease in this situation might state, "The annual rental increase shall be based on the CPI but will be no greater than 5 percent and no less than 3 percent."

When the parties to a lease agree that the minimum rent adjustment is to be based on the CPI, several specific issues must be resolved and stated in the lease. These issues are detailed below.

Base Year.   The first issue to resolve concerning CPI rent increases is a definition of the *base year*—the year from which the CPI increases will be measured. Landlords prefer the base year to be the year the tenant takes occupancy. Tenants negotiate for the base year to be the year after they take occupancy of the premises. Often the compromise is based on the time of the year the tenant takes occupancy of the premises to make the determination. For example, a tenant who takes occupancy in November may be granted the following year as the base year, but the tenant who takes possession of the premises in February will be encouraged to accept the year the lease begins as the base year.

Effective Date.   Along the same line, the next issue to resolve is the date the CPI rent increase becomes effective. The CPI increase may begin on the anniversary of the rent commencement date or on January 1 following that date. Thus, if a lease commenced on July 1, 2008, the base period for rent adjustment would be the first year of the lease—from July 1, 2008 to June 30, 2009. However, if the lease states that the CPI adjustment will be implemented "on January 1 after the lease commencement," the first lease adjustment would be for the period from January 1, 2009 to December 31, 2009.

Geographic Price Index.   A third issue to resolve is which geographic price index to use. The CPI—published monthly by the U.S. Department of Labor, Bureau of Labor Statistics—includes the national average (for U.S. cities) as well as the averages for many (but not all) major metropolitan areas. (The CPI for a few cities is published bi-monthly—some in even-numbered months, others in the odd months—or semiannually.)

The landlord is not able to compute the tenant's CPI-related rental increase until the CPI is published. The monthly reports are normally available three to four weeks after the adjusted month—i.e., the CPI for January is published around the end of February. For those metropolitan areas with CPIs that are published semiannually, the report may not be released until three or four months after the period ends. In a major metropolitan area with a CPI that is not reported monthly, the landlord may prefer to use the U.S. city average to expedite the adjustment of tenants' minimum rents. For CPI increases, the landlord may prefer to use "all U.S. cities and U.S. averages" while the tenant may prefer to use the "specific U.S. city and specific U.S. average." The tenant can minimize rent adjustments by searching recent CPI geographic history and negotiating to use the one with the smallest annual increases.

Adjustment Frequency.   The frequency of minimum rent adjustments is another issue to resolve. Landlords prefer annual adjustments, while tenants usually negotiate for less-frequent adjustments (e.g., every three years). Anchor retail tenants often negotiate for a fixed rental increase every five years.

Full or Partial Adjustments.   Also to be decided is whether the increase will be based on the full CPI (100 percent) or on only a part of it. In a partial adjustment, the agreement may be to increase the minimum rent based on a particular percentage of the CPI increase (e.g., 67 percent). Thus, if the CPI increase is 6 percent, rent is increased 4 percent (.06 × .67 = .0402). However, if the change in the CPI is negative—i.e., a decrease from the prior period—the minimum rent is not reduced. The landlord will not lower the rent in this situation because the building's operating costs do not decrease (this would not apply to a triple net lease) and the mortgage payment does not decline.

Rules and Regulations

The landlord is responsible for operating the property in a manner that is generally beneficial to all the tenants, their visitors, and their customers. To achieve this, the landlord usually sets rules for tenants and their operations that address issues of conformity and safety. Typically, these *rules and regulations* specify constraints on loading and unloading, shipping and deliveries, accumulation of garbage, maintenance of the environment (room temperature, use of loudspeakers, etc.), employee parking, and general housekeeping. Office buildings, medical office buildings, and multi-tenant industrial buildings provide extensive rules and regulations as an exhibit to the lease. Some shopping center leases insert these policies within several provisions throughout the lease.

As green leases are becoming more common, building rules and regulations are increasingly stipulating environmentally friendly guidelines. Preferred parking for hybrid or alternative fuel vehicles, mandatory use of green cleaning products, bans on energy-intensive equipment (e.g., space heaters), and designated smoking areas that are removed from the building are just a few of the regulations that are becoming more popular.

The rules and regulations provision requires the tenant to comply with the landlord's guidelines, and gives the landlord the right to modify them as necessary. It also states that the landlord is not responsible to the tenant for any nonperformance by other tenants, and that the rules and regulations are to be applied and enforced uniformly. The tenant wants the rules and regulations to be fair and reasonable, and may try to modify or negotiate some of them accordingly.

Sales Reports

If the lease has a percentage rent provision, it will also have a sales reporting provision. Even if a retail lease does not have a percentage rent provision, the landlord should negotiate for a sales reporting provision. This provision requires the tenant to submit sales reports monthly to the landlord. It may include a financial penalty if the tenant does not submit the sales report on time.

The monthly sales report is the best way for the landlord to know how a tenant is performing. The landlord and the property manager need this information to determine whether or not to renew the tenant's lease. Monthly sales reports also provide the landlord with advance warning if the tenant is having financial problems. All tenants report their sales monthly, except anchor tenants, who report their sales annually. These sale reports enable the property manager to better analyze the performance of the shopping center as a whole and each of its tenant categories. However, it is usually more difficult for the property manager to collect sales report than rent.

There are two issues for tenants to negotiate in regards to this provision. The first is the necessity of the provision. If the tenant has no percentage rent provision, there should be no sales reporting. The second is the penalty for late submissions. Tenants want to avoid a fee if their sales reports are submitted late; if they are not successful with this request, they can negotiate for the penalty to be waived the first time they are late.

Gross Sales Definition.   The percentage rent provision defines the gross sales to which the percentage rate will be applied and lists which items, if any, may be excluded from gross sales. Sales tax is one such exclusion; refunds and returns also may be deducted. Tenants seek to exclude as much as possible, while landlords want to include as many items as they can in the definition of gross sales in order to maximize their opportunity to collect percentage rent.

Tenants may attempt to exclude discounted sales to their employees from their reported gross sales, and landlords may be willing to grant this with limitations—e.g., the lease may refer to "sales to employees at a discount, not to exceed 2 percent of the tenant's total gross sales." Tenants also negotiate to exclude items that are sold as a *loss leader,* such as lottery tickets. They may want to exclude income from repairs and vending machines, credit loss, etc.

The Landlord's Auditing Rights.   Some leases allow the landlord to cancel the lease if the tenant deliberately understates sales. The percentage rent provision requires tenants to maintain sales records for a minimum of five years, and grants the landlord the right to audit the tenant's sales. The landlord is responsible for the cost of the audit unless the tenant's reported sales are inaccurate by a certain percentage or more, usually 2 percent.

Landlords want the right to audit not just the prior year's sales, but every year's sales. Tenants negotiate for the landlord to be required to notify them of the audit within a specific period (e.g., within 60 days of the time their December sales reports are submitted). The audit should be for prior years only, and each year may be audited only once. The results of the audit are confidential.

The Security Deposit

A *security deposit* is an amount paid by a tenant to a landlord, to be used as recourse if the tenant defaults on the lease. The purpose of a security deposit is to guarantee that the tenant pays all of the rent and charges required under the lease; it is not intended to be the last month's rent.

The tenant must also be sure that the security deposits are being handled in accordance with the lease provisions and returned promptly upon lease expiration, or sooner by joint agreement.

Anchor tenants and national tenants typically have established credit ratings, and they negotiate to omit the security deposit requirement. Local and regional tenants usually agree to pay a security deposit. In lieu of a specific deposit, the lease can require the tenant to provide a letter of credit valued at a certain amount.

The Amount of the Security Deposit.   The amount of the security deposit is typically one month's base rent. During a soft market, a landlord may waive the security deposit entirely. If the tenant's business is new or financially weak, however, the landlord may negotiate for a security deposit equivalent to two or even three months' rent. The tenant prefers as little a security deposit as possible. If the tenant must pay more than the standard one-month's-rent deposit, the terms may be negotiated.

Tenants may request that, if their rent is paid on time for 12 consecutive months, the amount of the security deposit in excess of one month's rent will be refunded. The landlord may agree to this but stipulate that the tenant must redeposit that amount if subsequent rent payments are late. Another approach for retail tenants is to have their excess security deposit refunded when their annual sales exceed a specific amount. If sales drop below the specified amount, they must increase the amount of their security deposit.

The Landlord's Use of the Security Deposit.   If tenants do not pay their monetary obligations under the terms of the lease, the security deposit may be used to cure the nonpayment. Should the landlord have the need to apply those funds to a delinquency, the tenant should be immediately notified by registered mail that they are being used and the reason for this use. A request for the tenant to replace those funds should be included.

The security deposit may also be used for required repairs or maintenance that the tenant refuses to perform. The security deposit provision should require the tenant to reimburse (or restore) the full amount of the security deposit held by the landlord if the deposit is used to cure a default by the tenant.

Return of the Deposit After Lease Expiration.   Depending on local laws, the security deposit provision usually concludes by stating that, if the tenant is not in default of the lease, the landlord will return the security deposit without interest and within a set number of days after the expiration of the lease term. Tenants should negotiate a specific procedure and date for the security deposit to be released. Unless required by law, landlords will not pay interest on a security deposit because of the amount of time needed to calculate this insignificant amount of interest.

Signs

An office tenant who leases a large amount of space may negotiate for the property's sole signage rights, desiring to be the only tenant allowed to place signs on the building's exterior. The landlord often negotiates to allow other tenants the right to display their signs. If the market is strong, the landlord may be able to negotiate a fee for the building's signage rights. Regarding signage on the building directory, the number of lines granted to a tenant and who pays for this cost are issues to be negotiated.

A tenant's signage provision (or a *sign restriction provision*) requires tenants to submit plans for their exterior signs for the landlord's approval. These plans must be based on the property's sign criteria, which are included as an exhibit appended to the lease. The lease requires the sign to be installed and maintained by the tenant. Signage is discussed in more detail in Chapter 8, "Profiting from a Commercial Location."

The Site Plan

A site plan showing the layout of the building is usually attached to the lease as an exhibit. The leased premises, including its dimensions, are identified on the site plan (crosshatched, outlined in red, or otherwise delineated). A ground lease may include a *metes and bounds* (boundary) description of the land parcel.

Landlords are advised to include a disclaimer on the site plan and in the body of the lease, stating that the site plan is not drawn to scale and that the landlord has the sole right to alter it without the tenant's approval. This disclaimer is very important to landlords in case they want to expand the property. This situation is most common with shopping centers, where the landlord wants the right to extend or add a building, create a separate parcel in the parking lot for a pad or outlot building, or remodel or rehabilitate the property without having to get each tenant's approval.

Adding a pad tenant on a ground lease will significantly increase the value of the shopping center. For example, if the annual ground rent is $60,000 and the shopping center is valued using a 10 percent cap rate, adding a pad tenant increases the property's value by $600,000. If the cap rate used is 6 percent, the value of the property increases by $1 million. These values may be reduced slightly if the management fee for the shopping center is a percentage of the property's income.

The site plan provision is also important for the tenant. In shopping centers, anchor tenants want to protect their sightline from the street and negotiate that a pad building can be located in a specific area of the parking lot. Anchor tenants will often negotiate for a predetermined amount of parking to be available in a defined area. Non-anchor tenants may attempt similar negotiations for parking but, unless the retailer is highly sought after, the landlord will not agree to this concession.

Storage

While this topic is crucial in industrial leases, it is also important in all commercial leases. Exterior storage is unsightly, can lead to fires and vandalism, and can be a hazard to traffic on the property. The lease should be very specific as to whether or not exterior storage is allowed and, if so, what can be stored, where, and for how long. The parties to the lease also need to decide if storage areas need to be enclosed with a fence, wall, or landscaping.

Store Hours

The store hours provision has evolved over many years. Originally, the retail lease stated that shop tenants would maintain the same hours as the anchor tenant. When anchor tenants—namely supermarkets—extended their hours, requiring shop tenants to maintain the same hours as the anchor tenants became impractical. Another approach was to require tenants to maintain the hours of similar businesses in the community. This allowed an outside influence to determine the merchant's hours of operation.

A store hours provision may also stipulate which days, if any, enclosed malls will be closed—usually for specific holidays (e.g., Thanksgiving and Christmas). Landlords do not want to open an enclosed mall if only a few tenants will be open. In an open mall or a strip shopping center, tenants have more flexibility because they can be open for business independently, without the entire premises having to be opened. If the lease states the days a mall will be closed, it should also provide for the landlord to have the freedom to change these days.

The most effective approach to store hours is to state the basic daily hours of operation in the lease and to allow the landlord to change them when necessary or appropriate. The tenant, however, does not want the landlord to be allowed to change the hours without the tenant's approval. The tenant should carefully read the minimum hours stated in the lease and, if they are unreasonable for the tenant's business, these hours need to be negotiated.

Taxes

Typically tenants reimburse the landlord for the property's real estate taxes and assessments. It is common for landlords to estimate the amount of these charges, bill tenants monthly for the estimated costs, and adjust these payments to the actual cost early the following year. Anchor tenants in shopping centers and industrial tenants in freestanding buildings negotiate for the right to reimburse the landlord for tax payments after the landlord has provided them with a copy of the payment. This may mean that the landlord fronts the tax payment for these tenants. The landlord prefers for tax payments to be submitted as soon as tenants are provided with a copy of the tax statement.

Tenants are almost always responsible for taxes on overstandard improvements. If a building's tax assessment increases because of a tenant's overstandard improvements, that tenant is responsible for the increase. The tenant should insist on receiving evidence that the improvements are what caused the tax assessment to increase.

A prudent property manager analyzes each successive assessment when it is received. If the analysis reveals that the property is over-assessed, the property manager may hire a consultant to appeal the assessment. If the appeal is successful, the savings will be passed on to the tenants—their pro rata shares of the taxes will be lowered. Because tenants are the beneficiaries of any tax savings, the landlord wants them to pay for the analysis and appeal of the assessment. Tenants may negotiate to reimburse the cost of an appeal if it is successful, but this may discourage the landlord from appealing. The lease may grant some tenants—usually major tenants and freestanding tenants—the right to directly contest real estate taxes on their premises, without landlord approval.

Tenant Improvements

If no work is to be performed by the landlord, the lease should indicate that the tenant is accepting the premises in "as is" condition. If the landlord is providing TIs, they should be specifically described in the lease. The lease or construction exhibit should then indicate that anything not specifically included as landlord work is to be paid for by the tenant.

Term or Duration of the Lease

A lease must have a finite term with fixed starting (commencement) and ending (termination) dates. For example, "The term of this lease shall be five years, beginning on November 1, 2008 and ending on October 31, 2013." The lease should not have an open expiration date—e.g., a date "to be agreed upon in the future." (See "Uncertain Commencement Date" below for steps to take if exact dates cannot be established at the time the lease is signed.)

Most landlords want tenants to open for business as soon as possible, but are not concerned with the specific month this occurs. Some retail tenants have blackout dates when they will not open a store. Depending on the retailer, the blackout period can extend from November 1st to March 1st, or it may include several specific periods during the year.

There are a few issues to be raised regarding the expiration date. To manage occupancy levels and the building's income, landlords do not want a large number of their leases expiring around the same time. The expiration dates should be staggered over different months and several years. Landlords and tenants of shopping centers agree that leases should not expire just before or during the Christmas holiday season. Both parties want to have the benefit of an additional best-selling season. Most retailers do not open during the Christmas season, making it difficult for landlords to lease vacant spaces during the last two months of the year. And since the majority of profits are earned by many retailers during the last six weeks of the year, they do not want the lease to expire during the year's last three months.

Title to Improvements

This provision gives the landlord title to the tenant's improvements, which remain with the premises when the tenant vacates. The tenant may negotiate to remove and keep some of the TIs.

Typical Lease Duration

The length of a lease varies depending upon several factors: property type, the amount of space being leased, whether the tenant is a national or local business, etc. At one time, landlords preferred shorter-term leases so that they could increase rents more frequently. But they soon realized how costly it is to replace tenants, and longer leases are now preferred.

Industrial tenant leases vary in duration depending on the size of the tenant and the costs of TIs, moving, and setup. Office building leases for Class A buildings are usually five to seven years, while for Class B or C buildings they are three to five years. Tenants who take large spaces in office buildings prefer leases of ten years or more. Medical office building spaces warrant longer leases (five to ten years, often with options) because of the high cost to build out a medical suite, which can be three to five times the cost of building out a typical office suite.

The length of retail leases varies more than any other type of commercial property. National shop tenants usually negotiate for lease terms of 7 to 11 years, and most local shop tenants negotiate for terms of three to five years. Retail tenants whose build-out costs are high (e.g., a restaurant) negotiate for longer leases—usually 10 to 20 years with options. These tenants require longer lease terms to amortize the cost of their TIs and fixtures; additionally, their loans to finance the purchase of equipment may be for periods longer than five years. Leases for pad and outlot tenants typically are for 20 to 30 years, often with multiple five-year lease options.

For years, anchor tenant leases were 30 years with six five-year options. Since the 1990s, however, many anchor tenants have negotiated 20-year leases with eight five-year options, allowing them to control the space for the same duration but with the right to terminate ten years sooner. It is in the best interest for all tenants to negotiate for lease renewal options that will give them the option to extend their lease if they so choose (see "Options" above).

Uncertain Commencement Date

When a lease is entered into before or during the construction of a building, or when the landlord reconstructs an existing space, it may not be possible to determine the exact commencement date. In such cases, the lease may state, "The commencement date shall be 60 days after the landlord turns the premises over to the tenant." Office tenants and many industrial tenants can move and set up within a day or two of their premises being built out, so these leases usually commence on day the premises are turned over to the tenant.

As an alternative for shopping center tenants, the lease might state that the commencement date will be either the day the tenant opens for business or a specific date, whichever occurs first. Another option is not to charge the tenants rent if the business opens before a specific date. This encourages opening early and benefits the entire shopping center.

Shopping center tenants are typically given 30 to 60 days after the turnover of the premises to prepare their store to open for business; if tenants are ready to open in less time, they would be wise to negotiate free rent for opening ahead of schedule. Some landlords want the rent the day the tenant opens for business and will not negotiate; others see the benefit of providing free rent in these situations. If a tenant opens after the date stated in the lease, the lease term and payment of rent still commence on the specified day unless special arrangements are made.

A lease with an uncertain commencement date should provide that the landlord and the tenant sign a *lease commencement letter* that ratifies the actual start date. If the landlord must alter when the lease begins, the building's property manager should send the tenant a letter (or written notice) that states the actual commencement date and the expiration date. To avoid any dispute over these dates, the lease commencement letter should provide a space for the tenant to sign (in acknowledgment); the letter should be sent to the tenant in duplicate, and a signed copy should be returned to keep on file.

Use of the Premises

The lease must state the tenant's use of the premises, and the use provision should be very specific about what business the tenant can conduct in the leased premises. The landlord's control over the tenant mix of any property is based on the allowable use(s) in each tenant's lease. This is especially important for shopping centers and retail properties, where the landlord attempts to create the best tenant mix for all the tenants, the property, and the trade area.

Shopping center landlords often want to avoid unnecessary duplication of uses in order to enable tenants to maximize their sales potential, thus increasing the possibility of percentage rent payments. In particular, a shopping center is likely to have only one dry cleaner, shoe repair store, barbershop, or drugstore. In some situations, however, having more than one tenant with the same use is desirable. Regional malls as well as lifestyle, specialty, and outlet shopping centers include several clothing, shoe, gift, and jewelry stores to provide consumers with a wide selection of merchandise and opportunities for comparison shopping.

The *use provision* in shopping center leases should limit the type of business the tenant may operate—and the products or services that can be sold—without being so restrictive that the tenant cannot operate successfully. For example, all types of shopping centers frequently have multiple restaurants, but this use should be tightly controlled. If a shopping center has three restaurants, the landlord does not want all three to serve the same type of food. To do so would dilute the sales of each restaurant, limit the variety of selection available to customers, and reduce or eliminate the potential for percentage rent. The likely result would be that one or all of the restaurants would go out of business.

The use provision in a restaurant lease states the type of food offered, whether alcoholic beverages may be served, and whether the food is eaten in the premises or not (i.e., carryout or drive-through). Such a lease provision might be phrased as follows: "Mexican restaurant with beer and wine for on-site consumption and takeout," or "Chinese restaurant with on-site consumption, takeout and delivery, and no hard liquor served." It is the exception to restrict carryout food.

Another way of limiting the use is to state what percentage of the store's entire sales a particular product may represent. A landlord who believes that only one candy store can be successful at the shopping center will be rightly concerned when a lease proposal is received from a card and gift store chain with a national format that includes incidental sales of candy. In order to allow this store to operate and still protect the sales and potential percentage rent of a candy store, the use provision could limit the square footage of the card and gift store's candy display or limit the store's percentage of candy sales. For instance, "Sales of candy may not exceed six square feet of display area" or "Candy sales cannot exceed 15 percent of the tenant's total annual sales volume." It is easier to monitor and enforce a restriction based on square footage than one based on sales. Another approach is to state that candy sales must be incidental to the sales of cards and gifts.

Retail tenants negotiate for the right to add merchandise. One common way chain store leases do this is to state that tenants may add merchandise sold in their other stores. This provision creates a problem for the landlord: The new merchandise may already be provided by another tenant and the market may not support both tenants selling this product. A more challenging situation arises when the landlord has given another tenant the exclusive right to sell that product; if the chain store tenant then adds the product, the landlord is in violation of the first tenant's exclusive provision.

In office buildings, a common mistake many landlords make is to state that the use is "general business purposes." This allows the tenant to conduct any legal business in the premises. A four-person firm in a 1500-square-feet space could become a 20-person answering service, thus placing a burden on the building's parking and other facilities.

The use provision for industrial properties should also be specific to the tenant's intended use. The landlord may be concerned that, if the use is changed, the new use will create a potential or possible hazardous waste situation.

An additional requirement for tenant uses in general is that *the tenant's use must be legal.* If the tenant's use of the premises is illegal (e.g., gambling in a state where gambling is prohibited), the lease is voidable and may be cancelled by the landlord.

The use provision can also establish a building as a green building, defining third-party certifications and the landlord's green practices. It sets the framework for green building operations and the importance of tenant cooperation.

Use provisions for all building types should be very specific regarding the tenant's use. However, tenants want to negotiate for a broad definition of their use or potential use. They prefer the option to add additional lines of business or even change their business.

Utilities

The utilities provision requires tenants to pay, in a timely manner, all utilities that are billed directly to them for their premises. The provision also grants the landlord the right to bill the tenant for a pro rata share of any utility that is not separately metered for each of the premises. Electricity and gas are commonly provided by private utility companies and metered directly to each tenant, but other arrangements may exist. Municipal or other governmental authorities often provide water, and charges for sewage disposal are usually based on water consumption. Many shopping centers have a common water meter for all the shop space.

Some tenants, such as restaurants and hair salons, use larger volumes of water than other tenants. Tenants will negotiate that, if another tenant uses more water or other utilities than the average, that tenant will be billed an extra amount for the excess consumption. This payment is then credited to the utility charges paid by all the tenants.

Waste Disposal

Garbage pickup (trash disposal) may be considered as a utility, or it may be addressed separately in shopping center or multi-tenant industrial property leases. Disposal service may be contracted for the entire property and charged in the CAM expenses, or individual tenants may contract for this service and pay the charges directly to the waste pickup service. Tenants want to be sure they are paying for their fair pro rata share of the waste disposal. If any tenants have more trash than is typical, those tenants should be billed for the extra trash they generate and the payments should be credited to the waste disposal bill.

For example, if waste disposal is charged to a shopping center's CAM expenses but some tenants pay directly for their pickup service, an adjustment must be made to the CAM billings. In such circumstances, tenants who contract directly for trash disposal are charged only for disposing of debris in the common areas—a small amount since only a small portion of the CAM expense is for emptying common area trash receptacles. One of the best ways to handle this issue is to create a separate charge for those tenants who use the common pickup services, and to exclude this charge from the general CAM costs.

Tenants who generate trash posing potential disposal problems—e.g., food wastes from restaurants, animal excrement and other materials from pet stores—may be required to have special water-tight containers. Some waste materials are potentially hazardous (e.g., medical wastes, dry cleaning chemicals, photo processing agents), and this provision must address the proper disposal of such waste.

The Substantial Completion Letter

A substantial completion letter informs the tenant that the TIs have been (or will be) completed on a specific date, and is used to state when the tenant's rent and other charges will commence. This letter can also remind the tenant that the *estoppel certificate,* proof of insurance, and *certificate of occupancy* must be provided to the property manager before the tenant can move into the premises. If the landlord is providing the tenant with a tenant improvement allowance, the release of these funds should be contingent upon the tenant providing the landlord with these items. A substantial completion letter is not needed when the tenant leases the premises in "as is" condition, but a letter requesting the aforementioned items is still necessary.

Exhibits

Finally, several exhibits are attached to and incorporated into the lease. They are usually appended in the order in which they are referenced in the body of the lease, identified as Exhibit A, Exhibit B, etc. These attachments usually augment or clarify specific aspects of the lease or spell out relevant details. The most common lease exhibits are listed below:

- *Site Plan of the Property.* This exhibit depicts the layout of all the buildings and the boundaries of the property. There may be changes to the site plan in the future, the most common being changes to the parking lot to accommodate expansion of the main building, the addition of a pad or outlot building, or changes in configuration when a shopping center is remodeled. The site plan may include a disclaimer that allows the landlord to make changes to it. The tenant negotiates what changes can occur in the common area, potentially an important issue for retail tenants.

- *Demising Plan of the Tenant's Premises.* The tenant's premises are marked on a layout of the building where the tenant's leased space is located. They may be outlined in colored ink or crosshatched in red or blue. The same disclaimer that appears in the site plan exhibit should be included in this exhibit.

- *Description of the Landlord's and Tenant's Work.* This exhibit, usually a standard form, lists the improvements to the premises that will be provided by the landlord and by the tenant. Usually this document also includes specifications for particular work.

- *Corporate Resolution of the Tenant.* If the tenant is a corporation, a corporate resolution authorizing one or more individuals to sign the lease should be appended to the lease. The resolution, which should be signed by two officers of the corporation, states that the officers who signed the lease on behalf of the tenant have the authority to bind the corporation to the lease. The tenant may request the same guarantee from the landlord.

- *Guaranty of the Lease.* If the landlord thinks that the tenant may not be able to perform lease obligations, especially those related to rent, the landlord will require one or more individuals to guaranty the lease. If the tenant is an individual who has a limited net worth, a friend or relative may provide the guaranty. If a corporation has a limited net worth, the landlord will require the owner (the officers or principal stockholders) or key employees of the corporation to personally guarantee the tenant's lease performance.

- *Sign Criteria.* The sign criteria restrict the size, location, and materials used for fabricating the tenant's sign. All exterior tenant signs must comply with the sign criteria in order for the property to maintain its image.

The discussions in this chapter highlight many of the specific provisions that are commonly found in commercial leases and present a sense of their respective importance to both landlord and tenant. The final contents and the terms and conditions of a specific lease depend not only on the parties to it (i.e., the landlord and the tenant) and their negotiating positions and skills, but also on the type and complexity of the property and the premises being leased.

13

Lease Administration

It is not the brick and mortar, or the land, but the lease document that creates value in income-producing commercial properties. This is the main reason why lease administration must be accurate, and the efforts to make it so reassure property owners that their property manager fully understands the inherent value in the property's leases.

A successfully administered lease has a positive impact on tenants and their perception of the property owner and property manager. Unless tenants have the perception of a competent and capable landlord, they are not likely to want to do more deals with that person. This is especially significant in retail properties, where multiple deals are quite common.

Lease administration is a tedious but essential activity. Lease administration comprises three very distinct areas that combine to enhance the value of a property: human relations factors, bookkeeping and record-keeping procedures, and fiscal issues. Each of these aspects is quite important to the entire process, and all must be done in a complete, accurate, and timely manner or the property will suffer.

HUMAN RELATIONS FACTORS

The lease document is a very precise legal document that sets forth the rights and obligations of the parties involved: the landlord and the tenant. In a perfect world, a well prepared and negotiated lease would resolve any issues between the parties. The administration of the lease would be a simple matter of checking the lease language. Unfortunately, it is not that simple. Dealing with people means dealing with those who have reactions and perceptions much different than our own, even when looking at the same document.

Establishing Good Communication

Although leases have evolved over the years to become quite comprehensive agreements, there is still ample room for interpretation. Communication becomes critical in resolving disputes without destroying the landlord–tenant relationship. That is not to say that the landlord or the tenant must "cave in" every time there is a disagreement with a tenant, but it is in the best interest of both parties to work hard to preserve their relationship.

Good landlord–tenant communication begins with the lease materials that are used in the initial contact of the tenant. They should be honest, accurate, and as complete as possible. The leasing personnel should not oversell. Tenants should not be promised things the landlord cannot provide. All information regarding the lease should be on the table before a tenant decides to enter into a lease. Rents, common area maintenance (CAM) charges, utility costs, marketing fund contributions, reserves, etc. should all be presented ahead of time and should be as accurate as possible.

Once the lease is signed, the leasing team should "hand off" the tenant to the property manager or project manager to prepare the space for the tenant's occupancy. It is best if this can be accomplished in person, but with many larger organizations this is not possible and either a phone call or a letter of introduction will suffice. When letters are used, it is a nice gesture for the property manager to contact tenants, welcoming them to the project and offering to provide any needed information.

Most larger projects have a tenant introduction package or "tenant kit" that is given to the tenant right after the lease is signed. This package introduces tenants to the project and tells them who handles various phases of their move-in and who will be in charge once they open for business. From that point on, the property manager or project manager should stay in close touch with tenants to be sure that everything is working well and that they are likely to open on time per the lease agreement. Any help that is needed—short of doing the tenant's work—should be done to expedite the process.

Once a tenant has completed all work and is open and operating in the premises, the property manager should visit the tenant and prepare a "punch list" of any construction items left to be done by the landlord. These items should be taken care of immediately. It is aggravating for a tenant to put up with a light fixture that is out or not having hot water once they are in business and paying rent. It is also a good idea for the property manager to visit new tenants and give them a gift (e.g., a food basket or potted plant) to welcome them to the project. At this time, the property management company's accounting department should provide the tenant with a letter indicating the starting and ending dates of the lease, as well as the amounts of the next rent payment and charges.

Once tenants are open for business, they should have a phone number and/or email address for the property manager that will allow 24-hour access if needed. Problems come up in properties 24 hours a day, and the property manager must be available to work with tenants and/or contractors if there is a need. All phone calls, emails, and correspondence should be responded to at the earliest possible time.

It is also a good idea for the property manager to visit the tenants at least periodically to chat about how they are doing and any problems of which the property manager should be aware. This provides the property manager with the opportunity to bring up items of mutual interest in a low-key fashion.

Tenant Requests

Good communication between the landlord or property manager and the tenant is likely to improve create a positive landlord–tenant relationship. There are two levels of communication between landlords and tenants. On the first level, landlords have information that they are required to provide the tenants and situations in which they are required to respond. When landlords are operating the common areas, for example, they are acting on behalf of the tenants in what could be considered to be a *fiduciary* obligation. The requirements for good communication are clear.

On the second level of communication, when a tenant asks for another copy of the lease, or asks for reduced rent or other incentives, the landlord is not obligated to do these things or even to discuss them. However, failing to address such concerns puts the landlord–tenant relationship at risk. Landlords should treat each tenant and each request seriously, even if they know they will have to say "no" to some requests. Positive communications make this relationship much more pleasant.

In most cases, landlords have long-term relationships with tenants in commercial properties. Landlords do not need to "give away the store" in order to please their tenants but, rather, they should listen to tenant questions, requests, and complaints; give tenants proper consideration; and provide them with pleasant, reasoned answers. It is not enough to quote the lease provisions that cover the items in question, but there is a sound business reason behind each lease provision that should be the basis of the final response to the tenant. A little empathy for the tenant's position goes a long way towards preserving the landlord–tenant relationship.

BOOKKEEPING AND RECORD-KEEPING PROCEDURES

There are many bookkeeping and record-keeping procedures to deal with as a part of lease administration.

The Process of Lease Administration

The entire lease administration process has evolved to encompass a very sophisticated, informational, and organizational approach. This course was largely set in motion by institutions and real estate investment trusts (REITs) owning properties. Such property owners have brought a sophistication level to lease administration that has allowed ownership and management to better understand the entire property as well as each individual lease.

Computers, as indispensable tools in property management and lease administration, have not made the administration of leases any less expensive. They have allowed, though, for the better evaluation and analysis of leases, resulting in improved leasing and property operations.

Good lease administration is more than just paperwork, and includes the entire property team. The property team consists of: the leasing agent, who goes out and finds tenants; the property manager, whose job it is to oversee the lease administrative process; the lease administrators, who are responsible for analyzing the lease and introduce it to the company accounting and administrative systems; the accountants, who are responsible for the income and expenses associated with the lease administration; the financial officers, who analyze the impact of the lease on the property's income and value as well as working towards maximizing the financial return to the property; ownership; and the attorneys, tax advisors, and property architects, who are all responsible in one way or another for the effective administration of the lease.

The administration of commercial properties requires well prepared and executed procedures, standard policies, and very specific routines. Daily interaction with tenants, clients, contractors, attorneys, accountants, leasing agents, city officials, and mortgage holders requires that business be conducted in a consistent and predictable way. Property owners—especially institutional owners—need to be confident that their property management firms and property managers are professionally equipped to handle every eventuality effectively and efficiently.

Often, when interviewing property management firms, property owners may request a review of the firms' procedures manuals. A prospective client is not likely to be impressed with "verbal" policies and procedures. Property owners want to know that the property management firm's operations and leasing responsibilities have been thoroughly analyzed to consistently maximize property potential.

The eight steps necessary to create an effective lease administration program are:

1. Establish forms, procedures, filing systems, and operating systems to handle all likely administrative tasks in an effective and efficient way.

2. Evaluate each lease to be sure that it is complete and ready to be input into the system.

3. Set in motion any requests for missing information to be sure it is obtained at the earliest possible time.

4. Have knowledgeable, trained personnel available to handle the input process.

5. Enforce measures for double-checking the input. This generally means that one person handles the input and another checks the accuracy of the information.

6. Implement procedures to uniformly administer all elements of the lease during its term, through its final termination.

7. Employ spot auditing procedures to ensure the quality of the administrative process.

8. Develop an internal mechanism to identify administrative problems and work towards solutions in the shortest time possible, consistently maintaining the quality of the operation.

The property management office should have a compilation of the company's forms, procedures, and standard letters on hand to establish their creditability and expertise and enhance the administrative process. For example, property owners want a property management company to have an established, company-wide procedure for approving invoices. This guarantees that the company has accounting procedures and controls to handle and disburse their funds properly and consistently.

Landlords and tenants want to see a well organized, systematic, secure system. Another example is the need for an established rent collection procedure. This top priority for property owners is less likely to be neglected if specific steps are in place and routinely followed. Quite often, these company policies will be augmented by the client's own requirements, but the client wants to know that there is a base program from which to work. It is equally important for the tenant to have an effective lease administration program.

Because so many administrative tasks are similar, standard letters are important in every property management office. They provide the opportunity to present consistent, complete, and reasoned communication. An additional benefit is that, if these letters are stored electronically, the property manager can ask an administrative assistant to send a specific letter (e.g., the "rent collection letter" to the tenant), and the assignment is accomplished in a uniform, pre-approved manner. This approach also minimizes the possibility of sending out "emotionally charged" letters in high-stress situations. For repetitive communications, the standard letter is an invaluable tool that provides an excellent economy of time and ensures a consistent response.

Generally, there are at least two copies of the final lease retained by the landlord and the tenant. Both have original signatures. These leases are most often kept in a secure file and are not used for day-to-day administrative chores, as they may be needed for court proceedings, refinancing, or the sale of the property. Generally, a copy of the lease is introduced into the administrative system. It is critical that any changes or amendments be distributed to the secure file as well as to the day-to-day file.

To make sure the original lease is complete, it is brought into the system and checked for proper signatures, insurance certificates, deposits (if required), lease guarantees, and the appropriate check. Many companies use a specific electronic format for this completion process. The lease administrator fills in the necessary items that are outstanding; once they are all accounted for, the lease is ready to be operational in the system.

Lease Files

Lease files are critical to the smooth operation of a commercial property's administrative system. Every effort must be made to ensure that they are complete, accurate, and up-to-date at all times. A standard procedure should be established for filing each tenant's lease and correspondence. This allows easy access to the information for anyone in the property management company. The larger the company, the more people are likely to need access to the individual tenant files.

File labels should identify tenants by trade name, property, and space or suite number. It helps to color code folders by project to reduce the chances of misfiling. It is also a good idea to have only one project per file drawer, but this can cause excess wasted space for a company with a large number of properties.

Within the folder, one organizational strategy is to keep the lease and all amendments on one side of the file, with the lease on the bottom and all changes and amendments ordered chronologically on top. All correspondence is kept on the other side of the file in chronological order. If the file becomes too large, a second file is prepared, but the lease always remains in the first file. This makes the basic agreement easy to find and correspondence easy to place. When a lease file is removed, the person removing it is required to place a signed and dated "lease out" card in the file. Files should be replaced as quickly as possible, and items are not to be removed from the file. If a paper is needed from the file, it should be copied so that the file remains complete at all times.

Project Files

Along with the tenant files, there is additional information that must be maintained in the project files. These files include, but are not limited to, retail tenants' sales and billing records, CAM or pass-through expense bills, project site plans, insurance and tax records, restrictive easements and agreements (if any), loan documents, certificates of completion, security deposit logs, security records and logs, marketing information, leasing reports, as-built drawings, photos of the property, any liability claims, business licenses, financial statements, hazardous materials information, and personnel records. It should be noted that confidential information, such as the financial and personnel records, may be locked up in a different set of files.

The tenant should also maintain a property-by-property file for each location. This file includes the lease as well as all correspondence, billings, underlying documents, plans, etc.

The Lease Abstract

The first step in getting a lease into the administrative system is the preparation of a lease abstract. This is a universal activity and is used to summarize the lease so that it is not necessary to consult a 20- to 60-page document each time an answer is needed. It is critical, however, that the abstract be an accurate reflection of the lease.

Once a lease is received from the leasing agents and is determined to be complete, the lease is abstracted by the landlord's and the tenant's representatives so that the salient points can be readily available. The landlord's property manager and accounting department, and the tenant's lease administrator, are provided with an abbreviated version of the lease.

The information needed for day-to-day lease administration includes lease terms, tenant or landlord information, rental information, and billback items. Most commercial property management software programs have a lease abstract report. Although these reports differ in form and layout, they all contain the same basic information. The length of the lease abstract depends on the complexity of the lease and the property. A lease abstract for a tenant in a small office building or shopping center may be one or two pages of information, whereas a lease summary for a tenant in a regional mall, mixed-use high-rise office building, or hotel, might take up four or five pages.

The property manager, the lease administrator, or the property accountant is generally assigned the responsibility of abstracting the lease. In very large companies it is not unusual for one person—a lease administrator—to be responsible for inputting lease information and overseeing the lease documents. Quite often that person will become the "keeper of the leases," and anyone in the company who wants access to a lease must sign it out and return it to the lease administrator. Landlords usually prefer to have only one person doing the lease abstracts for a particular building, because it familiarizes that person with the property's standard lease form and the tenor of all of the leases in the project.

Many firms prefer to have the property accountant abstract the lease, since the property accountant administers the tenant's billings and records the rental payments. Some firms have the property manager abstract the lease and the accounting department confirm that the abstract is an accurate reflection of the lease. Since tenants deal with multiple landlord leases, it is equally important for them to have easy access to the most important lease provisions. Having one person do the lease abstract and another check it provides a confirmation that the information is correct.

The landlord's effective lease abstract form includes:

- The tenant's legal name
- The store name (for retail tenants) or trade name
- The address and phone number of the tenant's location
- Any home office information
- The property manager's home phone number and address
- The phone number and address of the tenant's headquarters
- The lease commencement and expiration dates
- Any lease options
- Monthly and annual rent costs and rent step-ups
- The method in which the tenant is billed for operating expenses, CAM charges, taxes, insurance, and other items

Extra pages can be provided for recording additional information, such as a mall's marketing fund requirements, food court contributions, exclusives, co-tenancy agreements, etc.

The tenant's lease abstract includes the same information as the landlord's regarding rent, rent increases, options, billback formulas, and possibly marketing funds. It also includes the name of the property owners and the name of the property management firm, if applicable. From the tenant's perspective, the lease abstract provides an easy source of daily information, circumventing the need to research every lease question in a long lease document.

A lease abstraction error may lead to lost rents or charges for the landlord or overpayment by the tenant. At the very least, any errors will cause questions from landlords and tenants about the accuracy of the records. For example, a missing consumer price index (CPI) increase can result in incorrect billings, so it is prudent to have a second person (e.g., the controller or property manager) check the income section of the lease abstract by comparing the lease to rental increases, operating expenses, and CAM provisions. Reviewing the lease abstract also familiarizes the property manager with each tenant's lease terms. The tenant also must check to be certain the landlord is billing the correct rental rates, percentage rent calculations, and billback formulas.

While the lease abstract is being prepared, there are other schedules and logs that the landlord can easily complete at the same time. These administrative tasks are presented below in the order that they are likely to be completed, but a few of these chores do not necessarily have to be performed at a specific point in the process.

The Deferred Conditions Report

Over the term of any lease, there are undoubtedly changes that will take place. These include rent increases, possible changes in common area billing allocations, lease options, rights to cancel, rights of first refusal, expiration of insurance certificates, and the lease expiration. While the lease abstract is being prepared, the *deferred conditions report* is also updated to record these items.

The deferred conditions report is computer-generated and shows any future changes for all the property's leases. Notable event dates are set up on a monthly basis for the entire term of each lease. The reports are then checked at the beginning of each month and the appropriate action is taken. Lease expirations and lease options are generally set up in the deferred conditions report at least six months prior to the actual date to give the landlord and the tenant time to consider their course of action. Insurance certificate expirations are generally put in the system 60 days prior to their expiration, allowing time for the landlord to notify the tenant and the tenant to notify the insurance agent, ensuring that the new certificate is received by the landlord on time.

Tenant Rosters

For the landlord, it is almost universal that two different *tenant rosters* are needed for most properties to be effective. The landlord or property manager may have a very complete, several-page tenant roster that incorporates all changes in lease terms over the course of a lease. The property manager, however, generally needs a less detailed tenant roster that includes the basic information needed for day-to-day operations.

Each tenant roster should contain a listing of all spaces in the property (generally in the order that they appear); the names of the tenants, using the names on the door rather than corporate names; the unit numbers; square footage; current rentals; security deposits; percentage rent rates for retail tenants; lease dates; starting and ending dates; options; and the common area or pass-through expense billing formula. The roster should be changed each time a change is made in the basic information, and each roster should be dated to be sure that it is current. If two different rosters are prepared on the same date, they should be timed as well. Each version of the tenant roster should be retained, as these rosters can serve as a long-term overview of the property's occupancy.

The tenant is likely to maintain a property roster based on the overall portfolio within the tenant's operations, as well as a roster based on each district within the company. These rosters often contain much of the same information maintained by the landlord. They include the same information for the property manager and relevant financial terms of the lease, but also include the landlord's name, address, and phone numbers and specific individuals for legal notice.

The Lease Restrictions Summary

One of the more critical elements of the administrative process is to understand what lease restrictions exist and to keep a log of those restrictions so they are not violated. This is done with a lease restrictions summary. In a soft leasing market, it is not unusual for the landlord to give concessions in order to attract good tenants. Lease restrictions include exclusives, expansion rights, prohibited uses, etc. Additionally, some cities impose lease restrictions regarding allowable uses on a property. Some anchor or major tenants also require use restrictions. For these reasons, it is important to keep a separate listing of all lease restrictions that may have a future impact on leasing, management of the property, or tenant operations.

The list of restrictions can be maintained in a computer program, much like the deferred conditions report. The landlord or property manager checks the listing of restrictions each time a new lease is being considered to ascertain that no restrictions will be violated. The landlord's list should be distributed to the leasing agents, property managers, company counsel, and the owner of the property to be sure that all involved are fully informed.

Restrictions may include such items as a limitation on the size of certain uses, an outright ban on other uses, and restricted locations for certain uses that require long-term parking. If there are parking restrictions or a minimum number of parking stalls, tenants often monitor these closely to make sure they are in compliance with the lease provisions.

A violation of a lease restriction can lead to very costly legal action. Tenants want to be sure that their landlord is not violating any of the negotiated property restrictions, and consequently has a corresponding list for each location.

Options to Renew. The deferred conditions report should list the time-frame and terms for any options. Landlords prefer not to give options to tenants for a number of reasons, discussed in Chapter 11, "Lease Renewals." Options to either renew or cancel the lease (see Chapter 12, "Negotiating the Lease") can have a major impact on the property. Yet tenants are often able to negotiate options.

The listing for options should include the option notification date and any other restrictions that might prevent the tenant from exercising the option. The property manager and the tenant's lease administrator should look for restrictions placed on the tenant's right to exercise the option.

The *first right of refusal* is much like an option in that the holder of the right must be offered the option to lease additional space or purchase the building before a transaction can be concluded with another party. Generally, there is a limited window for the tenant to exercise this right, and this timeframe should be listed in the register. When a building has one or more tenants with this right, the property manager should indicate, on a site plan or floor plan, which tenants have the right and what spaces are encumbered by the restriction. This report should be checked prior to negotiating with anyone else for that particular space.

Exclusives. The granting of an *exclusive* to a tenant will have an impact on the landlord's future lease negotiations. An exclusive gives a tenant the sole and exclusive right to sell a particular product or provide a particular service. Generally, this right is granted to major or anchor retail tenants, and seldom to large, national chains. Though it is unusual, the same exclusive rights can be found in some office building leases and medical building leases.

If a tenant is granted an exclusive, the exact language of the right should be listed in the report. The tenant may be granted the right to be the only such use in a shopping center, to have the right to a given brand name, or to carry only so many lineal feet of a specific type of merchandise. The report should then be reviewed before a new lease is accepted.

Tenants are advised to monitor the products or services provided by other tenants in the building to guarantee that their exclusive provision is not violated.

Rental Income Records

Accurate rental income records are essential for the successful operation of commercial properties. A computer-based program is used to keep track of commercial tenant charges and payments. It is critical to set up each tenant's information accurately so accounting will know what to bill and when to bill it.

Basic information is entered into the rental records program and then tracked on a monthly basis. The program tracks base rent charges and payments, taxes, insurance, marketing funds, utilities, common area and/or office billbacks, late charges, parking fees, and any miscellaneous charges that may arise. The rental records are set up to provide a consistently updated reference about what is owed and what has been paid.

Tenants also keep their own records of what rent and charges are due and any limitations on those charges, such as caps or specific expenses excluded from their charges.

Percentage Rent Records

Because base rents are so high in most commercial properties, it is not common for retail tenants to owe percentage rents based on their sales. Percentage rents are most common in shopping centers and retail properties, but office buildings or industrial parks with retail or restaurant components also need to track tenant sales to determine if any percentage rents are due under the lease terms.

In order to keep track of the percentage rent, a summary should be prepared showing every space in the shopping center (or office building or industrial park, if appropriate), indicating the occupying tenant and any percentage rent lease provision. If the lease has no such provision, this should be noted on the record. The record should include the name of the tenant, the negotiated percentage rent rate, the breakpoint, the frequency of reporting and payment, and any special considerations such as limitations on what is included in the calculations of percentage rent and any deductions from the tenant's sales that are allowed.

The tenant must also keep track of the lease's percentage rent requirements to make sure that they do not pay more than the agreed-upon amounts.

Sales Report Forms

The collecting of tenant sales reports is a time-consuming and often difficult task for the landlord's property manager. Some smaller retail tenants often do not fully understand the percentage rent provisions, and any help that the property manager can provide will benefit both parties.

When the tenant is required to report sales on a monthly basis, it is suggested that the landlord send 14 blank monthly report forms at the start of each year. The forms should provide preprogrammed figures for the percentage rent rate, the gross sales, the breakpoint, the proper deduction of minimum rent, and a space for the amount of percentage rent due, if any. It is helpful for the form to include a reminder about when the form is to be returned and to whom it should be sent. Although it is suggested that blank report forms be prepared by the landlord and provided to tenants, tenants are obliged to provide their sales reports in a timely manner even if the landlord does not provide these forms.

Usually a monthly report is prepared by the accounting department showing each tenant who is obligated to pay percentage rent, the current month's sales for that tenant, the cumulative sales by month, and a two- or three-year running comparison of the sales figures. These reports are used to quickly evaluate how merchants are doing and are often reviewed prior to meeting with tenants. This type of report is used in analyzing the shopping center as a whole.

Quite often, shopping center management will calculate the tenant's sales per square foot, set up meaningful clusters (e.g., less than $150 per square foot, $150 to $250 per square foot, $250 to $400 per square foot, $400 to $600 per square foot, and $600 and above per square foot), and plot the sales on a site plan with different color codes. This helps to evaluate where the higher sales per square foot occur, equally as important, where lower sales levels can be found.

Sales reports are analyzed to determine if additional rent is due and, if so, that this rent is recorded and collected. Typically, sales reports are sent to the property management company's accounting department. The reports are analyzed to be sure they are accurate and that any monies due have either been received or have been entered in the ledger as a receivable and the tenant has been billed. Tenants also develop procedures to ensure that they pay only those amounts agreed to in the leases.

Information gathered from sales reports is used as a tool for evaluating opportunities for improvements, changes in tenant mix, and the renewal of leases about to expire. Sales report forms may be used to show weak areas in the merchandise mix or problems within certain areas of the property.

Some landlords opt to include a monthly sales reporting form at the bottom or back of their invoices to make it easier for tenants to include their sales report with their next month's rent. This form provides the tenant's sales breakpoint, percentage rent, and the address to which their report and percentage rent check should be mailed.

A disadvantage to including this form with the invoices is that, typically, the lease requires tenants to submit their sales to the landlord by the 20th of the following month (e.g., January sales reports are due to the landlord by February 20th). Thus, tenants send their January sales report, along with any percentage rent due, with the March rent check, making them ten days late (received on March 1st rather than February 20th). However, sales reports are more difficult to collect than rent. Since they seldom all arrive on the 20th of the month, receiving the report on the first of the month instead of the preceding 20th of the month is acceptable to most property owners.

Annual Sales Statements

When the lease requires the tenant to provide sales reports, there is almost always a requirement to provide a year-end sales report. Shop tenants generally are required to provide a year-end statement of sales signed by the owner of the business, but this does not necessarily have to be an audited statement.

The Security Deposit Log

Security deposits, as discussed in Chapter 12, may be required of tenants to safeguard against lease defaults. These deposits must be properly accounted for; they can be a bookkeeping liability. If the property is sold, the security deposits must be transferred to the new property owners. Most landlords are not required to put these deposits in a separate bank account or to pay interest to tenants. However, a listing or log of the deposits is nevertheless helpful. This log is prepared at the same time as the lease abstract and updated anytime there is a change. If a tenant pays a deposit and it is returned at a later date, the log should show both transactions so the record is complete. Showing only a zero balance after the fact does not provide a complete audit trail.

Tenants need to keep track of all security deposits as well. Some tenants negotiate to post a security deposit at the lease signing that will be returned in two years if they are not in default. In most cases, deposits are posted for the entire lease term, and tenants want to track these amounts to be sure they are returned according to the lease provisions.

FISCAL ISSUES

There are also many fiscal issues to be addressed in the process of lease administration.

Common Area Charges and Billback Administration

Tenant billbacks can be the cause of many tenant complaints and concerns as well as a major income source for landlords. Common area administrative fees and management fees can be the source of landlord–tenant disagreements. When the lease is clear as to how these charges will be applied, there are few problems; however, when the language is inconclusive or too general, problems may arise.

Tenant billbacks should be timely, fair (in accordance with lease requirements), and accurate. Slow billings can hurt a property's cash flow, and failure to collect monies due can reduce the value of the property. Tenants are concerned about inaccurate or overstated billings. Many tenants are able to negotiate limitations on or exceptions for their billback charges, and they want assurances that those limitations are being acknowledged.

It is very important that both parties to the lease have a complete understanding of all individual lease terms as well as the property's operational characteristics. Even though the theory behind common area maintenance charges is to bill the tenants for the cost of maintaining all of the common areas, the property manager, who administers these billings for the landlord, can bill a tenant for only those expenses allowed in the lease. In summarizing the tenant's lease, the property manager determines which charges are billable, how the tenant's share is calculated, and how the tenant will reimburse these expenses. The methods for billing expenses to tenants in different property types, are discussed in detail in Chapter 10, "Financial Issues."

Negotiated billback exceptions (also discussed in Chapter 10) are time-consuming and complex to administer. A separate operating expense budget (or budgets) must be developed to determine the correct amount to bill each tenant with negotiated exceptions. It is helpful to summarize the operating expense provisions for each tenant to be sure that there is an accurate listing of the specific lease provisions. The listing should include all spaces in the property, the name of the tenant, the square footage, management fee provisions and common area supervision fee provisions for shopping centers, and any exceptions to the billings. Even if certain tenants are not required to contribute to the operating expenses, they should be listed in the summary with the notation "no contribution required" so that everyone knows they are not supposed to receive a bill.

Tenants must establish a similar system to carefully monitor their billback charges, ensuring that their costs are accurate and that no credits are overlooked. If, for example, the landlord receives a payment from the property's insurance policy for common area damage, that payment should be credited to the cost to repair the common area. If a utilities refund is given at the end of the year to all the users, that refund should be credited to the CAM utilities. Tenant administration of billback charges consists of knowing what the lease provisions provide for and also what limitations or caps have been negotiated.

Billing Common Area Costs

Common area billings can be complicated and confusing, but an organized system helps significantly in the preparation of accurate and timely billings. The billings for different property types are discussed in detail in Chapter 10.

The easiest way to administer the common area charges or billback expenses is to set up an electronic spreadsheet with the bills and billings, as well as exceptions. As each bill for CAM charges arrives, it is entered into the system and allocated to the tenants within the spreadsheet. The spreadsheet may take some time to set up initially, but in the long run it will make the administration much easier and more accurate than that done by hand. The landlord should maintain CAM invoices in a separate file for use when the tenant billings are prepared. At the year's end, having all of the bills recorded and copied will make the final billings that much easier.

When common area bills are prepared, each invoice should be reviewed to be sure that the charge belongs in the tenant's billing. Great care must be taken to be sure that those charges are not billed to the wrong property. If copies of each invoice have been retained, it is easier to quickly grasp the situation and respond to tenant requests. Each month's total provides the basis for a straightforward comparison to budgeted figures. Year-to-date figures can then help the property manager to make responsible decisions for the balance of the year.

It is fairly easy to set up the CAM expense allocations on a spreadsheet for the final allocation. Tenants are listed by space number rather than alphabetically. The denominator for each category is the total square feet of all tenants who are being charged for that expense. For instance, if all tenants in a shopping center pay their pro rata share to maintain the common parking lot, the denominator for that category may be 550,000 square feet. However, the common area maintenance within the mall may only be covered by those tenants on the mall portion of the shopping center, leaving the denominator for these charges at 475,000 square feet. Thus, different denominators are used to calculate each tenant's charges.

Other exceptions can be set up in the spreadsheet and then checked for exceptions prior to the final billings. Marketing fund dues are usually calculated on a dollar-per-square-foot basis. The heating, ventilating, and air conditioning (HVAC) charge is usually a fixed monthly or quarterly charge based on the size of the tenant's HVAC unit.

Larger tenants often have administrative staff to review all CAM bills for compliance with the lease provisions. It should also be noted that some tenants engage companies to audit CAM charges. Landlords are advised to have lease language limiting the tenant's ability to audit old billings after a reasonable time has elapsed. Generally, the lease language indicates that the tenant may not audit more than one year in the past, the audit must be done by a competent auditor, and the auditor may not be engaged on a *contingency* basis. Lacking these lease provisions, the tenant may audit past bills at any point.

Other Tenants' Billings.   Commercial property owners enter into agreements with many different tenants; some tenants are granted concessions and some are not. If the concessions granted to one tenant do not cost the others anything, they are really none of their concern. The property manager's obligation is to show the tenants that they are paying only their fair share of the expenses and no more. Landlords are obligated to show tenants how they arrive at their allocations and that those shares are in accordance with their lease agreement. Beyond that, the concessions granted to others do not have to be divulged. Each lease is a private matter between the landlord and the tenant.

Year-End Reconciliations. The year-end reconciliation should be accomplished as soon as practical after the year's end. Some strong tenants include a certain date (e.g., March first of the following year) in their lease provisions for when such accounting must be completed. As always, all commitments should be fulfilled in a timely manner in order to maintain positive relations.

The typical commercial lease has the tenant pay a pro rata share of operating expenses. Most commonly, tenants receive an annual budget with their share indicated, and they pay a monthly estimate on that budget. At the end of the year, the landlord totals the tenant's share of the actual expenses and either bills the tenant for any balance due or refunds or credits any overpayment based on the actual expenses for the year. If a refund is considered, it is important to be sure that the tenant does not have an outstanding balance due before refunding the overpayment amount.

If tenants have made overpayments, there are advantages to both refunding the money and to crediting their account. Sending a check directly to a tenant is an acknowledgement that the money belongs to that tenant. Tenants rarely receive money from their landlord, and such payments foster good landlord–tenant relations. Sending refund checks also informs tenants that their landlord or property manager is operating the property effectively.

An advantage to crediting the tenant's future rent is that the landlord receives a partial payment for the next rental payment and has use of the tenant's money for a longer time. One possible disadvantage is that a tenant may overlook the credit and make the customary rental payment, creating a credit on the books that must then be communicated to the tenant and adjusted. Using an unusual credit can also confuse the amounts due and paid for future analyses.

Capital Improvements

Commercial property leases may include new signage, replacing the carpet in the common area, parking lot replacements, and energy conservation equipment and other capital expenses in the property's operating passthrough and CAM expenses. While these may be considered capital expenses in residential properties, appropriate lease language allows them to be billback items in commercial properties.

Some leases allow reserves for future replacements. If, for example, a parking lot will need a major, $100,000 resurfacing in five years, lease language that allows for reserves means the property manager could include a $20,000 reserve in the CAM budget for each of the next five years. The property manager may establish a reserve amount less than $20,000 per year if the reserve fund interest is credited towards the $100,000 needed. When the maintenance is undertaken, the funds are available and tenants need not be billed for a major expense all at once, or the landlord does not need to front the money and bill the tenants over the next five years.

The amount to reserve can be set by determining first which major maintenance or capital improvement items are allowed as pass-through expenses in the lease. The cost and timing of these expenses can then be anticipated. Major tenants seldom will contribute to a reserve; instead they pay their pro rata share of the expense when it is incurred. In such a case, the amount to reserve would be determined by subtracting the major tenants' pro rata shares. For example, if the major tenants were responsible for 75 percent of the CAM expenses, the landlord would need to reserve $25,000 of the $100,000 parking lot resurfacing costs. The smaller tenants would be billed for their portion of the $25,000 over five years, and major tenants would contribute their share of the expense ($75,000) when the resurfacing actually took place.

Real Estate Taxes

One of the largest expenses for most commercial properties is real estate taxes. Most leases require tenants to reimburse their landlord for the tenant's share of those taxes, and it is the property manager's responsibility to collect those payments. Property tax bills for office buildings and industrial buildings are usually included with the one pass-through operating expense billing. A single bill is sent to each tenant covering all of the building's expenses. If there is one tax bill for the entire property, it is up the property owner to allocate the tax charges to tenants based on their lease provisions.

There are many exceptions to how taxes are billed (e.g., anchor and outlot tenants having separate tax bills in some shopping centers). The property manager must be aware of these exceptions to be sure all property taxes are properly allocated and that the landlord is being properly reimbursed. Before starting any allocations, the property manager should obtain an assessor's map to determine how the property is segregated for tax purposes and reconcile that map to the leases. A property tax record can then be prepared to allocate the taxes per the lease agreements.

Another variation on tax billings is the base-year approach, which is used almost exclusively in office buildings. The base-year formula is more common in older leases. The landlord sets rent knowing what the taxes are for the year the tenant takes occupancy, and the base year (usually the same year that the tenant occupies the premises) is stated in the lease. Using this approach, if the taxes on the premises are $1,000 during the base year, the landlord pays $1,000 annually and the tenant pays the annual increase above $1,000. A 5 percent increase in the second year would mean that the landlord would still pay $1,000 and the tenant would pay $50 ($1,000 × .05).

Tax Appeals.   As a major expense for commercial properties, real estate taxes are often the source of disagreements between the landlord and tenant.

Because commercial buildings are valued via the *income approach* for tax purposes, low rents, high vacancies, and slow lease-up can result in overvaluations, which have quantifiable, negative effects on properties and can be the basis for effective tax appeals. In the recession of 1989, almost every commercial building qualified for a tax appeal, and those that did were often rewarded with a reduction in taxes.

The Cost of an Appeal.   The appeal of real estate taxes can be expensive, especially if it is contested by the taxing authority. Older leases often made no provision for the costs of tax appeals, so the landlord could appeal the taxes and pass on those savings to the tenants, but could not collect the cost of doing so.

There are companies that will handle the contesting of the taxes on a contingency basis. If there is no savings, they do not charge a fee. If savings are realized, the companies' fees may be 15 to 50 percent of the actual savings. The property owner or property manager may appeal directly, without any outside help.

If the lease does provide for reimbursement of the cost of appeals, real estate taxes can include all relevant expenses, "including fees reasonably incurred by Landlord in seeking reduction by the taxing authorities of real estate taxes applicable to the Property." Such statements place the burden of the appeal cost on those most likely to benefit from a tax reduction. Today's leases generally provide that the cost of an appeal is paid by the tenants. Resultant savings, if any, are passed along to them as well. This is a fair and reasonable approach to the situation.

Property Insurance

In commercial properties, the landlord is responsible for providing and billing back the property's insurance cost. The landlord's insurance does not cover the tenants' improvements, stock, fixtures, furniture, or equipment.

In office building and industrial properties, insurance covers all the buildings and common areas. In shopping centers, where anchor or pad tenants usually provide their own building insurance, the landlord's insurance policy excludes anchor and pad tenants' buildings. Liability insurance for the property, however, covers all buildings and requires a different expense pool for its allocation.

Shopping center leases allow the landlord to bill tenants for insurance on a full pro rata basis, and this cost is billed separately to the tenants. Insurance for office buildings and industrial properties is included in the building operating expenses and billed back to tenants, along with the other operating expenses of the buildings in one billing statement. In some office building leases, insurance has also been subject to base year considerations. This approach means that the insurance premium in effect at the commencement of the lease will be paid by the landlord throughout the lease term. Increases in premiums over the base year are shared pro rata by the tenants, as are all pass-through expenses above the base year.

A major issue between landlords and larger tenants is the level of coverage provided under the liability provisions. The lease may stipulate limits of $2 million in liability coverage, but landlords might have a policy with $20 million in liability coverage. If they are in a position to do so, tenants may refuse to pay the difference in premiums on the larger amount. Few tenants are in a strong enough negotiating position to obtain this concession.

Tenants' Insurance Certificates

An almost universal requirement of commercial leases is for the tenant to maintain insurance for the security of the tenant's business, the coverage of liabilities, and the protection of the landlord's property that is under the tenant's control. This includes *liability insurance, fire insurance, extended coverage insurance, boiler and machinery insurance,* plate glass insurance, etc. It is incumbent upon the landlord to be sure that each tenant provides the coverage required per the lease.

The property manager has the responsibility of collecting the necessary certificates of insurance and ascertaining that they reflect the lease requirements. The most effective approach is to create a summary of all insurance requirements for each tenant, and to then send letters requesting proof of insurance from each tenant. When proof of insurance is received, it is logged into the report along with the date of expiration. Sixty days prior to that expiration, the tenant is notified that the relevant certificate is about to expire and updated proof of insurance is requested.

Often tenants overlook the insurance provision when negotiating their lease. They should be aware of the insurance requirements in the lease and discuss during lease negotiations any required coverage or limits of coverage that seem inappropriate or excessive. The cost of insurance may be an unpleasant surprise to some tenants. Once the lease has been signed by both parties, the tenant must abide by the insurance provision. Tenants are advised to monitor the landlord's insurance and make sure that the limits are within the parameters set forth in their lease provisions.

Utilities

Providing a master meter for some utilities, such as water for a shopping center, produces cost savings when constructing a building. This situation, however, can create problems for the property manager in properly allocating the costs involved.

The billing of water to several small merchants in a shopping center can be a severe problem without the proper lease language. The most common language is "the cost is shared among the tenants based on a pro rata square foot." But what happens when one tenant has a restaurant, hair salon, or Laundromat and the other tenants have low water usage? Pro rata square footage is not a fair allocation for these different uses, but the lease language must be followed. Even if the lease language indicates allocation by a "fair means," this will not necessarily eliminate tenant arguments over how the billing occurs. The lease should allow for charging tenants extra for excessive water usage. In the end, it is best if each merchant has a separate utility meter.

This situation can be resolved in several ways. The first is to bill an overstandard utility charge to the tenants whose use is excessive, and then to credit this amount to the CAM budget. A consultant or utility company representative should determine the amount of overstandard utilities consumed by each tenant. Another approach is to segregate any tenants with excessive usage by giving them a separate meter to pay their charges directly. In this situation, these tenants should pay for the installation of the meter as well.

Another difficult situation arises when a supermarket (or restaurant) wants to maintain operating hours all night, but the parking lot lights for the rest of the shopping center go off at 11 p.m. The property owners then either have to cut out the supermarket tenant's lights and put them on a separate meter, or determine the extra expense and bill that directly to the supermarket, if allowed per the lease.

A profit can potentially be created if the landlord is allowed to purchase utilities at a bulk or wholesale rate and bill tenants at a higher market rate. In many jurisdictions, however, rate structures are such that the property owner cannot buy utilities in bulk at a lesser fee and sell them to tenants at a markup. Most leases provide that, if the landlord sells utilities to the tenants, the price cannot exceed what the tenant would pay to buy the utilities directly.

Billback Policy

Almost all commercial properties now use a monthly estimate to bill pass-through charges based on an annual budget, with a year-end adjustment. The main exception is when a tenant agrees to a "flat CAM," in which a set figure for billbacks is agreed upon by the landlord and tenant and there are no adjustments at the end of the year. Both parties take a chance that expenses will be either significantly higher or lower than the flat CAM amount. If the figures are carefully calculated, however, they should balance out over several years.

When preparing the common area or billback invoices, the property manager and/or landlord should take a very careful look at what is being billed. If it is questionable, it should not be billed. There is nothing in most leases that gives the landlord an "implied right" to charge for things not addressed in the lease language. Proper billings, however, create cordial relations with tenants and help future leasing efforts.

Approaches to Billing

There has been an ongoing debate for many years in the commercial property management field concerning whether or not to bill tenants on a monthly basis for their rent and charges (see Chapter 10). With modern technology, the billing process has become fairly easy and is an automatic part of many systems. Those against billing tenants argue that, if the bill does not arrive, a tenant might use that as an excuse not to pay the rent. They also do not want to incur the cost to send a monthly invoice to every tenant when the tenants know their obligations.

Three reasons are suggested in favor of monthly billings:

1. The monthly billing serves as an accurate reminder that the monies are due and gives the tenant the amounts and what they are for.

2. Since billing is done electronically, the invoice is a byproduct of the system and does not require much extra effort to produce.

3. The monthly invoice also can serve as a method of sending messages to retail tenants regarding sales increases, marketing activities, special holidays, etc.

Those who argue against monthly billings have several good points as well:

1. The lease indicates the rent and the tenant should not need a reminder. At the first of each year, landlords send out the charges for CAM costs, merchants' associations, utilities, etc., and tenants should not need further reminders.

2. All other items have to be billed separately anyway, so there is no need for a monthly billing.

3. Billing is expensive and there is no evidence that billing the tenants results in any higher payment percentages than not billing them.

There is a third billing method that is a compromise between these two stances. In this approach, the property management company prepares 12 invoices for the coming months and mails them to tenants all at once in December. The tenant can then use one each month and send it in with a check. Any increases during the year are included in the invoices, and tenants have everything they need to pay their rent. The cost of preparing and mailing the invoices is a small fraction of the cost of sending invoices every month.

Any of these billing approaches can be successful, but the final determinant of the success of rent collection ultimately rests in the collection process rather than the billing method.

CONCLUSION

Lease administration is not just the paperwork of overseeing the lease, but the full range of activities that ensures the lease agreement is being maximized for the property owner's benefit. It is often said that management is about money and relationships; and balancing the two can be a very difficult task in some cases. Maintaining a good tenant relationship while billing tenants for several charges—some of which increase unexpectedly—can be a challenging task, and yet every effort must be made to accomplish just that.

Mirroring the landlord's administrative programs, the tenant must have similar tracking devices and methods of checking for accuracy and compliance. This is not a case of the landlord and the tenant not trusting each other, but rather of good business sense and responsibility on the parts of both parties.

Glossary

absorption rate The amount of space of a particular property type that is leased compared to the amount of that same type of space available for lease within a certain geographic area over a given period of time, accounting for both construction of new space and demolition or removal from the market of existing space. Also used in reference to the rate at which a market can absorb space designed for a specific use (e.g., office space). Absorption rate can be computed as follows:

> Units or square feet vacant at the beginning of the period
> + units or square feet constructed new during the period
> − units or square feet demolished during the period
> units or square feet vacant at the end of the period
> = units or square feet absorbed during the period.

Americans with Disabilities Act (ADA) Enacted in 1990, the federal law that prohibits discrimination on the basis of disability. Of the five sections or titles, two are directly applicable to real estate managers: Title I (employment) prohibits discrimination in recruiting, hiring, promotions, compensation, training, and termination on the basis of physical or mental disability. If qualified applicants or employees who have a disability can perform the *essential functions* of a job, employers must make *reasonable accommodations* for them by improving access, restructuring jobs, adjusting work schedules, and the like. Title III requires all buildings that are open to public commerce to be made accessible to disabled people to the maximum extent possible by removal of architectural barriers in areas of public accommodation, provision of auxiliary aids and services to assist in communication, and modification of discriminatory policies, procedures, and practices. Title III affects all public areas of commercial properties and leasing offices, as well as other areas of residential properties that are open to the public.

anchor tenant A major shopping center tenant that will draw the majority of customers to the site. Normally an anchor tenant occupies a large space in a desirable location in the shopping center. Often there are two or more anchor tenants, depending on the type of shopping center.

arbitration A process of dispute resolution in which a neutral third party (arbitrator) renders a decision after a hearing at which both parties have an opportunity to be heard, often employed as a means of avoiding litigation. Arbitration provisions are common in collective bargaining (union) agreements and often required in commercial contracts. When arbitration is voluntary, the parties to the dispute select the arbitrator who has the power to render a decision, called an award, that is binding on the parties. See also *baseball arbitration.*

artificial breakpoint   An negotiated figure, agreed to by the tenant and the landlord, that requires the tenant to begin paying *percentage rent* either before or after the *natural breakpoint* is reached. See also *percentage rent.*

asset management   A specialized field of real estate management that involves the supervision of an owner's real estate assets at the investment level.

asset manager   One who is charged with supervising an owner's real estate assets at the investment level. In addition to real estate management responsibilities that include maximizing net operating income and property value, an asset manager may recommend or be responsible for property acquisition, development, and divestiture. An asset manager may have only superficial involvement with day-to-day operations at the site (e.g., supervision of personnel, property maintenance, tenant relations). Compare *property manager.*

assignee   One to whom some right or interest is transferred, either for the individual's own enjoyment or in trust. The person receiving an assignment.

assignment   The transfer, in writing, of an interest in a bond, mortgage, lease, or other instrument. The transfer of one person's interest or right in a property (e.g., a lease) to another. Also, the document by which such an interest or right is transferred. Specifically, the document used to convey a leasehold is called an *assignment of lease.* The assignor of a lease remains liable unless released by the landlord. Compare *sublease; sublet.*

assignor   One giving some right or interest. The person making an assignment.

baseball arbitration   An arbitration method in which each side presents terms for consideration and, if an agreement cannot be reached, arbitrators are brought in to determine which set of terms is closest to the actual market rate. See also *arbitration.*

base rent   The minimum rent as set forth in a (usually commercial) lease, excluding pass-through charges, percentage rents, and other additional charges. See also *minimum rent.*

base year   In a commercial (office, retail, industrial) lease, the stated year that is to be used as a standard in determining rent escalations. In subsequent years, operating costs are compared with the base year, and the difference determines the tenant's rent adjustment. Compare to *stop provision.*

billback   In commercial leasing, *billback items* (also called *billbacks*) include a property's operating expenses—such as real estate taxes, property insurance, and common area maintenance costs—that are paid by the tenants, usually on a pro rata basis. Also sometimes called *tenant charges, net charges, pass-through building expenses, pass-through charges,* or *billbacks.* See also *net lease; pass-through charges.*

boiler and machinery insurance   Property and liability coverage for loss or damage arising out of the operation of pressure, mechanical, and electrical equipment.

breakpoint   In retail leases, the point at which the tenant's volume of sales multiplied by a predefined percentage rate is equal to the base rent stated in the lease and beyond which the tenant will begin to pay percentage (overage) rent; also called *natural breakpoint.* (Natural breakpoint is calculated by dividing the tenant's annual base or minimum rent by the established percentage rate.) Sometimes a tenant and landlord will negotiate an *artificial breakpoint* that requires the tenant to begin paying percentage rent either before or after the natural breakpoint is reached. See also *percentage rent.*

broker   An agent with a real estate license who acts as a representative for an owner or tenant, within specific limits of authority. Also, an agent who buys, sells, or leases for a principal on a commission basis without having title to the property.

brokerage agreement   Another name for *leasing agreement.*

brokerage firm   An agency operated by a licensed real estate broker that employs licensed real estate personnel who bring in business by canvassing the territory for prospective tenants or for listings on properties. A full-service real estate brokerage firm may also provide property management services in addition to handling real estate sales and rentals.

Building Owners and Managers Association (BOMA) International   Membership organization of real estate professionals and others involved in all facets of commercial real estate, primarily serving the interests of the office building industry.

building rentable area   The sum of all the *floor rentable areas.*

building standard   A uniform specification that defines the quantity and quality of construction and finish elements a building owner will provide for build-out of space leased to commercial tenants. See also *tenant improvement (TI) allowance.*

business interruption insurance   A form of property insurance which provides coverage against the loss of profits (indirect loss) resulting from damage to the building or contents (direct loss), as by fire or other peril.

buyout   An arrangement in with either the tenant or the landlord pays a fee to cancel a lease before its expiration date.

capitalization rate   A rate of return used to estimate a property's value based on that property's net operating income (NOI). This rate is based on the rates of return prevalent in the marketplace for similar properties and intended to reflect the investment risk associated with a particular property. It is derived from market data on similar, recent sales (NOI ÷ property value/sales price = capitalization rate) or from calculations based on expected returns on debt and equity. Also called *cap rate* or *overall capitalization rate (OAR).*

cap rate   A shortened form of *capitalization rate.*

cash flow   The amount of spendable income from a real estate investment. The amount of cash available after all payments have been made for operating expenses, debt service (mortgage principal and interest), and capital reserve funds; also called *pre-tax cash flow* to indicate that income taxes have not been deducted.

certificate of occupancy   A document issued by an appropriate governmental agency certifying that the premises (new construction, rehabilitation, alterations) comply with local building codes and/or zoning ordinances.

clear height   The area between the floor and the ceiling that is unobstructed by lights, air conditioning ducts, etc. Some tenants need a minimum clear height to operate their equipment.

commercial multiple listing service   A listing of available commercial properties; a centralized database listing commercial real estate for lease in a specified market, often subscribed to by commercial brokers in the area.

common area maintenance (CAM) charges   The amount a commercial tenant pays to maintain the common areas of a shopping center or mall (e.g., public areas in a mall, landscaping, parking areas, sidewalks, and roadways). In leases for office buildings and industrial properties, CAM costs may be paid along with other property operating expenses as *pass-through charges*.

computer-aided design (CAD)   A computerized system used by architects, space planners, and building managers to facilitate space planning and building design; sometimes also called *computer-assisted design*. CAD makes it possible to create space plan drawings and make revisions to them more quickly than can be done using traditional methods.

conflict of interest   A situation that arises when the private interests of an individual in a position of trust (e.g., a broker or leasing agent) conflict with his or her official duties. Such conflicts must always be disclosed to the landlord.

construction area   Another name for *gross building area.*

consumer price index (CPI)   A monthly measure of changes in the prices of goods and services consumed by urban families and individuals. The CPI provides a way of measuring consumer purchasing power by comparing the current costs of goods and services to those of a selected base period; formerly *cost-of-living index.* Sometimes used as a reference point for rent escalations in commercial leases (i.e., as a measure of inflation). The CPI is published monthly by the U.S. Department of Labor, Bureau of Labor Statistics.

contingency   An event that may or may not occur within a designated time period or at all. In construction estimating, a contingency factor is commonly included to cover unexpected costs that arise as the job is in progress.

continuous operation   A shopping center lease provision that requires the retail tenant to operate the business throughout the term of the lease (sometimes including reference to established operating hours of the shopping center, but store hours are usually addressed in a separate lease provision); also called *operating covenant.* A continuous operation requirement may not be viable in jurisdictions where the courts will not enforce the lease provision but rather take the view that the landlord can recover money damages for a breach of the lease. In a shopping center, maintaining a continuously operating viable mix of retail business is key to the success of the shopping center as a whole and that of all the individual tenants; money damages paid to the landlord are not adequate compensation in the event a tenant does not comply. A shop tenant will sometimes try to negotiate to have the continuous operation requirement apply contingent on a specific anchor remaining in operation; if the anchor is allowed to *go dark,* the continuous operation provision in the shop tenant's lease would not apply. See *co-tenancy provision.*

corporation   A legal entity that is chartered by a state and treated by courts as an individual entity with the ability to buy, sell, sue, and be sued separate and distinct from the persons who own its stock. For purposes of taxation, the Internal Revenue Service differentiates regular corporations subject to corporate income tax under Subchapter C of the IRS Code from those whose taxable income is taxed to their shareholders per Subchapter S of the Code.

cost of living adjustment (COLA)   A method for determining increases in the cost of minimum rent based on the CPI's percentage increase. This increase can also apply to marketing fund contributions and some fixed CAM provisions.

co-tenancy provision   A provision in a lease that provides protection for a tenant who depends on other retailers to draw customers. For example, if a shopping center's anchor tenant would fail to open for business, delay opening, or cease to operate during business hours (i.e., "go dark"), the resultant adverse effects might allow a retailer with a co-tenancy lease provision to abate minimum rent, reduce common area maintenance (CAM) charges and property taxes, or even cancel the lease. This provision may also allow for such sureties if a certain percentage of a shopping center's leasable space is vacant.

declining percentage rent   A negotiated percentage rent structure such that the retail tenant pays a smaller percentage of gross sales after a specified sales volume is reached.

deferred conditions report   A computer-generated report that shows any future changes (e.g., rent increases, lease options, rights to cancel, rights of first refusal, expiration of insurance certificates, the lease expiration) in the lease. Landlords typically check this report at the beginning of every month.

demising wall   A partition or wall separating the leased space of one tenant from that of another tenant and from common areas.

demographics   The statistical analysis of populations, using information derived primarily from census records, including overall population size, density, and distribution, birth and death rates, and the impact of immigration and outmigration. Also included are age, gender, nationality, religion, education, occupation, and income characteristics of people who live in a geographically defined area. Used to characterize discrete markets. Residential property owners and managers are also interested in such concurrent data as household size, numbers of children and their ages, and levels of homeownership because they relate to requirements for living space in the form of rental apartments. Retail tenants are interested in population and household data within a prescribed *trade area* to help establish price points, merchandise mix, and marketing focus. A tool of *market research.*

double-net lease   Also called *net-net lease.* See *net lease.*

drip line methodology   An alternative method for measuring rentable area in industrial space, in which the *measure line* follows the most exterior drip line at the perimeter of the building's roof system. This approach is seldom used in the commercial real estate industry. Compare to *exterior wall methodology.*

dual agent   A single agent who, with disclosure to each party, represents both parties to a transaction (e.g., the landlord and the tenant in a lease transaction).

easement   An interest in or right to land that is owned by another person. A legal right to use land owned by another person or business for a specific purpose. An easement may be granted by a deed or created as a result of actual use that was not prohibited (*easement by prescription*).

effective rent   In residential property management, the rent paid by the tenant per month reduced by the monthly value of any leasing concessions computed on a per-month basis for that unit. The cumulative rental amount collected over the full term of a lease. Also, the amount of rent a commercial tenant actually pays after base rent is adjusted for concessions, pass-through charges, and tenant improvements. The effective rent differs from the quoted base rent set forth in the lease. Also called *effective rate.* See also *base rent.*

egress   The act of going out, especially from an enclosed place. In shopping centers, this is a critical parking issue for traffic flow. See also *ingress.*

eminent domain   The right of a government or municipal quasi-public body to acquire private property for public use through a court action called condemnation in which the court determines that the use is a public use and determines the price or compensation to be paid to the owner. (The owner of the property must be fairly compensated, usually based on an appraisal of the fair market value.)

endorsement   Signature placed on the back of a check transferring the amount of that instrument to someone else. An attachment to an insurance policy that provides or excludes a specific coverage for a specific portion or element of a property or makes additions or changes to the existing terms of a policy; also called a *rider.*

ENERGY STAR   A government-backed program that helps businesses and individuals protect the environment through superior energy efficiency.

estoppel   A rule of evidence preventing a person from asserting a claim or denial that contradicts a previously taken position or settlement.

estoppel certificate   A document by which the tenant states the terms of the lease and the full amount of rent to be paid for the entire term of the lease, commonly requested by the landlord in conjunction with a transfer of ownership or in relation to financing or refinancing.

ethics   The discipline dealing with good or bad, right or wrong, that provides a societal guide for behavior standards.

exclusive   A right granted to the tenant that restricts the landlord from leasing space in the same shopping center or office building to other tenants who sell similar merchandise or provide similar services, usually defined in an *exclusive use provision*. Care must be taken in granting exclusives because limitation of competition violates antitrust regulations. When granted, exclusives must be taken into account when prospecting for and leasing to additional tenants.

exclusive agency listing agreement   A type of listing agreement that is similar to the *exclusive right listing agreement*. The difference is that, if the landlord finds a tenant, a commission is not paid to the listing broker or brokerage firm.

exclusive right listing agreement   The most common listing arrangement used by landlords and brokers, this type of agreement gives the broker (or brokerage firm) the *exclusive right to lease* the specified property.

exclusive right to lease   The appointment of a broker as the exclusive agent to lease a property for a specified period of time. The broker is then owed a commission whether the property is leased by the owner, the broker, or any other agent during the specific period.

exclusive use provision   A clause preventing the landlord of a commercial building from leasing space to other tenants who sell merchandise or provide a service similar to that specified in the tenant's lease. See also *exclusive*.

extended coverage insurance   A policy that extends a basic fire policy to cover property loss caused by additional perils, usually windstorm, hail, explosion, riot and civil commotion, aircraft, vehicles, and smoke. May also be written as an *endorsement*.

exterior wall methodology   The most popular method for measuring rentable area in industrial space, in which the *measure line* follows the line of all the building's exterior walls. Compare to *drip line methodology*.

face rate   The rent paid by a tenant without any deductions for concessions such as free rent; the rate that is agreed upon up-front, without regard to allowances and concessions that are part of the deal.

fiduciary   One charged with a relationship of trust and confidence, as between a principal and agent, trustee and beneficiary, or attorney and client, when one party is legally empowered to act on behalf of another. Relating to a special relationship of trust or responsibility for another.

fire insurance   The most basic type of property casualty insurance. Insurance against all direct loss or damage by fire. See also *extended coverage insurance*.

first right of refusal   A right sometimes sought by a commercial tenant (and granted by the landlord at the initial leasing or lease renewal) that allows the tenant to lease previously defined additional space within a specific time period after the space becomes available for lease to another tenant or after the landlord has received a bona fide offer to lease that same space from another potential tenant (a third party). Usually the lease terms require the landlord to notify the tenant of the availability of the space or of the terms of the third-party offer, and the tenant must lease the space at market terms or under the terms of the third-party offer (if appropriate) or refuse the space so that it can be rented to the third party. This type

324   *The Leasing Process*

of lease provision may also be written granting the tenant the first right of refusal to lease a particular space within a defined time period at a negotiated rent (often market rate) when that space becomes available. This may be sought by the tenant as an alternative when the landlord will not negotiate an option to expand the tenant's space. See also *first right to negotiate; option.*

first right to negotiate   A provision sometimes sought by a commercial tenant (and granted by the landlord at the initial leasing or lease renewal) that gives the tenant the opportunity to negotiate for additional space before the landlord negotiates with any other prospective tenant concerning that space. See also *first right of refusal; option.*

floor area   Another name for *gross leasable area.*

floor load   The weight that a floor in a building is capable of supporting if such weight is distributed evenly, calculated in pounds per square foot; also called *floor-load capacity.* The *live load* of a floor.

floor plan   Architectural drawings showing the floor layout of a building, including precise room sizes and their interrelationships. The arrangement of the rooms on a single floor of a building, including walls, windows, and doors.

floor plate   An architectural drawing showing the layout (outline) of a single floor (or part of a floor), including details of exterior and interior walls, doors and windows, and precise room dimensions and their interrelationships; sometimes called *floor plan.*

floor rentable area   The area obtained by subtracting from the gross measured area of a floor the area of the major vertical penetrations on that same floor, making no deduction for columns and projections necessary to the building and excluding spaces outside the exterior walls. See also *floor usable area; building rentable area.*

floor usable area   The area enclosed between the finished surface of the office area side of corridors and the dominant portion or major vertical penetrations, including building common areas; equal to the sum of all usable areas in the given space, and expressed in square feet.

force majeure   An event or effect that cannot reasonably be anticipated or controlled. A clause commonly included in construction and other contracts to protect the parties in the event that part of the contract cannot be performed due to events or causes beyond the parties' control (e.g., weather, natural disasters, wars, strikes, or riots).

fully net lease   See *net lease.*

general contractor   An individual or company that undertakes the construction or renovation of a property and agrees to perform (provide) or procure all of the various construction disciplines necessary to complete building the structure and installing the necessary equipment and systems. A construction specialist who enters into a formal agreement or contract with the owner of real property to construct a building or complete a remodeling project.

go dark   A provision sometimes included in shopping center leases that allows a tenant to cease operations at the property if a predefined event occurs (e.g., sales at the location are below an agreed-upon dollar amount in two or more consecutive years or a specific anchor tenant leaves the shopping center). The tenant may be required to continue to pay the minimum guaranteed rent for the remainder of the lease term.

gray shell   Used in referring to the condition of the interior of a retail shell space that has been partially improved by the landlord (e.g., stubbed plumbing has been installed and concrete floors have been poured, but there is no finish on *demising walls*). Compare *vanilla shell.*

gross area   All the floor area inside a building.

gross building area   The area equal to the length times width of the building(s) times the number of living floors, including all enclosed floors of the building; computed by measuring to the outside finished surface of permanent outer building walls and expressed in square feet. Also called *construction area.*

gross leasable area (GLA)   The size of an individual tenant's area of exclusive use, usually expressed in square feet. The total square feet of floor space in all store areas of a shopping center, excluding common area space.

gross lease   A lease under which the tenant (lessee) pays a fixed rent. The landlord (lessor) is responsible for paying all property expenses (e.g., taxes, insurance, utilities, repairs, etc.), and these costs are factored into the rent paid by the tenant. Compare *net lease.*

gross sales   The total sales that the retailer makes during a specific period, usually a calendar or fiscal year.

gross up   In commercial leasing, adjustment of variable operating expenses that are passed through to tenants in a new building or one that is not fully occupied to more closely reflect those expenses under full occupancy.

guarantor   One who acts as a surety or gives security, as for payment of a debt. In real estate management, one who agrees to assume responsibility for a financial obligation of another in the event that the other person cannot perform (e.g., payment of rent under a lease).

guaranty   In real estate management, a pledge by a third party who agrees to assume responsibility for a tenant's obligations under a lease in the event of tenant default, including payment of rent and performance of all other terms, covenants, and conditions of the lease. The arrangement is specific to a particular tenant and the lease for specified premises. The individual or organization making such a pledge is called a *guarantor.*

heating, ventilating, and air-conditioning (HVAC) system   The combination of equipment and ductwork for producing, regulating, and distributing heat, refrigeration, and fresh air throughout a building.

holdover tenancy   A situation in which a tenant retains possession of leased premises after the lease has expired, and the landlord, by continuing to accept rent from the tenant, thereby agrees to the tenant's continued occupancy as defined by state law. Some leases stipulate that such holding over may revert to a month-to-month tenancy, often at a higher rent. See also *month-to-month tenancy.*

income approach   The process of estimating the value of an income-producing property by capitalization of the annual net income expected to be produced by the property during its remaining useful life.

incubator tenants   Retail tenants in a specific location for a trial period. If they are successful, these tenants go on to lease space on a permanent basis.

indemnify   To exempt from incurred liabilities or penalties. To secure against harm, damage, or loss. The leasing agreement usually includes a *mutual indemnity provision.*

ingress   The act of going in or entering. In shopping centers, this is a critical parking issue for traffic flow. See also *egress.*

Institute of Real Estate Management (IREM®)   A professional association of men and women who meet established standards of experience, education, and ethics with the objective of continually improving their respective managerial skills by mutual education and exchange of ideas and experience. The Institute is an affiliate of the National Association of REALTORS® (NAR).

insurance provision   A provision in commercial leases that requires the tenant to obtain specified types and amounts of insurance, including a certain amount of liability insurance, and to include the building owner as an additional named insured party on the policy.

International Council of Shopping Centers (ICSC)   Membership organization of retailers and owners, developers, and managers of shopping centers, as well as other professionals and businesses that provide services to those in the shopping center industry.

key money   In a desirable location, an amount paid to the landlord by a new tenant for the right to enter into a lease.

landlord's market   An "up" market, or one in which demand is stronger than supply, vacancies are few, and rents are rising.

late fee   A fee charged for late payment of rent.

Leadership in Energy and Environmental Design (LEED)   A rating and certification program administered by the U.S. Green Building Council (USGBC) that employs nationally accepted standards for the design, construction, and operation of high-performance, sustainable green buildings.

lease agreement   A contract between the landlord and tenant that establishes their respective duties and obligations. See also *leasing agreement.*

lease commencement letter   A written notice that ratifies the actual commencement and expiration dates for a lease, often used for leases with uncertain commencement dates. The letter includes a space for both the landlord and tenant to sign in acknowledgement of these dates, thus discouraging further disputes on the matter.

lease extension agreement   A covenant or other written and executed instrument extending or agreeing to extend the lease term beyond the expiration date as provided in the body of the original lease.

leasehold   Land or space held under a lease.

leasing agent   The individual in a real estate brokerage firm (or management organization or development company) who is directly responsible for renting space in assigned properties. In some states, leasing agents must have a real estate sales license unless they are employed directly by the property owner.

leasing agreement   A contract between the landlord and broker (or brokerage firm) that establishes their respective duties and obligations. Also called *brokerage agreement*. See also *lease agreement, listing agreement.*

letter of engagement   A letter used to formalize the agreement between a commercial tenant seeking space and the brokerage firm for which that tenant's leasing agent works. This letter recognizes the appointed brokerage firm as the exclusive agent to represent the business, and states how the leasing agent will be compensated.

letter of intent   A letter or document stating the intention of the party to take (or not take) a particular action, sometimes contingent on certain other actions being taken. In commercial leasing, a preliminary step to finalizing specific lease terms.

liability insurance   Insurance protection against claims arising out of injury or death of people or physical or financial damage to other people's property that is a consequence of an incident occurring on an owner's property. A form of coverage in which the insured (property owner) is the first party, the insurer (insurance company) is the second party, and the claimant (person who experienced the loss) is the third party; also called *third-party insurance.*

lien   A claim against property by a creditor under which the property becomes security for the debt owed to the creditor. The legal right of a creditor to have his or her debt paid out of the property of the debtor. Mortgages, mechanic's liens, and tax liens are monetary liens against a property for the satisfaction of debt.

limited liability company (LLC)   Created by state statue, a business ownership form that functions like a corporation (its members are protected from liability) but for income tax purposes is classified as a partnership. Income and expenses flow through to the individual members. The arrangement offers considerable flexibility in its organization and structure.

listing agreement   A contract between the landlord and broker that employs the broker to market and lease or sell a certain property. The agreement specifies the terms of the listing, including the specific timeframe and the commission to be paid. See also *leasing agreement.*

live load   The load (weight or force) on a structure that may be removed or replaced, including the weight of people, furniture, and equipment but not accounting for movement resulting from the force of wind against the exterior. See also *floor load.*

load factor   The percentage of space in a commercial building that is added to its usable area to account for lobbies, corridors, and other common areas; calculated by dividing the building's total common area by its total usable area. Sometimes also called an *add-on factor.* The relationship between a building's *gross area* and its *usable area.*

loss leader   In retailing, an item sold at a lower markup than would normally be obtained on that item in order to attract customers in the hope that they will buy more-profitable items as well.

macromarket   A market that is large in scale or scope.

management plan   The fundamental document for the short-term operation of a property that represents a statement of facts, objectives, and policies and details how the property is to be operated during the coming year. Such a plan usually includes the annual budget.

marketing fund   In a shopping center, an account controlled by the landlord that is specifically for funding shopping center promotions and advertising. Merchants in the shopping center contribute to this fund based on a predetermined amount stated in their lease. Compare *merchants' association.*

market rent   Rent that a property is capable of yielding if leased under prevailing market conditions; *economic rent.* Also, the amount that comparable space would command in a competitive market. Often used interchangeably with *street rent* and *contract rent.* (By definition, the latter is the rent stated in a specific lease.) For office buildings, the basis would be dollars per rentable square foot; for retail space, it would be dollars per square foot of gross leasable area (GLA).

market research   Collecting information about consumer wants, needs, and preferences by surveying consumers directly. A methodology used to explore product design, packaging, size (quantity), and other marketing-related issues, including price. In residential property management, a tool for identifying what apartment renters in a particular market want in terms of unit size, features and amenities, and rental price. In commercial management, the gathering of information about a trade area and a particular property pertaining to population, economy, local industries, per capita expenditures, competing properties, and sales potential. See also *market survey.*

market survey   A detailed and comprehensive evaluation of a given market that provides market research data. Collection and analysis of up-to-date information on other products distributed in a given area. See also *market research.* In real estate management, the process of gathering information about specific comparable properties for comparison to data about the subject property in order to weigh the advantages and disadvantages of each property and establish a market rent for the subject. In the office building market, a survey is made of comparable buildings located in the subject property's neighborhood and includes such information as number of stories, net rentable area, building features and amenities, rental rates, and load factors. For shopping centers, a market survey of competing shopping centers would include location specifics, gross leasable area (GLA), anchor and ancillary tenants, rental rates, and common area charges and concessions. Amount and availability of parking are important considerations in market surveys for all types of properties.

measure line   A conceptual line used for measuring commercial space, that generally runs to the outside of a building's exterior walls and to the center of its shared walls.

merchants' association   An organization formed in shopping centers and controlled by the tenants to plan promotions and advertisements for the good of the shopping center as a whole, usually established as a not-for-profit corporation. All tenants are required to participate, and both tenants and the landlord pay dues. In the past, this was the most common marketing format for shopping centers, but it has largely been replaced by the *marketing fund.*

metes and bounds   A method of describing land or property that uses compass directions, distances of the boundaries, and angles, resulting in what is called a "legal description" of the land. The boundary lines of land, with their terminal points and angles.

micromarket   A market that is small in scope, usually limited to a certain class of buildings within as specific area.

minimum rent   In retail leasing, the rent which will always be due each month in a tenant's lease term, regardless of sales volume and exclusive of any additional charges. Often used in conjunction with a percentage rent arrangement; sometimes called *fixed-minimum rent.* See also *base rent.*

month-to-month tenancy   An agreement to rent or lease for consecutive and continuing monthly periods until terminated by proper prior notice by either the landlord or the tenant. Notice of termination must precede the commencement date of the final month of occupancy. State law usually establishes the time period of prior notice.

mullion   A vertical framing member located between lights of windows, doors, or panels set in series, to separate and (often) support the glass.

natural breakpoint   The point at which the tenant's volume of sales multiplied by a predefined percentage rate is equal to the base rent stated in the lease and beyond which the tenant will begin to pay percentage (overage) rent; calculated by dividing the tenant's annual base or minimum rent by the established percentage rate. See also *artificial breakpoint; breakpoint; percentage rent.*

net cost   The cost after all incidental charges are added and all allowable credits are deducted.

net lease   A lease under which the tenant pays a prorated share of some or all operating expenses in addition to base or minimum rent. The terms *net* (or *single-net*), *net-net* (or *double-net*), and *net-net-net* (or *triple-net*) are also used, depending on the extent of the costs that are passed through to the tenant. Used most often for commercial tenants. The tenant pays a prorated share of property taxes under a single-net lease, prorated shares of both property taxes and insurance under a double-net lease, and prorated shares of all operating expenses (including common area maintenance) under a triple-net lease. Compare *gross lease.*

net operating income (NOI)   Total collections (gross receipts) *less* operating expenses; may be calculated on an annual or a monthly basis. More broadly, cash available after all operating expenses have been deducted from collected rental income and before debt service and capital expenses have been deducted.

net profit   The money remaining for an investor after income taxes have been deducted from the cash flow.

occupancy cost   The tenant's total cost for the leased space. For commercial tenants, this includes base rent plus a pro-rata share of property operating expenses (e.g., insurance, real estate taxes, utilities, common area maintenance, and management fees) and may include reimbursement of a tenant improvement allowance. In addition, retail tenants may pay percentage rent (also known as *overage*) and contribute to a marketing fund or merchants' association.

open lease listing agreement   A type of listing agreement that does not provide a broker with the exclusive right to lease the landlord's property. The landlord pays a commission to any broker who brings a prospect into a lease with the landlord.

option   The right to purchase or lease something at a future date for a specified price and terms. The tenant can exercise an option unless the tenant does something (or fails to do something) and consequently loses the option. Options may be received, negotiated, or purchased. In a lease, the right to obtain a specific condition within a specified time (e.g., to renew at the same or a pre-agreed rate when the lease term expires; to expand into adjacent space at a pre-agreed time when that space is expected to be available; to cancel the lease). Options are often incorporated in the lease as an addendum.

outlot   In a shopping center, a site that is located in the parking lot; also called *out parcel* or *pad space.* The term is often applied to freestanding space in the parking lot. Out parcel tenants usually include restaurants, gas stations, and banks.

out parcel   Another name for *outlot.*

overage   In retail leases, rent payments in excess of a guaranteed minimum, usually a percentage of the tenant's sales; also called *rent overage.* See also *breakpoint; percentage rent.*

pad   Short for *pad space* or *pad building.* Also, a parcel of rentable land in a residential development, with sewer and utility connections, designed to accommodate a mobile home; also called a *mobile home site.*

pad space   Another name for *outlot.*

pass-through charges   In commercial leasing, operating expenses of a property that are paid by the tenants, usually on a pro rata basis in addition to base rent, including real estate taxes, insurance on the property, and maintenance costs. Also sometimes called *tenant charges, net charges, pass-through building expenses, billback items,* or *billbacks.* See also *billback; net lease.*

percentage rent   Rent that is based on a percentage of a tenant's gross sales (or sometimes net income or profits), in excess of the guaranteed minimum or base rent under the lease and paid as *overage* rent (i.e., the amount of percentage rent in excess of the minimum or base rent due). See also *breakpoint*. A percentage rent provision may also be written such that the tenant is required to pay a percentage of gross sales in lieu of minimum rent under certain circumstances (e.g., loss of an anchor tenant).

performance bond   A guarantee or assurance by a third party (surety) that a contractor will perform and complete the contract as per agreement; a type of contract bond.

plan book   A book compiled by the building owner or property manager to keep track of how space is used in a building by showing each tenant's floor plans as well as all the floor plans by floor.

planned unit development (PUD)   A type of development that usually includes a mixture of open space, single-family homes, townhouses, community associations or cooperatives, rental units, and recreational and commercial facilities within a defined area under a specific zoning arrangement. Generally, PUDs are large in scale and built in several phases over a number of years. Typically, all infrastructure for the site is constructed before the improvements are built.

preleasing   The leasing of space in a project under construction before it is completed.

pro forma   In real estate development, a financial projection for a proposed project based on certain specified assumptions and reflecting construction costs, financing, leasing rates and velocity, and operating costs. An unofficial financial statement that projects gross income, operating expenses, and net operating income (NOI) for existing rental real estate based on specific assumptions; a *pro forma statement*. Also, a projection of gross income and net operating income of a stabilized property; a *budget*.

property manager   A knowledgeable professional who has the experience and skills to operate real estate and understands the fundamentals of business management. The person who supervises the day-to-day operation of a property, making sure it is properly leased, well maintained, competitive with other sites, and otherwise managed according to the owner's objectives. The chief operating officer or administrator of a particular property or group of properties.

psychographics   A qualitative methodology for compiling information about people's individual personalities and lifestyles, it goes beyond *demographics* to uncover personal preferences and attitudes that numbers alone do not reveal; a tool of market research. In leasing, used to determine what factors about a property are likely to appeal to particular prospective tenants (more specifically applicable to individual consumers in regard to apartment leasing). See also *market research*.

radius provision   A provision in a retail lease that prevents a retailer from opening and operating a similar—and therefore competitive—business within a certain radius (distance in all directions) from the shopping center, expressed in miles.

real estate investment trust (REIT)   An entity that sells shares of beneficial interest to investors and uses the funds to invest in real estate or real estate mortgages. Real estate investment trusts must meet certain requirements such as a minimum number of investors and widely dispersed ownership. No corporate taxes need to be paid as long as a series of complex Internal Revenue Service qualifications are met.

registration and commission agreement   An agreement between the brokerage firm and the landlord, in which the brokerage firm is appointed as the exclusive agent to represent the tenant seeking space. This agreement also includes the terms of the agreement and the commission schedule, and is formalized through the *registration letter.*

registration letter   A letter that the leasing agent presents to the landlord, stating that the brokerage firm and leasing agent represent the tenant. This letter includes the terms of the agreement and the commission schedule. It may be used in lieu of a *single party lease listing agreement.* See also *registration and commission agreement.*

registration list   A list of prospects that a broker registers with a landlord when an agreement for a certain property ends, so that the broker will receive a commission if one of the prospects he or she has contacted enters into a lease with the landlord within a certain timeframe. The leasing report may be used to ensure that only prospects who have shown serious interest or are involved in lease negotiations are included on the list.

rentable area   In an office building, the area on which rent is based and which generally includes the space available for tenants' exclusive use plus identified common areas less any major vertical penetrations (air shafts, stairways, elevators) in the building. The term is applied to the building as a whole, to individual floors, and to portions of floors. Compare *usable area.*

rentable/usable ratio   The relationship between the actual space that a tenant is able to use exclusively (the *usable area*) and the actual area—including the tenant's share of the building's common areas—that the tenant has to use (the *rentable area*).

request for proposal (RFP)   Written specifications for services to be provided by a bidder, often including the scope of work and details of design and use and asking for specifics regarding materials, labor, pricing, delivery, and payment.

reserves   Funds set aside for foreseeable expenses or charges.

retainer   A fee paid to an attorney or other professional for advice, or to be able to make a claim upon that person's services in case of need. Also, the act of employing an attorney.

return on investment (ROI)   The ratio of net operating income to the total investment amount, for a given time period, which provides a measure of the financial performance of the investment. A measure of profitability expressed as a percentage and calculated by comparing periodic income to the owner's equity in the property (income ÷ equity = % ROI). A measure of cash flow against investment, it can be calculated either before or after deduction of income tax. ROI measures overall effectiveness for management in generating profits from available assets; however, it does not consider the time value of money.

right to recapture provision   A lease clause that gives the landlord the right to take back space that the tenant chooses to sublet or assign.

rules and regulations   Guidelines for tenants who lease space in a building, usually outlining requirements specific to their occupancy and operating their business in the building and common areas; also called *house rules and regulations*. Specifics are usually incorporated in the lease, either as a specific provision or as a rider, and they vary by property type. These rules and regulations can be changed by the landlord during the lease term, whereas the lease provisions cannot.

security deposit   A preset amount of money advanced by the tenant before occupancy and held by an owner or manager for a specific period to ensure the faithful performance of the lease terms by the tenant; also called *lease deposit*. (Local or state law may require the landlord to pay the tenant interest on the security deposit during the lease term and/or hold the money in an escrow account.) Part or all of the deposit may be retained to pay for outstanding rent or charges, unpaid utility bills, and damage to the leased space that exceeds normal wear and tear. Limitations on withholding may be imposed by local and state ordinances.

shell space   The condition of a commercial tenant's space before occupancy and before any tenant improvements are constructed.

sign restriction provision   A provision in a shopping center lease that limits the use of outdoor and indoor advertisements and other graphic displays. More specifically, it requires the tenant to comply with specific sign criteria regarding sign placement, size, and graphics and to submit the plans for exterior signs for the landlord's approval; such signs are installed and maintained by the tenant. Sign criteria may be governed in part by local laws that regulate size, materials, and positioning.

single-net lease See *net lease.*

single party lease listing agreement   A type of listing agreement used when there is only one leasing agent involved in securing the lease. This may be used when a leasing agent represents a tenant, when the landlord gives the leasing agent an assignment to contact a specific prospective tenant, or when a leasing agent presents a prospective to a landlord with an open lease listing agreement. A *registration letter* may be used in lieu of a single party lease listing agreement.

site plan   A plan, prepared to scale, showing locations of buildings, roadways, parking areas, and other improvements. A drawing of a retail site as it will look when it is completed, including individual tenant spaces, common areas, elevators, escalators, food courts, service areas, parking, and access routes. Also called a *plot plan.*

smart building   An office building that has a single building-wide computer system to provide data processing and telecommunications and to control the HVAC, elevator, electrical, and security systems.

Society of Industrial and Office Realtors® (SIOR)   Membership organization of real estate brokers specializing in industrial and office properties and other individuals and businesses with interests in these types of real estate; an affiliate of the National Association of Realtors® (NAR).

space planning   The process of designing an office configuration for maximum functional efficiency based on a prospective tenant's space utilization needs, aesthetic requirements, and financial limitations.

specialty leasing agent   An in-house leasing agent employed by regional malls, responsible for leasing space in kiosks, carts, and vacant stores to temporary tenants for a short term during the holidays, special events, and the best selling seasons.

stop provision   In a commercial (office, retail, industrial) lease, the use of a stated dollar figure as a standard in determining rent escalations and pass-through charges. In subsequent years, operating costs are compared with this base figure, which is meant to represent the cost of operating the building during the initial year of the lease. Compare to *base rent.*

strip center   A type of shopping center designed in a single, unenclosed strip of stores set in a row facing a parking lot or the street.

sublease   A lease given by a tenant or lessee to another entity to use or occupy part or all of the tenant's leased premises for the duration (remainder) of the original tenant's lease term. The original tenant may retain some rights or obligations under the original lease and remains liable to the owner in case of default by the subtenant. See also *assignment.*

sublet   The leasing of part or all of the premises by a tenant to a third party for part or all of the tenant's remaining term. Under a *subletting agreement,* the original tenant is responsible for rent not paid or damages committed by the subtenant regardless of his or her agreement with the subtenant. Compare *assignment.*

substantial completion letter   A letter that informs the tenant of the specific date when improvements will be complete and rent and other charges will commence. This letter is not needed when the tenant leases the premises in "as is" condition.

tenant improvement (TI) allowance   In commercial leasing, an amount a landlord agrees to spend (for office and industrial buildings) or grants to the tenant (in retail properties) to improve the leased space before tenant move-in or as a condition of lease renewal. The exact amount, if any, is negotiable. A *standard tenant improvement allowance* is a fixed dollar amount allowed by the owner for items that may be installed in the leased premises at no charge to the tenant. Payment for tenant improvements is part of the lease negotiations. See also *building standard.*

tenant improvements (TIs)   Fixed improvements made to tenants' office space, usually based on specific building standards determined in advance by ownership; specifics are often negotiable, especially in a slow market. In apartment rentals, additions or alterations to the leased premises for the use of the resident, usually made at the cost and expense of the resident and becoming a part of the property unless otherwise agreed to in writing.

tenant mix   The combination (or types) of businesses and services that lease space in a commercial building.

tenant rep   Another name for a tenant-rep broker.

tenant-rep broker   A leasing agent who has made the commitment to represent the tenant in a real estate transaction. Also called *tenant rep* or *tenant-rep leasing agent.*

tenant roster   Compiled from the lease summaries at a retail property, a list of each tenant's square footage, the rental rate per month and per square foot, the percentage rate, and the amount of any security deposit along with the lease term (often including commencement and expiration dates). Usually this record does not show any payments made by the tenant.

tenant's market   A "down" market, or one in which supply exceeds demand, vacancies are fairly high, and rents are either falling or staying level.

tickler file   A record-keeping system that serves as a reminder of important dates. Today this function largely has been taken over by software programs.

trade area   The geographic area from which a shopping center obtains most of its customers. A trade area is generally divided into primary, secondary, and tertiary zones based on distance from the center of the area, travel time, and other factors. The size of the trade area depends on the type of shopping center, location of competition, natural and manmade boundaries, and other factors. See also *demographics.*

triple-net lease   Also called *net-net-net lease*. See *net lease.*

turnkey operation   A concession whereby the owner agrees to provide a completely finished space for a commercial tenant.

upset figure   In commercial build-to-suit leases, the specified dollar amount of costs at which the landlord has the right to cancel the lease or have the tenant pay the additional charges; a protection against cost overruns.

Urban Land Institute (ULI)   An independent nonprofit research and educational organization dedicated to improving the quality and standards of land use and development.

usable area   The area in an office building that is available for the exclusive use of a tenant; compare *rentable area*. On a multitenant floor, the area remaining after the area devoted to core facilities (public corridors, elevators, washrooms, stairwells, electrical closets) is subtracted from the gross area of the floor. On a single-tenant floor, usable area excludes ducts, stairwells, elevators, and the building elevator lobby on the floor if such exists, but includes washrooms and electrical closets.

use provision   A lease provision that restricts the use of the rental space. In an office or industrial lease, the type of business operation or intended use is cited. In a retail lease, the use provision restricts the tenant's use of the rented space by indicating what types of goods can and cannot be sold.

vanilla shell   Used in referring to the condition of the interior of a retail *shell space* that has been partially improved by the landlord. The improvements include only the drop ceiling, *demising walls* ready for paint, finished handicapped-accessible washrooms (an ADA requirement), floor covering, water heater, and basic electrical outlets. Compare *gray shell*.

work letter   An addendum to the tenant improvement clause of an office or retail lease that lists in detail all the work to be done for the tenant by the landlord; sometimes called a *construction rider*.

Index

A

Absorption rates
  of office building, 131
  of shopping centers, 116
Acceptance
  of keys, 240
  of premises, 240–241
Access as issue in office buildings,
  172
Accounting, pass-through operating
  expense, 250–251
Adjustments
  frequency of, 280
  full, 280–281
  partial, 280–281
Administrative assistant, 25–26
Administrative fee, 250
Advertising
  classified, 54
  display, 54
  employment, 51
  in lease, 241
  in leasing agreement, 64
  medical journal, 55
  merchant, 56
  print, 53–54
  radio, 53
  television, 53
  trade journal, 54
After-hours HVAC charges in request
  for proposal, 70

Age of shopping centers, 163–164
Alterations, 241–242
Alternative locations
  for office tenants, 150–151
  tenants evaluating, 148–151
Amenities for office building, 167
Americans with Disabilities Act (ADA)
  (1990), 15
  complying with, 71, 192
Amortization of improvements, 196
Anchor tenants
  advertising by, 141
  rent for, 134
Annual sales
  statements on, 307
  using, 199–200
Appearance for office building,
  167–168
Appraisers as information source, 118
Arbitration, 242–243
  baseball, 243
  typical, 243
Architect, 27–28
Architectural site plans, 92
Area amenities in request for pro-
  posal, 71
Artificial breakpoint, 198
Asking rates, 115, 117
Asset management, 24
Asset manager, 24–25, 97
  in leasing negotiation, 99

J
Janitorial services, 268
Journal of Property Management
(JPM), 12

K
Key money, 219, 268
Keys, acceptance of, 240

L
Landlord(s)
auditing rights of, 282
concessions of, 85–86
costs of not renewing lease, 225–228
cost to replace tenant, 226–228
decision to renew, 222–223
effective rent of, 194–195
entry by, 258
ethics and, 43–44
goals and objectives of, 81–86
credit rating, 82–84
tenant mix, 82
as in-house leasing agent, 22–24
investment of, 5–7
lease terms, 84–85
in lease transaction, 15–16, 103–104
leasing agent of, 98
in leasing process, 2–3
leasing report of, 36
in minimizing financial risk, 106
name and address of, in request for
proposal, 69
performance of, in lease renewal, 224
preparations in negotiating, 88–95
security deposit use by, 283
work of, 268
Landlord leasing agent, 19–20
Landlord leasing documents, 188–189
Landlord-provided improvements,
187–188
Landlord retention programs, 233–234
Landlord's market, 110
lease renewal in, 222
leasing in, 136
Landlord–tenant relationship
maximizing benefits of, 138
steps in good, 138–139

Late charge, 268–269
Leadership in Energy and Environmental Design (LEED) certification, 88, 233
Leasable area concept, 249
Leasable square footage, 249
Lease(s)
advertising in, 241
beneficiaries of completed, 1
business terms of, 10–11
commercial, 1, 178–179
double-net, 216
duration of, 287–288
final approval for, 105–106
fully net, 216
green, 88, 281
ground, 149, 217
guaranty of, 292–293
importance of, 5–7
length of, 204–205, 236–237
net, 216–217, 248
requirements and violations in renewal, 222–223
restrictions summary, 303–304
single-net, 216
tenant improvement (TI) under existing, 159–160
triple-net, 207, 248
vacation of tenant before expiration
of, 79–80
Lease abstract, 300–302
Lease abstraction error, 301
Lease addendum, 229
Lease administration, 294–316
bookkeeping and record-keeping
procedures, 297–307
fiscal issues, 307–316
human relations factors in, 294–297
process of, 297–299
Lease cancellation option in request
for proposal (RFP), 70
Lease commencement
letter of, 288
rental commencement versus, 269
tenant improvements and, 158–159
Lease concessions, 209–211
Leased area concept, 249